REGULATORY PROGRAMS

A Study Team Report
to the Task Force
on Program Review
May, 1985

Catalogue No. CP 32-50/20-1985E   Canada: $37.50

ISBN 0-660-11990-0   Other Countries: $45.00

Price subject to change without notice

(1) <u>too "legalistic"</u> - resulting in the private citizen being intimidated from intervening or being forced to hire legal counsel;

(2) <u>too expensive</u> - even major economic organizations complain about the cost of the hearings process;

(3) <u>too slow</u> - it is not uncommon for the decision-making process to be subject to extraordinary delays extending into years. This often is intolerable especially in instances of economic regulation where technology, information and markets simply move too quickly for the 19th century decision-making traditions. Indeed, this is one of the most fundamental questions in modern regulatory administration: as an instrument is regulation even capable of being adapted to today's fast moving realities? One of the strongest arguments for deregulation is that, however desirable or appropriate regulation might once have been to achieve some particular objective, it can no longer reasonably or economically be expected to do the job because the regulatory horse and buggy has been left behind by the space age. (While delay is a frequent criticism of regulatory boards, agencies and departments, the private sector is aware that this often reflects inadequate resources in relation to work volume rather than inefficiency).

D - <u>Small Business</u>

1. <u>Federal Regulatory Sensitivity</u>

- As small business is now the major engine of job creation in our economy, anything that impedes the small business sector could be regarded as an impediment to economic growth and job creation. For this reason, the Team's terms of reference included criteria intended to promote special attention to the effect of regulation on small business.

- The program and system review chapters of this report reflect the Team's views on a case-by-case basis. Taken together, there seemed to be quite a lot of evidence supporting the view that the federal government is insufficiently sensitive to the special characteristics of small business.

Among the points noted are the following:

(i) Small business operators are pressed for time and can be expected to have difficulty as individuals contributing to the consultative process and rseponding to any aspect of regulation requiring time or special effort on their part. There should be special sensitivity to small business time pressure.

(ii) The design of federal regulation appears often to have been directed conceptually at quite a large scale of corporate enterprise with the result that performance, reporting and other requirements are unrealistic for smaller operators. Getting the right balance is probably very difficult but greater efforts should be made including experimentation with tiering and flexibility concepts to avoid the differential impacts of regulation on large and small enterprise.

(iii) The design and implementation of federal inspection procedures need to be more sensitive to small business realities and, to that end, better coordinated both among departments and among levels of government.

2. The Emperor's Clothes

- A great deal is said about the burden of regulation on small business. Indeed, it has

28

CANADIAN HUMAN RIGHTS COMMISSION

FEDERAL COMMUNICATIONS REGULATION

THE TANGLED GARDEN OF ENVIRONMENT REGULATION

IMMIGRATION

CONTENTS

PREFACE

A MATTER OF FREEDOM

The Study Team wishes to comment on certain first principles which might act as an underpinning for a regulatory reform strategy and its explanation to the public.

Regulatory reform is all about freedom. The concept of personal freedom within the minimum constraints of community responsibility lies at the very heart of Canada's history and culture. The democratic traditions and rich economy of this blessed country have been built on that foundation.

Regulation is the removal of freedom, and when it goes too far, as it has, it risks threatening that foundation. When individuals become strangled by rules and red tape, they lose their sense of personal responsibility. If that persists, they then lose their sense of initiative. Not far behind comes stagnation of the economy and the decline of responsible government.

Perhaps, because we have grown accustomed to our gift of freedom, we forget that it is indeed a rare gift. When we allow regulation to run rampant, when we regulate any more than is absolutely essential, we have to recognize that we are striking at free citizens, free markets and the ideal of freedom itself.

There is no such thing as a free regulation.

11

ENERGY AND MINES

REGULATION OF THE FISHERIES

FINANCIAL SECTOR

HEALTH AND WELFARE

NORTHERN AFFAIRS REGULATION

JUSTICE PROGRAMS

LABOUR CANADA

REVENUE CANADA CUSTOMS AND EXCISE

TRANSPORTATION PROGRAMS

ROAD REGULATION

MARINE REGULATION

AIR REGULATION

RAIL REGULATION

GRAIN TRANSPORTATION AND HANDLING

OTHER REGULATORY PROGRAMS   579

FOREWORD

The Task Force on Program Review was created in September 1984 with two major objectives - better service to the public and improved management of government programs. Recognizing the desirability of involving the private sector in the work of program review, assistance from national labour, business and professional organizations was sought. The response was immediate and generous. Each of these national organizations selected one of their members to serve in an advisory capacity. These public spirited citizens served without remuneration. Thus was formed the Private Sector Advisory Committee which has been responsible for reviewing and examining all of the work of program review.

The specific program reviews have been carried out by mixed study teams composed of a balance of private sector and public sector specialists, including representatives from provincial and municipal governments. Each study team was responsible for the review of a "family" of programs and it is the reports of these study teams that are published in this series. These study team reports represent consensus, including that of the Private Sector Advisory Committee, but not necessarily unanimity among study team members, or members of the Private Sector Advisory Committee, in all respects.

The review is unique in Canadian history. Never before has there been such broad representation from outside government in such a wide-ranging examination of government programs. The release of the work of the mixed study teams is a public acknowledgement of their extraordinarily valuable contribution to this difficult task.

Study teams reviewed existing evaluations and other available analyses and consulted with many hundreds of people and organizations. The teams split into smaller groups and consulted with interested persons in the private sector. There were also discussions with program recipients, provincial and municipal governments at all levels, from officials to cabinet ministers. Twenty provincial officials including three deputy ministers were members of various study teams.

The observations and options presented in these reports were made by the study teams. Some are subjective. That was necessary and appropriate considering that the review phase of the process was designed to be completed in a little more than a year. Each study team was given three months to carry out its work and to report. The urgent need for better and more responsive government required a fresh analysis of broad scope within a reasonable time frame.

There were several distinct stages in the review process. Terms of reference were drawn up for each study team. Study team leaders and members were appointed with assistance from the Private Sector Advisory Committee and the two Task Force Advisors: Mr. Darcy McKeough and Dr. Peter Meyboom. Mr. McKeough, a business leader and former Ontario cabinet minister, provided private sector liaison while Dr. Meyboom, a senior Treasury Board official, was responsible for liaison with the public sector. The private sector members of the study teams served without remuneration save for a nominal per diem where labour representatives were involved.

After completing their work, the study teams discussed their reports with the Private Sector Advisory Committee. Subsequently, their findings were submitted to the Task Force led by the Deputy Prime Minister, the Honourable Erik Nielsen. The other members are the Honourable Michael Wilson, Minister of Finance, the Honourable John Crosbie, Minister of Justice, and the President of the Treasury Board, the Honourable Robert de Cotret.

The study team reports represent the first orderly step toward cabinet discussion. These reports outline options as seen by the respective study teams and present them in the form of recommendations to the Task Force for consideration. The reports of the study teams do not represent government policy nor are they decisions of the government. The reports provide the basis for discussion of the wide array of programs which exist throughout government. They provide government with a valuable tool in the decision-making process.

Taken together, these volumes illustrate the magnitude and character of the current array of government programs and present options either to change the nature of these programs or to improve their management. Some decisions were announced with the May budget speech, and some subsequently. As the Minister of Finance noted in the May budget speech, the time horizon for implementation of some measures is the end of the decade. Cabinet will judge the pace and extent of such change.

These study team reports are being released in the hope that they will help Canadians understand better the complexity of the issues involved and some of the optional solutions. They are also released with sincere acknowledgement to all of those who have given so generously of their time and talent to make this review possible.

TERMS OF REFERENCE

PURPOSE

To establish terms of reference for a mixed study team reporting to the Ministerial Task Force on Program Review concerning the federal government's regulatory structure and programs.

TERMS OF REFERENCE

In addition to programs already included in the terms of reference of other study teams, there are some 115 federal regulatory programs. These additional regulatory programs are administered with 11,400 person years in 33 departments and agencies at a direct cost to the government of $1.7 billion. These programs impose substantial indirect costs on the economy and are frequently perceived as excessive insofar as they obstruct growth and job creation or unduly limit the freedom of private individuals.

The study team will examine the federal regulatory system including the comprehensive list of regulatory programs contained in Annex A. In so doing, it will bear in mind the objectives of the Ministerial Task Force on Program Review and, in particular, its interest in developing a profile of government programs, including regulatory programs, which is simpler, more understandable and more accessible to their clientele, and where decision-making is decentralized as far as possible to those in direct contact with client groups.

With regard to the regulatory system, the study team will provide a report with its observations and advice concerning the efficiency, appropriateness and adequacy of

    (a)   the system as a whole, with special emphasis on regulatory prior assessment, approval and review procedures;

    (b)   private sector coordination and consultation practices;

(c)   interdepartmental and intergovernmental
      coordination and consultation procedures;

(d)   enforcement and compliance under existing
      regulations and consistency of administration.

With regard to its review of regulatory programs, the
study team will address both the substance and
administration of each program with a view to identifying
what either the team, the private sector or
provincial/territorial governments consider "problem
programs" as judged first of all against the criterion of
economic development that is:

(a)   does the program directly or indirectly constitute
      an obstacle to economic development or job
      creation?

And judged further against any or all of the following
criteria:

(b)   appropriateness - what is the program supposed to
      do, is it doing it and is a regulatory program
      (i.e. subordinate legislation) the best way to
      solve the problem?

(c)   adequacy - does achievement of the program's
      objective solve the problem it was directed at?

(d)   relevance - has the program become obsolete?

(e)   efficiency - can the program be done cheaper?

(f)   cost/benefit - do the administrative and/or
      indirect socio-economic costs appear to outweigh
      the program's benefits?

(g)   overlap/duplication - is there actual or perceived
      conflict or waste in relation to
      provincial/territorial programs?

(h)   consistency - are the rules commensurate with the
      risk and magnitude of the harm (problems) and are
      they applied on an equitable and consistent basis?

(i)   entrepreneurship - does the program stifle
      entrepreneurial initiative or create undue
      uncertainty, red tape or delays in the market
      place?

(j) good citizenship - does the program detract from good citizenship or otherwise bring regulatory administration into ill-repute?

(k) differential impact of regulatory regime on small or large corporations.

In conducting its examination, the study team should consult as appropriate with departments and private sector representatives and take full account of ongoing activities or initiatives which are relevant to the regulatory review. The team is expected to indicate to Ministers:

- where problems may exist in specific programs and the system as a whole, and

- what course or courses of follow-up action are open to further evaluate or remedy these problems.

A perceived "problem program" falling entirely within the responsibility of a single minister should be reported as such to the Ministerial Task Force with any observations that might assist the responsible minister to address the problem. However, where the study team identifies a regulatory problem area crossing departmental boundaries, it should seek to provide detailed suggestions on possible action plans for resolving the problem.

Except insofar as it might detract from the overall coherence of its review, the study team need not pursue regulatory programs which other team leaders have undertaken to examine within the scope of their terms of reference. However, these instances should be noted in the study team's report.

In reporting, the study team should provide details of the legislative and resource implications of any recommended program changes. In addition, the team should draw attention to regulatory developments or approaches in other countries which may be relevant to the study.

The study team will not address issues concerning the procedures or relationship to government of regulatory agencies except to identify problem areas, since these questions are the subject of a separate study.

LINKAGE WITH CONSULTATION PAPERS

Cutting horizontally across governmental activities as this study does, it will no doubt deal with issues to be covered by consultation papers. The team should examine and take note of these papers and, in its own consultations, ensure that the distinct focus of the regulatory review study is emphasized to prevent any confusion with consultations being conducted in any other context.

COMPOSITION OF STUDY TEAMS

The study team will be led by A. Campbell, Coordinator, Office of Regulatory Reform in the Treasury Board. He will report as appropriate through the Public Sector Advisory and the Private Sector Liaison Advisor serving the Chairman of the Task Force. The director will be supported by the staff of the Office of Regulatory Reform with up to 3 additional seconded government officers and a matching number of private sector representatives nominated through the Private Sector Advisory Committee. The team, or its director, shall meet with the Public Sector and Private Sector Liaison Advisors at their request.

WORK PLAN

The study team will submit for consideration by the Ministerial Task Force a detailed workplan reflecting these terms of reference.

The study team shall be afforded access to any evaluations or other relevant analysis which departments have with respect to programs covered by this review.

REPORTING SCHEDULE

The study team is expected to report its initial findings to the Ministerial Task Force on April 15, 1985. It will provide regular progress reports.

COMMUNICATION WITH DEPARTMENTS

The study team will initiate appropriate liaison and consultation arrangements with departments whose programs are affected by this study.

The Secretary of the Treasury Board and the Deputy Ministers of Justice, Transport, and Consumer and Corporate Affairs have been consulted on the proposed terms of reference.

REGULATORY PROGRAM INVENTORY

AECB	1	Administration of Atomic Energy Control Regulation
AGC	18	Agricultural Products Marketing Act
AGC	211	Race Track Supervision
AGC	213	Inspection & Control of Facilities & Food Products
AGC	214	Market Maintenance (RR) Reg-Related Support Services
AGC	215	Inspection & Protection of Crops, Livestock and Farm Input Supplies
AGC	902	Agricultural Products Board (RR)
AGC	223-6	Agricultural Stabilization Board - Deficiency Payments to Producers
CIT	1	Canadian Import Tribunal
CCA	2	Consumer Products - Product Information
CCA	4	Product Safety
CCA	5	Marketing Practices (Misleading Ads)
CCA	9	Corporations
CCA	10	Bankruptcy
CCA	12	Copyright and Industrial Design
CCA	13	Consumer and Corporate Affairs Patents
CCA	14	Trade Marks
CCA	31	Legal Metrology: Electricity & Gas
CCA	32	Legal Metrology: Weights & Measures
CCA	100	Consumer Services: Tax Rebate Disc. Act
CCA	101	Combines Investigation Act - Restraints to Competition
CCA	102	Metric Program
CCA	103	Regulated Sector (RR) Regulatory Intervention Activities
CCA	901	Regulated Industries Program (RR) Funding Consumer Int. Groups
CDC	200	Canadian Dairy Commission
CDIC	901	Canadian Deposit Insurance Commission
CGC	234	CGC Weighing Division
CGC	235	CGC Grain Inspection
CGC	901	Licensing, Registration, Documentation (RR)
CHRC	1	Canadian Human Rights Commission
CLRB	1	Canada Labour Relations Board
CMHC	1	Building Codes (Housing Standards)
CMHC	2	Mortgage Insurance
CPC	100	Canada Post Corporation: Letter Definition and Rates

CRTC	901	Broadcasting
CRTC	902	Telecommunications
CTC	2	Domestic Air Carrier Subsidies (RR)
CTC	10	Western Grain Transport (RR)
CTC	12	Water Transport Regulation
CTC	20	Air Transport Regulation
CTC	30	Motor Vehicle Transportation Regulation
CTC	40	Railway Economic Analysis & Quality of Service
CTC	45	Railway Safety
CTC	50	Rail Branch Line Subsidies (RR)
CWB	1	Canadian Wheat Board
DI	1	Insurance-Supervision of Companies
DOC	100	Spectrum Management (Radio)
DOC	901	Export/Import Cultural Property
EAC	1	The Passport Program
EAC	9	Export & Import Control Program (Special Trade Relations Bureau)
EC	18	Commercial/Toxic Chemicals
EC	903	Industrial Effluent & Emission Controls
EC	23	Ocean Dumping Controls
EC	25	Environmental Assessment Review Process (RR)
EC	97	Migratory Birds Conservation Program
EC	98	Wildlife Conservation Program
EC	901	Parks (Lands & Wildlife Regulation)
EIC	901	Immigration: Recruitment & Selection
EIC	902	Immigration: Enforcement
EMR	2	National Energy Policy Programs
EMR	12	Emergency Mandatory Allocation and Rationing Program
EMR	30	Petroleum Monitoring Agency (RR)
EMR	114	Explosives Act Administration
EPC	2	Emergency Planning & Resp. Coord.
F&O	1	Fisheries Prices Support Board
F&O	7	National Fish Inspection Program
F&O	8	Licensing & Resource Allocation
F&O	9	Small Craft Harbours
F&O	902	Monitoring, Control, Surveillance (Offshore, Coastal Inland)
FC	2	Inspector General of Banks
FC	901	Interest Act (with CCA)
HWC	17	Civil Aviation Medicine
HWC	18	Quarantine & Regulatory Services
HWC	22	Immigration Medical Services
HWC	100	Food Safety, Quality & Nutrition
HWC	101	Drug Safety, Quality & Hazard
HWC	102	Environmental Quality & Hazard
INAC	37	Funding for Band Government
INAC	58	Yukon/Northwest Territories Land Use Planning
INAC	74	Oil and Gas

INAC	79	Yukon/Northwest Territories Mining
INAC	201	Yukon/NWT Land, Forest & Water Resources Management
INAC	201.1	Yukon/NWT Land Resources Management
INAC	201.2	Yukon/NWT Forest Resources Management
INAC	201.3	Yukon/NWT Water Resources Management (Inland)
INAC	201.4	Yukon/NWT Water Resources Management (Offshore)
INAC	226	Canada Oil and Gas Lands Admin. (with EMR)
INAC	304	Institutional Support
INAC	306	Lands, Estates and Membership
INAC	307	Indian Natural Resources and Trust Funds
INAC	308	Institutions and Treaty Management
INAC	316	Comprehensive Community - Based Planning and Band Management
JUST	18	Statute Revision Commission
JUST	901	Review Statutory Instruments - Admin. Law Reform
JUST	902	Compliance Enhancement, Decriminalization (RR)
LC	4	Conditions of Work
LC	6	Occupational Health & Safety
LC	20	Mediation, Conciliation, Arbitration
LFBC		Livestock Feed Board of Canada
LRC	1	Law Reform Commission (RR)
NCPC	1	Northern Canada Power Commission (RR)
NEB	100	National Energy Board
NFPMC	1	National Farm Products Marketing Council
NFPMC	2	Agencies Established Under the Farm Products Market Agencies Act
NPAC	1	Regulation of Construction of the Alaska Highway Gas Pipeline
NRC	104	Research: Building Construction (RR)
PCO	100	Privy Council Office (Justice) (RR)
RCCE	2	Bonded Carriers
RCCE	3	Bonded Warehouses
RCCE	4	Licensing Custom House Brokers
RCCE	14	Customs Duty/Refund, Remission, Drawback
RCCE	29	Excise Duty
RCCE	34	Registration & Licensing of Vessels
RCMP	4	Firearms Registration
RCMP	100	Federal Law Enforcement Under Review (RR)
SC		Statistics Canada: Information Provision Requirements
SS	1	Citizenship Registration & Promotion
SSC	9	Canadian General Standards Board (RR)
STCC	11	Standards Council of Canada (RR)
TB	6	Office of Regulatory Reform (RR)
TB	901	Technical Advisory Group (SEIA) (RR)

```
TC      4     Air Carrier Operating Certificate
TC      27    Airworthiness/Aircraft
TC      47    Marine Aids to Navigation (RR)
TC      57    Pollution Regulatory (Marine)
TC      61    Marine Casualty Investigation
TC      67    Vessel Traffic Services/Traffic Management
TC      93    Transportation of Dangerous Goods
TC      275   Road Safety & Motor Vehicle Regulation
TC      310   Air Cushion Vehicle Regulation
TC      315   Personnel Regulatory (Marine)
TC      320   Ship Regulatory
TC      325   Ship Radio Inspection Regulations
TC      330   Navigable Waters Protection
TC      405   Aircraft Registration (RR)
TC      420   Air Traffic Services
TC      425   Air Navigational Aids (RR)
TC      430   Aviation Services
TC      435   Aviation Safety & Enforcement
TC      440   Licensing Registration, Training, Testing (Air)
TC      500   Insp. General - Transportation Safety
TC      600   Canadian Aviation Safety Board (RR)
TC      610   Four Pilotage Authorities
TC      999   Motor Carrier Reg. Coordination (RR)
DRIE    902   Textile & Clothing Board
TRFB    101   Tariff Board
```

KEYS:

(RR)   Regulatory-Related Programs

LIST OF TEAM MEMBERS

Team Leader

Antony Campbell
Coordinator
Office of Regulatory Reform
Treasury Board Canada

Private Sector Advisors

Jim Conrad
Executive Director
Canadian Federation of
   Independent Petroleum Marketers
Toronto

Reg Cook
Retired
Former Vice President
  Molson Industries
Toronto

Roy Olsen
Retired
Former President
Phillips Cable
Brockville

Robert Peel
Union Business Manager
258 International
   Brotherhood of
   Electrical Workers
   Vancouver

Beryl Plumptre
Reeve
Village of Rockcliffe
Ottawa

Tayce Wakefield
Government Relations
General Motors of Canada
Oshawa

Public Sector Advisors

John Blakney
Consumer & Corporate Affairs

Anthony Burgess
Department of Transport

Brian Carter
Department of Finance

Clara Dunning
Office of Regulatory
   Reform

M. Sylvain Dubois
Privy Council Office

Lee McCabe
Office of Regulatory
   Reform
Treasury Board Canada

9

Julianna Ovens   Denis Watson
Office of Regulatory Reform   Indian and Northern
Treasury Board Canada   Affairs

Research and Administrative Support

S. Brabant   A. Graham
A. Dale   E. Milligan
C. Dunning   C. Schwartz
B. Gagné

MAIN OVERVIEW

THE GOOD, THE BAD AND THE UGLY

Like the tuba in an orchestra, regulation can either be a harmonious instrument of government or, when played improperly or out of place, a device of torture.

Unfortunately, the analogy stops there. Orchestras rarely consider tubas appropriate, whereas governments tend to resort to regulation at the drop of a baton.

This has been increasingly the case since the 1930's when the public turned its faith to government as the protector of its interests. But it would be wrong to conclude that regulatory intervention is a new phenomenon; all governments have used regulation to achieve their purposes and Canada has never been an exception. From the stroke of midnight on July 1, 1867, Canadians inherited a mass of regulations many of which survive little changed to this day. Sir John A. might well have declared, "a regulator I was born and a regulator I will die". He was and he did.

This report is about the past and the future of regulation in Canada. The focus is on the federal government, but the principles apply to all governments in Canada. Indeed, an important view of the Study Team on Regulatory Programs should be stated at the outset:

> it is the combination of regulatory programs at all levels of government - federal, provincial and territorial and municipal - that is the number one regulatory problem in this country.

Canadians <u>are</u> overregulated and this report attempts to assess the federal contribution to that problem.

Similar work needs to be done covering all levels of government in Canada all at once. This was recognized at the outset of the regulatory reform movement in Canada when federal and provincial First Ministers initiated common action in 1978. It was an error when that initiative was allowed to wallow and eventually disappear, leaving governments to deal with reform as if it were thirteen

13

distinct problems as opposed to <u>one burden with multiple contributors</u>.

To paraphrase the Honourable Erik Nielsen, each regulatory program is a monument to a past problem. The first objective of the Study Team on Regulatory Programs, therefore, was to prepare a reliable regulatory inventory and to review the accumulation of federal regulatory programs introduced in the past. The focus of the review was to identify <u>problem areas</u>.

The Team's second objective was to look to the future by examining the federal government's system of regulation -- the mechanism which (1) develops regulatory policy, (2) implements it, (3) adjudicates it, and (4) evaluates it. Here again, the emphasis was on problem identification.

Thus, the Team's primary objective was to identify, among both federal regulatory programs and the regulatory system as a whole, "the good, the bad and the ugly".

The Team was also invited to suggest options to resolve any problems identified during its work. As a result, this report offers many options and suggestions to the problems identified within the federal realm of regulation.

A FISTFUL OF DOLLARS

Regulation, in the generic sense, is defined as the imposition of rules by the state or its agents backed by the threat of sanctions with the objective of modifying or controlling private behaviour.

The objective or beneficiary of a regulation is usually obvious. When regulation creates a "winner", as it usually does, the winner knows it. However, the cost of a particular regulation is rarely clear-cut and when it creates a "loser", as it usually does, the loser is often unaware of it. The taxpayer pays tax, buys butter or goes for a drive oblivious to the individual regulatory cost, but far from unaware or unconcerned about the aggregate effect. Of course, the victim in one instance can be the so-called winner in another; modern democratic government has a lot to do with achieving a positive balance of regulatory wins and losses for the individual voter.

The phenomenon that distorts the balancing act is that regulatory benefits are easily perceived, clearly focussed and immediately enjoyed while most of their costs are indirect, obscure and widely dispersed. It follows that it is usually much harder for government <u>not</u> to regulate than to regulate.

Thus, while Canada's economy surged ahead in the post-war period, it is not at all surprising that Canadians encouraged their governments to intensify their regulatory activities. The costs were buried deep in a growing GNP. However, as GNP growth began to shrink, people began to notice and be concerned about the costs of regulation. (Indeed, some schools of thought point to the plethora of regulation in the 1960-70's as a major cause of GNP shrinkage in the first place.)

Precisely because regulation is relatively cheap for government but expensive for the private sector and the economy as a whole, the Team concentrated on regulatory problems as seen and defined by the private sector and only secondarily as seen from the point of view of government. That is, the Team was not asked to seek cost savings to government but to identify cost savings to the economy as a whole.

The Team's point of departure for its regulatory review can be summed up in four principles:

(1) regulation is an important and useful instrument of government;

(2) its use in any particular situation should be a matter of balancing the benefits against the direct and indirect costs;

(3) there has never been a government regulation in history that had no economic cost; and

(4) you can't maintain champagne tastes with beer money.

In other words -- there's no such thing as a free regulation.

15

ANY WHICH WAY BUT LOOSE

In introducing the substance of the Team's work, it may be desirable to touch on three larger issues which have a profound influence on regulatory policy. Where one sits on these issues will have a lot to do with where one stands in the current regulatory reform debate.

(1) Deregulation is a word that is frequently used (actually, misused) in discussing changes in regulatory policy. Strictly speaking, the complete removal of regulation from a particular activity is deregulation. It is a rare phenomenon. Even in the United States, where instances of "economic" deregulation are quite advanced, there remains in place a substantial amount of "social" regulation. Such sectors as the airline, trucking, financial and communications industries are not truly deregulated at all. (Indeed, it may come as a surprise to many Canadians that California, home of Proposition 13, remains among the most heavily regulated jurisdictions in the world.)

Thus, deregulation is a word with a range of meanings and only rarely is it intended to convey its literal meaning. Most often the real meaning is reduced economic regulation -- that is, the reduced control by government or its agencies of such critical factors as prices, conditions of entry and exit and other competitive or market-related issues.

Whatever the meaning of the word deregulation, regulatory reform is not primarily concerned with the reduction or elimination of regulation. Its focus is on the improvement of regulation. Often this will mean less regulation or the same amount, but it can just as easily mean more regulation. When existing regulations are made better, the accurate description is apt to be "reregulation".

This discussion is not purely semantic. The Team found that many people already had their minds made up about "deregulation" -- one way or the other. This often inhibited the kind of practical, objective judgement that the Team found essential in carrying out its study.

(2)   How much trust to place in <u>market principles</u> is a
key question in approaching many regulatory
issues. It has been said that exactly contrary to
Americans, Canadians trust government and distrust
the market place. The Team found much evidence to
support this observation. Frequently during the
study, the best approach to a particular
regulatory issue boiled down to one's attitude to
the perceived benefits versus shortcomings of free
or fr<u>eer</u> markets.

(3)   Some contributors argued that, whatever one's view
of market theory, the geopolitical entity of
Canada does not lend itself naturally to
unfettered market precepts. Thus, longstanding
regional, political, economic and social realities
played a forceful role in the development of our
current regulatory structure and there is
reasonable cause for concern that, in some
instances, poorly managed regulatory reform can
have disturbing effects on the very fabric of the
country. Considerations of this nature underline,
in the Team's opinion, the critical importance of
much greater regulatory coordination, cooperation
and perhaps even consolidation, between the
various levels of government in Canada.

GENERAL FINDINGS

The Team's proposals constitute coherent and
significant regulatory reform. Overall, they would put the
federal government on a par or ahead of any other government
in Canada or elsewhere in the world. While the proposals
are balanced and reasonably cautious, the Team believes that
a reform package is needed to underline to the regulators
and public alike that the government is serious about
regulatory change in the interest of national economic
development and personal freedom.

The Team's general findings can be summarized as
follows:

1.   Canada is both over-regulated and badly
regulated. There is too much regulation relative
to the public's capacity to absorb it and relative
to the available resources for implementing and
enforcing it.

2. The cumulative effect of regulation at three
   levels of government constitutes an enormous
   impediment to initiative, enterprise and personal
   freedom. Accumulation leads to strangulation.

3. The process and much of the substance of federal
   regulation in recent years has been subject to
   insufficient administrative control and political
   supervision. Existing regulatory control
   mechanisms are inadequate, under-resourced or
   inefficient; regulators at all levels of
   government are largely insensitive to the hidden
   costs of regulation and unaware of alternatives to
   the use of the regulatory instrument.

4. Public access to and involvement in the
   development and review of regulation needs to be
   expanded.

5. Regulations once enacted need to be far more
   accessible to the general public. The primary
   clientele of government regulation is the public
   and not the legal profession. Indeed, the growing
   reliance on lawyers by ordinary citizens to help
   them cope with regulation should be seen as a sign
   of trouble, not success.

6. Regulatory programs have been subject to
   inadequate systematic review by responsible
   departments.

7. Parliament's role in the subordinate legislative
   process needs extension if there is to be any
   meaning to its democratic legislative function.

8. A large proportion of existing regulatory programs
   is in need of improvements - the Team offers
   suggestions concerning two-thirds of them.

9. Federal economic regulatory programs are monuments
   to circumstances that have radically changed or
   are changing too fast for 19th century regulatory
   methods to keep up. To one degree or another many
   federal economic regulations need to be
   deregulated-- i.e. altered, reduced or phased out.

10. The entrenched Canadian tradition of promoting social policy objectives through economic regulation is a luxury with a high but hidden price tag. Our economy and international developments are making it less and less tenable "to have our cake and eat it too". A strong social safety net is only possible if, first, there is a strong economy. There should be no mistake about the multi-billion dollar cost we incur by mixing the two.

11. There is something ironic about a country contemplating free trade with the United States while tolerating innumerable regulatory barriers to trade inside its own borders. As one of the Team's provincial contacts put it, the biggest benefit to Canada's economy from a deal with the U.S. might well be the dismantling of those interprovincial barriers.

12. Whether or not we move to free trade, there is a need for greater sensitivity in Canada to the importance of regulatory structures and shifts in the U.S. and other major trading countries. We have no choice but to adapt to them on a continuing basis. Adaptation does not mean imitation, but Canadian solutions have to bend to international realities.

13. Regulatory activity by provinces and municipalities is no less of an impediment to economic growth than is federal regulation. Municipalities, in particular, need to be encouraged to embrace regulatory reform.

14. Overlap and duplication exists between layers of government and is significant.

15. It is the total cumulative burden of regulation in Canada that is the number one regulatory problem. Individual programs need improvement or deregulation, overlaps and duplication need attention, but, above all, we need intergovernmental cooperation to shrink the overall regulatory burden on individual freedom and the smooth working of the economy.

THE NEED FOR A STRATEGY

If regulation "is the main business of government", these general findings are a serious indictment and they call for serious action. The difficulty is in moving from the general and cumulative to the specific and immediate.

Every individual regulatory program exists because legislators or regulators saw a specific problem that, in their judgement, required attention through regulation. It follows that no regulatory program lacks supporters. Most programs have created vested interests and their beneficiaries will fight vigorously to prevent change. Moreover, it is a characteristic of Canadians to be generally supportive of the "goodness" of regulation and, as a consequence, to be susceptible to the case by case arguments of those who wish to see no change in this country's regulatory status quo. It is not an easy matter for a government to provide leadership in these circumstances.

Taking these realities into account, the Study Team is of the view that the regulatory change needed by the country cannot be expected from or left to random and piecemeal efforts and initiatives. Instead, the Team suggests the adoption of a Regulatory Reform Strategy which could bring about long-term change for the good of the country.

The essence of the proposed Strategy is to place emphasis on the future. Reversing past regulatory errors and radically altering the present regulatory structure is not a practical proposition.

However, the Strategy could emphasize the establishment of principles and procedures for harnessing, controlling, improving and reducing all future federal regulatory activity. If there is a radical improvement in how government handles future regulation and if it can work bit by bit on what already exists, that would be a regulatory achievement whose effects would be felt for years to come.

HORIZONTAL REGULATORY ISSUES

The terms of reference of the Regulatory Programs Team focussed on program and systems review at the federal level. While appropriate, this vertical orientation placed the Team in some difficulty with regard to some issues which were neither purely program nor system related. These issues were dubbed "horizontal issues" since they tended to cut across the regulatory spectrum and they came up repeatedly during the course of the Team's work. A complete understanding of the regulatory status quo probably requires some awareness of many of these issues. The development of future policy and program directions should not ignore them.

This section lays out briefly a number of such horizontal issues or themes. Some relate to problem areas, some to solutions, some to a combination of both. Also included are several of what might be called "crazy ideas". In any exercise of reform one finds that traditional concepts, limitations and accepted ways of doing things tend to rein in the scope of possible change. With the intent of stimulating thinking with some unorthodox views, some "crazy ideas" received or conceived by the Team during its work are recorded.

A - Issues Affecting the Quality of Federal Regulation

1. Inadequate Appreciation of the Regulatory "Sink-Hole Effect"

   - Just as some investments end up requiring more and more infusions of capital to the point one has to decide if it is wise to throw "more good money after bad", so too in regulation one can reach the point where, however worthwhile the objective, the cost of achieving it through traditional regulation is clearly excessive.

   - A variant of this problem is the sometimes difficult decision for governments of where to draw the line in achieving a particular regulatory objective. Sometimes 70 per cent of a regulatory objective can be achieved with relatively small fiscal expenditure but the remaining 30 per cent can only be accomplished by geometric resource increments. This is an especially serious problem in areas of health, safety and environment where the public naturally expects a very high level of protection.

   - Thus, even where it otherwise makes sense to use regulation to achieve an objective, it

21

may be unwise because of the sink-hole effect.

2. **Inadequate Appreciation of Regulatory Sedimentation**

    -   In a federal system there seems to be a particular propensity for layer upon layer of individual initiatives to be introduced over time, each of which seems justifiable but together creates an unsystematic bundle of constraints and disincentives that can supplant the marketplace and remove regulatees from economic reality.

3. **Split Regulatory Responsibilities**

    -   The Team was somewhat surprised to discover the number of instances in which responsibility for a particular regulatory area is intentionally or effectively split between or among various departments and agencies. There are cases, for example, where National Health and Welfare carries out research on a chemical and concludes that it poses an unacceptable hazard, yet responsibility for implementing that judgement or not resides in another department - e.g. Agriculture. Similarly, there is frequent splitting of policy and operational responsibility.

    -   No doubt there are good reasons for the prevalence of this phenomenon, such as the need for the "practical" viewpoint of a line department to be balanced with the more "objective" approach of the policy departments or vice versa. On the other hand, the effect of splitting responsibility can be to encourage duplication, internal red-tape and diffusion of responsibility and accountability.

    -   Examples of this problem or its variant encountered in the regulatory area included: Finance/National Revenue, Environment/Fisheries, Health and Welfare/ Labour/Canadian Transport Commission,

Agriculture/Consumer and Corporate
Affairs/Health and Welfare.

- The costs and benefits of these internal
  splits of responsibility deserve to be
  subjected to special scrutiny. Most were
  probably good or unavoidable when introduced
  but maybe some have outlived their usefulness
  especially in the tight fiscal environment of
  the 80's.

4. Inadequate Penalties

- The Team encountered numerous instances in
  which penalties provided by law for
  regulatory infractions were clearly so
  inadequate that they entirely nullified the
  effect of the regulation or regulatory regime
  in question. There is no doubt that a
  primary reliance on criminal sanctions can
  have a similar nullifying effect by virtue of
  being so heavy that the burden of proof
  becomes extremely difficult and legal
  proceedings commensurately too expensive and
  judges and juries too reluctant to convict.
  But in the regulatory area, the Team found
  more instances of excessively lenient
  penalties than the obverse.

- There is no point in large expenditures to
  establish, maintain and enforce a regulatory
  regime if the maximum sanction amounts to an
  easily absorbed "cost of doing business".

- An especially pernicious impact of inadequate
  penalties is the tendency in government to
  add additional regulations to bolster the
  original regulation which was undermined by
  an inadequate penalty structure. Fisheries
  regulation is a good example of this problem.

- In addition to further work along the lines
  of the Federal Decriminalization and
  Enforcement project currently underway in the
  Department of Justice, there should be a
  directed initiative to identify all
  regulatory statutes whose penalties have
  become inadequate and omnibus amending

23

legislation should be put before Parliament as soon as possible.

5. <u>Obsolete Statutes and Regulations</u>

- The Team's review involved active regulatory programs as determined from government fiscal records. As a result, obsolete statutes and records were missed in the review because they were not captured by the "fiscal computer".

- In itself, this is not a particular problem. Yet, even dormant regulations are not free of cost since, like sleeping dogs, they take up space, require occasional upkeep and sometimes are seen as a continuing potential threat in the private sector.

- The Team estimates that there are about 80 obsolete or redundant regulatory and other statutes. It suggests that omnibus repeal legislation can be introduced either separately or in combination with other regulatory reform legislation to remove the cadavers.

- Similar redundancy and obsolescence no doubt exists among regulations (subordinate legislation) under statutes that are otherwise alive and well. In the Team's view, Departments and agencies should be encouraged to do a spring cleaning of their regulations. Perhaps such a task could be centralized (e.g. in Justice) to minimize the number of orders in Council that would be necessary to repeal the obsolete regulations.

B - <u>Parliament</u>

1. <u>Legislative Delay</u>

- Parliament is the key actor in the regulatory system, yet, for all sorts of understandable reasons, it constitutes something of a stumbling block to efficient and effective regulation. The heart of the problem has been Parliament's ability to cope on a timely or reliable basis with the volume of

24

legislation placed before it. In the regulatory area this has three implications:

i) existing regulatory legislation urgently needing amendment gradually becomes obsolete and sometimes even a serious impediment to economic development or other significant interests (e.g. copyright legislation);

ii) in turn, this encourages the drafting of "umbrella" legislation which delegates very broad subordinate legislation -- moving power from Parliament to the government and administration. While this offers flexibility, it frequently transfers power that should remain in the hands of elected representatives;

iii) a related effect is the tendency (if not need) for government to stretch to the maximum the subordinate legislation-making authority of existing statutes to overcome the extreme difficulty of pursuing amended authority through Parliament. Sometimes the stretching quite consciously exceeds statutory authority; this can place citizens in the extraordinary position of defending themselves or litigating at their own expense against all the resources of government even where government has good reason to doubt the legality of the regulation in question.

- Parliament also plays an important "after-sight" role in the regulatory process through the functions of the Standing Joint Committee on Regulation and Other Statutory Instruments. Notwithstanding the utility of this role, if there were a choice between spending Parliamentary time on regulatory legislation or regulatory after-sight, the Team would prefer the former.

- Current reform initiatives by Parliament will undoubtedly have positive implications for improved regulation.

C - Regulatory Tribunals and Agencies

While the major boards and regulatory agencies were examined by the Team from a policy point of view, the terms of reference specifically excluded review of relationship issues between regulatory agencies and the government. Because of their importance to the efficiency and effectiveness of the regulatory system, the Team wishes to note the importance of the following issues which came up repeatedly during its work for further attention either by the agencies or by a further study team on regulatory agencies.

1. Appointments

    -   There was frequent private sector comment on perceived shortcomings in the appointments to some tribunals and regulatory agencies.

    -   Criticisms were made about the occasional lack of (1) expertise (2) "merit" or (3) representativeness. Some criticism was directed to the inadequate number of full and/or part-time positions in some instances (e.g. AECB).

    -   Given the important regulating role of adjudicators where their interpretations of statute and subordinate legislation can have regulatory effect well beyond the original intentions of Parliament, the "right type" of appointments to Boards and agencies deserves case by case definition and implementation.

    -   In some jurisdictions outside Canada, there are special career streams and programs to develop and train administrative judges or arbitrators. This concept might be explored for Canadian application.

2. Procedures

    -   Whether established as "buffers" to costly and lengthy litigation in courts or not, the procedures of regulatory agencies and tribunals are frequently perceived as:

become common at all levels of government to justify the need for regulatory change by reference to this burden. In some governments regulatory reform is treated almost exclusively as a small business concern.

- It is the Team's opinion that there may be a risk of distortion in placing too much weight on the small business dimension of regulatory reform and especially so at the federal level.

- Although small business contacts indicated strong concern about several federal programs (the following were the subject of specific concern by order of priority: Revenue Canada, Human Rights Commission, Consumer and Corporate Affairs, Agriculture, Immigration, waste management and health protection regulations in Environment Canada) the Team received the impression that provincial and especially municipal regulations have a greater impact on small business operators. Moreover, the federal programs complained about by the small business sector were in most cases the same complained about by larger organizations.

- The Team received significant evidence that established small businesses are often quite comfortable with and feel protected by regulation. In other words, the emperor clearly has clothes but maybe not as many as those who would have us believe that small business operators would be very happy to see all regulation disappear overnight.

E - Regulatory Effects of Non-Regulatory Programs

- Of the various instruments of government, taxation and expenditure programs are, broadly speaking, on the same level of importance as regulation. Over the years a substantial blurring among these instruments has taken place. As a result, a totally comprehensive review of contemporary

regulation would need to examine several tax
and expenditure programs which have a
distinctly and sometimes intentional
regulatory effect. Perhaps the most stark
example of this kind of disguised or hybrid
regulation is the Unemployment Insurance
Program whose regulatory repercussions are
profound and widespread.

- In the Team's opinion, the instruments of
government should not be mixed without
careful attention to the hidden costs and
impacts. For example, it may appear
sensible to use the government's purchasing
leverage (e.g. consulting contracts) or the
monopoly it enjoys over certain services
(e.g. airports) to force behaviour change,
but there are bound to be economic and
possibly socio-political costs from such a
blending of objectives (e.g. in terms of the
efficiency of purchasing procedure or cost of
goods) and those costs should be calculated
in detail before such programs are initiated.

- As a related point, the Team was
uncomfortable with the idea of using
taxation or expenditure programs to control
private behaviour without explicit
Parliamentary approval.

F - Internationnal Regulation

- Another dimension of regulation not directly
captured within the Team's terms of
reference is the growing phenomenon of
regulation under international covenants and
agreements. To an important extent, this
development is to be welcomed as a desirable
extension of international legal and
regulatory harmony. To that extent, it is
important that Canada's regulatory programs
reflect its international commitments and
interests. However, it needs to be
recognized better than it is now that when
the federal government is itself a regulatee
this can sometimes have important economic
and other implications (e.g. government
procurement codes, whaling bans,

international shipping conferences, etc.).
Consequently, no international regulatory
commitments should be entered into without
careful regulatory impact analysis to ensure
that international proposals are in tune with
Canada's interests.

- A particular and sensitive dimension to this
  issue which perhaps needs attention is the
  current trend in the United States government
  towards calling into question the work of
  many international organizations, and
  especially those in the UN system. It will
  take fairly sophisticated regulatory and
  diplomatic skill for Canada to avoid getting
  "whip-sawed" in many regulatory areas if this
  trend goes very far. For example, Canada is
  already somewhat caught in the position of
  one foot on each of two diverging icebergs in
  the area of dangerous goods regulation where
  U.S. and "international" approaches differ.

G - United States Regulatory Relations

- At a time when Canada's economic development
  is particularly vulnerable to developments in
  the United States, the Team notes the
  importance of and potential dangers in our
  "bilateral regulatory relationship". That
  term has been coined by the Team to reflect
  the broad range of regulatory linkages
  between Canada and its major trading
  partner. These are by no means a recent
  phenomenon. However, there is a need for the
  External Affairs and Finance departments to
  recognize this as a distinct dimension of
  bilateral relations requiring special
  management. The need emerges from the fact
  that the United States has adopted a clear
  regulatory policy which in recent years has
  differed markedly from Canada's approach.

- The move to "deregulation" in the United
  States is important both in regulatory and in
  more general terms, and the implications for
  Canada are bound to be important.

-    The corollary of this concern is that Canada
     can learn a lot from American (and other
     foreign) experiments in new approaches to
     regulation. In the Team's view, these should
     be monitored both for lessons that we should
     emulate as for experiments we should avoid.

H - Compliance Issues

-    All of the regulatory programs reviewed by
     the Study Team include measures intended to
     influence the behaviour of the regulated
     private sector and to foster compliance with
     the policy objectives of the program. Not
     surprisingly, the Study Team found a number
     of compliance problems which are common to
     many regulatory programs.

     -    Uncertainty of Mandate: Imprecision of
          the policy objectives of a program makes
          it difficult for regulators to focus
          their efforts and for regulatees to
          agree on the reasons for regulation
          (e.g. the Export-Import Control Program
          includes two very disparate purposes:
          to stabilize the domestic supply of
          goods and to prevent foreign sales of
          certain strategic goods). The policy
          purpose of a program should be clearly
          stated, preferably in the statute
          itself. The Team believes that, where
          there is more than one purpose, those
          purposes must be distinguished and
          priorities set.

     -    Costly and Inefficient Monitoring
          Practices: Many programs depend too
          heavily on direct government
          inspection. In the Team's view,
          self-reporting and third-party
          monitoring should be put to greater use,
          always backed by statistically sound
          spot-checking.

     -    Perceived Unfairness of Monitoring and
          Enforcement: This includes treating
          similar situations differently and
          treating different situations the same.

32

Public regard for enforcement can be fostered, and compliance enhanced, by written procedures and policies which structure the discretion of officials.

- Inadequate Array of Responses to Non-Compliance: Many regulatory statutes provide inadequate means for officials to respond appropriately to the varying situations of non-compliance they encounter. Officials often must decide between a disproportionate sanction and none at all. A modulated array of responses is desirable.

- Inadequate Sanctions for Serious Non-Compliance: Where penalties are too low in relation to the proceeds of a violation, serious offenders get an unfair economic advantage. For example, this is apparently a problem with Fisheries enforcement. In general, serious non-compliance must be made unprofitable.

These and other compliance problems are being dealt with by the government through the Federal Statutes Compliance Project.

SOME WORTHWHILE IDEAS

- A study team that plunges into contacts across the country comes across a lot of ideas. Some deserve to be recorded for further consideration. Here is a selection:

    1. Decennial Sunset Clauses should be introduced into all regulatory legislation or at least all legislation that is oriented to providing a regulatory framework for economic activity. This would help ensure regular review by Parliament and would guarantee regular updating.

    2. Regulatory Flexibility Act (similar to one in the U.S.) should be legislated to provide for the tiering of regulations, administrative procedures and federal program delivery to

33

recognize the limited financial and managerial capacities of small business.

3. Regulation-Free Zones are a variant of the free-trade zone concept. Of course, a totally unregulated geographic area is hard to imagine, but an essential minimum of regulations could be defined beyond which enterprise would be free. This concept could prove even more stimulative than a tariff-free zone given how low tariffs are moving under the GATT.

   Such zones would also allow limited experimentation on the effects of greatly reduced regulation. This could provide lessons that might then be applied or not applied on a wider geographic basis.

4. Departmental and Agency Responsibility for Financial Costs of Litigation refers to the notion (correct in the Team's view) that departments and agencies should be made to "feel" the costs of their regulatory litigation. At present, their direct legal costs are absorbed by the Department of Justice and have no effect on their own financial "bottom lines".

   - The idea has two variants:

     (i) departments should pay their legal costs from their budgets to provide an incentive to regulators to ensure that their regulations are as well prepared (and enforceable) as possible and to prevent "shaky" prosecution.

     (ii) departments should pay the legal costs of private citizens and small entities when a prosecution is unsuccessful to provide an incentive against questionable prosecutions or prosecutions intended to intimidate.

5. <u>Regulatory Honeymoon</u> is how one might
    describe the idea of allowing a three-to-five
    year period in which new business would be
    exempted from complying with labour
    standards. This could be combined with
    another idea from the March National Economic
    Conference whereby, during that honeymoon
    period, any (voluntary) expenditures for
    occupational, health and safety would be
    allowed as a business tax write-off.

6. <u>Reverse Onus</u> refers to the concern among
    business people about what they perceive as
    the relatively frequent assumption of guilt
    in federal regulations and procedures, an
    assumption which can put them to considerable
    cost regardless of how innocent they may be.
    There is a need at all levels of government
    to review statutes and weed out reverse onus
    provisions. A variant of this idea is that
    the onus could be placed on government to
    prove that a particular development project
    contravenes environmental principles, failing
    which the developer would be allowed to
    proceed. If this idea were combined with
    time-limits and the government department in
    question had to absorb its legal and other
    costs, a remarkable change might come about
    in some of the current tortured approval
    procedures which economic developers must
    undergo.

<u>ACKNOWLEDGEMENTS</u>

With all the competing considerations that come into
play in the review of regulatory programs and systems, one
might have expected a Joint Study Team composed of a broad
range of private and public sector representatives to have a
great deal of difficulty arriving at a consensus. In
reality, this was not the case. On the contrary, as this
report indicates, the Team was able to arrive at important
findings notwithstanding its diversity. This was because a
conscious effort was made by each member to set aside
preconceptions and to arrive at practical and reasonable
judgements in light of the current economic and social
priorities of the country. This sometimes required walking
a tight-rope, but the results of the study show, in the

Team's view, that a sensible balance can indeed be found in the field of regulatory policy.

The members of the Study Team include six volunteers from the private sector who left the comforts of home and hearth to work very long hours during some of the bleakest months of the year. In addition to the public servants listed as members of the Team, there were a number of important contributors to the Team's work from several corners of government, the private sector and even foreign governments. Special gratitude is due to the Treasury Board for putting a complete support unit at the disposal of the team (Office of Regulatory Reform), the Department of Justice for providing the ready assistance of several of its legal experts, and the Department of Supply and Services which, together with technical assistance from the United States Government, provided a computerized system to cope with the mass of regulatory information generated by the study.

The Team would like to express warm appreciation to the Ministerial Task Force for the privilege of serving the public through this important study. It would also like to express appreciation to the "mother ship" under the command of Mr. Darcy McKeough and Dr. Peter Meyboom. They provided a perfect blend of direction and freedom which left the Team with a clear guide to the galaxy but plenty of room to fly.

Our deepest gratitude goes to our spouses, friends and families who probably paid the highest price while we were engrossed in a unique and fascinating experiment.

REVIEW OF REGULATORY PROGRAMS

I   INTRODUCTION

This section reports on three key objectives of the Regulatory Program Team:

1)   to identify and describe all federal regulatory programs;
2)   to determine where problems in specific programs might exist as judged by the team, the private sector or other levels of government; and
3)   to indicate to the Task Force what course or courses of follow-up action are open to remedy or further evaluate these problems.

A)   Regulatory Program Inventory

The compilation of an accurate and authoritative inventory of federal regulatory programs (see Annex to Terms of Reference) was not an easy task since existing program descriptions were based on operational or budgetary imperatives unrelated to regulatory considerations.

A second difficulty stemmed from the ambiguity of the terms "regulatory" and "program", which resulted in departments arriving at different approaches in describing their regulatory activities, some subdividing a broad regulatory area into several component mini-regulatory programs while others took a sector in its entirety and called it a program. Faced with quandaries of this sort, the Team decided to invite the departments and agencies to determine the regulatory program descriptions that best suited their experience and requirements.

Some agencies objected to being singled out as regulatory programs. In these cases the Team made a judgement based on this test: other than on a purely adjudicative basis, has the agency been given power by statute to establish or legislate rules of public behaviour subject to penalties? This test resulted in the elimination of some programs from the original inventory and the retention of a few programs, notwithstanding the reluctance of the agencies in question.

The resulting inventory contains a total of 146 regulatory and regulatory-related programs (the latter term was coined to allow for grey-area programs whose main raison d'être is associated with regulation even if they do not strictly speaking regulate) costing $2.7 billion dollars and involving some 34,500 persons. The inventory is a significant achievement in itself since it provides the federal government for the first time with a reasonably up-to-date basis for monitoring and management of its regulatory activities.

II   PROBLEM IDENTIFICATION

The Study Team's Terms of Reference required it to identify "problem programs" on the basis of 11 criteria. The Ministerial Task Force expressed its dominant criterion as follows:

"first of all against the criterion of economic development"; that is, does the program directly or indirectly constitute an obstacle to economic development or job creation".

The Team was expected to identify problem areas among federal regulatory programs in relation to these criteria and with the help of views and comments from the private sector (see Record of Consultation), the provinces and territories, and the department responsible for each program. All the comments have been taken into careful account by the Team in compiling its report.

However, it is perhaps important to note that the Team did not necessarily agree in each case with the comments received from other sources. In the end, the Team decided that its duty was to act very much like a jury in advising the Ministerial Task Force. That is, "without fear or favour" and on the basis of all the information available to it.

Except for native regulatory programs, which were the subject of another team, the profiles, overviews, and backgrounders provide a comprehensive picture of current federal regulatory programs. The first page of each profile is strictly factual and represents the first ever comprehensive description of these programs. The Team suggests that the Department of Supply and Services, or a designated minister, prepare a compendium of factual descriptions of the federal regulatory programs prepared by the Regulatory Programs Team for publication.

Although this report is by no means definitive, the Study Team is confident that the key problem areas and many useful suggestions have been identified. In that respect, the Team believes it has met its objective of establishing a sound basis for future improvements of regulatory program management by the federal government.

OVERVIEW

AGRICULTURAL REGULATION
(Excluding Grain)

The totality of government agricultural programs includes direct subsidies, research, management information and assistance, subsidized loans, loan guarantees, crop insurance, domestic and export product promotion, product grading, product health and safety regulation, land quality improvement expenditures, domestic agricultural production controls and import control. The provinces have developed many duplicative or parallel agricultural assistance or subsidy programs.

Regulatory programs form a relatively small subset of this complex web of interrelated programs developed and managed by Agriculture Canada or for which the Minister of Agriculture is responsible. Although these programs are not big users of tax dollars compared to agricultural expenditure programs, their impact on economic development is significant, because they affect interprovincial and international trade, private sector innovation and entrepreneurship.

The regulatory programs studied can be grouped as follows:

I   NATIONAL SUPPLY MANAGEMENT

CDC 200	Canadian Dairy Commission
NFPMC 1	Farm Products Marketing Council
NFPMC 2	Agencies Established Under the Farm Products Marketing Agencies Act

These programs operate independently of Agriculture Canada. They employ border controls on imports and centrally planned national and provincial production limits (called quotas) for industrial milk, eggs, chickens and turkeys to control domestic supplies and thereby increase producer prices and incomes. They have severely restricted efficiency improvements in the affected industries. The Economic Council has estimated that in 1980 the total wealth transfer to producers from consumers under these programs was about $500 million per year (with another $300 million going from taxpayers to producers through the industrial milk subsidy).

However, producers and the department contend these programs serve a social purpose of helping to preserve the family farm, that they assure domestic self-sufficiency in the regulated product, and that consumers are assured a secure supply of high quality product. By maintaining the family farm, it is contended, integration of farms with farm input or processor interests is avoided, thus maintaining a more decentralized and competitive food production system.

In the Team's opinion, there is a lack of accountability in these programs which has allowed the producer-dominated marketing agencies to use regulatory protection to divert substantial economic benefits to their producer-constituents. Better supervisory legislation and a liberalized import policy are proposed. (See related Background papers.)

II FOOD PRODUCTS AND FOOD INPUT REGULATION AND INSPECTION

AGC 213	Inspection and Control of Facilities and Food Products
AGC 214	Market Maintenance (Grading, Research)
AGC 215	Inspection and Protection of Crops, Livestock, and Farm Input Supplies.

These inspection programs enforce government regulations that touch on practically every aspect of food and food input production and international trade. These regulations set out detailed rules concerning grading, labelling, nutritive value, product composition, product healthfulness, and plant hygiene.

The Agri-Food Regulation and Inspection activity of Agriculture Canada which runs these programs employs 3,600 people and will spend $165 million in 1985/86 on regulatory program delivery. On balance, the extensive inspection provided under these programs is accepted by producers and processors (especially for exports and imports) even though considerable irritation with inspectors' behaviour was expressed by regulatees.

Outside health, safety, and hygiene regulation, the Study Team concluded that the taxpayer was funding quality control and product information monitoring through inspectors which should be the responsibility of the private sector. Government inspection is the most costly way of enforcing regulatory compliance, can inhibit private sector innovation in production processes and inevitably politicizes day-to-day production activities as government inspectors represent a third interest, in addition to managers and labour, on the job site.

We suggest that product quality monitoring in all three programs should be privatized or otherwise cost-recovered. In our view, there should be more industry self-regulation in these areas. However, government regulation and inspection in food, health and safety and with respect to exports and imports should be retained for the time being.

III   INCOME AND PRICE STABILIZATION

        AGC 902   Agricultural Products Board
                       (regulatory related)
        AGC 901   Agricultural Stabilization Board
                       (regulatory related)

Both programs provide subsidies to farmers when market prices for their products drop below the previous year's average levels. If farm income support is considered to be in the public interest, then these programs provide a more desirable option than national supply management - but they should be redesigned to increase coordination with provincial support payments, introduce some producer co-insurance and make eligibility criteria more explicit.

IV   Miscellaneous

        AGC 18   Agricultural Products Marketing Act
        AGC 211   Race Track Supervision

No substantial problems exist with respect to these programs.

AGRICULTURAL PRODUCTS MARKETING ACT - AGC 18

Objective

To improve the orderly marketing of agricultural products governed by provincial marketing boards, by granting extra provincial jurisdiction on the sale and marketing of these products.

Authority

Agricultural Products Marketing Act (APMA).

Description

The provinces have created a large number of marketing boards to control the intra-provincial production and/or marketing of agricultural products. However provincial marketing board legislation cannot extend to products moving interprovincially or internationally. Regulatory jurisdiction over such movements rests with the federal government.

The provinces wishing to act as a sole or first receiver of all agricultural products subject to provincial marketing board legislation or to collect levies from producers to cover marketing board costs on their entire production (and not just production sold intra-provincially) require regulatory authority to do so to be delegated by a federal Act. This is the function of the APMA.

Under the Act, provincial marketing orders relying on delegated federal jurisdiction require Order-In-Council approval. The administrative resources of this oversight function are provided through the Marketing Services Division of Agriculture Canada.

Resources

($000's)	82/83	83/84	84/85	85/86	86/87	87/88
Person-Years		0.5	0.5			
Operating Exp.		18	23			
- Salaries						
- O & M						
- Other Expenses						
Revenue						
Subsidies						
Capital						

Problem Identification

Producers and provincial marketing boards are supportive of the Act and consider it to be necessary for the effective and fair operation of provincial agricultural products marketing schemes. This is also the view of the department which has indicated that the legislation:

1) makes provincial marketing boards and provincial agricultural sectors more stable and efficient; and

2) provides a mechanism to increase provincial board resources for market promotion of Canadian agricultural products.

However, the Department and the provincial boards consider that the current requirement of Order-In-Council approval of all provincial marketing orders, including the most routine, made under delegated federal powers is costly, cumbersome and reduces the management flexibility of provincial boards.

Observations

There is a consensus that delegated federal jurisdiction is needed to permit provincial marketing boards to apply their regulatory policies to all production within a province. Generally speaking, such boards do not possess significant power to disrupt the influence of market forces on production and pricing decisions as do national supply management regimes. In many instances they have improved market efficiency by increasing market information available to producers and increasing producer bargaining power vis-à-vis large or highly concentrated food processors. Thus they contribute to economic development and job creation.

There appears to be no need for Order-In-Council approval of all provincial marketing orders which rely in whole or in part on delegated federal jurisdiction. However, the removal of all federal oversight would not be desirable. For example, a provincial marketing board which was authorized under the APMA to become a first receiver of all interprovincial or international shipments of a product into the province could employ such a monopoly power to restrict supplies within the province in order to raise commodity and producer incomes. Such a practice would encourage further balkanization of the agricultural sector and reduce agricultural efficiency in the same manner as has occurred under national supply management schemes.

Options

The Study Team recommends to the Task Force that the government consider the following:

1. Determine which types of provincial marketing orders are purely routine and would not create any barriers to interprovincial or international trade. Eliminate Order-In-Council approval of such orders.

2. Give closer scrutiny to those provincial orders which may have the effect of creating barriers to interprovincial or international trade or unreasonably increasing commodity prices and reject orders having such effects.

RACE TRACK SUPERVISION - AGC 211

Objective

To protect the wagering public at race tracks from faulty or fraudulent betting systems and race conduct, and to assist in ensuring a viable race track industry through the provision of efficient pari-mutuel and race supervision services according to uniform national standards.

Authority

Criminal Code (s.188).

Description

The program is conducted by the Race Track Division of the Department of Agriculture. Regulatory powers are given to the Minister of Agriculture pursuant to the Criminal Code exemption from gambling offences for pari-mutuel betting at lawful horse races. The program develops and enforces regulations concerning the operation of pari-mutuel systems, the method of calculating the amount payable in respect to each dollar bet, the conduct of race meetings in relation to photo finish, race patrol and drug control, and the provision and maintenance of facilities for the operation of pari-mutuel systems.

The number of race days operated by each track is indirectly controlled by the authorization of a limited number of pari-mutuel betting days. Provincial racing commissions also regulate the operating day of race tracks, creating some federal/provincial overlap and duplication.

The program is self-financing through a levy of 0.8% on all pari-mutuel bets.

Resources

($000's)	82/83	83/84	84/85	85/86	86/87	87/88
Person-Years		90	90	103		
Operating Exp.						
- Salaries						
- O&M		12,021	12,107	13,206	14,137	14,391
- Other Exp.						
Revenue		13,198	12,690	13,206	14,137	14,391
Subsidies						
Capital				352	55	58

Problem Identification

The Program provides fraud prevention and quality control services directly and through subcontractors which would, in all likelihood, be required under provincial race track regulation if they were not already covered in the Criminal Code.

The Race Track Division recognizes that the overlap in authorizing racing days with provincial authorities can be an irritant and consults frequently with the provincial bodies to minimize inconsistent authorizations. Only a few disputes have arisen and all appear to have been satisfactorily resolved.

Through the levy system, the 12 largest tracks cross-subsidize the Division's supervision of the smaller (115) tracks. The large tracks are aware of this effect but support it on the ground that it helps to maintain the size and credibility of the industry in the face of stagnant demand.

The betting public is largely unaware of the program. The levy has, relative to provincial taxes, an insignificant impact on funds available for distribution as winnings.

Daily on-site supervision by government personnel is non-discretionary under the Criminal Code. However, supervision is tailored to meet the circumstances of the track and its betting system.

Observations

The program does not create an obstacle to economic development or job creation. Rather, it contributes to public confidence in an industry which provides one of the few lawful gambling activities in Canada while also generating considerable tax revenues.

There is no articulated desire by the industry in favour of self-regulation or provincial regulation with respect ot the services provided by the Program.

With actual federal/provincial overlap being negligible, the only issue of concern would appear to be the efficient delivery of supervisory services. Apart from pari-mutuel supervision (which must be conducted by government officials under the Criminal Code), the Race

Track Division is relying increasingly on subcontractors in the private sector for the provision of services to the Program. These contracts are let pursuant to competitive tenders, thus reducing the opportunity for inefficient provision of services.

Options

The Study Team recommends to the Task Force that the government consider the following:

1.   Continue Program as is within Agriculture Canada.

2.   Amend Criminal Code to allow periodic instead of constant on-site pari-mutuel system supervision.

3.   Amend Criminal Code to pass regulatory responsibility to provinces.

INSPECTION AND CONTROL OF FACILITIES AND FOOD PRODUCTS - AGC 213

Objective

To ensure the safety, quality and nutritive value of edible agricultural products.

Authority

Humane Slaughter Act, Meat Inspection Act, Animal Disease and Protection Act, Fruit, Vegetable and Honey Act, Canada Agricultural Products Standards Act, Livestock and Livestock Products Act, Food and Drugs (by reference in Regulations), Consumer Packaging and Labelling Act (by reference in Regulations).

Description

The Program has three principal activities:

1. ## National Inspection Services

    a) This element includes the National (Meat) Inspection Service, as well as Import, Foreign and Federal/Provincial Inspection Programs. All animals are inspected before and after slaughter, while site inspection and monitoring ensures that the environment in which meat products are produced, stored and transported meets legislated requirements in regard to construction, sanitation, operation and hygiene.

    b) A meat inspection service is provided on a cost recovery basis to some provinces, under federal/provincial agreement, in meat plants which would not otherwise fall under federal inspection (i.e. where meat and meat products do not move into intraprovincial trade). Meat inspection systems of countries exporting meat products to Canada are evaluated to ensure that Canadian standards are met.

2. ## Plant Registration and Inspection

    This element aims at compliance with regulations governing operations, sanitation and hygiene standards in food processing plants. Physical inspection are conducted on domestic dairy, poultry, egg, honey, maple, and processed fruit and vegetable plants registered with the Department.

3. Scientific Analysis

This element provides composition, chemical and microbiological testing services in support of food product inspections (including meat, dairy, fruit, vegetable and poultry product samples) to ensure that the products comply with federal standards for safety, quality and composition for domestic and export markets.

Resources

($000's)	82/83	83/84	84/85	85/86	86/87	87/88
Person-Years		1,380	1,371	1,398		
Operating Expenses		57,030	59,644	62,906		
Revenues		3,770	4,157	13,920		
Subsidies						
Capital		120	359	303		

Problem Identification

The regulations and methods of enforcement in these areas are not questioned in principle by agricultural producers. Processors have questioned in general terms the current need for as extensive a system of product quality and product information regulation as presently exists and, with respect to such regulation, the need for regulatory enforcement and compliance monitoring using government inspectors. They do not take issue with health and safety regulation under these programs or using government inspectors to monitor compliance with such regulations or with more intensive inspection of exports.

The Department believes that much of the quality and grading regulation development and compliance enforcement through inspectors amounts essentially to a free service to industry which industry should either pay or assume responsibility for. The FOIL program (see Background Paper on inspection-based compliance) is an effort to do so. This program has been severely criticized by the inspectors' union as leading to lower quality and unhealthy processed meats.

Observations

Opportunities exist to utilize technology to shift quality control and quality assurance responsibilities more to the private sector, thus decreasing reliance upon rigid product regulations and/or the subjective judgment of government inspectors. This could reduce private sector irritation that inevitably flows from the constant presence of government inspectors at plants and grading stations, improve citizenship, and allow for greater innovation in production processes. To date, the Department's approach has been incremental and fragmentary. A comprehensive approach to reform of quality standards development and enforcement is needed to supplement current product-specific initiatives. The inspectors union's concerns about reduced regulatory compliance resulting from a shift of compliance-monitoring responsibility to processors can, in the Team's view, be addressed by making less discretionary existing measures to deter non-compliance (prosecution and fines, deregistration or registration suspension of processing plants, publication of observed compliance performance of plants) and requiring processors to use their own, not government, grading stamps.

Options

The Study Team recommends to the Task Force that the government consider the following:

1. Reduce inspection based compliance and rely more on industry self-monitoring.

    a) Systematically develop FOIL inspection/monitoring systems for all quality standard enforcement activity in the processing area as an intermediate step towards adopting a voluntary total quality control approach to agricultural product quality maintenance.

    b) Adopt a sliding scale to recover plant inspection costs which is integrated with FOIL inspection intensity levels (i.e. as compliance deteriorates, inspection costs increase).

    c) Contract out routine laboratory analyses.

    d) As a model for other products, encourage the implementation of electronic hog grading as soon as possible and stimulate experiments in using robotics for hog grading (At present human hog inspectors are expected to grade 360 hogs per hour, or one hog every 10 seconds).

e)   Establish and publicize guidelines for the prosecution, suspension of registration and deregistration of plants which are serious and/or repeated compliance problems. Remove administrative discretion as fully as possible from these guidelines. Publicize widely action taken under them.

f)   Increase the level of fines available and sought in prosecutions under the Acts.

g)   As employee inspection increases, phase out the use of government certification stamps by employees of processing plants, and replace them with processor-identified attestations.

2.   Continue as is but devote more resources to health and safety inspection.

FRUIT, VEGETABLES AND HONEY REGULATIONS
AGC - 213 (SUPPLEMENTAL)

Objective

To control the importation of fresh fruit and vegetables from the United States.

Authority

Fruit, Vegetables and Honey Act.

Description

The Act and its Regulations were established in 1935 to provide quality standards for produce and honey and to regulate trade in these products. The Regulations were amended in 1942 to prohibit the importation of produce without a confirmed sale within 24 hours of shipment from the point of production as part of the wartime effort to discourage inefficient use of rail cars. They were also amended in 1947 to include trucks in the prohibition and in 1949 to limit the range of products affected to only those kinds grown in Canada. There is an exemption for small lots of produce not exceeding 1000 pounds per vehicle, per importer, per day. In mixed loads, importation is permitted if the produce of a kind grown in Canada does not exceed 1/3 of the load.

The effect of the Regulations is to allow produce imports from the U.S. from areas far from the border but not from close to the border.

Canadian Agricultural Products Standards Act of 1955 and its regulations have consolidated all federal quality and trade regulations first enacted under specific sectoral legislation with the exception of the import restricting provisions of the Fruit, Vegetables and Honey Regulations.

Resources*

($000's)	84-85	85-86	86-87	87-88
Person-Years	10	10	10	10
Expenses	300	312	324	337
Revenue	-	-	-	-

* Departmental estimate in the event the Regulations were enforced.

Problem Identification

In May 1984, the Standing Joint Committee on Regulations and Other Statutory Instruments reported that the regulations were _ultra vires_ and should be revoked. Shortly afterwards the government decided to stop actively enforcing the Regulations.

The Department considers that the regulations should be kept in order to avoid a flood of low cost U.S. produce imports which would harm Canadian producers. It has suggested that the regulations be kept as part of the Regulations of the Canadian Agricultural Products Standards Act. The department's position is supported by processor representatives.

Other departments consider the regulations to be:

(1) an unwarranted restraint to trade which keeps produce prices too high in Canada and,

(2) an emerging irritant in U.S.-Canadian trade relations.

Since the Regulations were enacted 40 years ago, both the federal and provincial governments have set up a variety of price and income support programs to deal with serious, unexpected drops in domestic producer prices.

Observations

The regulations are anachronistic and possibly illegal but a handy way to protect producers from competition. They are a barrier to trade, invite retaliatory action under the GATT and push up Canadian food prices.

Domestic fresh fruit and vegetable prices have not dropped since the government stopped enforcing the Regulations.

Agriculture Canada has provided no empirical evidence to support the view that repeal of regulations would wipe out Canadian fresh fruit and vegetable producers. These producers will have been helped by the recent decline in the value of the Canadian dollar relative to the U.S. dollar.

Options

The Study Team recommends to the Task Force that the government consider the following:

1.(a)   Repeal the regulations and evaluate the impact of their absence on Canadian producers at the end of the 1985 growing season,

   (b)   If necessary, provide price or income support under the Agricultural Stabilization Act or the Agricultural Products Act.

2.(a)   Re-enact the regulations under the Canadian Agricultural Products Standards Act.

MARKET MAINTENANCE - AGC 214

Objective

To assist in the maintenance of existing national and international markets for Canadian agricultural products.

Authority

Animal Disease and Protection, Meat Inspection, Seeds, Canadian Agricultural Products Standards, Livestock and Livestock Products, Fruit, Vegetable and Honey, Plant Quarantine Act, Hay and Straw Inspection, Feeds, Fertilizers, Pest Control Products, Food and Drugs, Consumer Packaging and Labelling, Weights and Measures, Import and Export Permits.

Description

This Program provides regulatory-related support services for AGC 213 and AGC 215. The principal areas of the Program are:

1. Negotiating zoosanitary and phytosanitary standards for exports of agricultural products (animal and plant).

2. Inspecting, testing, quarantining, and certifying animal and products, and ensuring they meet requirements of importing countries.

3. Inspecting and certification of exports of seeds and seed potatoes.

4. Assuring adequate agricultural input labelling to permit safe agricultural outputs (feed, fertilizer and pesticide).

5. Ensuring compliance with grade and composition standards for domestic and imported agricultural products.

6. Ensuring that a national livestock grading system maintains a uniform national standard and constitutes a good basis for marketing livestock carcasses.

7. Inspection and phytosanitary certification of plants, plant products and any other things that can carry plant pests.

Resources

($000's)	82/83	83/84	84/85	85/86	86/87	87/88
Person-Years		974	976	984		
Operating Expenses		38,390	41,538	44,018		
Revenue		740	554	8,359		
Subsidies, etc.						
Capital		734	650	1,531		

Problem Identification, Observations, Options

The regulatory activities for which this Program provides technical and scientific support services are examined under AGC 213 and AGC 215.

INSPECTION AND PROTECTION OF CROPS, LIVESTOCK AND FARM INPUT SUPPLIES - AGC 215/R

Objective

To ensure the protection of animals and plants necessary for food and agricultural production, and to ensure the availability and quality of basic inputs (feed, seed, fertilizers, pesticides) for this production.

Authority

Livestock and Livestock Products, Animal Disease and Protection, Fertilizers, Pest Control Products, Pesticide Residue Compensation, Feeds, Seeds, Plant Quarantine (Also International Plant Protection Convention), Food and Drugs, Consumer Packaging and Labelling, Weights and Measures, Import and Export Permits, Appropriation (Rabies), International Plant Protection Convention.

Description

The general areas of Program activity are:

1. <u>Animal disease control and eradication:</u> (including zoonotic diseases) to protect the health of Canada's livestock and poultry, to reduce the risk of transmission of animal diseases to humans, to ensure animals are treated humanely, and to ensure the viable domestic and export marketability of livestock, poultry and agricultural products. This includes the control of imports to prevent disease introduction, while facilitating the importation of essential animal genetic material and other commodities.

2. <u>Control of plant pests:</u> (diseases, weeds, insects) which can have a negative economic impact on agricultural and forestry production and marketing.

3. <u>Agricultural input assurance:</u> quality hay seeds and seed potatoes; safe and effective pesticides, livestock feeds, fertilizers, and the introduction of healthy genetic stock.

Pursuant to the various enabling acts, the Program develops and enforces, through inspection activities, regulations concerning product quality and safety standards, label designation, product and business licensing, product and business registration and certification, quarantine, compensation, testing, grading and information reporting. The sanctions available under the legislation include permission/refusal to import or sell, detention, prosecution (fines and/or imprisonment), destruction and seizure, registration and deregistration of plants, delisting of plants.

Resources

($000's)	82/83	83/84	84/85	85/86	86/87	87/88
Person Years		1,131	1,140	1,235		
Operating Expenses		55,886	58,901	66,948		
Revenue		1,673	1,595	9,248		
Subsidies, etc.		365	1,682	635		
Capital		3,445	3,178	5,978		

Problem Identification

The regulations and methods of enforcement in these areas are not questioned in principle by agricultural producers. However, processors and consumers have questioned in general terms the current need for as extensive a system of product quality and product information regulation as presently exists and, with respect to such regulation, the need for regulatory enforcement and compliance monitoring using government inspectors. These groups do not take issue with health and safety regulation under these programs or with reliance on government inspectors to monitor compliance with such regulations. There is also consensus among producers, processors and consumers that health, safety and quality assurance regulation and enforcement of a high order are warranted in the case of agricultural exports to maintain and improve access to international markets for agricultural products.

In a 1984 A-base review, the Department identified inadequate resources as presenting effectiveness and adequacy problems in the following regulatory areas: plant health, fertilizer, feed, seeds and pesticides. In each case substantial resource increases were proposed as a short term response. Long-term proposals varied in each area. At the same time the Department has recognized that much of the quality and grading regulation development and compliance enforcement through inspectors amounts essentially to a free service to industry. It, therefore, considers that the industry should become responsible for quality control and assurance, leaving the Department to concentrate on control of health, safety and wholesomeness.

Observations

The variety of long-term options presented by the Department, coupled with large resource increase proposals for the short term to deal with resource restraint problems, suggests that the Department has not taken a comprehensive approach to assessing regulatory reform and optimal program design. With respect to fertilizer, feed and seed regulation, a number of regulatory innovations now being considered by the Department with respect to a specific area in relation to quality and information provision could well be applied in a comprehensive fashion in all three areas. These initiatives would allow resources to be concentrated more effectively on safety matters.

Private sector reliance upon government inspectors to maintain adequate product quality (at a given price) would be decreased, and in its place would be substituted more informed private decision-making. Such an overall approach would require initially a clear identification by the Department of which regulatory controls are necessary to ensure health and safety. This approach would improve the adequacy, relevance and efficiency of regulation in the above areas while allowing for improved citizenship and entrepreneurial intiative.

With respect to pesticide regulation, a current departmental practice known as Product Specific Regulation (PSR) has apparently been employed to grant a form of patent protection for the source companies of new active pesticide ingredients. This has been achieved through the department's pesticide registration procedure by permitting the source company to have exclusive use of the supporting data for a new product for 15 years from the date of commercialization. This practice, according to some representatives of the pesticide formulating industry, has had the effect of restricting competition in the Canadian pesticide industry and increasing pesticide prices to farmers. In the Team's view, such a policy is outside the spirit, if not the letter, of the enabling legislation which is to regulate pesticide safety and quality and amounts to the creation of a new intellectual property right akin to patent protection.

Options

The Study Team recommends to the Task Force that the government consider the following:

1. Instead of increasing resources to department, adopt different regulatory methods such as:

(a) Introduce a program of publishing compliance test results to replace enforcement by inspectors;

(b) Increase cost recovery for all government tests directed at product quality (but not safety-oriented tests);

(c) As a substitute for plant-level inspections, amend all farm input legislation or regulations to provide for government approval of minimum quality control standards for plant processes to be monitored by plant employees subject to periodic audit by inspection staff; and

(d) Increased accreditation of private testing laboratories (subject to government monitoring) with government labs continuing to provide official testing for export products and plant health-related testing.

2. For pesticides:

a) Stop providing any exclusive registration under the Pest Control Product Act; rely on Patent Act for invention protection.

SUMMARY OF AGRICULTURE CANADA A-BASE REVIEW
RECOMMENDATIONS: INSPECTION PROGRAMS (AGC 215)

The specific areas identified by the Department as being in need of significant resource increases to meet workload demands and program objectives are:

1. Plant Health (administration of the Plant Quarantine Act and International Plant Protection Convention): existing resource base insufficient to adequately service increased trade volumes to protect the continued marketability of $8 billion of exports in agricultural and forest products and to protect the health status of the plant population for efficient production.

2. Fertilizer quality packaging and labelling standards development and regulation (Fertilizers Act):

    a) compliance rate of fertilizer products in the marketplace has dropped from 82.3 per cent in 1976 to 75 per cent in 1983.

    b) poor quality fertilizers reduce farm productivity, yet fertilizer costs increased 243 per cent over this period.

    c) improve compliance in short term with resource increase and in long term by:

        (i) introducing a program of publishing test results to replace quality standards enforcement by inspectors;

        (ii) implementing and extending a cost recovery program based on a tonnage fee.

3. Feed safety and quality packaging and labelling standards regulation (Feeds Act, Hay and Straw Inspection Act, Pesticide Residue Compensation Act, Food and Drugs Act):

    a) increasing safety concerns due to greater use of medications and by-products such as recycled livestock manure as feed ingredients, increasing number of on-farm mixers using drug premixers.

b)   greater volume of producer complaints, low
      compliance level of fertilizers tested.

c)   improve compliance in short term with a shift in
      program emphasis from quality to safety and in
      long term by:

      (i)   amending Feeds Act to institute minimal
             quality control standards ("Good
             Manufacturing Practices") for manufacturers
             subject to periodic audits by inspection
             staff,

      (ii)   accreditation of private testing
             laboratories,

      (iii) increase cost recovery for feed registration
             from 25 per cent to 100 per cent.

BACKGROUND

REGULATORY ENFORCEMENT: INSPECTION-BASED COMPLIANCE SYSTEMS - AGC 213-215

I   INTRODUCTION: RELATIONSHIP TO STUDY TEAM ASSESSMENT CRITERIA

Many regulatory programs, especially those in the agri-food and consumer protection fields, have traditionally relied on visits to or even the continuous presence of government inspectors on the premises of businesses subject to mandatory product standards regulation as the primary means of ensuring compliance with the relevant regulations. Whether the inspector's task is to be present to verify, to attest to compliance with respect to each product, or to perform random or periodic "spot-checks" of production processes or products, the role of the inspector is essentially: (1) to replace the businesses' senior management in looking over the businesses' employees to monitor their day-to-day regulatory compliance and (2) replace competitors and consumers in initiating government action to remedy or discipline instances if non-compliance.

As government reliance on inspectors to ensure regulatory compliance grows over time, other methods of ensuring compliance, such as fines following criminal prosecution of serious offenders and licence or registration suspensions, tend to be eclipsed.

The use of inspectors is, however, one of the most costly, if not the most costly, measure available to governments for monitoring regulatory compliance. Moreover, inspection-based compliance systems can:

(1)   Over time, result in increasing, and possibly excessive, reliance by businessmen on government employees to identify problem areas leading to a failure to comply and to present solutions to such problems.

(2)   Result in government inspectors becoming intermediaries between management and labour and between sellers and buyers (e.g. hog producers and hog processors with respect to the quality and hence value of individual hogs).

63

(3)   Cause increasing and perhaps undue reliance by
        consumers (both household and business) of the
        regulated product on the assumption that
        "government", (through its inspectors) has
        attested, or even guaranteed, that not only is the
        product safe, but that it is good or appropriate
        quality and that all relevant information
        concerning it has been presented by the seller.

In these instances, the effect of relying on government
inspectors can well be a lessening of the extent to which
actors in the marketplace take direct responsibility for
their economic decisions. Not only does this impinge on the
achievement of the good citizenship goal as defined in the
Terms of Reference of the Study Team, it may also create a
tendency on the part of businessmen and the public to seek
more government intervention through inspection when things
are perceived to "go wrong" with the products or services in
question or when products or production processes change or
seem to become "more complex".

On another plane, inspection-based compliance systems,
like stringent product design regulations, can have the
effect of unduly inhibiting the ability to innovate in
production processes and thereby impede increased business
productivity and economic development within particular
industries. This can occur in the following ways:

(1)   In making decisions to introduce new technologies
        or simply to rearrange the way a business goes
        about producing things, managers must not only
        take into account the structure of their business,
        including the aspirations and abilities of its
        workforce and existing labour agreements, but also
        the interests of a second workforce not directly
        under their control – the government inspectors.
        This can increase the difficulty in making major
        process changes if the inspectors or the managers
        are unable or reluctant to adapt to the change.
        In effect, through the power to amend regulations
        or change policies and practices, government holds
        a veto power over major production process
        decisions.

(2)   Because management is no longer directly
        performing certain "hands-on" quality and safety
        monitoring functions (where inspectors perform
        them) managers do not have sufficient knowledge to

affect productivity improvements in a timely fashion.

(3)   Economic actors who perceive that certain innovations are not in their economic interests (because employees may be displaced or some jobs will change or become more difficult) may effectively politicize inspectors against the change through a myriad of job-site actions directed at demonstrating that the innovation is doomed to result in regulatory breaches or that the only practical way to do things is the way they are done now.

Still inspection-based compliance enforcement tends to elicit the greatest incidence of business irritation and complaint. Typically this irritiation is articulated as:

(1)   meddling in management affairs,

(2)   arbitrary and capricious judgement calls,

(3)   inspectors appearing to issue orders or give advice which goes beyond the four corners of the regulation they're enforcing,

(4)   arguing with employees or being pushy with respect to remedying a non-compliance situation,

(5)   being unreasonably "nitpicky", or

(6)   interfering with managements' or employees' other responsibilities.

In light of the above considerations, it would appear that any general re-examination of the effects of government regulation should look particularly closely at existing inspection-based compliance systems to determine whether current economic circumstances might allow regulatory compliance to be achieved through less onerous or costly measures which place greater responsibility on the private sector economic actors involved to ensure effective compliance monitoring and, at the same time, provide greater scope for innovation and entrepreneurial initiative. In the following sections two alternative approaches to constant hands-on inspection in the agri-food sector are outlined.

II VOLUNTARY TOTAL QUALITY CONTROL (TQC)

This is a new approach to the health, safety and quality regulation of processed meat and poultry products introduced by the U.S. Department of Agriculture (USDA) in 1980. Under it, processing firms submit comprehensive plans to the USDA for the in-house production and operating control of food quality, sanitation, net weight, labelling and similar variables. The role of the USDA shifts from being an inspector to primarily giving approval to a firm's quality control plan, including the identification by the firm of problems and the design of the testing and reporting mechanisms proposed for key "control" points in the production process. Once the plan is approved, plant management becomes responsible for checking these control points and documenting its findings. USDA inspectors periodically monitor these records and conduct occasional spot checks, thus distancing themselves considerably from the worklife of the plant. Plant inspection activity no longer forms the bulk of their work and it is generally ancillary to process monitoring by the firm. In this manner plant regulation shifts from being detection-oriented to prevention-oriented.

The change in approach was largely in response to the following factors:

(1)   a recognition by the USDA that, over time, greater volumes of food processing, and an increasing variety and complexity of processed food products, had outstripped the capabilities of traditional plant inspection methods, and, given departmental resource constraints, was jeopardizing the relevance and adequacy of such methods;

(2)   industry submissions that internal quality control methods available with increased plant automation could also, with minimal modification, meet regulatory requirements;

(3)   departmental studies which raised serious concerns over the objectivity and reliability of judgemental compliance and enforcement decisions of on-site inspectors and concluded that statistical sampling and lab-testing would provide a more objective and reliable measure of compliance for subsequent enforcement action.

(4)   a general recognition in the industry and
        government that the appalling plant conditions
        observed at the turn of the century had been
        eliminated and that firms were now strongly
        motivated by increased competition from larger
        markets, more efficient transportation and storage
        systems, and greater consumer awareness, to
        maintain high standards on their own;

(5)   USDA officials were concerned that plants were
        tending to take inspectors for granted.

A 1984 USDA assessment of the first 4 years of the
program reported the following industry responses:

(1)   92 per cent of plants started TQC to demonstrate
        self-responsibility over their operations.
        Product quality and operational flexibility were
        also important motivational factors.

(2)   Plant operations generally showed improvement
        after TQC was implemented. A majority of the
        plants reported improved employee and management
        attitudes in their work. Seventy-three per cent
        also experienced greater control over production
        since starting TQC. Product safety and quality
        showed improvement as well.

(3)   TQC had a positive effect on plant-inspector
        relations. Sixty per cent of the plants reported
        an improved relationship. Where plants did report
        problems with the inspector, the reasons given
        were inspector difficulty in adjusting to TQC and
        in accepting the new roles inherent in the
        program.

(4)   Plants reported greater management control and
        quality awareness as important benefits of TQC.
        Savings in USDA inspection overtime charges was a
        significant benefit for many plants as well.
        Sixty-nine per cent reported saving money on
        overtime expenditures. The median cost per plant
        avoidance was U.S. $5,017, and ranged from
        U.S. $50 to $50,000.

(5)   The greatest initial cost for most plants to enter
        the program was, primarily, developing the TQC
        program. The median cost was U.S. $1,377 per

plant. Seventy-five percent of the plants
reported development costs of U.S. $3,100 or
under. Additionally, 14 per cent of the plants
were required to purchase laboratory or production
line equipment to enter TQC. The one-time median
cost for this equipment was U.S. $2,050.

(6) Continuing cost in TQC participation is primarily
the recordkeeping requirement. The daily reported
median requirement was 2 hours. A few plants also
reported hiring one or two additional workers or
incurring added overtime cost as a result of TQC.

The conclusion of the USDA assessment is as follows:

"Overall, TQC appears to be a net benefit to
plants in the program. Initial cost expenditures do
not seem a burden to most plants, and are often offset
by first year USDA overtime savings. Even the best
managed plants report improved operating procedures and
product quality after TQC involvement. In many cases,
the daily regulatory relationship between the plant and
inspector is improved and more clearly defined. If the
participation rates of large plants, who produce most
of the inspected product, and small plants, who require
the greatest inspection resources, continue to
increase, TQC will have a significant effect on meat
poultry products and inspection."

Detected quality control problems and instances of
regulatory non-compliance result in written USDA requests
for proof that corrective action is being taken by the
plant. The USDA retains its statutory powers to deregister
or prosecute in the event of serious non-compliance. It has
also recently introduced a special program known as
Intensive Regulatory Enforcement (IRE) for problem plants.
Under IRE special quality control plans must be drawn up and
additional inspector surveillance may be provided.
Compliance for six months removes the plant from the
program. Plants under IRE are excluded from bidding on
federal contracts.

The USDA is also actively encouraging more vigorous
prosecution of infractions and is asking Congress for
greater powers to shut down violators.

These actions have been taken in response to concerns that TQC has transferred too much responsibility to plant personnel too quickly. The USDA has not, however, changed its plans to implement TQC as widely as possible.

TQC represents a program designed to rely to the fullest extent possible on self-regulation, self-control and integration of regulatory monitoring processes within the firm's own production process while still maintaining a comprehensive product regulation scheme having health, safety, quality and consumer information aspects. It suggests that not only can greater self-regulation work in the areas of quality assurance and the provision of adequate product information, but, even in the critical areas of agri-food health and safety regulation, there is also greater scope for greater self-regulation and less use of government inspection.

III   FREQUENCY OF INSPECTION LEVEL (FOIL)

This alternative to continuous on-site inspection was developed by Agriculture Canada, originally for the dairy product industry, beginning in 1970. FOIL has subsequently replaced monitoring programs for fresh fruit and vegetables, poultry and egg products.

The department is currently studying pilot FOIL systems for meat processing and storage inspection. FOIL is a statistically-based methodology to direct traditional inspection resources to higher risk commodities and establishments. Under it, commodities and establishments are, on the basis of past compliance performance (as determined by the incidence of regulatory non-compliance observations), designated for reduced, normal, or tightened inspection visit frequencies instead of having government inspectors present throughout working hours.

However, relative to TQC, FOIL must be viewed as largely a half-way measure. It provides greater flexibility to public service managers in resource allocation and thereby improves program productivity, but it retains the traditional on-site monitoring role for government inspectors. Apart from rewarding high business compliance with less inspector coverage and a reduction in inspector overtime payments by processors, it does not systematically shift responsibility for compliance monitoring from government to industry as does TCQ.

FOIL does place full responsibility on plant employees for grading when inspectors are not present. However, government grading stamps continue to be used. The union representing federal meat inspectors has expressed concerns over this practice, contending that this creates the false impression with consumers that impartial government employees have done the grading and may permit the plant to "hide" behind the government inspection program if grading problems arise. The union has also alleged that, without a continuous inspector presence at the plant, compliance to health and safety regulations will also deteriorate.

The extent to which FOIL can be extended further in the direction of TQC would appear to depend on the development of clear supplementary deterrents to regulatory non-compliance (e.g. publication, prosecution and fines, and plant deregistration), particularly with respect to health and safety matters.

AGRICULTURAL PRODUCTS BOARD - AGC 902

Objective

To stabilize markets, prices and producer incomes by buying commodities which are in temporary over-supply and reselling them later.

Authority

Agricultural Products Board Act.

Description

The Agricultural Products Board (APB) comprises three senior officials from the Department of Agriculture. They are presently the same members as the Agricultural Stabilization Board. The APB is empowered by the Agricultural Products Board Act to buy, sell or import agricultural products, and to administer food contracts and other commodity operations. It may purchase and hold stocks of agricultural products for later sale, emergency relief in Canada or assistance programs abroad. The Act is most often used in support of the Agricultural Stabilization Act as a vehicle to remove a calculated amount of a product from the market to firm up prices, and thus, perhaps, to avoid the need for a general deficiency payment program. The Act has also been used to provide purchase and resale price support to a number of agricultural commodities, such as sweet cherries, solid pack apples, grape juice, grape concentrate, and canned tomatoes. Through past programs, the Board has supplied the World Food Program with canned turkey, dehydrated potatoes, canned beef loaf, and canned whole egg powder.

As a generalization, the APB deals with matters ancillary to price support operations, but not coming specifically under the authority of the Agricultural Stabilization Act.

Where it provides purchase/sale assistance, the APB negotiates purchases from producers at a price below recent year's average levels which is calculated to result in a 50/50 sharing of anticipated losses between producers and the federal government. The program has been directed at commodities which are not readily storable in their natural form (where marketings are more readily controlled by producers) and where storage for later resale is feasible

after some processing. As a result the program has
concentrated on horticultural produce and avoids overlap
with departmental expenditure programs aimed at improving
on-farm storage facilities to avoid post-season distress
sales by producers.

The APB calls upon resources of the Agricultural
Stabilization Board and the department as needed.

Resources

($000's)	82/83	83/84	84/85	85/86	86/87	87/88
Person-Years	2	2	2	2	N/A	N/A
Operating Exp.	N/A	N/A	N/A	N/A	N/A	N/A
Purch.& Handling	10,500	12,600	12,600	5,600	N/A	N/A
Sales	2,900	7,700	11,900	5,600	N/A	N/A
Net Losses	7,600	4,900	700	0	N/A	N/A

Problem Identification

The program has received no adverse comment either in
principle or with respect to its operations from the private
sector. It has the support of producers.

The Department considers it to be a complement to the
Agricultural Stabilization Act which has helped reduce
overall government income stabilization payments in Canada
more than it has cost the taxpayer. In particular, the
ability of the APB to act quickly to deal with product
perishability or acute producer financial problems has been
cited as a positive attribute.

A 1984 Departmental Program Evaluation on Market Risk
Programs (which included the APB) observed that the Act has
been used to provide continuing financial support for a
turkey processor despite its intended producer-
orientation. The evaluation concluded that there was a lack
of clarity in the APA as to its purposes which made it
difficult to articulate clear program objectives and
performance indicators. It also concluded that a major
indirect effect of the program was to strengthen producer
returns although this is not an intention of the program.

Observations

This is not a regulatory program per se but a
regulatory related commercial marketing activity by
government. The net losses of the program could be viewed
as a producers' expenditure through the negotiated

commodity purchase price. As a complementary program to the Agricultural Stabilization Board, the APB comprises part of the policy alternative to national supply management which creates much less of an obstacle to economic development than supply management and entrepreneurial activity.

In the view of the Study Team, the Program appears to have performed well as a quick-response, short-term market stabilizer. However, such market interventions do result in higher prices for consumers and processors even though the taxpayer cost can be minimal when compared to possible subsequent ASA outlays to raise producer incomes. Nevertheless, internalizing the "cost" of the program through higher commodity prices is a more desirable approach than subsequent taxpayer-funded support payments, as provided by the Agricultural Stabilization Board, since it allows for a direct market response to the supported price through altering consumption patterns.

The APB has repeatedly intervened in certain sectors (grapes, B.C. turkeys). In these cases the Program runs the risk of overlapping with the role of the Agricultural Stabilization Board or, at worst, artificially propping up chronically declining sectors whose resources should be directed at other areas of agriculture.

Options

The Study Team recommends to the Task Force that the government consider the following:

1. Amend the Act to clarify purpose to provide only short term intervention and to foreclose any further continuous year-to-year assistance under this Program.

2. Alter purchasing arrangements to make producers fully or partly responsible for net losses arising from subsequent product sales by Program.

3. Encourage increased direct producer responsibility for product marketing, e.g. through co-ops or long-term agreements with processors.

4. Make Program eligibility criteria more transparent. Require Program to report costs and benefits of individual purchase initiatives.

AGRICULTURAL STABILIZATION BOARD - AGC 902

Objective

To provide deficiency payments to producers for named or designated commodities under the Agricultural Stabilization Act (ASA).

Authority

Agricultural Stabilization Act, 1958; revised 1975.

Description

The Agricultural Stabilization Board, a Crown Corporation, is comprised of several senior public servants within Agriculture Canada. It reports directly to the Minister of Agriculture and is essentially administrative in nature. The Board is advised by a committee of farmers and representatives of farm organizations across Canada. The aim of the Board is to help farmers obtain a fair share of the national income and to achieve an equitable balance between the prices farmers receive for key agricultural products and the cost of the goods and services they buy, more specifically to keep producers in business when farm returns for a particular commodity fall significantly or when input costs have risen at a faster rate than market prices.

Under the terms of the Act, prescribed prices for the following commodities must be calculated annually at not less than 90 per cent of their average price over the previous five years, with adjustments according to production cost changes: cattle, hogs and sheep; industrial milk and cream; corn and soybeans; and oats and barley not produced in the area designated in the Canadian Wheat Board Act. These prices remain in effect for 12 months. The Board makes support payments for deficiencies between market and prescribed prices. Other commodities may be supported at a price determined by the Governor in Council and for periods prescribed by the Council.

While tying the support level directly to what the farmer has received on average for his commodity in the marketplace and to what it cost him to produce the crop, the Act also seeks to maintain incentives for individual farmers to achieve the best return they can from the marketplace.

It is for this reason that a deficiency payment is made on an average basis for a marketing period and all eligible producers receive the same rate per unit.

The bulk of the Board's annual payments, approximately $300 million, is made up by the on-going subsidy for industrial milk (see CDC 200) which should not be viewed as a price or income stabilization measure. This payment is not included in the Resource Profile below but is included in the government's Expenditure Estimates.

Resources

($000's) Years	82/83	83/84	84/85	85/86	86/87	87/88
	60	56	66	59		
Operating Expenses	2,200	2,300	2,100	2,200	N/A	N/A
Stabilization Pymts						
Named Commodities	2,600	12,400	149,000	75,000		
Designated Commodities	3,500	70,900	14,900	11,000		
TOTAL	6,100	83,400	163,900	86,000		

Problem Identification

The program has not been questioned on principle by the private sector. There appears to be a general acceptance among food processors and retailers and consumers of the desirability of some government support to stabilize farm incomes. Indeed, as the costs of federal supply management schemes become more fully appreciated by these groups, they have placed increasing emphasis on improving upon the ASB model in order to address farm income stability problems caused by international price fluctuations through such a scheme as opposed to implementing more supply management schemes. In order to improve on the ASB a number of private sector representatives have advocated adopting a "tripartite stabilization" program for all named and designated commodities under the Act.

Modelled along the lines of the proposed red meat stabilization plan this new approach would involve shared federal, provincial and producer funding and would be designed more along the lines of business insurance. Senior department officials are also displaying an increasing preference for income stabilization over supply management as under the ASA the formal incentives for increased farm efficiency are affected much less and payments are made only at times when an income support need has been identified from actual developments in the marketplace.

A 1984 Departmental Program Evaluation of Market Risk Programs (including the ASB) concluded that federal ASB payments should be reduced by adopting the tripartite approach. Beginning in the 1970's the provinces became increasingly involved in making stabilization payments to significant agricultural subsectors in their economies. Over the period 1974-82 annual total provincial stabilization program expenditures averaged $74 million while the average federal (non-dairy) stabilization outlay was $49 million.

Observations

This is not a regulatory program per se but a regulatory related expenditure or subsidy program offering an alternative to supply management schemes with respect to farm income stabilization or maintenance. Given the defects of supply management, increased reliance on direct income stabilization measures can, in appropriate cases, do more to facilitate economic development than its "next best" policy alternative. ASB payments are uniform to all producers and therefore create no greater disincentive to increased producer efficiency or incentive to creating excess productive capacity than would any other irregular subsidy programs. However, to be a more attractive policy alternative to national supply management, the ASA could be improved by:

(1) integrating provincial support measures: Current independent provincial stabilization programs have distorted inter-provincial comparative advantages, have engendered competitive payment escalation in which large, high ability-to-pay organizations become probable winners, and have resulted in problems with our trading partners who consider stabilization payments to be nothing more than subsidies. (The most recent example is the U.S. decision to erect a countervailing tariff against Canadian hog exports).

(2) requiring some producer cost-sharing: At present payments are made when producer prices drop below a calculated threshold but producers are not required to contribute towards the stabilization scheme when prices are high. This makes the program look more like an outright subsidy than an income stabilization scheme. A producer

contribution requirement would (a) reduce taxpayer costs, (b) create an incentive for increased information sharing among producers, (c) increase incentives for greater producer efficiency, and (d) re-orient the program towards income stabilization.

Options

The Study Team recommends to the Task Force that the government consider the following:

1. Incremental Change

    (a) Amend the Agricultural Stabilization Act to make federal payments contingent upon adoption of a tripartite stabilization program under which the provinces agree not to fund beyond a specified limit per unit of commodity produced or to create other independent income support measures.

    (b) As a focus for further tripartite consultations and a model for a revised ASA, adopt the new red meat stabilization legislation.

    (c) Encourage to a greater extent, the formation and development of producer cooperatives to provide a vehicle for a degree of producer self-insurance against market risks.

2. Major Change

    (a) Remove the Act from the Department of Agriculture; merge administration with the administration of the Fisheries Prices Support Act (F&O) in a non-sectoral department (eg. Finance).

    (b) Develop a strategy for full producer self-insurance against price-induced income fluctuations and elimination of government support payments.

CANADIAN DAIRY COMMISSION: DAIRY SUPPORT PROGRAM
CDC 200

Objective

To provide efficient producers of milk and cream with the opportunity of obtaining a fair return for their labour and investment and to provide consumers of dairy products with a continuous and adequate supply of dairy products of high quality.

Authority

Canadian Dairy Commission Act.
Agricultural Stabilization Act.

Description

To ensure sufficient returns to producers, the Canadian Dairy Commission administers dairy support programs composed of an offer-to-purchase program for butter and skim milk powder and a federal subsidy program. The subsidy program is funded through the Agricultural Stabilization Act. The subsidy of $6.03 per hectolitre is paid directly to producers. Interest, storage and transportation costs associated with support purchasing and re-sale of butter and skimmed milk powder are also partially funded under the program. The amount of the subsidy has remained constant since 1975. The maximum subsidy available to an individual producer is $30,000.

Since 1979, some of the subsidy has been paid on a limited amount of production for export. National industrial milk production is set in a manner which leads to surpluses of skim milk powder, a by-product of butter production. Under supply management, domestic prices for both butter and skim milk powder are kept well above international prices. Dairy product surpluses are sold on depressed world markets at international prices. Federal dairy policy assigns to producers financial responsibility for selling surplus dairy products offshore. However, the government pays storage and related inventory costs ("marketing" costs) for certain products, including all skim milk powder surplus to Canadian needs.

The Canadian Dairy Commission is a Crown corporation and Crown agent in administering the federal dairy program for industrial milk, i.e. milk processed into dairy products other than retail milk such as butter, cheese and skim milk powder. It performs the role of the national marketing agency in administering national production quotas and marketing plans of the Canadian Milk Supply Management Committee and federal-provincial committee (see Background Paper on National Supply Management). Individual provincial milk marketing boards regulate the supply and price of milk destined to be sold as fluid milk. There is negligible interprovincial trade in the provincially regulated product. The Canadian Dairy Commission reports directly to the Minister of Agriculture and is not supervised by an independent body, as are other national supply management programs.

Resources

($000's)	82/83	83/84	84/85	85/86	86/87	87/88
Person-Years	72	72	77	78	78	
Operating Expenses	5,600	5,500	6,500	4,400	4,600	
Transfers Under the Agricultural Stabilization Act (ASA) Subsidies for production consumed domestically	*266,000	294,800	282,000	276,100	274,900	
Subsidies for production for export*	13,300	15,200	13,300	8,000	6,700	
Marketing costs (storage, interest & handling)*	15,700	37,500	22,000	13,000	13,000	
Sub-Total (ASA)	295,000	347,500	317,300	297,100	294,600	
TOTAL EXPENDITURES	300,600	353,000	323,800	301,500	299,200	

* Estimates, confirmed by the CDC

Problem Identification (See also Background Paper on National Supply Management)

Among the national supply management programs, views pro and con are most polarized in relation to industrial milk. Canadian milk costs are estimated by Ariculture Canada to be 55 per cent above those of the European Economic Community and 25 per cent above the U.S. Calculations for the Economic Council of Canada have indicated that, in 1980 dollars, the regulation of industrial milk through quotas and price supports caused a transfer of $400 million to producers from consumers (from high prices caused by inefficiency), $256 million from buyers of quota to sellers of quota, and $300 million from taxpayers to producers (the subsidy).

Senior Agriculture Canada staff have stated that the current regulatory structure has reduced producer interest in increasing efficiency and redirected their efforts towards just matching their quota allocation almost on a daily basis. The CDC's support price program, coupled with its quota setting and management policies, has resulted in frequent excess supplies of butter and skim milk powder and shortages and/or high prices of industrial milk for cheese and other specialty products (markets where consumer demand is increasing).

In a 1982 report the Auditor General made the following observations concerning the accountability of the Commission: (a) Effective review and challenge of the Commission's budget submissions do not take place between Agriculture Canada and the CDC. At the same time the CDC does not acknowledge a functional relationship between itself and Agriculture Canada. (b) It is debatable whether the Canadian Milk Supply Management Committee (the federal-provincial signatories) is an appropriate forum to elicit accountability from an agent of the Crown. The CDC chairs the Committee and provides it with staff support. The Committee has no executive powers over the CDC. (c) Although the Act makes the CDC's exercise of its corporate powers subject to any regulations of the Governor-in-Council made under the Act, this control has not been exercised, with the exception of a regulation for cheese.

The Canadian Dairy Commission has also been criticized by the Auditor General for not adequately controlling its export marketing operations. Dairy producers are one of the most politically active and effective agricultural lobbies.

In particular, Quebec industrial milk producers and vertically integrated producer co-ops have argued that preservation of the family-owned dairy industry in that province is a lynchpin of rural society.

Observations

In the view of the Team, this program creates severe economic distortions, is very costly to the federal government, and is bad for consumers. The domestic subsidy only serves to insulate producers from the natural market response to high prices caused by supply management-reduced demand and increased pressure to improve efficiency. Its elimination would increase the price of butter by about 34 cents a pound.

With such high stakes involved, the Canadian Dairy Commission cannot itself serve both as marketing agency and supervising body. The Commission's accountability at present is weakly defined and needs clarification. The CDC also needs to be effectively supervised. Otherwise, the national industrial milk supply management program will continue to be regarded by many as being skewed against non-producer interests and providing massive windfall gains to producers.

Options

The Study Team recommends to the Task Force that the government consider the following:

To improve accountability:

1. Make the Canadian Dairy Commission subject to National Farm Products Marketing Council supervision.

2. Governor-in-Council passes supervisory and management accountability regulations.

To increase efficiency:

1. Steadily increase cheese imports and make the issuance of import permits more transparent (see Background Paper on National Supply Management).

2. Remove the export subsidy immediately and phase out the domestic industrial milk subsidy over no more than a five-year period.

NATIONAL FARM PRODUCTS MARKETING COUNCIL - NFPMC 1

Objectives

The maintenance and promotion of a strong, efficient and competitive production and marketing structure for regulated products, while balancing the interests of producers and consumers.

Authority

Farm Products Marketing Agencies Act, 1972.

Description

The principal statutory duties of the National Farm Products Marketing Council are:

1. Advising the Minister of Agriculture on all matters relating to the establishment and operation of marketing agencies under the Farm Products Marketing Act.
2. Reviewing the operations of agencies with a view to ensuring that they are promoting and maintaining a strong, efficient and competitive production and marketing industry for the regulated product or products and have due regard to the interests of producers and consumers of the regulated product or products.
3. Consulting with the agencies and provincial governments in promoting more effective marketing of the regulated farm products through interprovincial and export trade.

The Council is composed of three to nine members, at least 50 per cent of whom must be primary producers. Members are appointed by the Governor-in-Council who also names the Chairman and Vice-Chairman, one of whom must be a primary producer. The Council staff is structured into the following groups: Agency Operations Review, Economic Research, Executive and Administrative Services, Information Services.

In providing advice to the Minister on the advisability of establishing a national agency, the Council must take steps to ensure that the proposal to form such an agency conforms to the objectives and requirements of the legislation. This requires an economic analysis of that part of agriculture involved and the existing marketing problems, the holding of hearings so that all parties concerned may submit their views and cross-examine each other, the complete review of the proposed marketing plan to see if it will work and achieve the objectives set out in the Act. This may mean lengthy discussions with the proposers, who themselves may have to hold further interprovincial discussions, in order to develop and agree to necessary changes to the proposals.

In monitoring and supervising existing agencies, the Council is required to review their operations and report at least annually to the Minister, review all orders and regulations proposed by agencies to implement the product's marketing plan (with the power to approve or set aside), and enquire into and take action on complaints concerning the agencies. The Council can withold prior approval of regulations or revoke agency regulations which have been designated for post approval or seek criminal enforcement in the event of Agency non-compliance with the Act.

Resources

($000's)	82/83	83/84	84/85	85/86	86/87	87/88
Person-Years		25	27	28		
Operating Expenses		1,484	1,635	1,839		
Revenue						
Subsidies						
Capital		6	24	N/A		

Problem Identification

The arguments for and against the National Supply Management programs within which the Council performs supervisory and limited regulatory duties are presented in the Background Paper. As noted in that paper, these programs are strongly supported by producers subject to them, but are severely criticized by consumers, food processors and retailers, organized labour, and many academic experts. The Council is also a strong supporter of national supply management. The member provincial marketing boards also support the schemes but have, nevertheless, at times disagreed with national marketing agency decisions concerning quota allocation (especially new or overbase quota) decisions through appeals to Council. Producers consider these programs have helped preserve independent family farms. The Economic Council has calculated that in 1980 the annual cost to consumers of these programs is over $56 million for eggs ($20,000 per producer) and $77 million for chickens ($30,000 per producer). The Council itself has indicated that it has had in the past some difficulty working within its existing legislative framework to effectively supervise the marketing agencies, but that creative use of its supervisory powers in recent years has led it to have an effective supervisory role. Much of its work takes the form of diplomatic intervention and behind-closed-doors moral suasion grounded upon its power to disallow marketing agency regulations. Some of these initiatives, such as Council's 1981 publication of guidelines for the updating of cost of production pricing formulae, have been actively resisted by some agencies.

Observations

The accountability of national marketing agencies to the Council has been vague, with the result that the adequacy of the Council's supervision over the supply management schemes has suffered. In May 1983 the Minister of Agriculture told the joint marketing plan signatories they were not cooperating with each other or the Council and threatened putting the agencies into trusteeship and winding them up. Provincial cooperation has improved in the last two years as the Council has established reporting guidelines for agencies, and obtained greater Ministerial and agency support for its supervisory role, but the economic damage of these programs persists. The Council's role and powers could be clarified and strengthened. This is necessary to improve the regulatory structure and public credibility of a severely criticized regulatory program.

Options (For discussion see Background Paper on Reforming the Council)

The Study Team recommends to the Task Force that the government consider the following:

1. ## No Change

    (a) Let Council continue to test its existing powers until successfully challenged in the courts.

2. ## Moderate Change

    (a) Strengthen the Council by amending the Farm Products Marketing Agencies Act to:

i) remove the primary producer quota in Council membership. Merit should be the only appointment criterion for all members.

ii) provide the Council with the express power to compel information and affidavit evidence from national marketing agencies (in the form best suited to the circumstances) with respect to the fulfilment of any of the Council's statutory duties.

iii) expand power to disallow agency orders and regulations to situations where Council is of the opinion that the order or regulation either:

    (1) cannot be reasonably expected to promote a strong, efficient and competitive production and marketing industry for the regulated product, or

    (2) does not take due regard of the interests of producers or consumers of the regulated product.

iv) require agencies to establish and adequately fund a consultative committee representing producers, consumers, processors and retailers.

v) expressly allow the Council to establish and enforce rules of procedure for its supervisory activities.

vi) expressly require agencies to issue regulations on "overbase" quota allocation.

vii) in general, confirm Council's supervisory authority.

viii) provide for agency audits by the Auditor General.

(b) Increase regulated product imports; make the issuance of import permits more predictable and transparent; eliminate import controls on further processor; and retail level product. (See Background Paper on National Supply Management.)

(c) Fund Council through agencies' administration levies assessed against producers.

3. Radical Change

(a) Eliminate Council National Supply management and border controls; leave regulation to the provinces.

(b)   Give the Council full regulatory powers over price and supply similar to the CRTC.

Reforming the National Farm Products Marketing Council

Current Situation

The Council has consistently contended that it is a "supervisory and monitoring agency" and not a regulator, and that, if there are regulators within the national supply management programs, they are the national marketing agencies. Nevertheless the Council does clearly exercise some regulatory powers: (1) approval of global production quotas proposed by the agencies, (2) disallowance of agency orders and regulations which are not necessary for the administration of the marketing plan, and (3) to make enquiries and "take such action within its powers" (see (1) and (2)) to deal with complaints from persons affected by the operations of an agency. The Council's statutory duties with respect to the operations of the agencies require it to:

(1)   provide advice "with a view to maintaining and promoting an efficient and competitive agriculture industry" (emphasis added),

(2)   review the operations of agencies to ensure they carry out their own statutory objects, and

(3)   work with agencies in promoting more effective marketing of farm products.

The Council is therefore expected to have a more hands-on and collaborative relationship with the agencies than would be expected of an "independent board" such as the NEB or CTC.

To aid in its public hearings, the Council is given all the powers of a Commissioner appointed under the Inquiries Act including the power to subpoena witnesses and written evidence and to compel testimony, and to retain consultants to perform audits of parties called to testify. However public hearings can be held only in specified circumstances and the Council possesses no statutory power to require the production of information outside a public hearing. Nor do full public hearings necessarily provide the best format for dealing with all regulatory responsibilities of the Council.

Alternative Models

Critics of the Council's current manner of operation have suggested two alternatives:

(1) pluralist Council membership

(2) making Council a pure regulatory body with powers similar to the CRTC.

For its part, the Council would generally prefer to work within the existing statutory framework (to first test the effectiveness of its current authority) including:

(1) making greater use of its Inquiry Act powers in public hearings having broad public involvement;

(2) the issuance of guidelines to agencies concerning matters which are subject to Council review as agency orders and regulations (e.g. the nature and extent of information required when considering levy orders and agency budgets, information requirements and time frames relating to quota orders, annual reviews of agency programs and financial accountability of agencies);

(3) expressing its views in a more hard hitting fashion in its Annual Report to the Minister.

Examination of Alternatives

(a) Pluralist Council Membership: This alternative may give certain identified interest groups (consumers, labour) a sense that they are getting a direct say in Council's decision-making. However, by itself, expanding on the statutory membership quota for the Council would not improve or clarify its regulatory role. A more pluralist Council would also, in the Team's view, inhibit its effectiveness as a participant in the regulatory structure for the following reasons:

(1) The credibility of its public hearing processes would diminish as hearing participants would conclude that the decision would turn less on the quality of the presentations and more on behind-closed-door deal-making among identified factions when Council makes its decision.

(2) The credibility of Council as an "honest broker" in inter-provincial dispute arbitration would suffer.

(3) Given the current polarization of views retention of producer control of the Council would be viewed as meaningless by its critics, while shifting control to non-producers would alienate the Council from primary producers and most provincial agricultural ministries and supervisory boards.

In short, a pluralist Council might look better but no problems would be solved and many more would be created.

Instead, in the Team's view, much could be done to diffuse criticism that Council has a pro-producer bias if the current statutory requirement of at least 50% of members being "primary producers" were removed. This would permit the Governor in Council to appoint Council members more on the basis of merit and objectivity while still leaving the federal government full flexibility to appoint a sufficient number of primary producers to provide expert input and to satisfy the provinces and producer interests.

To deal with concerns about inadequate non-producer input to the system, all national agencies should be required to establish a general advisory committee consisting of representatives of all interested parties to provide general input on agency operations. Permissive authority is given to agencies under subsection 26(1) of the Act to make bylaws to do so. This concept could be strengthened by amending the Act to state that agencies shall provide for such committees and that these committees shall be funded from producer levies (with the adequacy of committee budgets being reviewed by Council) as part of its responsibility to ensure agencies fulfill their statutory duties. Agencies have established such committees for specific purposes but appear to have been reluctant to set up and fund a general oversight group.

(b) Public Utility Model: Under this approach Council would have a broad power to disallow and vary agency orders and regulations and also to prohibit or direct agency action to fulfill the agency's statutory responsibilities or duties. The Council's exercise of its responsibilities would occur more through public processes (such as public hearings) in which interested parties would have a legal right to a fair opportunity to present their views and to

analyse and challenge the views of other parties. Public
hearings could be held concerning cost of production formula
approval and global quota approval.

In the Team's view, this model is not sufficiently
sensitive to the unique structure of national supply
management programs. Under these programs the agencies, as
creations of the Governor in Council, are ultimately
accountable to the federal government, but they administer a
marketing plan the terms of which form a contract between
the federal and provincial governments.

If the Council were given the above regulatory powers,
it would be in the position, as a federal body, to direct
the management of the marketing plans to be consistent with
its interpretation of an agency's duties under the Act.
This would amount to a significant shift in the balance of
power among the provinces, the federal government and the
Council, to the Council. An appeal route from Council's
decisions would, as a result, become politically necessary.
If it were to the federal Cabinet or Minister of
Agriculture, the provinces would become concerned that only
one party to the federal-provincial agreements would be
interpreting and enforcing the agreement. If it were to the
signatories of the agreement, then, in practical terms,
Council's policies would have to be justified in terms of
the agreement and not the standards of the Act, no real
enhancement of Council's role would occur, and the Council
would lose some of its existing statutory independence.

(c) Continued Experimentation With Existing Powers: The
Team agrees with the Council that, if only because of its
ambiguity, the Act provides Council with room to expand its
role beyond that which made it subject to heavy public
criticism in the 1970's. Still, a number of relatively
minor statutory changes could do much to improve Council's
effectiveness and help re-orient national supply management
programs to operate more in the public interest and less
exclusively in the interest of producers. These changes
would, in our view, not disrupt the "creative tension" that
exists between the Act, the marketing plan, and the
federal-provincial agreement with respect to each agency.

(1) Access to Agency Information: The Council's
Inquiry Act powers of production, now restricted
to public hearings, should be extended to all
supervisory functions to ensure it has adequate
agency information to effectively discharge all
its supervisory activities.

(2) Clarify agency order and regulation veto power:
The Act should clearly indicate that agency orders
and regulations may be disallowed by Council if
they would be inconsistent with the agency's
statutory duties. However, Council should not be
provided with powers to vary orders or regulations
or direct that certain orders or regulations be
promulgated by agencies as this could shift
marketing plan management responsibilities from
the agencies to the Council.

(3) Rules of Procedure: Council should be expressly
granted the power to establish and enforce rules
of procedures for all its supervisory activities.
These rules would take the place of "guidelines"
it presently issues on an informal basis to
agencies. Council should be encouraged to
establish information requirements for agency
filings that place the onus on agencies to
demonstrate that their orders, regulations, and
quota proposals are consistent with their
statutory duties.

(4) Quota reallocation standards: Council has
repeatedly been faced with the need to adjudicate
complaints from provincial supervisory boards
concerning new or above-base quota allocations.
No agency at present has an established formula
for overbase quota allocation. The tendency has
been to expand and contract provincial allocations
of global quota according to historical shares as
global quota expands and contracts and not
according to comparative advantage (i.e. relative
efficiency). The Act should be amended to require
agencies to establish by regulation a method of
allocating "over base" quota in a manner which
reflects relative producer efficiency among
provinces. Such regulations would be subject to
Council disallowance. At present section 24 of
the Act only requires agencies to "consider the
principle of comparative advantage" but not to
apply it or to implement quota reallocation by
means of regulations. Another, more desirable but
perhaps more extreme, alternative, would be to
require renegotiation of base quota allocation

among the signatories every five years. The base allocation for eggs, as an example is taken from production shares 15 years ago and is probably obsolete.

In addition, further processor complaints concerning the unwarranted expansion of the scope of product regulation under national supply management requires careful and systematic examination. In the Team's view, it should not be the purpose of such schemes to protect processors of regulated primary products from import competition through border controls on semi-processed and processed product. Nor should supply management insulate primary producers from having to evolve or innovate in the quality mix of products leaving the farm gate. An increasing amount of the Council's workload has been taking up in mediating processor complaints, with provincial supervisory boards or the agencies, to the effect that inadequate domestic supplies of the right kind of primary products are available for processing in order to efficiently supply consumer restaurant and prepared food industry needs, or to permit timely product innovation by these firms.

AGENCIES ESTABLISHED UNDER FARM PRODUCTS
MARKETING AGENCIES ACT — NFPMC 2

Objective

To promote a strong, efficient and competitive production and marketing industry for the regulated product or products in relation to which an agency may exercise its powers.

To have due regard to the interests of producers and consumers of the regulated product.

Authority

Farm Products Marketing Agencies Act
Orders in Council establishing agencies

Description (See also Background Paper on National Supply Management)

To date three marketing agencies have been created under the Act:

Canadian Egg Marketing Agency (CEMA)
Canadian Turkey Marketing Agency (CTMA)
Canadian Chicken Marketing Agency (CCMA)

They operate as Commercial Corporations.

An Agency is operated by its Board of Directors, which is composed of representatives from each member provincial commodity board. As well as the commodity board representatives, there are also two federal appointees on the Board of Directors of the Egg Agency, one of whom is the Chairman, and of the Chicken Agency. The Agencies are also advised on policies and operations by consultative committees, composed of representatives of various interest groups.

The National Marketing Agencies act on behalf of their provincial members to coordinate production through national supply management programs by establishing national and provincial production quota for the regulated commodity. In arriving at a national quota figure for a particular product, provincial commodity boards gather estimates of their market needs which are then considered by their representatives on the Agency's Board of Directors, and by the Agency's consultative committee. The figure that is struck is then forwarded to the National Farm Products Marketing Council for approval. Each agency allocates provincial quotas according to the different criteria laid down and agreed to in their marketing plan.

Agencies have differing powers with respect to producer price-setting. The producer price for eggs is set centrally by the Canadian Egg Marketing Agency, according to a cost of production formula plus a reasonable return to producers. The Canadian Turkey Marketing Agency uses a national cost of production formula to assist provincial turkey boards in establishing provincial producer prices. The Chicken Agency is in the process of developing a national formula but at the moment prices are set provincially using the Ontario price as a benchmark. The agencies' cost of production formulae are based on national surveys commissioned by the agencies.

The agencies are financed through the collection of producer levies, and also through the collection of fines for over-production where these occur. The egg agency also includes a consumer levy in its producer price for eggs, which is used to clear eggs surplus to table market requirements. These eggs are sold at a reduced price to the egg processing industry on a contract basis.

Resources

Except for an initial federal start-up grant of not more than $100,000 an agency is not entitled to federal funding. Agencies are financed through producer levies.

Problem Identification (See Background Paper on National Supply Management, NFPMC 1 profile, and Background Options Paper on NFPMC 1)

Two independent studies of the CEMA and two internal studies (one by a CEMA committee and one by the Council) have found that the producer-dominated board has been preoccupied with short-term, producer-oriented and provincial interests. Some individual directors have expressed concern about these preoccupations.

A study of the CCMA, commissioned by the Council, revealed similar preoccupations on the part of its board. Such a study of the CTMA if conducted should be expected to produce comparable findings: the CEMA and CCMA studies confirmed observations of the Council, in its day-to-day monitoring and supervision, common to all three agencies. The Council considers there has been a continuing agency resistance to Council supervision but that this resistance is disappearing (see NFPMC1).

Observations

There are a number of factors contributing to these agencies' short term focus. Only the CEMA has a significant budget for advertising and promotion. The CCMA and CTMA are starved for funds to engage even in this limited marketing strategy. None of the three devotes effort to new product development and marketing. There are grounds to suspect that the decline in turkey consumption in Canada, compared with the upward trend in the U.S., relates to a failure in Canada to make progress in further processing.

Within the Agency boards, interprovincial rivalries continue although the agencies are intended to be vehicles for greater provincial cooperation. Provincial commodity boards regard their appointees to the national boards as delegates to the agencies, rather than directors of national corporations with responsibilities that extend well beyond the farm gate. Internal rivalries can stifle agency boards and result in decisions based on compromise rather than economic principles: for example, penalties for overproduction forgiven or reduced, sometimes under threats of withholding of funds or withdrawal from the Agency -- what the Minister of Agriculture called "blackmail" in an address to all signatories of the national agencies in May 1983.

Attempts of the Agencies to develop satisfactory formulas for allocating overbase quotas have amounted to political compromises and have not applied straightforward economic principles.

In recent years, the main problem has been the chicken marketing agency. Inadequate supplies caused by centrally planned production limits are most likely to appear when consumer demand for the product is expanding. This problem exists for chickens where further processors and fast food chains have experienced serious shortages. Also, since the

CCMA doesn't control farm gate prices through a cost of production formula, many producers have received returns well above the provincial boards "benchmark" prices because of the shorted market. Allowing "supplementary" chicken imports hasn't kept prices down and doesn't provide the secure supply processors and restaurants need to make investment decisions.

Options (See Background Paper on National Supply Management, NFPMC 1 profile, and Background Paper on NFPMC 1 Options)

The Study Team recommends to the Task Force that the government consider the following:

1. Regulatory Reform.

    (a) Encourage boards to direct efforts more towards market development and product innovation, especially with respect to the processing and fast food sectors.

    (b) Adopt recommended amendments to strengthen and clarify Council's supervisory role.

    (c) Create greater pressure for increased efficiency by allowing increased chicken imports.

2. Eliminate National Supply Management programs; leave to provincial regulation.

BACKGROUND

NATIONAL SUPPLY MANAGEMENT SCHEMES

I   INTRODUCTION

The farm production of industrial milk, eggs, chickens and turkeys in Canada is governed by a set of complex and uniquely Canadian regulatory schemes which are, in fundamental respects, quite similar. These Programs are often referred to as National Supply Management.

The common elements of National Supply Management programs are:

1)   A Federal/Provincial Agreement providing that:

    (a)   A federal/provincial committee will be established to set the "global" annual production "quota" in the commodity (usually based on average production shares over the five years prior to the agreement). This, in practice, is usually done on the recommendation of the marketing agency or through actual delegation to the agency, subject to a right of appeal.

    (b)   Provincial production shares of the global quota are established (the shares are allocated and administered in each province by a provincial marketing board).

    (c)   The committee is assigned the responsibility to allocate new or "overbase" quota among provinces and to calculate provincial shares in the event of a global quota reduction.

    (d)   The federal government agrees to a policy of "national self-sufficiency" in the commodity.

    (e)   A producer-controlled national marketing agency is established to hold and clear surplus product (domestically preferably, but if necessary, internationally), to advise and/or chair the federal-provincial committee, deal with the provincial boards, and otherwise implement the agreed-to marketing plan for the product.

96

2) A federal Act or Order-in-Council creating the marketing agency.

3) The imposition of import limits on the regulated product (and some processed forms of the regulated product) under the Export and Import Permits Act.

4) With the exception of industrial milk, a statutory body, the National Farm Products Marketing Council, advises on the desirability of proposed National Supply Management programs and the terms of the marketing plan, and supervises and reports publicly on the operations of the marketing agencies.

The two critical and unique elements of national supply management schemes, therefore, are: (a) fixing a <u>national production quota</u> and managing <u>provincial shares</u> and (b) imposing <u>border controls</u> on lower-priced imports of the regulated products. The aim of quotas is to increase producer prices and incomes, and to stabilize production (i.e. reduce cyclical swings).

Without both measures national supply management schemes would, over a period of years, fail to provide the full intended income benefits to producers since supply limits would be by-passed through interprovincial or international trade.

II OPPOSING VIEWPOINTS

A - Arguments Against

National Supply Management programs have been the focus of considerable private sector (consumer, academic experts, and processors) criticism. In contrast these parties have generally viewed periodic price or income stabilization programs and purely provincial marketing boards as either beneficial to, or at least not unduly restrictive of, competition, efficiency, and structural change in the industry.

The common problems identified with these programs by these parties are:

(1) The presence of high trading values for quota - This, it is argued, indicates that:

    (a) Original owners of quota have reaped windfall gains.

    (b) Total industry output has been unreasonably constrained by global quotas.

    (c) Purchasers of quota must recover this cost through excessive farm gate prices.

    (d) The cost of getting into the business on the part of new entrants is made very high, thus perpetuating indefinitely high prices, jeopardizing the ability of small farmers to enter, creating a barrier to exit, and encouraging, over time, farm concentration (as only larger or vertically integrated farms can finance quota costs).

It is argued by many economists that there is no more objective or better measure than high quota values of the existence of industry inefficiencies, excessive prices and profits, and transfers of wealth from consumers to producers. Moreover, the capitalization of quota in farm costs (such as land prices if quota enures to the farm or is grandfathered with farm assets in some fashion) makes it almost impossible for government to get out of the scheme because to do so would require massive quota-compensation payments to producers if farm bankruptcies or eradicated life savings are to be avoided.

(2) Unreasonably high prices:

    (a) Commodities subject to such schemes are much more costly in Canada at the farm gate than in our major trading partners, principally the U.S.

    (b) Trying to hold down farm gate prices to quasi-competitive levels through complex "cost of production" formulae (as has been attempted for eggs) doesn't work. It is argued that, where these formulae exist, they are controlled by the producer-controlled agency and are, in any event, subject to manipulation and a host of "judgement" calls. Farmers will find ways of getting the market price paid to them (e.g. by payments in kind) if the "cost of production price" is below the market price. Trying to induce efficiency and lower prices with such formulae, therefore, becomes a resource-intensive and fruitless game for economists and bureaucrats.

(3)   Farm Scale and Location Becomes Inefficient:

Although there is a tendency towards increased concentration over time in each regulated commodity sector, restraints on interprovincial quota reallocation, high quota costs, and the levels of farm gate prices allowed under existing cost of production formulae, will together restrain farms from reaching the size of truly efficient operations which exist in the U.S. and will prevent production from being optimally located in relation to consumer markets. It is also suggested that "cost of production" formulae returns when coupled with provincial market board intra-provincial trading policies have eliminated incentives or opportunities for even interprovincial trade.

(4)   A Permanent Seller's Market:

The cyclical ebb and flow between buyers and sellers markets in most industries tends to encourage greater efficiencies, and a reasonable balance of bargaining power. However, it is argued, global quotas coupled with border controls under National Supply Management create a permanent seller's market which hurts consumers and processors by:

(a)   discouraging product innovations by producers,
(b)   inhibiting product innovations by processors since new products cannot be introduced unless reliable, long-term supplies of the right type of agricultural product are available,
(c)   reducing the efficiency of new processing systems, which must be designed to be compatible with the wide

range of products "forced" on processors
by the National Marketing Agency.

    (d)   gearing producers' behaviour to meeting
quota limits, sometimes on a day-to-day,
week-to-week basis and not meeting
processor demand patterns.

(5)   <u>Regressive Taxation</u>:

Shifting wealth from consumers to producers
through agricultural product price increases
amounts to a "regressive tax" because such
products form a higher portion of low income
consumers' budgets than those of high income
consumers.

B - <u>Arguments in Support</u>

Supporters of National Supply Management have cited a
number of advantages which they contend are not available
under individual provincial marketing boards:

(1)   Elimination of competition between provincial
agriculture ministries and instances of
retaliation against extra-provincial shipments
(e.g. the Ontario/Quebec "chicken and egg war" of
the early 70's).

(2)   Retention of family farms in the face of low-cost
imports (often allegedly "dumped") from other
countries' "factory-style" operations.

(3)   Redressing bargaining power between producers and
large, concentrated nation-wide food processors
and retailers.

(4)   Stabilization and improvement of farmers' incomes,
without having to call upon government funds, by
eliminating excessive or destructive competition
among producers. Income stability has the
indirect effect of encouraging greater farm
investment, greater technological change on the
farm, and better product quality. Quota value
provides a form of pension fund for retiring
farmers.

(5)   Through the national marketing agency producers
find cooperative, national solutions to their
problems.

(6) Consumers receive the assurance that the regulated product will always be of high quality and in adequate supply throughout the country.

C - Observations

From these considerations it is evident that national supply management schemes have been created and maintained in order to improve the relative economic position of farmers, and to achieve a social policy goal of slowing the rate of decline of our rural population. The means selected for doing so (supply control) achieves this end in a "hidden" fashion through product prices.

III   RELATIONSHIP WITH TRADE POLICY

Outright import restrictions on agricultural products (prohibitions or maximum per year, as opposed to tariffs) are the most effective means of controlling domestic supplies in order to improve the incomes or wealth of Canadian producers. Under Article 11 of the General Agreement on Tariffs and Trade (GATT), Canada's trading partners may respond to such border control either through countervailing action (against the product) or retaliatory action (against any other Canadian exports) unless the product in question is the subject of a national supply management scheme.

In Canada agricultural product border controls are administered by the Minister of External Affairs under the Export and Import Permits Act through the issuance of import permits to dealers of products designated under the Act. Section 5 of the Act empowers the Governor in Council to establish an Import Control List to restrict imports for a number of purposes including "to implement any action taken under...the Canadian Dairy Commisstion Act... and the Farm Products Marketing Agencies Act". Products subject to the Act include not only the regulated primary or farm gate product but also some processing stages of the product.

The volume of affected imports given permits in a given period of time is entirely within the Minister's discretion. Government statements as to the amount or value of an agricultural product which can be imported in a given year are, therefore, not enforceable against the Minister through legal action.

In practice, the Department of External Affairs, through the Special Trade Relations Bureau, relies upon the advice of the affected "line" department with respect to the issuance of import permits and exercises little independent control over the process. The Minister has a broad discretion to attach terms and conditions to any import permit.

The Governor-in-Council may also make regulations concerning a number of matters including information and undertakings to be furnished by applicants for permits, the application procedure, the terms and conditions upon which permits may be issued, and exempting products from the operation of the Act.

Two types of import policies exist for products subject to national supply management:

(1)   absolute volume ceiling (cheese under the Dairy policy), and

(2)   an import floor plus discretionary "supplementary" import permits issued to processors on a "proven need" basis (chicken, eggs, turkeys).

No explicit eligibility criteria or fairness rules have been established with respect to regularly issued or supplementary permits although holders of permits for "within ceiling imports" expect to receive the same import authority from year to year and generally do. Nor does the volume of such permits appear to bear any direct systematic relationship to actual domestic supply shortages, quota value increases or farm gate price rises although supplementary permits have been employed as a short term offset to global quota not expanding to meet rising demand, as in the recent dramatic expansion of domestic demand for processed and "fast food" chicken.

Although national supply management is intended to protect producers, import controls have been expanded to cover such a broad range of products that processors and further processors are also protected.

In the past some national marketing agencies have argued that, in order to fully manage supplies, all import permits should be issued to them and that they would then act as a "fair broker" of imports or be the importer themselves. These requests have, to date, been resisted by the federal government.

IV   OBSERVATIONS

Of all regulatory programs in agriculture, the national supply management programs have been subject to the severest and most consistent negative comment from the private sector (all affected interests, with the exclusion of farmers themselves). These comments focus on the restraints to innovation and efficiency caused by national and provincial quotas, the costs to society of high quota values, and the lack of accountability of the marketing agencies themselves. These programs are clearly viewed by their critics as obstacles to improved national productivity and long term economic development. Moreover, senior Agriculture Canada officials are now expressing similar concerns that national supply management has acted as an undue brake to increased producer efficiency, and, hence, long-term viability and they are expressing a preference for a combination of ad hoc support and subsidized income insurance programs.

In the Team's view these programs have excessively favoured producer interests, have blunted entrepreneurial initiative at both the producer and processor levels, and have been inadequate in protecting consumer interests. To the extent they have engendered long-term production efficiencies they have reduced national productivity and have thereby become an obstacle to economic development. As indicated in the Program Profiles, national supply management programs currently transfer around $1 billion per year from consumers, processors and taxpapers to primary producers.

However, regulatory reform measures directed to redressing the current imbalance in benefits flowing to producers from consumers and processors under these programs must take the following important factors into account:

   (1)   the capitalization of quota value in farms' cost structure and the resulting need to have government buy producers out of the program if quota value disappears;

   (2)   shared federal/provincial jurisdiction over agriculture;

   (3)   strong regional identification with the industry (industrial milk in Quebec, eggs and chickens in Manitoba);

(4)   an absence of taxpayer savings coupled with a
       likelihood of some immediate tax revenue losses;

(5)   a likelihood of some short-term unemployment among
       workers who have a low chance of being
       successfully retrained, resettled, and
       re-employed;

(6)   the fact that these programs were originally set
       up largely to get government out of direct
       producer income support payments in these sectors.

OVERVIEW

CONSUMER AND CORPORATE AFFAIRS

THREE DEPARTMENTS IN ONE

Since its inception in the late 1960's, the Department of Consumer and Corporate Affairs has been a conglomerate. Much of its legislative base was acquired from other Departments. Some administrative responsibilities were assigned to it by interdepartmental agreement. To this was added new regulatory legislation on consumer products information and hazardous products, policy analysis resources and funding for a variety of consumer groups.

The Department is now divided into three largely autonomous Bureaus (Consumer Affairs, Corporate Affairs, and Competition Policy) each having a distinct mission and clientele. If there is a common thread among the three Bureaus and a "mission" for CCA's regulatory activity, it is to make the marketplace work better. Rules and regulations are the means used by CCA; it has few incentives or subsidies at its disposal. In this respect it is unique among federal economic-oriented departments.

The Study Team reviewed a total of 13 CCA regulatory programs and two regulatory-related programs covering all three Bureaus.

(1) ## BUREAU OF CONSUMER AFFAIRS:

This Bureau develops and administers regulatory programs aimed at protecting consumers against hazardous products and product misrepresentation and ensuring accurate measurement of products. As well, Consumer Affairs conducts consumer research, provides consumer information, promotes metrication, and funds consumer groups ($700,000 in total in 1984-85 for the Consumers Association of Canada alone). Consumer Affairs represents about half of CCA's ongoing program delivery budget and over half of CCA's program-oriented person years.

The Study Team reviewed the following Consumer Affairs Programs:

CCA 2	Consumer Products
CCA 4	Product Safety

CCA 31	Legal Metrology - Electricity and Gas
CCA 32	Legal Metrology - Weights and Measures
CCA 100	Tax Rebate Discounting Act
CCA 102	Metric Program (with closing of Metric Commission, responsibility in Policy Coordination Branch.)
CCA 901	Funding of the Regulated Industries Program of the Consumers' Association of Canada (regulatory related).

In the Team's view, two major problem themes emerge:

(a) <u>Consumer Affairs is too interventionist in dealing with product information matters</u>. Much consumer information regulation is not needed and could be replaced by voluntary industry standards. Competition among suppliers can also be relied on more to produce accurate and adequate product information. Product misrepresentation problems can be handled better by a law of general application (for example see Marketing Practices) or provincial consumer protection laws.

(b) <u>In large measure, current measuring-devices inspection by government is unnecessary and, if provided, should be cost-recovered</u>. Device monitoring and certification should be privatized, with responsibility for monitoring devices and ensuring compliance with the law being left to the owners of measuring devices. The first priority should be to privatize gas and electricity meter monitoring and certification.

(2) BUREAU OF CORPORATE AFFAIRS:

This Bureau is responsible for much of the federal framework legislation that establishes many of the rules of the game for commercial relations in Canada. Its client is business. Corporate Affairs' Programs are:

CCA 9	Corporations
CCA 10	Bankruptcy
CCA 12	Copyright and Industrial Design
CCA 13	Patents
CCA 14	Trade Marks

While the Study Team found these programs to be
well-regarded and necessary for orderly private
commercial relations, and largely well run, their
legislative underpinnings are by and large too old, in
clear need of updating, and are losing their relevance
to the business market place.

In the Team's view, needed amendments to these
framework laws have been needlessly delayed. Antiquated
framework laws represent an almost undetectable but
nevertheless pervasive obstacle to economic development
and job creation by increasing investor and business
uncertainty and making the basic rules of the game
unclear.

(3) BUREAU OF COMPETITION

This Bureau develops and administers Canada's
competition law, the Combines Investigation Act. It
has three programs:

        CCA 5   Marketing Practices
        CCA 101   Combines Investigation Act
        CCA 103   Regulated Sector Branch (regulatory
                    related)

The Bureau's clientele is both business and consumers.
Its mission is establishing and enforcing rules
concerning unwarranted restraints of trade and
anti-competitive abuses of market power to improve the
functioning and efficiency of Canada's market economy.

The Combines Act is a general law of general
application and is a complementary framework
legislation to the laws administered by Corporate
Affairs.

The Study Team found Marketing Practices to be well-run
and effective in preventing public product
misrepresentations. It has a well thought-out
compliance program and restricts criminal prosecution
to the most significant cases.

However, other important provisions of the Combines Act (mergers, monopolies, anti-competitive agreements and pricing) were found to be outdated and ineffective. The Act must be modernized; its relevance to business and consumers has been seriously eroded. A practical compliance and education program is also urgently needed for restraints to competition provisions. Competition Policy has been too prosecution-oriented in the enforcement of these provisions and has taken too long to investigate and lay charges with respect to anti-competitive agreements meriting prosecution.

CONSUMER PRODUCTS - CCA 2

Objectives

To identify, control and prevent product misrepresentations in the marketplace and to ensure adequate product information is available to facilitate effective consumer choice.

Authority

Exclusive Responsibility

Consumer Packaging and
  Labelling Act
Textile Labelling Act
Precious Metals Marking Act
National Trade Mark and
  True Labelling Act
  packaging, labelling
  and advertising of foods.

Administration at Retail Level

Canada Agricultural
  Products
  Standards Act (CAPS)
Fish Inspection Act
Provincial Agricultural
  Legislation

Description

The program administers and enforces legislation and coordinates the development of and monitors voluntary programs covering a wide variety of food and non-food consumer products. In addition to conducting approximately 40,000 trade level inspections, some 65,000 complaints and enquiries are handled each year, 15,000 advertisements for radio and television are pre-approved and, as a pre-market service to the industry, 8,000 labels are examined for regulatory compliance.

The program establishes and maintains regulations and voluntary guidelines applicable to foods, textiles, precious metals and pre-packaged non-food consumer items. The program implements a compliance strategy which includes the inspection of regulated products at all levels of trade and the provision of consumer and trader information programs. In addition, program administrators approve food advertisements for radio and television prior to airing and reviews draft labels in relation to regulatory compliance.

The Program is decentralized in district offices and five regions (85 per cent of PYs), with headquarters in Hull, Quebec.

The Program is currently the subject of a comprehensive departmental program evaluation which will be completed in 1986. This evaluation does not include the Marketing Practices Branch.

Resources

(000's)		82/83	83/84	84/85	85/86	86/87	87/88
Person-Years		278	275	275	275	275	275
Operating Expenses							
- Salaries		6,745	8,115	8,882	9,169	9,169	9,169
- O&M		1,871	2,029	1,938	1,612	1,521*	1,521*
- Other Expenses							
Revenue		60	60	60	60	60	60
Subsidies		NONE					
Capital	H.Q.	13	19	4	0	0	0
	Field			290	766	766	766

Problem Identification

Some business representatives have questioned both: (1) the need for the extent of mandatory product and packaging regulations developed and/or enforced by this Program, and (2) the manner in which regulatory compliance is monitored and enforced. These concerns were strongest in the area of food products. Specific criticisms include: unneeded duplication of inspections at the plant and retail store levels; arbitrariness, and intrusive behaviour by inspectors; government preclearance of broadcast food product advertisements; differential treatment of domestic and imported food product labelling and packaging; Food and Drug Act content and labelling regulations are inhibiting product innovation and consumer choice. However, some businesses support continued regulation where CCA personnel perform activities which, without government regulation, would likely have to be conducted to some extent within the firm, with the costs being borne by the firm. Consumer representatives are generally supportive of the program.

The Department considers that the regulatory Acts under its exclusive responsibility do not inhibit innovation and that the program as a whole does not constitute an obstacle to economic development. It considers that current resources are minimal to achieve regulatory compliance but it notes that wherever possible voluntary programs are pursued and implemented. The Department has also stated that the early business interview results in the internal

evaluation of this Program indicate a positive and
supportive attitude to the Program and that inspectors'
manuals have already been updated to deal with interpersonal
relations with traders, provide information packages to
traders, increase educational meetings with traders, and
develop a form of "showcase" hearing in lieu of formal
prosecutions.

No adverse provincial comment has been received. With
the exception of Quebec which has its own food legislation,
there is no overlap or duplication of food inspection
activity with other levels of government.

Observations

A main objective of the Program, the prevention of
misleading or inaccurate consumer product information is the
same as the Marketing Practice Branch of the Department.
The Program's second main objective - to improve upon the
quality and extent of product information - assumes that
competition among producers and sellers, self-regulation, or
consumer research cannot be relied upon to generate
sufficient product information for consumers. This
assumption is disputed by some business representatives,
with some validity in the Team's view.

A review of the guidelines and regulations under the
Consumer Packaging and Labelling Act indicates that, apart
from the bilingual information requirements, firms would
probably quickly lose customers if they did not meet the
minimum product information standards on a voluntary basis,
in the absence of mandatory regulations.

The activities of this Program and the Marketing
Practices Branch appear to be largely uncoordinated and to
operate in isolation from each other.

In the Team's view, the regulations administered by the
program constitute barriers to entrepreneurial activity and
product innovation, may well have lost their relevance in
today's marketplace and could to a significant extent be
supplanted by industry self-regulation and consumer
self-help (aided by the media and consumer publications).

Options

The Study Team recommends to the Task Force that the
government consider the following:

1. Maintain program but do not increase regulation in this area. Give priority to establishing a compliance and enforcement policy that takes full account of the business objectives, performance and compliance records of the regulated firms, identifies industry areas suitable for self-certification and monitoring, and targets the Branch's inspection and enforcement activities.

2. Maintain program but consolidate responsibility for enforcement of provisions aimed at preventing willful misrepresentation, i.e., fraud, together with the activities of the Marketing Practices Branch.

3. With the exception of bilingual packaging requirements, phase out program's information regulation and product representation activities while leaving the existing legislation and regulations on the books.

   (a) Rely on the marketing practices program, provincial consumer protection activities and increased industry self-regulation through voluntary consensus standards.
   (b) Turn remainder of food product regulation over to Department which regulates food safety and wholesomeness.

4. Repeal all consumer protection regulation not required for health or safety purposes and place responsibility in this area on provinces.

MARKETING PRACTICES BRANCH - CCA 5

Objective

Administration of the provisions of the Combines Investigation Act governing advertising and deceptive marketing practices. Punishment of violations under the relevant provisions of the Combines Act. Deterrence from the commission of other violations. Assist business, through a Program of Compliance, in complying with the law by providing opinions on the application of the Act to proposed advertisement. Restore the marketplace balance that deceptive practices distort.

Authority

Combines Investigation Act

Description

The Program forms part of the Bureau of Competition Policy of the Department of Consumer and Corporate Affairs. The Combines Investigation Act is the only federal statute of general application to all representations by sellers to the public, including all media advertising. The Act contains a general prohibition against materially misleading representations backed up by criminal law sanctions. In considering whether the law has been broken, the courts are required to assess the overall impression created by the representation. In addition to this general rule, the Act also contains specific prohibitions against particularly deceptive and unfair marketing practices, including: performance claims not based on adequate and proper tests, misleading warranty/guarantee representations, ordinary price misrepresentations, double-ticketing, non-availability of advertised specials, sale above advertised price, pyramid selling, and referral selling.

Under the Act, the Director of Investigation and Research must conduct an investigation if he has reason to believe that a marketing practice offence has occurred or if he receives a written complaint. Under the Program of Compliance, the Program provides opinions on the application of the rules in the Act to proposed advertisements. The Misleading Advertising Bulletin, published quarterly, contains summaries of prosecutions that resulted in convictions and policy statements on various emerging issues. This bulletin, together with the Program's guidelines ("How to Avoid Misleading Advertising"), are designed to help the business community avoid practices which might contravene the Act and to educate the general public.

The Program also conducts over 1000 Information Visits annually wherein Program staff inform businesses of an infraction and request voluntary compliance in situations where proceeding with the case would not benefit the marketplace and would place an undue hardship on the business.

The largest fines to date under this Program ($1.7 million) were recently assessed against a major department store chain for promoting jewellery with false appraisal certificates. The Program is largely decentralized in five regional offices and has a core management and policy staff in Hull.

Resources

($000's)	82/83	83/84	84/85	85/86	86/87	87/88
Person-Years	66	66	76	79	79	79
Operating Expenses						
– Salaries		2,157	3,086	2,985	2,985	2,985
– O&M		368	551	576	576	576
– Other Exp.		--	--	--	--	--
Revenue	600	1,700				
Subsidies						
Capital		70	40	40	40	40

Problem Identification

Unlike a number of other federal regulatory programs directed at preventing economic fraud but having application to specific economic sectors, this Program has not been questioned in principle by the private sector. Nor has its method of compliance enforcement (summarized in Background Paper) been identified as a significant irritant. Consumers are supportive of the Program, particularly where it has yielded well publicized, successful prosecutions and substantial fines against major firms which have systematically misinformed the public. The Department considers that the Program facilitates economic development by fostering fair competition, clarifying the rules of business behaviour, and increasing consumer confidence in the Canadian marketplace.

However, there is considerable overlap in the legal rules administered by the Program with many of the elements of the Consumer Products program of Consumer and Corporate Affairs, other federal regulatory programs directed at preventing economic fraud (such as grading and labelling agricultural inputs and products) and consumer protection legislation in a number of provinces (see Background Paper). The Department considers that these overlaps have not resulted in administrative duplication because the Program has been directed largely at areas not addressed by specific regulatory programs (principally the retail level for consumer products) and Program staff closely cooperate through regional offices with provincial officials.

No adverse comment from the provinces has been received.

Observations

The Program represents a model of how general legal principles affecting all parts of the economy can be translated into a well received administrative program of compliance which relies to the fullest extent possible on industry self-monitoring and self enforcement. However, there has been no effort within CCA to date to systematically compare or integrate the duplicative and potentially conflicting approaches of this program and the Consumer Products program. Rather, there appears to be a tacit understanding at the managerial and operating levels not to invade the other program. There appears to have been little effort by Branch managers to integrate the Program's compliance activities with private or government remedies available under provincial consumer protection legislation other than to act as a referral point for complaints from provincial officials.

The Branch operates separately from other activities of the Bureau of Competition policy. However, resource levels are determined in conjunction with other Bureau of Competition Policy enforcement activities and not apparently in relation to similar activities within the Bureau of Consumer Affairs.

Despite the preference within the Department for general laws of general application, no efforts are underway to alter the "bureaucratic equilibrium" between this Program and other federal sector-oriented "economic fraud" prevention programs for which this Program may present an effective alternative.

Options

The Study Team recommends to the Task Force that the government consider the following:

1. Maintain program as is.

2. Merge and consolidate Consumer Products with Marketing Practices with:

    i) the merged activity to be located under the Department's consumer program; and

    ii) the necessary legislative amendments to ensure that this new consumers protection activity is under the direct authority of the Minister of Consumer and Corporate Affairs and not the Director of Investigation and Research.

BACKGROUND

CONSUMER PRODUCTS – MARKETING PRACTICES
PRODUCT INFORMATION REGULATION

1. ## RATIONALE AND ALTERNATIVES

Just as there can be "market failures" with respect to the production and distribution of products justifying regulatory intervention, there can also be market failures concerning the provision of product information from producers or sellers to buyers. This can occur in a number of ways:

(1) Producers or sellers provide an insufficient amount of product information to buyers and this prevents buyers from making purchase decisions which maximizes their well-being.

(2) Producers provide an adequate quantity of information but it is presented in a fashion calculated to misinform and deceive, thereby preventing purchasers from making rational purchasing decisions.

(3) Producers provide so much disparate information that informed product comparisons are either simply not possible or cannot be made without additional costs which are too high relative to the cost of the product.

(4) The purchaser is not the ultimate consumer and cannot make the kinds of purchasing decisions that are in the best interests of the ultimate consumer.

Case (4) is frequently encountered with respect to purchases for children or infants of products which may be unsafe. In this instance, information regulation is frequently accompanied by mandatory or voluntary product safety standards aimed at eliminating serious safety problems from the marketplace.

Cases (1) to (3) can be addressed in a number of ways:

(1) Patience - Despite identified information failures, competition among businesses and purchaser self-education are relied on to correct the failure, over time.

117

(2) <u>Private Remedies</u> - Contract law (which provides remedies for misrepresentation) is fortified to provide purchasers clearer or easier-to-enforce compensation rights with respect to information failures they have identified.

(3) <u>Criminal Sanctions</u> - Especially in the second case, the state may intervene to deter and punish intentionally deceptive behavior through actual and/or threatened criminal prosecution.

(4) <u>Self-regulation</u> - Producers and sellers, recognizing the potential for information failures, agree to voluntary disclosure, advertising or product design standards, to improve the quality of product information (and to avoid direct government intervention).

(5) <u>Mandatory Standards</u> - Embodied in government regulations, such standards can require producers to:

   (a) provide a specified minimum of information according to specified formats,
   (b) refrain from making specific kinds of statements or representations, and/or
   (c) follow a specified product design in order to sell the product under a commonly used name (e.g. apple juice)

These alternatives are not mutually exclusive and have been relied on by governments in varying combinations to solve identified problems in the provision of product information. However, in the field of consumer products (i.e. products being sold to the ultimate household user), direct government intervention (alternatives 2, 3, 5) has been particularly pronounced with respect to matters which do not give rise to product, workplace or environmental safety issues. This intervention has been at both the federal and provincial levels and has, largely because of different approaches taken by each level (which in part flow from different constitutional responsibilities), not been coordinated or evaluated in a systematic fashion. (See Sections 4 and 5).

2. AN APPROACH TO REGULATORY REFORM

Product information is never perfect or costless to acquire. In this sense, product information market failures are ever-present. The critical issue is to identify when patience or self-regulation cannot be relied on and some government intervention is required and, if so, what regulatory instrument is appropriate. Similarly, the first question which should be asked with respect to substantively reforming existing product information regulation programs should be: "Can we now rely on industry competition, purchaser self-help or self-education, or industry self-regulation to overcome product information inadequacies, inaccuracies or disparities?"

If the answer to these questions is no, then the next question should be: "Can the problem be satisfactorily overcome through enhanced civil remedies and/or general statutory rules to correct industry behaviour?" These measures leave considerably more freedom to industry relative to mandatory standards and should be the first line of government intervention. These measures can also encourage improved industry behaviour through self-regulation but, depending on their design, they may create a disincentive to consumer self-help and self-education.

Only as a last resort should mandatory information or product design standards be relied on. These reduce business flexibility the most and are the most costly to government.

In the Team's view, the need for such mandatory standards may not exist where:

(1)   health or safety concerns do not arise;
(2)   several similar products or product substitutes are available;
(3)   an industry trade association exists to formulate common minimum disclosure standards;
(4)   consumer purchasing decisions are frequent (to allow a consumer "learning curve" to evolve);
(5)   individual purchasing mistakes caused by wrong or insufficient information do not have a substantial impact on a consumer's well-being or wealth.

The continued appropriateness of mandatory product information standards should be assessed against these considerations.

On this basis, a comprehensive assessment of the current relevance and usefulness of the large number of mandatory federal consumer product information regulations which are not health or safety based would appear to be the most useful starting point. To a large degree consumers are better educated, more aware of sales techniques, have better lines of communication through the media and volunteer groups than when these regulations were put in place. As well, there appears to be a greater awareness on the part of industry to provide accurate product information (see next section) and few consumer products are provided by industries in which competition is not present.

3.   ADVERTISING SELF-REGULATION

A number of Canadian trade associations have established codes or guidelines for their members with respect to advertising practices to avoid public misrepresentation. This form of self-regulation flows not only from a desire to obey the law, but also the mutual economic interest of association members to avoid industry goodwill with the public being eroded by the product misrepresentations of an individual member. Following is a partial list of advertising codes of practice:

Product	Association
Cosmetics, Toiletries, Fragrances	Canadian Cosmetic, Toiletry and Fragrance Association
Non-Prescription Medicine	Advertising Standards Council
Horticultural Products	Advertising Standards Council
Feminine Sanitary Protection Products	Canadian Association of Broadcasters
Food-Comparative Commercials	Advertising Standards Council

The Advertising Standards Council also publishes a "Canadian Code of Advertising Standards" and the Canadian Association of Broadcasters publishes a "Broadcast Code for Advertising to Children".

The increasing numbers of such codes (the enforcement of which relies largely on moral suasion and a "gentlemen's agreement" among members to adhere to them) suggests that an improved industry awareness of the desirability of providing adequate and accurate product information has developed in

Canada and that, as a result, government concern over information market failures (unrelated to health and safety matters) may no longer need to be as great as it was in the last two decades.

4. PROVINCIAL CONSUMER PROTECTION LEGISLATION

A number of provinces have enacted and actively administer legislation directed at preventing and providing consumer remedies for "economic fraud" or "deceptive marketing practices".

This legislation is not duplicative of the legislation administered by the Consumer Products and Marketing Practices Programs of the Department of Consumer and Corporate Affairs since it does not impose disclosure standards by regulation, nor does it provide purely for criminal penalties in the event of the breach of a statutory prohibition. Instead, these Acts establish new contractual rights which are privately enforceable in the regular civil courts by individual consumers. Some also provide for government initiated "cease and desist orders" where unfair practices are involved. This largely reflects the fact that the provincial Acts are founded on the constitutional "property and civil rights" power and are conceived as an extension of the statutory law on commercial relations administered by the provinces under this power. The federal laws derive from federal authority to regulate trade and commerce and to enact criminal law.

While the machinery differs, the object of the provincial laws is nevertheless much the same as the federal laws: to create informed consumers and honest and forthcoming sellers and thereby to redress a perceived imbalance in bargaining power favouring sellers.

In broad terms the provincial legislation differs from the federal legislation principally because the provincial approach relies less on direct government intervention and much more on individual or collective self-help through enhanced and/or codified consumer rights. Generally speaking, the provinces have not enhanced buyers rights at levels of trade other than the retail level.

The relevant provincial legislation can be summarized as follows:

Province	Legislation	Enforcement
British Columbia	Trade Practices Act (1974). Remedies include private civil action contracts, the option of quasi-criminal proceedings. The Act is limited to "consumer transactions".	During the late 1970's, there was considerable interest and activity related to misleading advertising issues. The level of activity has declined in the last few years and the focus has shifted to the conventional provincial concern for abusive direct sales prac tices (e.g. home repair scams). Approximately 20 enforcement proceedings take place each year. The annual budget for activity in this field is about $250,000.
Alberta	Unfair Trade Practices Act (1975). Remedies are limited to administrative orders and the Act is limited to "consumer transactions".	Provincial interests include misleading advertising by intraprovincial entities as well as the conventional provincial concerns of unconscionable practices and abusive direct sales practices (e.g. auto repairs). The province will generally not act on competitor complaints.
Manitoba	There is a Consumer Protection Act which covers such issues as improper disclosure of credit. However, no general legislation exists dealing with misrepresentation.	

Newfoundland	Trade Practices Act (1979). There is partial overlap in coverage vis-a-vis the misleading advertising provisions of the C.I.A.	Private Enforcement relied on a Director responsible for the Act but it does not appear that he has any staff.
New Brunswick	There is a Consumer Products Warranty Act which codifies consumer warranty rights. However, no general legislation exists dealing with commercial misrepresentations.	Private actions
Saskatchewan	Consumer Products Warranty Act. No general legislation exists dealing with commercial misrepresentations.	Private Actions
Prince Edward Island	Business Practices Act (1977).	Private right to damages against unfair business practices, including (public and private) misrepresentations. No active enforcement. There is a Director responsible for the Act, but it does not appear that he has any staff.
Ontario	Business Practices Act (1974). The Act is limited to "consumer transactions".	The focus of provincial government efforts is on fraudulent business practices, in particular, car repair frauds, home repair, and vacation land scams.

Province	Legislation	Enforcement
		The Province is very active in the above-noted areas with a budget of $2,000,000. However, involvement in false and misleading advertising issues is minimal with less than 5 per cent of resources directed in that area.
Nova Scotia	None	
Quebec	Loi sur la protection du consommateur (1980).	The Act provides both rights and government cease and desist powers. The Province is interested in misleading advertising issues as well as the conventional areas of provincial concern. The Province remains very active although there has been a dramatic decline in formal proceedings (from 150/ year to about 25/year). Approximately, 25-30 persons are engaged in this activity.

5. FEDERAL STATUTES

There are a number of federal statutes, which regulate the manner in which certain products or goods are required to be marked, packaged and labelled. In many cases they also contain prohibitions against product misrepresentations. These statutes often relate to specific products (e.g. foods), for which the government has established various grades or classifications. These statutes generally state that such products may not be marked, labelled or described as being of a certain grade or classification unless the product conforms to the standards prescribed for the product, grade or classification. Some statutes relate to products which are considered to be dangerous or hazardous. The following statutes are not administered by these programs.

Act and Administering Department	Subject Covered
1. Bank Act	Regulates bank advertising directed to interest rate cost of borrowing.
2. Canada Elections Act	Prohibits publishing false statements affecting personal character or conduct of candidates.
3. Copyright Act (Consumer & Corporate Affairs)	Creates an offence to knowingly infringe copyright of literary dramatic, musical works, or engravings.
4. Criminal Code (Provincial Attorneys-General)	Prohibits lotteries, forgeries of trade marks, "passing-off", advertising illustrations of Canadian currency etc.
5. Hazardous Products Act (Consumer & Corporate Affairs)	Regulates advertising of certain hazardous products.
6. National Defence Act Royal Canadian Mounted Police Act	Prohibits unauthorized use of words "Canadian Forces", their insignia or any RCMP name, member or insignia.

7. Trade Marks Act (CCA)   Prohibits the making of a false or misleading statement which may cause confusion between competitive wares and services. Prohibits unauthorized use of government crests, flags, marks etc.

8. Weights and Measures   Regulates representations marked on products or packaging regarding quantity, volume etc.

These statutory summaries rely upon primary research conducted by the Marketing Practices Branch.

The product information legislation administered by these programs is as follows:

Act and Administering Department	Subject Covered
Broadcasting Act (C.R.T.C., CCA2)	Regulatory provisions for the advertising of alcoholic beverages, food and drugs, and patent medicines.
Consumer Packaging and Labelling Act (CCA2)	Regulates representations on "pre-packaged products".
Food and Drugs Act (Health & Welfare, CCA2)	Prohibits certain kinds of advertising in relation to food, drugs, medical devices or cosmetics
National Trade Mark and True Labelling Act (CCA2)	Prohibits falsely advertising any commodity as having a national trade mark applied to it.
Textile Labelling Act (CCA2)	Prohibits the advertising of certain textile articles unless the Act's requirements are complied with.
Combines Investigation Act (CCA5)	Prohibits misleading public representations and specific practices such as bait and switch selling, double ticketing and pyramid selling.

CONSUMER PRODUCT SAFETY — CCA 4

Objective

1. To provide for a marketplace that recognizes the public's right to know of hazards associated with household chemicals and other products.

2. To ban or regulate products where it is deemed that labelling or other sources of hazard information are not adequate to achieve the ends of public safety consistent with the spirit of the Act.

Authority

Hazardous Products Act (1969)

Description

The Program forms part of the Bureau of Consumer Affairs of the Department of Consumer and Corporate Affairs. The Program is responsible for the administration and enforcement of the Hazardous Products Act and its regulations, as well as the monitoring of voluntary programs undertaken by industry to protect the public against hazardous products in the marketplace. These efforts are reinforced by encouraging industry and importers to market products of safe design in the first instance to minimize the need for regulatory intervention and the promotion of safety awareness amongst consumers. Supported by field inspections and other compliance activities, it identifies hazards in consumer products, proposes regulations where necessary and ensures that non-complying products are removed from the marketplace.

The Act deals with what might be referred to in general terms as consumer goods and makes specific mention of such product categories as those designed for household, garden, or personal use, for use in sports or recreational activities or for use by children. It also mentions, without reference to end use, poisonous, toxic, flammable, explosive and corrosive products, but excludes from its purview food, drugs, cosmetics, pest control products, radioactive materials and explosives within the meaning of the Explosives Act. Thirty-five product areas are banned (e.g. lead pigments in paint and asbestos in textiles) and 36 others are regulated under the Hazardous Products Act (e.g. children's toys and furniture, the labelling of

household chemicals and fire hazards in textile products).
Major operations include the identification of hazards
(through laboratory testing and analysis of accident data),
the conduct of consumer and trader information programs and
the inspection of products in the marketplace to ensure
compliance with existing regulations.

The Program is decentralized in district offices and
five regional offices (46 per cent of PYs) with headquarters
in Hull, Quebec. The assistance of provincial fire
marshalls, coroners and other professionals is sought as
required, to cope with special consumer problems and
distribution of preventive information. Health and Welfare
Canada, Energy, Mines and Resources and other federal
departments provide scientific, medical and other
specialized assistance as required.

Resources

($000's)	82/83	83/84	84/85	85/86	86/87	87/88
Person-Years	90	87	89	89	89	89
Operating Expenses						
– Salaries	2,428	2,740	3,440	3,260	3,260	3,260
– O&M	795	729	770	878	878	878
– Other Expenses						
Revenue						
Subsidies						
Capital – H.Q.	129	292	234	218	218	218
– Field			11	123	123	123

Problem Identification

The Program is generally supported and well regarded by
both business and consumers. However, some business
representatives have expressed concern that the Program has
inhibited product innovation and discriminated against
imported consumer products. Consumer representatives have
for some time been concerned that the Program does not
systematically identify consumer product hazards and that,
as a result, regulatory coverage may be too narrow.

The Department considers that the Program has been
effective in reducing product-related accidents and hence
health care costs to society, although it admits there is no
systematic or statistical way of measuring whether the
Program is doing the best possible job with the best mix of
regulatory instruments. It also considers that, at its
current resource level, the Program is restricted to a

reactive, rather than a pro-active, mode of operation. The Department notes that, to the fullest extent possible, regulations are developed in close consultation with the industry and consumers and that Program staff seek voluntary compliance by manufacturers and retailers first and foremost. There is no duplication of effort with the provinces or municipalities. No adverse comment has been received from any province.

Observations

The Program's emphasis on consultation, voluntary compliance and encouraging industry self-regulation through voluntary consensus standards foster consistency, and good citizenship. While some barriers to innovation are caused by the regulations, this is minimized by the Program's reliance on consultative performance-oriented standards rather than those that are design- or formulation-specific. Compliance costs appear to be low. The Program itself remains reactive and its activities are often driven by "media issues". This can also contribute to inadequate coverage. Without a systematic process for identifying consumer product risks and actual broad-based consumer accident data (such as exists now in the U.S.), the Program may come to rely on selective information which provides misleading indications of product problems. The federal government hazardous products programs are fragmented among several Departments. As a result regulatory gaps may exist, but consumers may mistakenly be relying on full regulatory coverage of hazardous products.

Options

The Study Team recommends to the Task Force that the government consider the following:

A)   To improve the scope of this Program:

1.   Attach priority to the development of product information systems and a consumer accident data base to permit a more proactiave regulatory stance.

2.   Provide a greater amount of consumer information concerning what the Program does not regulate to encourage:
(i) greater consumer self-help in appropriate cases, or
(ii) industry self-regulation.

3. To aid in compliance and enforcement activities, widely publicize instances of non-compliance with the regulations to act as an incentive by publicity-sensitive industries (such as the toy industry) to assume a greater responsibility in reducing involuntary product risks through self-regulation.

B) **To improve the overall coverage of federal hazardous products programs:**

1. Take steps to eliminate fragmented federal hazardous products regulation and, if necessary, merge the administration of all federal hazardous product legislation within one department.

2. For proposed regulatory initiatives not subject to SEIA's, develop a less detailed and less costly method for broad socio-economic analysis by the Program. This analysis should expressly address:
   i) the extent to which the initiative would raise product prices and thereby encourage regulatory bypass,
   ii) whether the initiative would create a non-tariff barrier,
   iii) whether the problem could equally be solved through increased or better product information disclosure.

3. Conduct an interdepartmental assessment of all federal hazardous products regulation programs to determine:
   i) the resource allocation priorities to be attached to each program and,
   ii) whether all of society's regulatory needs in the area are being adequately addressed by the current program mix.

CORPORATIONS - CCA 9

Objective

To provide an institutional framework for the orderly conduct of business and the accumulation of capital. To regulate the creation and existence of federal corporations. To maintain order and fairness in the corporate environment.

Authority

Canada Business Corporations Act, Canada Corporations Act

Description

The Corporations Branch forms part of the Bureau of Corporate Affairs of the Department of Consumer and Corporate Affairs. Excepting financial intermediaries, all federal business corporations, including investment and small loans companies, are incorporated under the Canada Business Corporations Act (CBCA).

It is responsible for the administration of several federal acts, including the Canada Corporations Act and the Canada Business Corporations Act. Under the latter are incorporated all federal business corporations, including investment and small loan companies. The Canada Corporations Act applies to the establishment and functioning of all federal non-profit corporations. In addition to providing legal instruments of incorporation, the Program has a monitoring/regulatory role in ensuring compliance with the Act and regulations in such matters as annual filing of financial statements and insider trading activities. The Program also deals with relaxation of public disclosure requirements where market conditions dictate and investigates complaints of abuse of minority shareholders, unusual market activity or malfeasance.

The total number of federal corporations has grown from 81,000 to 155,000 between 1979 and 1983. The Program now receives a monthly average of 2,800 articles of incorporation, 12,000 statutory filings and 11,000 information requests.

Resources

($000's)	82/83	83/84	84/85	85/86	86/87	87/88
Person-Years	63	61	56	59	59	59
Operating Exp.						
- Salaries*	1,600	1,600	1,600	1,700	1,700	1,700
- O&M	500	500	700	400	400	400
- Other Exp.						
Revenue**	6,300	7,800	8,300	17,700	17,700	17,700
Subsidies	NONE					
Capital ($000's)	0	5	8	8	8	8

* Excludes employee benefits
** Assumes fee increases by Order-in-Council in effect in
   1985-86

Problem Identification

The program is not questioned in principle. The
increasing number of federal incorporations indicates an
increasing preference for federal incorporation in the
business community.

The Department considers that the program has no
significant problems. However, as the result of discussions
with the provinces, the Department is considering increasing
the threshold for activating the takeover bid provisions of
the CBCA to bring these provisions more into line with
provincial securities and corporation law. The Department
also intends to seek amendments to the CBCA to make the
powers of the Director of Corporations consistent with the
Charter of Rights and Freedoms and to clarify some
compliance and reporting provisions of the Act.

Higher CBCA incorporation fees are proposed by the
Department to create a greater incentive for businesses not
having national objects or activities to incorporate under
provincial corporation Acts.

Increased automation of program delivery, coupled with
the privatization of corporate name search activities has
allowed the program to deal with a significantly increased
workload without increasing total resource requirements.

All provinces also have corporation legislation. A
business's decision as to whether to incorporate
provincially or federally is largely determined by whether
the business will have substantial interprovincial activity

and the flexibility, rights, and obligations afforded under alternative incorporation laws. There is, therefore, a choice but no overlap or duplication among federal and provincial corporation laws. However, there is some overlap between the CBCA's stock trading rules and provincial securities laws.

Observations

The program provides an essential legal framework for businesses and non-profit organizations operating on a national basis and has been well received by the private sector.

The continued relevance and usefulness to the private sector of these framework laws will rest on the timely enactment of updating amendments of a "housekeeping" nature.

Options

The Study Team recommends to the Task Force that the government consider the following:

1.   Reform Parliamentary practices to develop a "fast track" procedure for enacting relatively non-controversial or "housekeeping" legislation which is not subject to speedy enactment under the Miscellaneous Statute Law Amendment Act.

2.   Attach priority to passage of Amendments currently being proposed by CCA with 1985-86 Legislation Plan.

BANKRUPTCY – CCA 10

Objective

To restore to more productive use resources which have been locked up in an insolvent business. To ensure the fair and equitable treatment of debtors and creditors. To prevent fraud in insolvent estate administration.

Authority

Bankruptcy Act, Criminal Code provisions relating to commercial fraud.

Description

The Bankruptcy Branch forms part of the Bureau of Corporate Affairs of the Department of Consumer and Corporate Affairs. The Bankruptcy Branch, under the supervision of the Superintendent of Bankruptcy, oversees the administration of bankruptcy in Canada. Bankruptcy and insolvency are constitutionally designated federal responsibilities. However, certain functions may be devolved to the provinces, as has been done with the orderly payment of debt provisions of the current Act. The Branch regulates the insolvency process, licenses and supervises bankruptcy trustees and conducts investigations to detect offences under the Bankruptcy Act or the Criminal Code.

As of March 1984, there were 575 licensed individuals and 100 licensed corporations under supervision. During the 1970's and early 1980's, bankruptcies in Canada increased, peaking at 43,000 per annum at the height of the recession in 1982-83. The estimate for 1984-85 is 33,000.

The regulatory services provided under this Program include registration of bankruptcies, chairing of creditors' meetings, examination of bankrupts, trustee licences, audits and small debtors referrals.

The Program's services are being provided through 15 regional and district offices across Canada. Estate administration is being performed by private trustees.

Resources

($000's)	82/83	83/84	84/85	85/86	86/87	87/88
Person-Years	153	146	143	143	143	143
Operating Exp.						
- Salaries*	3,700	4,400	4,600	5,100	5,100	5,100
- O&M	900	900	1,200	1,400	1,300	1,300
- Other Exp.						
Revenue**	1,700	1,800	1,400	3,800	3,800	3,800
Subsidies	NONE					
Capital ($000's)	21	74	18	18	18	18

* Excluded employee benefits
** Assumes fee increases by Order-in-Council in effect in
    1985-86.

Problem Identification

The need for a national bankruptcy law is not
questioned. However, both the department and the private
sector consider there is a strong need to update the Act.

The private sector has raised the following concerns:

(1)   Commercial Crown corporations should not be given a
      priority over other business creditors simply because
      they are government owned.
(2)   Employees of a bankrupt company should have a
      preference over secured commercial creditors for a
      larger portion of their wages and benefits owing,
      subject to a maximum per employee.
(3)   The Act should provide for business rearrangements
      short of full liquidation as is currently provided for
      under U.S. Bankruptcy law.
(4)   Unpaid suppliers of merchandise should have a right to
      reclaim the merchandise.
(5)   There may be a need to regulate receivership by a
      creditor pursuant to a debenture with the debtor
      business in order to fairly protect the interests of
      all creditors where a creditor's petition for
      bankruptcy is not feasible or desirable.
(6)   Special rules may be appropriate for insolvent farmers
      and fishermen.

As a result, the Minister has proposed that revision of
the Act form part of the Department's legislative plan for
1985-86. Amendments had been introduced by the previous
government but were not enacted.

Despite a doubling in bankruptcies over the last five years, program efficiency has improved by 204 per cent in throughput terms as total person-years have been reduced by 38, largely through attrition.

Observations

A bankruptcy law providing for easier and orderly business exit upon insolvency is generally regarded as facilitating economic development and entrepreneurial initiative by easing entry into small business and improving the availability of commercial credit to new businesses.

While the overall scheme of the Act or the quality of its administration are not subject to criticism, it is apparent that the Act has not kept pace with changing commercial realities and attitudes concerning fair treatment of creditors.

The increasing use of private receivership arrangements in commercial affairs is a symptom of the declining relevance of this framework law. Such private arrangements may not provide for fair and democratic treatment of all creditors' interests. Rather, they are likely to primarily benefit the most powerful creditors who are in a position to negotiate and administer such arrangements.

In the Team's view, the Bankruptcy Act requires modernizing. Otherwise, public confidence in the fairness of its priorization of creditors' claims and its commercial relevance will fade.

However, it should be recognized that not all interested parties will ever be fully satisfied with the Bankruptcy law because it adjusts competing creditors' rights.

Options

The Study Team recommends to the Task Force that the government consider the following:

1. A high priority should be attached to speedy passage of amendments to this important framework law.

2. Parliamentary time should be allocated for the next few years in a way which gives clear preference to essential legislation related to the economy.

COPYRIGHT AND INDUSTRIAL DESIGN – CCA 12

Objective

To grant equitable and exclusive intellectual property rights.

Authority

Copyright Act and Industrial Design Act.

Description

The Copyright and Industrial Design Office forms part of the Bureau of Corporate Affairs of the Department of Consumer and Corporate Affairs.

The Office is responsible for the registration of copyrights for original artistic, dramatic, literary or musical works and industrial designs that are original shapes, pattern or ornamentation applied to an article or manufacture, as provided in legislation and maintains a record of same. Approximately 8,400 copyright certificates and 1,560 industrial design applications are handled each year.

Copyright and industrial design legislation is intended to provide protection for intellectual property rights much as common law does for real property. Copyright is automatically conferred upon creation of the work and remains in force during the life of the creator, and for 50 years thereafter. Registration under the Act allows for easier and less costly private enforcement of such rights. Industrial design protection is extended initially for five years and is renewable for a further five-year term.

The Copyright Appeals Board determines royalties payable to copyright owners of musical works.

Resources

($000's)	82/83	83/84	84/85	85/86	86/87	87/88
Person-Years	15	15	14	14	14	14
Operating Exp.						
– Salaries*	400	400	500	500	500	500
– O&M	100	100	100	100	100	100
– Other Exp.						
Revenue**	600	700	600	1,400	1,400	1,400
Subsidies	NONE					
Capital	200	600	000	200	200	200

* Excluded employee benefits
** Assumes fee increases by Order-in-Council in effect in 1985-86.

Problem Identification

The need for some form of proprietary rights to protect the income-earning potential of creative effort is not questioned in principle. Arts groups and other creators have expressed criticism for many years that the range of intellectual and artistic activity subject to property rights under the Copyright Act has become too narrow as the result of technological and industry structure changes. Publishers, broadcasters and other resellers and transmitters of artistic endeavour have suggested that expanded artistic property rights are not necessary because competition for valuable artistic output now ensures satisfactory returns to artists, etc. These parties have also expressed concern over the uncertainty caused in the marketplace of continuous re-examination of the appropriateness of the current Copyright Act without any legislative amendments actually being enacted.

The previous government tabled a White Paper on copyright law reform co-signed by the Ministers of CCA and DOC. This same document has been tabled in Parliament for Committee reports by the current Ministers of CCA and DOC as a discussion paper and not a White or Green Paper. The paper proposes a variety of new rights and redefinition of the scope of certain existing rights directed at increasing creators' incomes. The issues of greatest potential controversy are:

a) attaching copyright liability to broadcast retransmission;

b) attaching first ownership of copyright in works created by employees in the course of employment to the employees and not the employer; and

c) expanding the ability of the creator to control the form or manner in which his or her efforts are re-used.

No concerns have been received with respect to the operations of the Copyright Appeals Board.

Observations

While specific proposals for copyright reform are numerous and individually complex, there does not yet appear to be a consensus between the originators of creative effort (who benefit from copyright) and the resellers of such effort (who make payments for use of copyright material). Moreover, as between the principal government departments involved there does not appear to be an agreement as to whether copyright law revisions should be viewed as a tool of arts policy (private copyright payments as a substitute for government grants) or of broad economic development policy (encouraging the ready and low-cost resale and reuse of creative output, and, hence, the diffusion of new ideas) through greater reliance of contractual arrangements between creators and users of their products.

To remove the present uncertainty over the future role of copyright law and its relationship to new media technologies, speedy and final reconsideration of the Act is needed. A Parliamentary Committee with sufficient funds to be well staffed with experts in the field is, according to the Study Team, the appropriate forum for such a review.

Options

The Study Team recommends to the Task Force that the government consider the following:

1. Amendments to the Copyright Act should be legislated by early 1986 at the latest.

2. Provide funds for adequate expert support to the House Communications Committee examining copyright law

reform. Set an early deadline for the Committee's
report.

3.   Make the amended legislation subject to decennial
      review by inserting a sunset clause.

PATENTS - CCA 13

Objective

1. To encourage invention in Canada and abroad by granting exclusive intellectual property rights.

2. To facilitate technological information dissemination to potential Canadian users.

Authority

Patent Act

Description

The Patent Office is responsible for all aspects of the Act -- examination of applications, granting of rights, recording of patents issued and maintenance of search files of Canadian and foreign patents in force. There are some 20 million patents on file. Around 26,000 applications are filed and 22,000 patents issued each year, 95 per cent to foreigners. In turn, other governments may grant patents to Canadians.

A patent can be viewed as a contract between the inventor and the state. In return for granting a limited monopoly on the production and sale of a product or process for a specified period of time, commercially valuable, technical information is made publicly available. The term of a Canadian patent is 17 years from the time it is issued.

An invention is eligible for patent protection if the Patent Office is persuaded it is new, useful, and commercially exploitable.

The Patent Office classifies and examines applications for patents and publishes those granted in a weekly periodical. Additionally, the Patent Office facilitates the dissemination of patent disclosures to the public, conducts technology searches, provides scientific assessment and forecast and disseminates technological information. Also, the Patent Office considers and disposes of compulsory license applications.

Services are provided centrally from the national capital, yet filings are accepted in departmental regional offices. Private patent agents (solicitors) in most cases represent applicants with the office.

Canada is a signatory to the Paris Convention for the Protection of Industrial Property, and is party to international treaties on patents.

Resources

($000's)	82/83	83/84	84/85	85/86	86/87	87/88
Person-Years	332	269	264	268	268	268
Operating Expenses						
- Salaries	8,400	8,100	8,600	9,200	9,200	9,200
- O&M	900	900	900	1,700	1,500	1,500
- Other Expenses						
Revenue	13,900	14,000	13,000	25,400	25,400	25,400
Subsidies	NONE					
Capital	35	41	27	30	30	30

* Excludes Employee Benefits
** Assumes fee increases any Order in Council in effect in 1985-86.

Problem Identification

The manufacturers of patented drugs have for many years strongly objected to provisions in the Act which make the licensing of their drug patents compulsory in Canada. They contend that this provision results in less R&D being conducted by them in Canada with an attendant loss of high tech jobs and less technological diffusion in the health sciences field. Consumers and some provinces support the provision since it has allowed a low cost "generic" drug industry to develop in Canada, thereby bringing health care costs down. However other provinces support abandoning compulsory licensing and using other means to help keep drug costs down.

The department contends that the present legislation does not create a sufficiently clear mandate to the Patent Office to develop a program to actively disseminate the vast amount of public technological information available in the office's files along the lines of Japan's office. As a result, it feels that Canada's patent system is not living up to its responsibility to disclose information which would allow more rapid technological change and would prevent unnecessary duplication of R&D (as researchers would become more aware of existing inventions and other discoveries).

Getting a patent in Canada presently takes an average of 34 months. The Study Team on Services and Subsidies to Business has calculated that an examiner takes on average a half a day to determine whether an invention is unique to the world. The Office's practice is to rely on U.S. examination results which must be appended to the application. Eighty per cent of Canadian applications have a U.S. counterpart. The remainder are largely applications previously accepted in other jurisdictions. Less than 500 patents per year are filed solely in Canada. The department has identified a number of relatively minor amendments to the Act which it feels will make the Program more efficient. These are supported by the private sector.

Observations

Compulsory licensing of drug patents will be the subject of a special inquiry report to be published in the near future (Eastman Commission). The Department plans to enact legislation in the area this year. Compulsory licensing has kept drug costs down. Published CCA studies indicate that relatively few jobs are at stake over this issue and that patent drug industry R&D in Canada has not declined in real terms since the measure was introduced in 1969.

The proposal to use the Patent Office as a clearing house for technological information must be considered in the context of the current multiplicity of government-funded specialized technology information sources including the NRC. Computerizing the patent files for this purpose in the U.S. has proven very costly. Linking the Patent Office with other existing technology banks at NRC may be more useful and less costly. Some distance can be travelled by arranging electronic access to U.S. technology databases.

In the Team's view there is considerable duplication and repetition of effort by Canadian patent examiners vis-à-vis their counterparts in other industrialized countries which Canada's becoming a member of the international patent-pooling agreement would help to avoid.

Options

The Study Team recommends to the Task Force that the government consider the following:

1. **To improve operation of Program**

   (a) Mandate the Patent Office to develop an information dissemination program in cooperation with other Canadian and foreign technology databases (no new legislation required). Design program to be capable of delivery by private firms as are corporate name searches.

   (b) Ratify and accede to the Patent Cooperation Treaty to reduce examination duplication.

   (c) Change patent protection to 20 years from date of filing to conform to most industrialized countries and encourage earlier working of inventions.

   (d) Adopt a two-tier fee structure with reduced fees for smaller entities.

2. **For compulsory licensing**

   (a) Introduce legislation in the fall to implement recommendations of Eastman Commission.

   (b) Other options are:
      (i) Set drug patent licence royalties according to patentee's level of Canadian R&D which is not incurred for Canadian safety approvals.
      (ii) Provide drug patentees a limited period of market exclusivity following initial marketing.
      (iii) Exempt companies providing performance and low price commitments from compulsory licensing.

TRADE MARKS - CCA 14

Objective

To grant equitable and exclusive intellectual property rights by granting an exclusive, privately enforceable right to use a distinctive trade mark to identify a business's goods and services in the marketplace.

Authority

Trade Marks Act.

Description

The Program is carried out by the Bureau of Corporate Affairs of the Department Consumer and Corporate Affairs. The Trade Mark Office receives and processes applications for registration of "a word, symbol or picture or a combination of these used to distinguish the goods and services of a person or organization" from those of others in the marketplace. Approximately 16,500 trade mark and 16,700 registered user applications are received annually. The initial term of a trade mark is 15 years, although it may be renewed every 15 years indefinitely.

Regulatory services provided include trade mark and registered user registration certificates and proofs thereof. The Program's benefits consist of the creation of business goodwill and providing a ready means of identifying a supplier's products in the marketplace. The Program's activities include the disposal of trade mark and registered user applications, and the dissemination of information, in accordance with statutes, and in response to public demand. The Program's staff examines applications for trade marks and registered users, publishes a weekly periodical of marks approved and provides searching facilities to the public.

Services are provided centrally from the national capital, however, filings are being accepted in departmental regional offices. Private trade mark agents (solicitors) in most cases represent applicants with the office. A Trade Mark Opposition Board resolves disputes over the registration of trade marks. Apart from the arbitration activity of the Trade Mark Opposition Board, the program relies upon the self-regulation of registered trade mark rights by their owners through the civil courts, such as actions to prevent the use by competitors of similar trademarks which would confuse the public. Resources were increased in 1983-84 to deal with a serious application backlog problem which has now been resolved.

Resources

($000's)	82/83	83/84	84/85	85/86	86/87	87/88
Person-Years	28	94	82	84	84	84
Operating Exp.						
- Salaries*	700	2,800	2,700	2,900	2,900	2,900
- O&M	100	300	900	400	400	400
- Other Exp.						
Revenue	4,000	4,500	4,400	16,800	16,800	16,800
Subsidies	NONE					
Capital**	5	33	39	9	9	9

* Excludes employee benefits.
** Assumes fee increases by Order-in-Council in effect in 1985-86.

Problem Identification

The program is not questioned in principle. Trade mark applications numbered about 18,000 in 1983-84 and are estimated to be about 19,500 in 1985-86, indicating increasing business demand for the program.

However, costs per application in 1983-84 were about $150 and are expected to be about $185 in 1985/86, representing a real cost increase when adjusted for inflation. Over the same period the trade mark application inventory will have risen from about 29,000 to about 35,000, an increase of 20 per cent, indicating a substantial increase in total elapsed time of handling applications.

The Business Programs Study Team has calculated that, despite some improvement in the application handling rate per person-year, applications still average 19 months before the trade mark is granted, of which 10 months represents the time the application spends in the Trade Marks Office prior to publication.

Observations

The Program facilitates economic development by allowing businesses, through an easily identified mark, to distinguish their goods and services in the marketplace and to protect and enhance the goodwill associated with their products. Trade marks help to prevent the "passing off" of one supplier's products for another's, thus improving opportunities for entrepreneurial activity. Trade mark rights are privately enforced at no cost to government. Private enforcement of trademark rights appears to provide satisfactory trademark protection to the private sector. This approach is preferable to government intervention as it fosters good citizenship.

However, in the Team's view, steps should be taken to improve the application processing efficiency of the Trade Marks Office. Delays in granting trade mark registration can inhibit product innovation, the entry of new businesses, and entrepreneurial activity generally while making unfair competition through "passing off" easier.

In this regard, the Team agrees with the suggestion of the Business Programs Study Team to proceed quickly with planned amendments to the Act, establish and meet higher processing standards and providing for telecommunicated filings from trade mark agents' offices.

Options

The Study Team recommends to the Task Force that the government consider the following:

1. Reform Parliamentary practices to develop a "fast track" procedure for enacting relatively non-controversial or "housekeeping" legislation which is not eligible for enactment under the Miscellaneous Statute Law Amendments Act.

2. To reduce processing time, develop and adhere to application processing performance standards.

LEGAL METROLOGY — ELECTRICITY AND GAS — CCA 31

Objective

To ensure accurate measurement and equity in trade of electricity and natural gas as mandated under the Electricity and Gas Inspection Acts.

Authority

Electricity Inspection Act, Gas Inspection Act, to be replaced by Electricity and Gas Inspection Act, 1981 (not yet proclaimed).

Description

The Program forms part of the Bureau of Consumer Affairs of the Department of Consumer and Corporate Affairs. The Program determines and enforces standards of measurement, establishes specifications for, and approves energy metering devices used in trade, calibrates and certifies measurement standards, verifies meters and ancilliary equipment to ensure accuracy and resolves disputes between buyers and sellers of electricity and gas.

The Program deals with the measurement of gas from wellhead to consumer, including export and the measurement of electricity sold from transformer stations to consumers, including export. This involves working with over 1,100 electricity and gas utilities, electricity and gas meter manufacturers and the control of 14 million metering devices. The frequency for the re-verification of in-service meters is legislated and all new metering devices used for billing purposes must be approved as meeting established performance criteria prior to being used in the marketplace.

Meters are verified for accuracy within prescribed tolerances before use and are sealed to prevent tampering. Almost 2 million electricity and gas metering devices were verified in 1983/84, largely on a sampling basis, and some 116 approvals were granted for prototypes for new/modified metering devices. These activities are undertaken to ensure equitable transactions between suppliers of electricity and gas and their customers in an area of trade where suppliers have exclusive right of distribution and sale of an essential, invisible commodity.

The sub-activity also calibrates industry and government standards (more than 1,100 such standards were calibrated to 1983-84) used for verification of measuring devices and maintains traceability to NRC standards. The sub-activity also provides expert and independent arbitration of disputes between sellers and consumers of energy as prescribed by law.

The program is decentralized with district, area and five regional offices (84 per cent of PYs) with headquarters and testing laboratories in Ottawa, Ontario.

Resources

($000's)	82/83	83/84	84/85	85/86	86/87	87/88
Person-Years	208	199	194	193	193	193
Operating Expenses						
– Salaries	5,012	6,023	6,074	6,363	6,363	6,363
– O&M	842	1,090	1,182	956	956	956
– Other Expenses						
Revenue	1,316	1,168	1,300	1,800	1,800	1,800
Subsidies						
Capital	113	127	105	340	340	340

Program Identification

The Program has not been questioned in principle by the private sector, nor have criticisms of its administration been raised. It is supported by energy utilities and consumer groups. The department considers that government electricity and gas meter verification and inspection is necessary to prevent economic fraud, given the inability consumers to verify the amounts of gas and electrical energy consumed against the invoice. It notes that the Program's 1984-85 per capita cost was $0.29 and is relatively insignificant considering the value of measurement/billing errors which can (and do) occur even at the domestic (consumer) level.

New legislative authority was passed in 1981 to replace legislation enacted early in the century. It will allow utilities and manufacturers to certify that their meters meet federal standards of accuracy. However, the Department considers that current resources are insufficient to ensure accurate measurement and equity at commercial and industrial levels of trade. It is concerned that privatizing meter certification and verification will result in poorer compliance. No provincial concerns have been raised. The enabling legislation flows from an area of exclusive federal jurisdiction.

Observations

While arguing that the Program is needed to prevent "economic fraud" and significant measurement errors, the department also readily acknowledges that accurate measurement is a "sacred" matter among businessmen and that reputations as honest and reliable traders can be seriously harmed or lost by reports of measurement inaccuracies, even in the absence of evidence of fraudulent intent. The incentives for effective self-regulation and self-enforcement therefore appear to be very strong in this area. The new Act, in fact, contemplates private meter verification.

In addition, changing technology has resulted in metering devices which are more reliable at the time of manufacture and remain reliable longer. These factors suggest that the level of government resources required to provide adequate regulatory coverage in this Program could well be decreasing. However, resource levels are proposed to remain the same for the next several years. The absence of a significant level of detected fraudulent metering by the department suggests that the Program's actual role is to provide a form of maintenance management to electricity and gas sellers.

In the Team's view, this Program is a prime candidate for a shifting of compliance activity out of government and into the private sector. A modest incentive in this regard has already been created by accreditation fee increases to utilities. However, some smaller electricity and gas sellers may require government assistance at the start-up stage to absorb accreditation responsibilities and to prevent a differential impact from such reorientation. The Team is not persuaded that meter certification and verification would not be well handled by private firms serving smaller electricity and gas businesses. The latter's strong compliance incentives, coupled with ease of business entry into certification/verification should mitigate against continued survival of certification/ verification businesses that do not perform well.

Options

The Study Team recommends to the Task Force that the government consider the following:

1. Leave Program as is but move to full-cost recovery in three years.

2. Move on phased basis to privatization combined with increased sanctions against fraudulent non-compliance.

3. Facilitate reduced government inspection of the accuracy of electricity and gas meters:

   a. Move to full cost recovery to create an incentive for greater self-verification and the adoption of more reliable metering technologies.

   b. Encourage the development of private meter verifying services. Conduct an experiment in contracting-out government inspection activities.

   c. Shift the time limit for meter re-verification from the Act to the regulations to permit greater flexibility to adapt re-verification to improved reliability brought about by changing technologies.

   d. Give greater publicity to significant instances of non-compliance and announce a policy that, in cases involving fraudulent intent, offenders will automatically be prosecuted.

   e. Speed proclamation of new Act and passage of regulations allowing for privatization of certification and verification.

LEGAL METROLOGY - WEIGHTS AND MEASURES - CCA 32

Objective

To ensure accuracy of measurement and equity in the trade of commodities and services sold on the basis of measurement.

Authority

Weights and Measures Act, Fertilizers Act, Feeds Act, Seeds Act, Pest Control Products Act.

Description

The Program forms part of the Bureau of Consumer Affairs of the Department of Consumer and Corporate Affairs. The Program examines and approves weighing and measuring devices used in trade, calibrates and certifies measurement standards, certifies test equipment used by industry and government, verifies, through a field inspection program, the accuracy and appropriate usage of all weighing and measuring devices used in trade, and defines units of measurement to be used in trade.

Weights and Measures' effectiveness is predicated on inspection activity to identify and correct instances of non-compliance. The Weights and Measures Act requires that device designs be approved, and that, once installed, new devices be initially inspected before use and then periodically verified for compliance. While the Act does dictate the frequency of inspection of in-service devices, the sub-activity attempts to verify all devices used in trade once every two years and provides for more frequent inspection of weighing devices located in primary grain elevators which must be inspected every year). The frequency for calibrating government-owned standards is legislated.

Estimates indicate that some 600,000 weighing and measuring devices are used in trade in Canada. In 1983-84, more than 270,000 device inspections were conducted (more than 50,000 devices were found to be operating beyond acceptable limits of error and were corrected) and 370 devices were approved for use in trade. These activities are undertaken to ensure the highest compliance possible of devices with the provisions of the Weights and Measures Act on the premise that the accuracy of devices is essential to

152

equitable transactions between traders and traders and consumers. Furthermore, some quarter million package and bulk commodity inspections were conducted in 1983-84. Here, more than 50,000 (20 per cent) of these were found to be in error beyond acceptable limits and were corrected before sale. Weights and Measures also calibrates standards used by industry and government to verify device accuracy and maintains traceability to NRC standards. More than 64,000 standards calibrations were performed in 1983-84.

The Program is decentralized with district, area and five regional offices (90 per cent of PYs) with headquarters and testing laboratories in Ottawa, Ontario.

Resources

($000's)	82/83	83/84	84/85	85/86	86/87	87/88
Person-Years	300	311	334	335	335	335
Operating Expenses						
- Salaries	6,991	8,735	10,258	10,553	10,553	10,553
- O&M	2,072	2,421	2,644	2,880	2,880	2,880
- Other Expenses						
Revenue	947	918	1,000	1,600	1,600	1,600
Subsidies						
Capital	149	253	1,163	410	410	410

Problem Identification

The Program has not been questioned in principle by the private sector. Some concerns have been raised that it has a differential impact on small business, that its current method of compliance checking may not be fully adequate and that weights and measures regulation can be more efficiently conducted.

The Department considers that the Program as it is currently delivered could not be done less expensively without jeopardizing effectiveness and that at present it does not have sufficient resources to inspect and monitor trade closely at all transactional levels. As a result, the Program is employing a "tiered approach" which directs resources more to retail and commercial trade levels and less to large industry (i.e. to the areas of trade where buyers are least able to protect themselves). The Department contends that "third party protection" is necessary from fraudulent and inaccurate trade measurements and that the benefits of this protection are high given its 1984-85 net cost of $0.64 per capita.

The Department has indicated that the Program's relevance and effectiveness could suffer if non-controversial technical amendments to the Weights and Measures Act regulations are not quickly acted on by PCO (the regulations have been with PCO for about two years).

There is no provincial overlap as weights and measures is an area of exclusive federal jurisdiction. No adverse comments have been received from the provinces.

The Department contends that it has not had satisfactory results from certifying repair agencies to attest to measurement device re-verification, and that privatization of verification activities is therefore problematic.

Observations   (see also CCA 31)

The Department readily acknowledges that accurate measurement is "sacred in trade", that the Program has detected only a few instances of fraudulent measurement and that non-compliance disclosure is a powerful disciplinary tool in this field. This indicates that there are very strong incentives for effective self-regulation and self-compliance in this area. Consequently, the Program's lab testing and spot-checking for measurement accuracy should largely be viewed as a form of measuring device problem identification service for businesses, the costs of which, in the Team's view, should be directly borne by business in accordance with the level of service received.

A 1982 Program study indicated that very few compliance problems existed for retail level scales and that most problems occurred in relation to more complex "installed" devices (e.g. at processing plants and scales used in transportation of goods). Despite the finer identification of problem areas, the nature of the service delivered and the strong likelihood that self-enforcement is a viable option, the Program's level of cost recovery remains low and its overall resource level is proposed to be constant over the next several years.

The Team is not persuaded that opportunities to privatize verification through repair agency certification are limited - in light of the close identification of business integrity with accurate measurement and the power of "adverse publicity" in the area.

Options

The Study Team recommends to the Task Force that the government consider the following:

1. Leave the Program as is.

2. Increase inspection/verification charges to full-cost recovery in 5-10 years to act as an incentive for the entry of certified repair agencies. Establish higher fees for instances in which non-compliance is detected but do not cost recover where spot-check shows compliance.

3. Move to private certification with continued spot-checks.

4. Give greater publicity to significant instances of non-compliance and announce a policy that, in cases of fraudulent intent, offenders will automatically be prosecuted and substantial fines requested.

TAX REBATE DISCOUNTING - CCA 100

Objectives

To protect consumers from excessive discounting of their rights to an income tax rebate by businesses who purchase this right in return for an immediate cash payment.

Authority

Tax Rebate Discounting Act.

Description

The Program is carried out by the Bureau of Consumer Affairs of the Department of Consumer and Corporate Affairs. This program seeks to protect those who "sell" the rights to their anticipated income tax refunds to tax rebate discounters, for a portion of the refunds' value, in exchange for immediate cash. The function is performed through extensive information disclosure by discounters and discounters' associations, examination and inspection of the documentation relating to a sample of discounting transactions, the gathering of general statistics on the discounting market, and responding to clients' complaints and enquiries. The number of transactions covered by the Act has doubled every year since 1979. The legislation requires that one who "sells" an anticipated tax refund receives:

1. At least 85 per cent of the refund's value;
2. A clear statement of the transaction, in writing and signed;
3. Notification of the actual refund; and
4. The full value of the excess of the actual refund over the anticipated refund (if the actual refund is less than that calculated by the discounter, the "seller" of the refund must still make up the difference).

In B.C., Alta., Sask., P.E.I., N.S., and the Yukon, the provincial or territorial governments administer the Act, aided by information provided by the federal government. In Manitoba, administration is a joint federal/provincial responsibility. In the other provinces, the federal government has sole responsibility. Discounters' compliance is monitored primarily through sample document inspection and through complaint response. There are no federal

licensing or certification requirements though these do
exist in some provinces. All federal administration
functions are carried out from headquarters in Hull, Quebec.

An internal audit is planned for July to September
1985. A review of the legislation itself is almost
completed.

<u>Resources</u>

($000's)	82/83	83/84	84/85	85/86	86/87	87/88
Person-Years	3	3	3	3	3	3
Operating Exp.						
- Salaries	60	65	70	74	74	74
- O&M						
- Other Exp.*	76	100	65	60	60	60
Revenue						
Subsidies						
Capital						

* Includes primarily computer service costs, and the costs
  of printing forms.

<u>Problem Identification</u>

Anti-poverty groups, while supporting the legislation
in principle, have recommended that the maximum discount
rate of 15 per cent should be significantly reduced having
regard to the decreased processing time for tax rebates by
Revenue Canada and the resulting reduction in discounters'
interest costs.

Tax Rebate discounters support the current scheme and
the 15 per cent limit on the ground that the "discount" is
now increasingly used to cover the processing costs of
providing a complete tax preparation service to the consumer
which includes guaranteeing the income tax filing for the
client and dealing with Revenue Canada for the client.

The Department observes that the market for tax rebates
is largely artificial since it arises because government
collects too much income tax from many low income consumers
(especially those having periodic or part-time income and
those eligible for the Child Tax Credit) and that the
legislation is tailored to protect consumers with pressing
cash flow needs from unscrupulous businesses. The
Department considers that, if the federal legislation were
not in place, many provinces would outlaw tax rebate

discounting entirely with a resulting loss of choice for consumers.

Observations

The Program does not have a materially positive or negative impact on economic development, job creation or entrepreneurial initiative. However, if tax rebate discounting were prohibited, it is likely that the market for tax preparation services would decline and jobs would be lost.

On balance the tax rebate discounting industry does not appear to be opposed to the paper burden, additional costs or discount constraint imposed by the Act.

With the evolution of tax rebate discounting from being strictly a consumer loan business towards being more of a by-product of legitimate tax preparation services for individuals, self-regulation by the industry is becoming a viable option to continued government regulation of tax rebate discounting contracts.

Options

The Study Team recommends to the Task Force that the government consider the following:

1. Amend the Act to establish the discount maximum under regulations to allow the effective rate of interest reflected in the discount to be readily adjusted to market interest rates as rebate processing times and consumer loan rates vary.

2. Amend the Act to make it subject to a sunset clause (termination in 5 or 10 years) to provide time to develop a program of industry self-regulation with the aid of consumers and the provinces.

3. To reduce need for Program, increase Revenue Canada's speed in processing and sending tax refunds coupled with publicity that this is occurring.

4. To reduce need for Program, opportunities should be sought for curtailing collection of excessive income tax revenues in advance.

5. Take no action.

BUREAU OF COMPETITION POLICY: RESTRAINTS TO COMPETITION - CCA 101

Objective

To administer the Combines Investigation Act. "An Act to provide for the investigation of combines, monopolies, trusts and mergers".

To establish and enforce rules governing, and to promote policies improving the efficient and equitable functioning of a competitive and dynamic market economy.

Authority

The Combines Investigation Act

Description

There are two principal areas of focus: the administration of the provisions of the Combines Investigation Act; and the promotion of competition policy considerations in the development and implementation of economic policy. In addition, the Bureau promotes public understanding of the content and scope of the Act and of the economic and social significance of an effective competition policy, and represents Canada's interest in international competition policy issues.

The chief executive officer is the Director of Investigation and Research, who reports to Parliament through the Minister. The incumbent is also the Assistant Deputy Minister, Competition Policy, responsible to the Deputy Minister for the resources of this Bureau.

There are three areas of emphasis:

1. Restraints to Competition: involves the administration of the criminal provisions of the Act relating to conspiracy, merger, monopoly, price maintenance and other pricing practices; and the non-criminal provisions relating to matters reviewable by the Restrictive Trade Practices Commission, such as consignment selling, market restriction and tied selling.

2. Economic Analysis and Policy Evaluation: involves development of enforcement policy and economic analysis

of competition policy issues in support of the Bureau's policy and enforcement activities; participation in the development of federal economic policy; advice to the Minister on competition policy issues and support to the development of competition-related legislation; representation of Canadian interests relating to competition and trade issues in international forums.

3. Administration: includes general management, planning and reporting, coordination and central support services and supports amendments to the Combines Investigation Act.

(Additionally, there are two other areas of emphasis: Marketing Practices, and Regulated Sector.)

Mandatory demands for service include Requests for Information, Compliance Requests (provides to business sector opinions as to whether a proposed plan of action might contravene the provisions of the Act), FIRA Reviews, Education Requests, and Handling of Complaints from business sector on allegations that the provisions of the Act may have been contravened.

Resources

($000's)	82/83	83/84	84/85	85/86	86/87	87/88
Person-Years	241	241	262	264	265	265
Operating Expenses						
- Salaries	7,523	8,661	10,391	10,649	10,690	10,690
- O&M	4,263	4,005	3,508	3,455	3,403	3,403
Revenue	531	2,380	1,000	1,000	1,000	1,000
Subsidies	--	--	--	--	--	--
Capital	53	86	57	57	60	60

Problem Identification

1. Attempts at Reform: The department considers that elements of the Act (monopolies, mergers, conspiracy) are ineffective and need to be modernized. There is a lengthy history of recent attempts to reform the Combines Act: Economic Council of Canada report in 1969, passage of so-called Stage I amendments in 1976, and introduction of several bills into Parliament since 1976. An elaborate system of consultations has been carried out over this period with active business and consumer associations. The

current Minister of Consumer and Corporate Affairs commenced another round of consultations on March 20, 1985, with the comment that "reform is long overdue". Nevertheless, there are important segments of the Canadian business community who are less than enthusiastic about reform. Small business groups are generally supportive, but with varying degrees of enthusiasm. Consumer groups are supportive, but with an emphasis different from the small business representatives.

2. <u>Public Education</u>: The Bureau has a program of Information and Compliance which involves speeches by the Director, as well as non-binding opinions on Compliance requests. However, public awareness of and faith in the Act is low. The department considers not enough attention has been given to providing compliance guidelines to industry.

3. <u>Enforcement</u>: The principal function of the Bureau is the enforcement of the Act. Most enforcement actions stem from complaints. There are various steps, with safeguards (Preliminary Study, Formal Inquiry) which can lead to discontinuance, or reference to the Restrictive Trade Practices Commission or the Attorney General. Many inquiries and cases hearings take an inordinately long time (5 to 10 years).

4. <u>Charter Amendments</u>. The decision of the Supreme Court of Canada in <u>Southam</u> indicates a need to modify the Act to ensure compliance with the Charter especially in respect to search and seizure powers.

<u>Observations</u>

1. <u>Attempts at Reform</u>: Any regulatory reform which reduces direct economic intervention by government creates a pressing need to reform and modernize Canada's Combines Act. A credible Combines Act is a necessary prerequisite to substantive regulatory reform.

2. <u>Public Education</u>: Although the Bureau responds to requests for information and compliance, this tends to be from a small group who know "the system". The Bureau has not done enough to broaden public education (high schools, colleges, universities), nor to encourage compliance by taking a proactive stance to

interpretation of Act and jurisprudence. There is a tendency to be too prosecution and complaint oriented. This can distance Program staff from the private sector and marketplace realities.

3.   Delays in Enforcement: Excessive delays in prosecuting major cases reduces deterrent effect of Act and overall credibility of the Program.

Options

The Study Team recommends to the Task Force that the government consider the following:

1.   Give the highest priority to speedy changes to meet Charter requirements and to ensure rapid passage of significant reforms to Canada's Combines Act which make it clearer, easier to enforce, and relevant to the current economic environment.

2.   Develop a comprehensive and proactive public education program on the benefits of the maintenance of competition on economic development, job creation, viability of small and medium sized enterprises and entrepreneurial initiative.

3.   Develop a proactive compliance program modelled along the lines of the Marketing Practices Branch.

4.   Significantly speed up the handling and disposition of the enforcement case load. Strengthening the Act, in itself, won't be effective unless the whole process of inquiry is greatly speeded up.

5.   Increase use of "out-of-court" settlements and inquiry suspension agreements in which would be included voluntary compliance provisions, and develop means to ensure that parties comply to such settlements.

METRIC PROGRAM — CCA 102

Objective

To initiate, coordinate and undertake investigations and prepare plans for metric conversion.

Authority

Order-In-Council PC 1971-1146 which established the Metric Commission.

Description

The Metric Commission was created to initiate, coordinate and undertake investigations and prepare plans for metric conversion. It was to act as a catalyst and facilitator of conversion. The Commission consisted of a committee of not more than 20 commissioners and a chairman who are Governor-in-Council appointees. The Commission will phase out its operations and close out its administration as a separate entity by March 31, 1985. At that time, a small metric office is expected to be established within the Policy Coordination Bureau of the Department, to look after the interests of over 20 sectors whose conversion will not be completed and to provide metric conversion information to business, industry and consumers.

The Metric Commission possessed no independent regulatory authority. However, in response to recommendations of the Commission, many departments and agencies have amended existing social and economic regulations and legislation to accommodate metric conversion. These included Public Works, Transport, Statistics Canada, Health and Welfare, National Defense, DRIE, Agriculture and Canadian Transport Commission.

The provinces and territories have agreed to use their facilities for disseminating information provided by Metric Commission Canada and consequently cost-sharing agreements were signed with six provinces and two territories. In four provinces, public, industrial and government relations offices for the dissemination of metric information is provided through service contracts. Within individual industry sectors specialized metric information applicable to that specific industry has from time to time been prepared by the sector members and distributed through their association and/or corporate offices.

The Program is centralized in the National Capital Region.

Resources

($000's)	82/83	83/84	84/85	85/86	86/87	87/88
Person-Years	98	88	51	18	9	9
Operating Exp.						
- Salaries	2,834	2,682	1,744	878	489	318
- O&M	5,398	5,119	4,728	2,163	684	584
- Other Exp.						
Revenue						
Subsidies	11,087	4,196	6,500			
Capital	15	13	0			

Problem Identification

Over the years, many business groups have questioned the pace and mandatory nature of the Metric Conversion Program overseen by the Metric Commission. Similar concerns were raised by some private sector interests in the course of this Program Review.

Consumer representatives and representatives of large businesses and businesses heavily involved in international trade have, however, supported metrification.

In 1982-83 Consumer and Corporate Affairs, using independent consultants, evaluated the overall status of metric conversion. This evaluation established that by 1984-85 the momentum of conversion in most economic sectors would be self-sustaining, and that the Commission should be phased out and replaced by a small metric office.

The Department has identified possible differential cost impacts on small retailers and is now studying solutions to this problem.

Observations

Some business groups continue to oppose the mandatory substitution of metric measurements for the Imperial system in principle.

However, adoption of the metric system is now widely viewed by the private sector as facilitating economic development by improving access of Canadian goods and services to international markets and lowering technical communication costs. Consumer groups consider that, on balance, the metric system is simpler to understand, thus improving consumer product information.

The government's recent policy announcement on metrification has been well accepted in the private sector as providing greater choice and flexibility for businesses in adopting metric and co-posting Imperial equivalents.

Options

The Study Team recommends to the Task Force that the government consider the following:

1. To maintain momentum towards metric, provide promotional and research resources within CCA as proposed by the Department.

2. Eliminate all metric promotion resources; rely on existing private sector momentum to further expand metric conversion.

BUREAU OF COMPETITION POLICY: REGULATED
SECTOR BRANCH — CCA 103

Objective

By intervening as a party in regulatory proceedings to alter the nature and scope of regulation so as to place a greater reliance on competition and market forces.

Authority

Combines Investigation Act, s.27.1.

Description

The Bureau of Competition Policy forms part of the Department of Consumer and Corporate Affairs. This Program conducts the bulk of the regulatory intervention activity of the Director of Investigation and Research. Section 27.1 of the Combines Act authorizes the Director to make representations before any federal board, commission or other tribunal which affects the production, supply or other economic aspects in respect of the maintenance of competition. The Director has also intervened before provincial regulatory bodies at their request, or with their concurrence.

Since its creation in 1980, the Branch has been active mainly in the fields of telecommunications, broadcasting, transportation, and financial institution regulation.

As an intervener, the Director possesses the same rights as any other party to the proceedings in question. For example, in quasi-judicial hearings the Director, through legal counsel, will generally cross-examine witnesses, present expert opinion evidence, and file final arguments.

Other branches of the Bureau of Competition Policy have also conducted interventions in other regulatory fields including insurance, the professions, energy resource transmission, and agricultural product supply management.

Resources

($000's)	82/83	83/84	84/85	85/86	86/87	87/88
Person-Years	16	17	21	27	27	27
Operating Exp.						
- Salaries	535	696	894	1,199	1,199	1,199
- O&M	127	397	379	499	499	499
- Other Exp.						
Revenue						
Subsidies						
Capital			2			

Problem Identification

The Department considers that the Program's interventions have encouraged regulatory decisions which have allowed easier competitive entry into regulated industries and have inhibited regulated companies, from foreclosing competition or unjustifiably expanding the range of markets subject to economic regulation.

Some private sector representatives have argued that other parties are capable of adequately presenting pro-competition viewpoints in a manner which displays greater pragmatism and industry knowledge. They argue that the Director's interventions are largely duplicative and, therefore, unduly increase the costs of regulation. They have also suggested that the Director's intervention authority should be repealed or be made subject to Ministerial consent.

Other private sector representatives have strongly supported the Program's interventions on the grounds that: (1) private parties seeking regulatory reforms which increase competition need the support of a competition advocate having the resources to engage experts, and (2) the Director often brings a perspective to regulatory issues which improves the regulator's appreciation of the extent to which market forces can be relied upon.

Observations

Other bodies intervene before regulatory boards in their own interests and on occasion these coincide with the positions taken by the Director. However, only the Director intervenes strictly in the interest of reducing regulatory interference in the operation of markets in favour of maintenance of competition and its attendant economic development and job creation benefits.

To date, the Director may have concentrated his intervention resources too much in telecommunications and transportation.

Requiring the Director to obtain Ministerial consent before intervening would make the Director, in effect, the voice of government policy, thus: (1) placing in doubt the freedom of the Director to act independently under the Combines Investigation Act, and (2) imperilling the independence of the regulatory board.

On balance, agents capable of moving the regulatory system more towards market-based measures and away from direct detailed intervention, deserve to be strengthened, not weakened, at this time.

Options

The Study Team recommends to the Task Force that the government consider the following:

1. Maintain the program as is while the Director establishes broader priorities in deciding whether to intervene or not in particular regulatory settings.

2. Require all federal regulatory agencies to render decisions which are least restrictive of competition and, in deciding, to give weight to the expected benefits of competition (in lieu of the Director intervening).

FUNDING OF REGULATED INDUSTRIES PROGRAM OF THE CONSUMERS' ASSOCIATION OF CANADA - CCA 901

Objective

To provide funds for interventions on behalf of consumers before federal regulatory agencies.

Authority

Department of Consumer and Corporate Affairs Act

Description

The Regulated Industries Program (RIP) is a separately funded committee of the National Executive of the Consumers' Association of Canada (CAC). CAC, with a membership of 160,000, is the largest national general interest volunteer consumer interest representative. RIP represents CAC before federal regulatory boards and other bodies examining regulatory issues.

Government funding has been provided for RIP since its inception in 1974 on the ground that effective advocacy of the consumer interest before regulatory bodies is costly and that individual consumers are not likely to contribute to such interventions when they know that they will not be excluded from the benefits obtained for consumers as the result of the intervention.

Since its inception, RIP's regulatory interventions have largely been confined to the areas of telecommunications and transportation (in particular, airlines).

RIP's major policy initiatives are considered by CAC's Board of Directors although there is no formal requirement for Board approval.

Resources

RIP has received the following awards for the past
three years:

1982/83 $283,000
1983/84 $300,000
1984/85 $300,000

In 1984-85 RIP's funding consisted of a $100,000 grant
and $200,000 in contributions for specific projects.

RIP's interventions before the CRTC have, in some
cases, been partially funded by costs awards assessed
against the regulated telecommunication carrier.

Problem Identification

By providing professional consumer representations
before federal regulatory boards to balance the presence of
the regulated industry, CAC and Consumer and Corporate
Affairs, as well as many active private sector interveners,
consider that RIP's interventions can improve the economic
efficiency and innovativeness of industries subject to
economic regulation.

On the other hand, some regulated industries have
complained that a proliferation of "public interest
interveners", often representing similar viewpoints, has
increased the costs of regulation to themselves and to the
regulatory agency.

Observations

RIP has been credited by CCA and many private sector
and academic observers with having provided effective
advocacy of the consumer interest over its 10 year life and
having acted as a stimulant of regulatory reform in general.

RIP calculates that the taxpayer/consumer earns a very
high return on the funds "invested" in RIP since the program
has contributed to regulatory decisions which have allowed
regulated companies to collect hundreds of millions of
dollars less in revenues than the regulated companies had
contended they needed. The exact extent to which RIP caused
these cost-savings for consumers cannot, however, be
determined due to the nature of the regulatory process

170

(multi-party, and boards can make their own assessment of the merits of a regulated company's application).

Although many U.S. consumer advocacy groups have successfully funded their operations through private donations, RIP has been unable to do so. With a decline in cost award revenues in recent years, RIP has, in effect, become more dependent upon government funding in the last three years.

RIP has not significantly diversified its intervention activities in the last several years. It is, consequently, running a risk of becoming a "captive" of the regulatory environment and machinery in which it has operated. The areas in which it has been most active, primarily telecommunication and transportation regulation, are also likely candidates for significant regulatory reform and deregulation. RIP may, in the absence of a more diversified role, resist the loss of its traditional intervention forums and thus resist both substantive and procedural regulatory reforms in these sectors.

RIP is currently attempting to diversify its advocacy activities beyond telecommunications and transportation. However, it is doubtful that, under its current terms of reference to CAC, RIP's more professional approach to consumer advocacy within CAC can be extended to areas of social (health, safety, information) regulation or international trade regulation. On the other hand, comments received by the Team strongly suggest that CAC has been a less than effective advocate of consumer interest and regulatory reform in the fields of social and trade regulation.

In addition to the RIP funding, CCA provided $450,000 to CAC in grants and contributions in 1984-85. Of this, $200,000 was used to subsidize CAC's magazine ("Canadian Consumer") and testing operations and $250,000 was used by CAC's policy and activities department, largely to support CAC's political infrastructure.

Options

The Study Team recommends to the Task Force that the government consider the following:

1.   Terminate CCA funding of RIP.

2.   Retain the program at the current level of funding.

3.   Retain the program and increase its government funding.

OVERVIEW

CANADIAN HUMAN RIGHTS COMMISSION

The Canadian Human Rights Act which prohibits private acts of discrimination on ten grounds is administered by the Canadian Human Rights Commission (CHRC) and applies to departments, agencies and undertakings under federal jurisdiction. It is distinct from Charter of Rights equality provisions which apply to law (state acts). Thus, for example, federal and provincial (except Quebec) laws cannot contravene the rights set out in the Charter. On the other hand, under the Canadian Human Rights Act, departments, agencies and federally-regulated public and private enterprises (e.g. Bell Canada, banks) cannot discriminate either against employees or members of the public whom they serve on any of the ten prohibited grounds for discrimination (e.g. sex, race, religion, handicapped).

The CHRC has a broad mix of powers and roles, but basically it is advocate, referee and enforcer. It issues guidelines for compliance with the Act, investigates and resolves complaints, and through the Tribunal, adjudicates cases based on standards it sets in its interpretation of the legislation. Because of this breadth of scope, its activities are viewed with apprehension by the regulated who contend that there is insufficient regard for the costs or the difficulties involved in compliance.

In Quebec, the problem of combining the multiple roles of advocate, referee and enforcer has been addressed through a unique system. The province's human rights commission can investigate complaints, but cannot enforce. However, in order to avoid the inequity of costly litigation for the individual complainant, the provincial commission can represent the complainant in the courts where the merits of a case have been established. Thus, the commission is an advocate but the court adjudicates.

The current Omnibus legislative package before Parliament (Bill C-29) proposes an independent Human Rights Tribunal (currently appointed by the Commission). Although this is a positive step in terms of disentangling conflicting roles, it may be desirable to consider further reduction of CHRC powers in resolving cases which in its view need not be referred to the Tribunal. Its role could be limited to that of investigating complaints leaving decision-making entirely to the Tribunal.

In the Team's view, its advocacy function which is particularly onerous to the regulated, could also be restricted through various mechanisms (e.g. regulated departments and enterprises could be required to inform employees and the user public of their rights; improved public communication by CHRC of cases and decisions could reinforce the information flow and encourage compliance). Its regulatory powers, including the issuance of guidelines to employers would consequently be curtailed. The resulting, more focussed role would probably also require fewer resources although these may have to be partially reallocated to the Tribunal.

CANADIAN HUMAN RIGHTS COMMISSION - CHRC 1

Objective

To foster the constitutional precept that every individual should have equal opportunity to participate in all spheres of Canadian life consistent with his or her duties and obligations as members of society.

Authority

Canadian Human Rights Act (1976); amended in 1980, 81, 82, 83.

Description

The Canadian Human Rights Commission (CHRC) administers the legislation which applies to federal jurisdiction (federal departments and agencies, the Yukon and Northwest Territories, interprovincial and international transportation, telecommunications undertakings, banks, companies dealing with radioactive materials, interboundary pipelines) and which prohibits discrimination on 10 grounds. It maintains close liaison with similar provincial agencies which administer provincial human rights legislation through a national association of human rights agencies.

The CHRC has a diverse, broad mix of powers and roles: it adjudicates, makes regulations, provides policy advice to the government (e.g. regarding amendments to the Act), investigates, monitors and promotes the human rights issues under its purview through public education initiatives. There are various options involved in the CHRC's operations once a complaint has been determined to fall within its jurisdiction. An investigation is initially conducted. The findings are submitted to Commissioners who can make the following decisions: not take further action on the complaint, dismiss the complaint, appoint a conciliator to bring about a settlement, and approve settlements where agreement has been reached by the parties or appoint a tribunal. Part of the current Omnibus legislative package before Parliament proposes an independent tribunal.

The CHRC is composed of the Chief Commissioner, a Deputy Chief Commissioner who are full-time members and three to six other members who may be full- or part-time. There are seven regional offices (Halifax, Montreal,

National Capital Region which includes headquarters, Toronto, Winnipeg, Edmonton and Vancouver). The main organizational components are: complaints and compliance, public programs, and research and policy. In 1983-84, the CHRC received over 30,000 enquiries, investigated 359 complaints of which more than half were dismissed. The majority of cases in that year dealt with discrimination based on sex, disability and race. The complaints and compliance sector uses about one-third of total person-years and almost one-quarter of budgeted resources.

Resources

($000's)	82/83	83/84	84/85	85/86	86/87	87/88
Person-Years	127	130	156	159	159	159
Operating Exp.						
- Salaries	4,411*	4,823	6,484	6,687	6,687	6,687
- O&M	1,576	2,153	2,691	2,643	2,643	2,643
- Other Exp.						
Revenue						
Subsidies						
Capital	105	390	32	14	14	14

* Includes employee benefit plans

Problem Identification

Although there is agreement by the groups contacted on the substantive merit of human rights legislation and on a need for an agency like the CHRC to avoid costly litigation, the following concerns were noted:

1. The economic costs of implementing certain CHRC guidelines issued to promote compliance are regarded as excessive for employers and therefore constitute obstacles to economic growth and job creation.

2. Employers noted that their rights over the management of their human resources are too severely restricted, and that CHRC seems to be biased in favour of complainants.

3. Delay and uncertainty are substantive issues. For instance, when there is a change of CHRC personnel in the course of an investigation, the entire process is resumed from the starting point. Certain instances were cited in terms of "the CHRC never completely closes a file".

4. There is some perceived overlap and even conflicting objectives with respect to other operations in the federal government. For example, Canadian Transport Commission and Labour Canada's occupational safety and health provisions can be and have been in conflict with human rights legislation.

    The CHRC notes that its workload has increased as a result of a Supreme Court decision (the Leitiff Case) which imposed additional procedures on complaints received. When asked about the high number of enquiries which it receives from the public (30,000 per year), the CHRC agreed that its mandate must be very unclear to the public.

Observations

1. In the Team's view, when an agency is both "police and judge", there are resulting, justifiable apprehensions by the regulated. Bill C-29 would ameliorate this situation by removing from the Commission the power to appoint members of Human Rights Tribunals when attempts at a settlement have failed.

2. The CHRC is not sufficiently responsive to regulated employers' concerns regarding costs and management prerogative. The Team found that it has a potentially major impact on economic development and job creation interests, but there seems to be little evidence that these are taken into full account by the CHRC.

3. The high number of enquiries (30,000 last year) suggests either limited knowledge of CHRC mandate, or perhaps that the name Canadian Human Rights is misleading. The general application of the Act is valid only to the user-public which avails itself of federally-regulated services; otherwise, it is directed to the federally-regulated employer-employee situations with respect to prohibited grounds of discrimination.

4. The equality provisions of the Charter of Rights apply to law (state actions) and not to private acts of discrimination. Repeal of the Human Rights Act would have the effect of permitting acts of discrimination by federally-regulated private sector undertakings (e.g. Bell, Canadian Pacific, banks etc...) which are not covered by provincial human rights legislation.

Options

The Study Team recommends to the Task Force that the government consider the following:

1. <u>Status quo</u> (as it will exist after the enactment of <u>Bill C-29</u>).

2. Procedural and substantive changes could be made:
   i) Abolish the CHRC and provide that henceforth discrimination complaints shall be dealt with by the courts, with provision for legal aid.
   ii) Maintain the CHRC but allow a complainant the option of instituting proceedings before the courts, with provision for legal aid.
   iii) Maintain the CHRC in the role of ombudsman. This would require further review, including an analysis of other jurisdictions' experience when they have opted for this route.
   iv) Maintain the CHRC, but ensure that complainants and defendants are treated equally. Since complainants are represented by the Commission when a case is before a Human Rights Tribunal, defendants should enjoy a similar benefit if the appearance of equality is to be maintained.
   v) Steps should be taken to reduce delays, possibly including regulatory time-limits.
   vi) The CHRC could address costs of compliance when developing regulations.

OVERVIEW

FEDERAL COMMUNICATIONS REGULATION

A. SYNOPSIS

Technological change has made regulatory policies and methods in broadcasting and telecommunications obsolete. Continuing regulation as is will continue to inhibit innovation and economic development in each industry and, especially for telecommunications, the economy as a whole. Industry and regulatory developments in U.S. broadcasting and telecommunications will continue to be the most innovative and dynamic in the world and provide the model for the Canadian private sector.

In broadcasting, programming regulation is excessively detailed and burdensome. Volume-based Canadian content quotas have diluted Canadian program quality and marketability. Given the mature state of the Canadian industry and the range of services available throughout the country, a fundamental restructuring of regulatory policy which relies more on management incentives and market forces is needed in the view of the Team.

In telecommunications, competition has been rapidly developing in some areas of the industry (both in the U.S. and parts of Canada) for the last several years. This industry is becoming an increasingly vital part of Canada's "post-industrial" infrastructure. Moving away from regulatory practices developed in the old monopoly environment, coupled with major planned reductions of regulation in competitive areas, is critical if telecommunication industry innovation and productivity is to keep up with our southern neighbour. Compared to the U.S., Canada's regulated long distance rates are too high; this decreases the competitiveness of our service sector and increases the cost of doing business in Canada. Universal household telephone service can be maintained, even with increased competition, through innovative local service rate structures such as local measured service. The present regulated rate structure depresses local service rates for all subscribers, whether they need this help or not.

B. FEDERAL REGULATORY PROGRAMS

The Study Team reviewed
three programs: DOC 23/102-108, Radio Frequency
                                    Spectrum
                 CRTC 901, Broadcasting
                 CRTC 902, Telecommunications

(1) Department of Communications:

(a) Radio Frequency Spectrum: DOC administers the
     Radio Act. Radio Spectrum management is an
     exclusive federal activity. A licence from the
     Minister is necessary to operate any radio
     transmitting device including broadcast towers,
     microwave systems, satellite systems and cellular
     radio systems. DOC's licensing acts as much as an
     entry control for new broadcasting and
     telecommunication businesses as do the CRTC's
     policies. Under the Telegraphs Act, DOC regulates
     access to Canada by marine transmission cable.

     On the broadcasting side, DOC's licensing
     decisions are a prerequisite to the CRTC issuing a
     broadcasting licence. In telecommunications,
     DOC's policies act as the first economic hurdle
     for new firms. For example, competing cellular
     radio service applicants had to prove their
     economic worth to DOC into order to get the
     necessary facilities licenses before going to the
     CRTC for authorization to interconnect with the
     local networks of the federally-regulated
     telephone companies. DOC's microwave licensing
     policy has to date foreclosed the emergence of
     private microwave telecommunication systems and
     has restricted microwave spectrum to one full
     service network (Telcom Canada) and one specialty
     carrier (CNCP Telecommunications). This is not an
     economic development problem now but probably will
     be within five years. Examination of alternative
     licensing practices should therefore begin now.

(b) Government ownership: While not included as
     regulatory programs, government ownership of the
     CBC and Teleglobe has in effect become a
     substitute for agency regulation.

(i) CBC: Although the CRTC must review the CBC's network license from time to time, the CBC is primarily accountable to the Department for its programming, advertising and station location policy and its relationship with its affiliates through the Estimates process which determines the size of the government subsidy to the network.

(ii) Teleglobe Canada: Canada's overseas telecommunication monopoly is not regulated by the CRTC because it is a Crown Agent. Although it reports to the CDIC, DOC retains the policy lead over Teleglobe by virtue of expertise and its facilities licensing powers. DOC ensures Teleglobe has the monopoly on overseas signal carriage. If privatized, Teleglobe would probably be subject to CRTC regulations. This in turn will require decisions on the degree of regulation and competitive access to its facilities.

(2) <u>CRTC</u>

(a) Broadcasting: Whereas DOC licenses certain critical facilities, the CRTC licenses all broadcasting services pursuant to the Broadcasting Act (radio and TV stations and networks, Pay TV services, and cable companies). The Act sets out a number of policy objectives for the Commission and is essentially an instrument of social and cultural policy aimed at ensuring that the broadcasting system is predominantly Canadian in control and content. The CRTC exercises its mandate through licensing (i.e. entry control). Entry restriction is viewed as necessary to allow licensees to cross-subsidize the presentation of less remunerative Canadian programming and cultural, community and current affairs programming. However, once a firm receives a licence, a licence renewal is virtually assured in perpetuity as long as the firm remains solvent and no record of serious breaches of licence conditions is established.

Through the power to attach conditions to licences, and licence renewal and suspension, the CRTC has established rules concerning:

i)   product design (Canadian content, market
      segment orientation of radio stations,
      program mix of TV networks and promotion of
      local services);
ii)   horizontal mergers and industry
      concentration;
iii) cable service (rates, territorial markets,
      stations carried, U.S. advertisement
      substitution, and community channel
      provision);
iv)   cross-media (e.g. newspaper-radio) ownership;
v)   licensee exit (by sale of license, a
      corollary of entry control);
vi)   advertisement content (especially foods and
      beverages)
vii) programming ethics (racial, sexual, and
      religious matters).

By far the most detailed regulation concerns
programming design, mix, and content. This is
achieved through reporting requirements, and
monitoring audits, and "promises of performance"
which may influence licence renewal decisions.

(b) Telecommunications: Jurisdiction is shared with
     the provinces. The CRTC regulates Canada's two
     biggest telephone companies (Bell Canada, BC Tel –
     70 per cent of the market), CNCP
     Telecommunications (a specialty carrier which
     competes with the telephone companies in business
     services) and Telesat Canada (the domestic
     satellite carrier). Its principal powers are over
     rate price levels and rate structure, and the
     terms and conditions of service offerings access
     to carriers' facilities (by competitors such as
     CNCP, cable companies, and other telephone
     companies). Through the terms and conditions and
     access powers the CRTC has authorized
     customer-owned connection of "terminal equipment"
     (both single-line sets and multi-line private
     business exchanges), and interconnection with the
     local network by paying, mobile phone, and
     specialized business services (such as CNCP's
     private line and data services). Through these
     decisions, the CRTC has taken the lead among
     Canadian telecommunication regulators in allowing
     competition in specific areas of an industry once
     viewed to be a natural monopoly. Some provincial

182

telecommunication regulators have followed the CRTC's initiatives but others (Saskatchewan and Manitoba in particular) strongly feel there should be only one carrier providing "network services".

Telephone company rates approved by the CRTC are designed to allow the companies to cover all expenses and earn a reasonable after-tax profit. Approved rate levels and structures have reflected primarily considerations of intersubscriber equity and comparative value among services and not the relative costs of providing services. Little data are available or service costs; the data and estimates of costs which are available is subject to considerable debate among industry experts. Through its price control power, the CRTC has also established monitoring schemes for telephone company quality of service (including public access to basic service) and construction program activities.

C.   REGULATORY REFORM:

Issues are tightly interrelated in both broadcasting and telecommunications regulation. They have been studied for years by both the federal and provincial levels. No clear governmental plan of action has yet emerged. This probably reflects the fact that industry realities are changing faster than policy-makers can keep up.

It is clear to the Study Team that regulation of both industries should be reduced and reoriented towards greater reliance on management incentives and market forces and away from the extensive direct controls which currently exist. This is necessary to allow the industry the flexibility it needs to adapt, innovate, increase productivity and grow. This would require acceptance of: (1) less government cultural planning and local station protection in broadcasting, and (2) rate structure and industry structure changes in telecommunications which would be opposed by groups who regard telephone service more as a social tool than an economic tool.

The Study Team suggests that consideration be given to the following action:

(1)   Broadcasting:

    (a)   Eliminate volume of time-based Canadian content quotas – they encourage dilution of Canadian program quality and reduce program marketability.

    (b)   Instead of issuing broadcast licences through public hearings and automatic licence renewals, move to a system of marketable licences which is supported by market-based spectrum allocation policy.

    (c)   Drastically reduce detailed programming requirements and monitoring practices.

    (d)   Allow the development of private radio networks (presently prohibited).

    (e)   Leave merger control to the Combines Act.

    (f)   Make the CBC primarily responsible for ensuring "Canadianness" of system.

(2)   Telecommunications:

    (a)   Continue phased introduction of competition in industry submarkets initiated by the CRTC.

    (b)   Develop a strategy for ensuring telephone service benefits which provides subsidized or cross-subsidized rates only for subscribers requiring them.

    (c)   Adopt the policy that all telecommunication rates should be cost-based and take immediate steps to reduce long-distance rates of federally regulated carriers (domestic and international) down to cost-related levels.

    (d)   Develop alternative spectrum management policies aimed at facilitating greater network competition.

Options are presented in the Program Profiles which would allow detailed implementation plans to be developed over a short time-frame.

RADIO FREQUENCY SPECTRUM – DOC 23/102-108

Objective

To manage the utilization and development of the radio frequency spectrum in Canada and to protect Canada's rights regarding the use of the spectrum through international agreements and regulations.

Authority

The Radio Act, Department of Communications Act, The Telegraph Act, The National Transportation Act, the Railway Act.

Description

In all countries of the world, a National Government Agency regulates the spectrum. Internationally, radio frequency spectrum is managed by the International Telecommunications Union (ITU) to which Canada is a signatory member and to which decisions and regulations carry treaty status.

Licences of frequency are organized within various categories of services. Spectrum services include: AM and FM radio; citizen's band; short-wave and cellular radio; UHF and VHF television; micro-wave and satellite telecommunications; etc. Licences are issued by the Department of Communications on a demand basis subject primarily to technical conditions of performance. Radio frequency spectrum is managed as a common natural resource. Regulations are of an engineering nature and are operational, designed to facilitate equitable sharing of spectrum among the greatest number of users in an environment free from harmful frequency interference.

Licence applications are centralized but spectrum control is undertaken through local department representatives. The program is labour intensive with only partial cost-recovery.

Resources

($000's)	82/83	83/84	84/85	85/86	86/87	87/88
Person-Years	983	981	972	975	974	974
Operating Exp.						
– Salaries	29	32	34	37	37	37
– O&M	6	7	7	8	8	8
– Other Exp.	–	–	–	–	–	–
Revenue	0.6	0.6	0.6	0.6	0.6	0.6
Subsidies						
Capital	2	2	2	2	2	2

Problem Identification

There is consensus that this is not a problem program. The private sector did however, express some irritants with the delivery mechanism.

1. greater detailed engineering documentation is sometimes requested than might otherwise be required;

2. often, a lengthy response time by DOC to various requests; and

3. at times, lack of synchronization between CRTC's decisions re broadcast or telecommunications performance, and DOC's certification of technical equipment or approval of technical standards.

Observations

1. In spectrum management, the party regulated is also the consumer/user which suggests an element of monopoly protection afforded the licensee.

2. Academic economists and some prospective licensees have expressed criticism of DOC spectrum management as a natural resource and the process of "command-and-control" regulations. Recent literature focuses upon spectrum as a government-issued permits market, with initial allocation by auction and freely transferable use rights by the licensee. This would allow the potential user the option of obtaining a new license or buying or renting an existing one. More efficient allocation of spectrum and greater utilization could be accomplished with less detailed regulation. Use of frequency, quality of technical

service and introduction of new technology would reflect market trends. Government would function as the broker and gatekeeper, and manage international spectrum relations.

3. Any change to telecommunications policy that would involve satellite or microwave transmission will also encompass spectrum management. This program should probably be considered when examining telecommunications issues.

4. Full cost recovery is planned by the Department of Communications in fiscal years 1987-88 and 1988-89. A recent "A Base" Review pointed to the cost-effectiveness of the program and the general lack of problem identification by the industry.

Options

While spectrum management is not considered a problem program, the Study Team recommends to the Task Force that the government consider the following:

1. Simplify documentation and filing procedures;

2. Review the co-ordination procedures on joint applications to CRTC and DOC; and

3. Assess the emerging literature on alternative regulatory approaches which is gaining importance at the U.S. Federal Communications Commission.

BROADCASTING – CRTC 901

Objective

To encourage implementation of the national broadcasting policy set out in the Broadcasting Act through the regulation and supervision of the Canadian broadcasting system. Specific objectives include: Canadian ownership and control; varied and comprehensive programming using predominantly Canadian talents; provision of English and French services to all Canadians; contribution of the CBC to national unity and expression of Canadian identity; and responsiveness of regulation and supervision to scientific and technical advances.

Authority

The Broadcasting Act (April 1968), The Canadian Radio-Television and Telecommunications Commission Act (April 1976), Elections Act.

Description

The CRTC licenses broadcast services, (for a term of five years) through a competitive application public hearing process and examines both economic and social factors. These include: the financial viability of the applicant; the potential economic impact on existing licensees; demographic, regional and cultural needs; and categories of programming. "Promises of performance" are attached and monitored for compliance. Sanctions include suspension, licence revocation, non-renewal or short-term renewal, attachment of specific conditions to licences, issuance of reprimands either privately or by public notice and the imposition of fines. The Commission also regulates competition policy (mergers, acquisitions, exit) in the broadcasting sector. It establishes the rates that cable television undertakings can charge their subscribers. Additionally, the CRTC can undertake, sponsor, promote or assist in research relating to any aspect of broadcasting.

The decisions or orders of the CRTC are final and conclusive except insofar as matters of law are appealable to the Federal Court of Appeals and issue, renewal, amendment of broadcasting licences may be referred back to the Commission for reconsideration by Order-In-Council.

Activities of the Commission are centralized with the exception of public hearings held in various locations across Canada. All Commission activities are advertised in regional or local papers affected by its decisions. Liaison offices are located in Halifax, Montreal, Winnipeg, Vancouver and planned for Toronto and Edmonton.

In total, the CRTC supervises over 1,500 radio stations, about 1,500 television stations, and over 850 cable television systems. This includes pay television, specialty and educational television and the CANCOM satellite network. The CRTC operates on a cost-recovery basis.

Broadcasting has long been judicially recognized as residing in federal jurisdiction.

Resources

($000's)	82/83	83/84	84/85	85/86	86/87	87/88
Person-Years	426	417	400	425	425	425
Operating Exp.						
- Salaries	17	18	19	20	20	20
- O&M	5	5	6	5	5	5
- Other Exp.						
Revenue	21	22	25	32	32	32
Subsidies	0.1	0.1	0.1	0.1	0.1	0.1
Capital	0.2	0.4	0.2	0.1	0.1	0.1

NOTE: Total CRTC operations of which broadcasting constitutes half the person-years.

Problem Identification

1. Detailed and complex regulations leave little managerial control over business operations (particularly FM radio programming and AM radio/pay TV technology-use).

2. High compliance costs include the paper burden involved in submitting to detailed analyses of "promises of performance".

3. Public hearing process and regulatory lag (one year) inhibits adjustment to market trends and adds significantly to administrative costs. Appropriateness is questioned for program content change, transfer of ownership and license renewals.

4. Volume-based Canadian content rules distort the flow of advertising dollars, contribute to the high cost of program production and retard the competitiveness of Cable TV with alternative technologies of satellite reception and video-tape.

5. Licensing process protects existing licensees and often helps those survive even if ill-managed and not adequately serving the intended market.

6. Cable TV suffers by its dual role as a broadcaster and its function as a carrier. This has also permitted some provincial overlap in the licensing of Pay TV networks and the carrying of non-programming services.

7. CANCOM's role in the competitive marketplace.

8. Bill C-20 establishing executive direction to the CRTC politicizes the process and may result in confused accountability.

Observations

1. The prime regulatory issues are competition policy in the sector and detailed control over programming. Broadcasting is a highly dynamic media which must adapt quickly to listening and viewing tastes. The main problems focus on detailed regulation without regard for what the public wants and what the public can now obtain through non-Canadian sources.

2. CRTC's desired policy is more supervision and less regulation. Monitoring systems should not be so detailed and complex (e.g. Radio Analysis Program) as to add to compliance costs.

Options

The Study Team recommends to the Task Force that the government consider the following:

1. Adoption of a "permits market" licensing process where the value of a license reflects the competitive impact of a new broadcaster and the tastes and desires of consumers are better served as existing licensees attempt to increase their economic value which is transferable;

2. Leaving mergers and acquisitions to the Combines Act;

3. Permission for radio (AM/FM) program networking;

4. Abolition of program logs, Radio Analysis Program, TV scheduling and program category requirements, using where possible broadcast data collection agencies;

5. Equity across the components of the broadcast media on advertising and commercial content guidelines,

6. A cost pass-through mechanism on Cable-TV rates; and

7. Determining Canadian content rules on a market or managerial incentive system, e.g.
    i)   extend capital cost allowance to the production of TV programs;
    ii) link Canadian content to broadcaster's gross revenue base;
    iii) tier license renewal terms (i.e. 1,3,5,7, years) to Canadian content share of total programming hours;
    iv) assign points by category of difficulty, expense, risk associated with Canadian production, with the broadcaster expected to achieve a total point score over some specified time period.

TELECOMMUNICATIONS — CRTC 902

Objective

To ensure that tolls charged by federally regulated telecommunication carriers are just and reasonable and that carriers do not make any unjust discrimination or give any undue preference in the provision of their services and facilities.

Authority

Railway Act, National Transportation Act, Canadian Radio-Television and Telecommunications Act, Telegraphs Act, Bell Canada Special Act, British Columbia Telephone Company Special Act, Canadian National Railways Act, Canadian Pacific Limited Special Act.

Description

The Commission is a statutory regulatory agency independent from the executive arm of government (Lambert Report). This would change with the passage of Bill C-20 which authorizes executive direction to the CRTC.

The Commission regulates Bell Canada, B.C. Telephone, CNCP Telecommunications, Northwest Telephone, Terra Nova Telecom and Telesat Canada, who collectively provide service to 70 per cent of total Canadian telephones. Rates for new services and rate changes are set and approved upon determination of an appropriate return on equity capital. CRTC attaches conditions to the provision of services and facilities, permits the degree of interconnection or agreements between companies, determines and approves limitations of liability and approves capital stock issues.

Compliance monitoring is undertaken through regular and detailed carrier reporting of financial, quality of service and performance data. Subscriber complaints and those of applicants for service are also recorded. The Commission directs corrective action as appropriate, enforcing its orders itself or through the Federal Court of Canada.

Telecommunications Regulation relies heavily upon the public process, be it through oral hearings or paper proceedings. The Commission's decisions are appealable to the Governor in Council and to the Federal Court. Formal accountability would be enhanced with the passage of

Bill C-20. Resources and activities are centralized in the national capital with the regional offices promoting public accessibility.

While there is no actual duplication of regulation (only one agency regulates any given carrier) there is a "crazy quilt" of telecommunications regulation in Canada. In addition to CRTC activities, provincial public utility boards generally regulate provincial, crown and other private carriers.

Resources

($000's)	82/83	83/84	84/85	85/86	86/87	87/88
Person-Years	426	417	440	425	425	425
Operating Exp.						
- Salaries	17	18	19	20	20	20
- O & M	5	5	6	5	5	5
- Other Exp.						
Revenue	21	22	25	32	32	32
Subsidies	0.1	0.1	0.1	0.1	0.1	0.1
Capital	0.2	0.4	0.2	0.1	0.1	0.1

NOTE: Total CRTC operations of which telecommunications constitutes half the person-years.

Problem Identification

1.   Determination of telecommunication markets where competition is sufficient to allow deregulation. The extent to which competition could flourish, how quickly it could be phased-in, and what regulatory means would ensure discrimination does not occur.

2.   Rate rebalancing across the tariff schedule, specifically between long distance and local services where the former currently subsidizes the latter.

3.   Union concern about the impact of competition on jobs and the skill mix.

4.   Internationalization of the telecommunications market. Advanced technology allows bypass of Canadian telecom services.

5.   Divided federal and provincial jurisdictions create difficulties in setting trans-Canada rates, settlement

procedures for intercompany traffic and cost-effective product design and marketing for manufacturers or suppliers.

6. The intensity and detail of regulations raises the issue of <u>de facto</u> management of the carriers by the CRTC.

7. Regulatory Methods. The existing tools of regulation were originally designed for a non-competitive "natural monopoly" environment and are becoming inappropriate to the mixed competitive and non-competitive telecommunications marketplace.

Observations

1. The major regulatory issues are the extent of competition, the "crazy-quilt" of jurisdiction and regulatory processes.

2. The Commission is mindful of competitive markets. It has permitted competition in the interexchange private line market (1979) telecommunications terminal equipment market (1980), enhanced services (1984) and is presently considering CNCP access to the public long distance message market.

3. Reregulation in Canada means enhanced competition in specific markets and new processes to ensure fair competition, not the mandated break-up of large companies as in the U.S.

Options

The Study Team recommends to the Task Force that the government consider the following:

1. Employ directive power to accomplish step-by-step reduction in regulation as markets warrant increased competition.

2. Review Telecommunications Policy with a view to arriving at a reduced regulatory intervention policy through reform in relation to the following issues: universality of local service, role of Telesat and Teleglobe in provision of competitive services, transmission resale and sharing, national terminal equipment attachment rights, foreign specialty carrier

access and equipment supply, regulatory means of
ensuring non-discrimination and fair competition, and
jobs.

3. Develop a strategy for ensuring telephone service
    benefits which provides subsidized or cross-subsidized
    rates only for subscribers requiring them.

4. Adopt the policy that all telecommunication rates
    should be cost-based and take immediate steps to reduce
    long-distance rates of federally-regulated carriers
    (domestic and international) down to U.S. levels.

5. Develop alternative spectrum management policies aimed
    at facilitating greater network competition.

BACKGROUND

BROADCASTING AND TELECOMMUNICATIONS

TECHNOLOGY VS. REGULATION

The challenges to regulatory process, policy and techniques/methods are always the greatest when the regulated industry is subject to rapid technological or structural change or consumer expectation of the industry is rapidly evolving. There is no better illustration of this fact than the communications industry. Over the last two decades an unprecedented growth in electronics technology has revolutionized both the consumer electronics industry (VCR's, home computers, home stereos, colour TV) and the industrial electronics industry (microwave, satellites, coaxial cable, digital technology); this has allowed the broadcasting and telecommunications industries to offer a host of new services and to produce them in dramatically new ways.

In broadcasting the developments include: superstations which broadcast through the country from one city, national and regional pay television, cable services having a wider signal mix and capable of growing "non-programming services" such as security-monitoring and specialty advertising.

In telecommunications, there have been dramatic productivity gains by telecommunication "carriers", an explosion of service offerings especially in data communications and other specialized business applications, and increasing pressure to introduce competition in an area which a decade ago was considered best served by geographic monopolies largely offering "Plain Old Telephone Service".

As a result, fundamental questions are being asked about the way the federal government regulates each industry. Many contend that the way these industries have traditionally been regulated:

(1) restrains developments which would benefit consumers (including businesses);

(2) is out-of-date and largely ineffective; and

(3) cannot meaningfully be modified to address the
       changes and should be replaced by new policies and
       methods, or even abandoned altogether.

In contrast, where technology is slow to change and
there is little potential for product diversity, such as in
electrical energy production and transmission, such
fundamental questions tend not to be asked.

INFLUENCE OF U.S. REGULATORY CHANGES

More than in any other industry, the U.S.-Canada border
is porous in communications. Canadians close to the border
(by far the majority) access U.S. broadcasting through cable
and home receivers. Even Canadians not living close to the
U.S. border have successfully demanded equivalent choice
through cable service. Leading edge information-intensive
services industries are influenced in their investment
decisions by the comparative prices and product choices of
the Canadian and U.S. telecommunications industries
(especially in long haul services). Short of outright
border controls (which would probably be ineffectual) there
is little that can now be done to prevent Canadian business
from bypassing Canadian carriers when U.S. transmission and
related data storage and processing services (both with the
continent and overseas services) are better.

Of equal importance is the demonstration effect of
U.S. regulatory reform in communications. Over the last 10
years, the United States has taken the lead among nations in
reforming communications regulation. While many have
described this as "deregulation", no major regulatory laws
or institutions have been changed. The situation remains
one of "regulated competition" in both sectors. While many
changes have flowed from new policies of the U.S. federal
regulator, the Federal Communications Commission (FCC),
these changes have often been reluctantly adopted by the FCC
as the result of strong industry and/or executive branch
representations, a failure of established interests to
submit pursuasive evidence in support of the status quo, and
even court rulings overturning the FCC. Anti-trust decisions
have also been a major influence (most notably the ATT
Divestiture).

The major elements of the new orientation in U.S. communications regulation are:

(1) A recognition that the broadcasting and telecommunication industry had undergone great structural change and no longer needed as much direct control to achieve socially desirable performance;

(2) The development of techniques to identify those aspects of the industry which could be made competitive, to prevent dominant firms (such as ATT) from unfairly using their corporate power to overwhelm these areas, and to then stand back and see whether competition worked;

(3) A recognition that traditional techniques of public utility and cultural regulation just would not work in the modern environment.

The principal regulatory changes included:

(1) Broadcasting: reduced horizontal merger restrictions, reduced programming and advertising content controls, removal of policies aimed at restricting TV network ownership of production facilities and program production, removal of entry controls on Pay-TV and "superstation" services;

(2) Telecommunications: permitting competition in the provision of telephone equipment, long distance, and specialized business services, allowing the construction of competing microwave, cable, and satellite transmission networks, reducing the regulatory burden for price changes and new service offerings for dominant firms and forbearing such regulation for new suppliers, and allowing competition in international and telecommunication facilities and services.

The results have been somewhat different in each sector. In broadcasting, there has been greater horizontal and vertical integration within the established TV and radio industry, but there has also been tremendous growth in consumer choice from new specialized services delivered by municipally regulated cable companies. In telecommunications, the end-to-end telephone company monopoly has been replaced except in local services by competitive industry of specialized suppliers. There has also been an explosion of new products at lower prices for business. However, to date residential telephone service consumers have obtained fewer benefits (largely through cheaper telephone sets and lower long-distance rates where competition exists). Consumer representatives fear that, as long-distance rates continue to drop, telephone companies will make up revenue deficiencies from their most captive market, local residential services.

EXPORT OF MOVEABLE CULTURAL PROPERTY – DOC 901

Objective

To preserve in Canada the best examples of Canada's heritage in moveable cultural property.

Authority

Cultural Property Export and Import Act

Description

The Moveable Cultural Property Secretariat in the Department of Communications oversees the processing of all cultural property export permits. The Secretariat also maintains records and advises the RCMP on enforcement.

A control list is made available by the Secretariat on approval by the Governor in Council and is specific as to type of cultural property subject to control, age, and monetary value. The Cultural Property Export Control List is updated periodically. Export permits are required for all objects included on the Control List.

Expert examiners from curatorial institutions first review permit applications relative to criteria determining cultural heritage. Upon denial of applications, appeals are made to the Canadian Cultural Property Export Review Board.

When an export permit is ultimately denied, after a sanctioned delay period, federal grants or loans are made available to Canadian cultural institutions to effect purchase of the heritage property.

The administrative cost of the program is low. There are only four person-years allocated, with assistance provided by officers of Revenue Canada and employees of curatorial institutions.

Resources

($000's)	82/83	83/84	84/85	85/86	86/87	87/88
Person-Years	4	4	4	4	4	4
Operating Exp.						
- Salaries	0.1	0.1	0.1	0.1	0.1	0.1
- O&M	0.1	0.1	0.1	0.1	0.1	0.1
- Other Exp.						
Revenue						
Subsidies	1	2	2	2	2	2
Capital						

Problem Identification

None

Observations

1. On occasion there has been opposition to the imposition of export controls on classes of objects. The Canadian Archaeological Association opposed the inclusion of archaeological objects in the Control List in 1983-84. The problem was solved by employing members of the Association as expert examiners.

2. A review of the Act was last undertaken in 1981.

3. In the Team's view, this is a social/cultural program in the national interest for which the economic costs appear to be low.

Options

None

OVERVIEW

THE TANGLED GARDEN OF ENVIRONMENT REGULATION

INTRODUCTION

Though protection of the environment is a prime concern for companies, interest groups, governments and indeed, all Canadians, the issue of who should protect our natural heritage remains unresolved. Instead, there are significant overlaps in environmental regulations between provincial and federal programs, and among several federal programs in most areas.

Jurisdiction for the environment is not clearly enunciated in the British North America Act, although it has been tied to the provincial resources power and several areas of federal legislative competence including Fisheries, Oceans, and administration of Crown lands.

The provinces generally seek to retain control over environmental protection within their boundaries. However, there are numerous types of deleterious substances which recognize no boundaries, (including toxic chemicals, such as PCB's, and acid-rain generating emissions). Many argue that these should be regulated nationally to ensure greater protection for humans and environment, and in fact the federal government has enacted residual legislation to help control pollution where the provincial legislation has not been adequate. But too often, the dual controls result in confusion, overlap, and even conflict.

The federal government often duplicates its own efforts as well, particularly in the North, where environmental concerns are addressed by numerous departments and agencies. (A non-exhaustive list includes, DOE, DFO, DIAND, COGLA, AWAC, RODAC, EARP, NEB...). This often results in excessive cost and confusion to the private sector, and generates an ethic of conflict between development proponents and environmentalists who fear that controls are insufficient. There is a danger as well that amidst the regulatory panoply with its diverse administrators, serious environmental impacts may be overlooked (e.g. low level radioactive wastes).

The question of adequacy is compounded by the discretion allotted to enforcement officers. The Fisheries Act for example, makes the introduction of any substance into the water an offence, the enforcement of which is left at the discretion of Fisheries Officers. Even properly trained officers cannot be expected to determine in all cases which substance in what concentration will be harmful to the environment. But businesses face continual uncertainty whether they will be found in breach of the Act, even where they may have obtained provincial licences to emit a substance.

Even where environmental assessment is included in plans for development, these latter problems may not be averted, notwithstanding the considerable costs which may have been incurred by proponents. For example, a developer who undergoes the EARP panel process often incurs significant expense without certainty that the project's environmental effects will not be reviewed at a later stage, or that by complying, he or she will be immune from prosecution under environmental legislation upon project completion. Thus, developers may be deterred from marginally-economic projects, and are consistently frustrated by the regulatory burden they bear.

However, environmentalists argue that their interests remain largely unprotected as well, since the complexity of regulation may still allow deleterious substances to enter the environment in significant and detrimental amounts.

CONCLUSION

Effective environmental protection and management, of which regulation is an essential component, requires clear jurisdictional lines and accountabilities, reflected in sound legislation, consensus on objectives and standards, co-operative measures for monitoring and compliance, and reliable, accurate methods and data for determining the compliance, and for determining the trade-offs between benefits and costs. In Canada, there are serious deficiencies in practically all of these regulatory prerequisites at all levels of government.

The program profiles in this report should be considered in relation to the Northern Development programs. It is clear that federal environmental regulation, both in its content and its confusion, is a significant obstacle to economic growth and job creation. Yet, no one suggests that environmental regulation be abandoned. The challenge is to determine a better and more efficient way to balance the interests in this area when they are conflicting and to greatly reduce regulatory conflicts and overlaps.

While the Team has identified the problems and some suggested solutions, it has not been able in the time available to map out a comprehensive plan of action. However, it is certain that such a plan of action is a matter of urgency for the government. Among the subjects of possible further study are the following: a role for a single department or agency to be the champion of the environmental cause, possibly a joint federal-provincial policy and jurisdictional review which could address existing conflicts and overlaps. Clear performance objectives for developers and other users of the environment would remove the uncertainty associated with current regulations. Regulations must be drafted to allow equitable application and enforcement, while protecting the environment. The tangled garden of environmental regulation must be pruned to ensure both the protection of the environment and the reasonable administration of the regulations.

INDUSTRIAL EFFLUENT - EMISSION CONTROLS - EC

Objective

To control industrial effluent and emissions from plants, and thereby to: 1) protect the health of persons against airborne pollutants, and 2) protect the fisheries resources.

Authority

Fisheries Act, Clean Air Act.

Description

The Clean Air Act prescribes national emission standards for four classes of stationary sources: chlor-alkali plants (five plants), asbestos mining and milling operations (12 plants), secondary lead smelters (eight plants with another 50 plants that have some process components subject to regulation), and vinyl chloride plants (six plants). These regulations are based on economically achievable technology with a view to reducing pollutants that pose a "significant danger to human health" or jeopardize international obligations.

The Clean Air Act also regulates lead content in gasoline. (Automobile emission standards are prescribed by regulations under the federal Motor Vehicle Safety Act and corresponding provincial statutes.)

The authority to deal generally with water pollution problems as they relate to protection of the fisheries resource is found in Section 33 of the Fisheries Act and regulations made pursuant to this section. The Act prescribes national effluent standards for six major industrial sectors, including pulp and paper mills (123 mills in 1982), metal mines (132 in 1982), petroleum refineries (36 in 1980), chlor-alkali mercury plants (five in 1985), and potato, meat and poultry processing plants. Both regulations and guidelines are prescribed for each sector; numerical values in the regulations are based on best available technology with a view to reducing the impact of pollutants on fish habitat and the fisheries resource.

Regulations under the Clean Air Act and the Fisheries Act were developed by Task Forces composed of federal, provincial and industrial representatives.

Resources

Enforcement is achieved by Fishery Officers (whose budgets are allocated to the Department of Fisheries and Oceans) and to other public officials (e.g. provincial Fishery Officers and RCMP) empowered to be Fishery Officers under the Fisheries Act.

Problem Identification

Clean Air Act: The federal role in air pollution control has been largely confined to the area of information collection and analysis rather than enforcement. The actual enforcement of air pollution control rests principally with provincial pollution control agencies exercising specific provincial statutory authority.

Fisheries Act, s.33: There are a number of significant problems with the water pollution control provisions of the Fisheries Act. These include:

1. Industrial sectors affected by the Act assert that existing regulations require review and up-dating together with new regulatory initiatives for industries not currently covered by regulation or guideline (i.e. gold mines); a legal mechanism is needed to permit older operations time to comply with prescribed requirements.

2. Jurisdictional ambiguities between federal agencies with a mandate to deal with various aspects of the water pollution problem. Major overlaps occur here on the question of protection of fish habitat (DFO), protection of the northern aquatic environment (DIAND), and protection of coastal marine environments (DOT, COGLA).

3. Lack of clarity in the specification of legal requirements. Section 33(2) is a general prohibition against the deposit of deleterious substances in water frequented by fish. Interpretation of this all-embracing general prohibition varies by region and is reflected in enforcement patterns under the Act.

4. Enforcement of the provision is uneven. The Fisheries Act is actively enforced by federal authorities in coastal regions; in inland waters the actual

enforcement of water quality control principally rests with provincial agencies exercising their authority under specific provincial statutes and under the Fisheries Act. Where provincial effluent licences permit the deposit of a deleterious substance the operation is exposed to the continuing threat of prosecution by a prosecutorial authority other than EC or the province for the breach of s. 33(2).

5. Industrial sectors affected by s. 33 assert that the single resource focus of the Act is too narrow and impedes the development of projects with wider socio-economic value.

Observations

Clean Air Act: The central role of the federal government in the collection and dissemination of information is particularly critical as air pollution can have significant transprovincial and international effects.

Fisheries Act, s. 33: Section 33 of the Act is used to control water pollution generally although it is closely tied, for constitutional purposes, to protection of the fisheries resource. DOE and DFO share significant responsibilities in this regard. Administrative arrangements between the two departments are being developed to alleviate certain jurisdictional ambiguities. As a general principle, it is also clearly desirable to coordinate the delivery of federal and provincial water and air quality standards, with a view to minimizing duplication of regulatory requirements, keeping in mind federal constitutional responsibilities in these matters.

Options

The Study Team recommends to the Task Force that the government consider the following:

1. Review s. 33 of the Fisheries Act to assess feasibility of full implementation of all provisions of the section as drafted or, in the alternative, determine required amendments to Act/regulations needed to address compliance problems with the Act.

2. Encourage federal/provincial cooperation on the question of industrial effluent control, possibly through the development of specific agreements on enforcement policies for section 33.

3. Use s. 33(13)(f) as a vehicle to delegate discretionary powers to provincial officers (subject to Ministerial approval).

4. Encourage early completion of the inter-departmental development of a clear unambiguous compliance and enforcement policy for s. 33.

5. Provide national training standards for all officers with enforcement responsibilities under the Fisheries Act.

6. Delete s. 33 from the Fisheries Act and assign control of all industrial effluent to the provinces.

COMMERCIAL/TOXIC CHEMICALS — EC 18, 22

Objective

To evaluate and control the effects of toxic chemicals on the environment.

Authority

Environmental Contaminants Act, Clean Air Act (fuel additives), Canada Water Act (phosphates), Pest Control Products Act, Transportation of Dangerous Goods (Advisory Services).

Description

Manage the entry of dangerous chemicals in harmful quantities into the environment by assessing their environmental effects, controlling their entry, developing and implementing control measures, and by advising other governments and agencies with regulatory responsibilities of the existing or potential effects of the chemicals. Comply with international obligations under the International Convention for the Protection of the Ozone Layer, and input other international initiatives on toxic chemicals under the OECD and UNEPO.

Resources

($000's)	82/83	83/84	84/85	85/86	86/87	87/88
Person-Years	59	59	65	66	66	66
Operating Expenses						
- Salaries	1,859	1,947	2,367	2,425	2,425	2,425
- O&M	1,099	379	1,581	1,412	1,412	1,412
- Other Exp.						
Revenue						
Subsidies						
Capital	7	6	25	34	34	34

Problem Identification

The program is based on the premise of residual authority. Control measures are only involved when perceived problems are not addressed by other federal or provincial statutory authorities.

No serious concerns were expressed about the program, although environmentalists would encourage more research on the possible deleterious effects of new and existing chemicals.

Observations

The program provides a high standard of research into toxic chemicals at a relatively low cost and provides a sound, rational safety net for dangerous chemicals.

Canadian cooperation in the development of international testing and standards for toxic chemicals is a positive trend in chemicals management.

Re Toxic Chemicals: The problems of managing toxic wastes are very significant, having international as well as national, regional and local impact. Responsibility for toxic wastes lies largely with the provinces; federal legislation is residual. Therefore, while we can accurately describe the regulation of toxic chemicals, by itself, as a non-problem, the bigger and serious questions of toxic waste management through regulation and other means are not being addressed here.

This area of regulation, taken as a whole, is characterized by a lack of coherence among programs and by a lack of overall priorities. The Environmental Contaminants Act has insufficient powers to deal with this area of increasing public concern. A 1982 report by Treasury Board identified some 58 Acts administered by some 24 departments as having something do with toxic chemicals.

The Inter-departmental Committee on Toxic Chemicals, reporting to the Minister of Environment, currently has a mandate to define policy in the area of toxic chemicals, establish priorities, and integrate departmental resources. The Committee has eleven member departments, with seven others on observer status. Preliminary consultation has begun on the toxic chemical policy.

Options

The Study Team recommends to the Task Force that the government consider the following:

1. Retain the Program as is.

2. Develop national standards and contingency plans for inadvertent spills of toxic chemicals.

3. Undertake a comprehensive policy review to determine the adequacy/appropriateness of relevant statutes and regulations.

OCEAN DUMPING CONTROL - EC 23

Objective

To prevent environmental impact in the marine environment from ocean dumping, and to comply with Canada's international obligations under the 1975 Convention on the Prevention of Marine Pollution by Dumping of Wastes and Other Matter ("London Dumping Convention").

Authority

Ocean Dumping Control Act and Regulations.

Description

Under the Ocean Dumping Control Act, administered by Environment Canada (Environmental Protection Service) disposal of wastes at sea is regulated through a system of permits.

The terms and conditions of these permits vary with the type of substance being dumped. These substances are divided into three schedules based on danger to human health, to marine life and other legitimate uses of the sea. Permits typically govern such things as timing, handling, storing, loading and placement at the disposal site.

Permits to dispose of waste at sea are required for all Canadian ships, aircraft, platforms, or other artificial structures in all waters. Foreign vessels require such permits if they wish to dump in Canadian waters.

Inspectors are designated under the ODCA, and inspections are carried out to ensure compliance with the Act and terms and conditions of the permits. This activity is administered by four regional offices in Vancouver, Yellowknife, Montreal and Dartmouth.

Sanctions for violation vary according to the schedule, and include fines up to $100,000 for each offence, seizure or detention of the ship or aircraft.

The Act does not apply to discharges resulting from offshore mineral/petroleum exploration and development, from normal operation of ships and other craft, or from land-based sources such as effluent pipelines. These are

covered by other legislation, such as the Canada Shipping
Act, the Oil and Gas Production and Conservation Act, the
Fisheries Act, the Arctic Waters Pollution Prevention Act,
and the Northern Inland Waters Act.

The Act <u>does</u> apply to dumping all other materials at
sea, or destroying them at sea by incineration. It applies
to loading waste on ships, aircraft, platforms or other
artificial structures for disposal at sea. All ocean
dumping permits and amendments must be published in the
Canada Gazette before they come into force. The Act applies
to a distance of 320 km offshore. Interdepartmental liaison
is provided through four Regional Ocean Dumping Advisory
Committees (RODAC), chaired by EPS.

<u>Resources</u>

($000's)	82/83	83/84	84/85	85/86	86/87	87/88
Person-Years	40	44	72	62	62	62
Operating Expenses	3,504	2,253	4,913	3,995		
Revenues						
Subsidies	--	179	5			
Capital	1	--	14	18	18	18

*   Waste Management Sub-Activity (includes Ocean Dumping
     Control)

<u>Problem Identification</u>

Private sector (oil and gas industry) opinion of the
Ocean Dumping Control Act is unfavourable, not so much of
its objectives but of its administration and overlap with
other legislation. A specific irritant is the actual or
potential invoking of ODCA to regulate abandonment of
artificial islands in Beaufort Sea offshore drilling. On
abandonment, the islands could pose a hazard to both the
environment (if toxic substances and debris are left on
them) and navigation. Industry views OCDA as "stand alone
legislation"; it in fact constitutes a legislative back-stop
if other federal or provincial agencies specifically charged
with regulation offshore fail to measure up. Thus,
satisfying the environmental provisions of the Canada Oil
and Gas Lands Administration (COGLA) may not be enough to
satisfy Environment Canada on cessation of exploration with
respect to ODCA.

The legislation associated with ODCA, and the
concomitant advisory bodies, comprise a tangled web of

regulation and regulatory process, especially in the North. There, the Arctic Waters Pollution Prevention Act, its advisory body Arctic Waters Advisory Committee (AWAC), COGLA, DFO and the Fisheries Act and RODAC, all converge to bemuse and confuse the private sector proponent of an exploration or development project. The latter often perceive Fisheries and Environment personnel as using their legislation to prevent and thwart economic development activity that has been legitimately licensed elsewhere.

To a lesser extent the problems of overlap exist in provincial offshore areas. One environmental interest group was of the opinion that, with respect to British Columbia, the overlap, or backstop, provisions were necessary because B.C. does not effectively enforce its own regulatory controls offshore.

Observations

There appears to be no quarrel with the fundamental objectives of ODCA and the fact that Canada has an overriding "obligation" to live up to the London Convention preventions.

There is a process problem to resolve; ODCA must defer to, or be deferred to by, other Acts/agencies that have jurisdiction offshore.

In the time available, the Team was unable to untangle the problems underlying this program sufficently to identify firm solutions. The problems are compounded by evolving judicial rulings. The matter is important since private sector economic interests see the program as a major economic impediment.

In 1984, the B.C. Court of Appeal in the Crown Zellerbach case ruled S.4(1) of the ODCA ultra vires. Section 4(1) is the general prohibition against dumping without a permit. An appeal to the Supreme Court of Canada in the case is pending. In the meantime, the ruling is binding in B.C. where the Fisheries Act, s.33, is currently being relied on to specify environmental operating conditions for waste disposal at sea.

In the event of an unsuccessful appeal to the S.C.C., amendments to the Act or, in the alternative, new draft regulations under another statute such as the Fisheries Act,

215

will have to be considered if the federal government wishes to continue this program.

Options

The Study Team recommends to the Task Force that the government consider further study in this area, possibly in terms of considering the possibility of establishing one environmental body through which all environmental offshore requirements would be satisfied. Options: DFO, DOE, DIAND (in the North), COGLA, provincial/territorial government.

ENVIRONMENTAL ASSESSMENT REVIEW PROCESS - EC 25

Objective

To promote environmentally sensitive, publicly responsive resource and project planning in areas of interest to the federal government.

Authority

Government organization.

Description

The Environmental Assessment Review Process is essentially a three-stage process. First, the federal department with the lead involvement in a development project undertakes an initial environmental screening to determine if there are significant environmental effects. If the department concludes that there are no significant adverse effects, the project proceeds, subject to mitigative measures. Second, where the department concludes that the probability of significant adverse effects is uncertain, a more detailed initial environmental evaluation takes place. Third, where the department decides that the environmental effects may be significant, the matter is referred to the Executive Chairman of the Federal Environmental Assessment Review Office who establishes an assessment panel comprised of public servants and independent experts. Each panel develops guidelines for the preparation of an Environmental Impact Statement (EIS) by the department and proponents initiating the project, studies the EIS, holds public consultations, and reports to the Minister of the Environment who confers with the Minister of the initiating department.

The EARP process applies to projects undertaken directly by government departments, or, where a project may have an effect on lands administered by the federal government, or where a financial commitment has been made to the project by the Government of Canada.

Resources

The following resources are for the Federal Environmental Assessment Review office activities. The number, size, and complexity of projects reviewed affect resource requirements.

($000's)	82/83	83/84	84/85	85/86	86/87	87/88
Person-Years			25	24	26	29
Operating Expenses						
- Salaries			1,220	1,184	1,184	1,868
- O&M			1,504	2,437	1,823	2,364
- Other Expense						
Revenue						
Subsidies						
Capital			4	15	5	7

Problem Identification

Despite recent revisions to the EARP process, there remain a number of significant problems that can result in uncertainty, unnecessary delay and excessive cost. These include:

1. Since initial assessment of environmental effects and the decision to refer a project to FEARO is made by the initiating department, and because "significant adverse affects" are not defined, the potential exists for a department to accelerate or delay the development of a particular project. Since departments are not required by legislation to submit proposals to EARP, there is little further recourse to judicial review.

2. EARP panel reviews are site and project specific, and may result in duplication of assessment for similar projects in similar areas. (The Beaufort EARP addressed this issue in reviewing development in an area where forty licences might operate, but its findings were considerably narrower than expected, and did not address similar concerns in other regions, e.g. tankers off Labrador.)

3. EARP processes focus on planning methods to mitigate potential deleterious environmental effects, but consider neither alternative uses for the resources nor optimization thereof.

4. There are no constraints placed on the EARP process to require assessments to be completed within a specific period of time. In the absence of such parameters, the Beaufort review lasted five years and cost $20 million; some assert that the findings of that review might have been arrived at after a few weeks of internal meetings.

5. Much of the cost of EARP panels falls to the private
    sector proponents, while interested groups or
    individuals may receive government funding to appear
    before an EARP panel. In many cases, both are the
    beneficiaries of the process, but both do not share the
    costs.

Observations

The public is not aware in most cases that the EARP
process has been initiated for a project until it reaches
the panel stage.

The most significant problem with the EARP process is
the overlap and duplication of environmental assessments.
EARP reviews occur during the initial planning stage of
project development, and may be duplicated fully, or in
part, by provincial assessments, native group reviews under
land claims settlements, land use planning, Water Board
permit procedures, and NEB reviews. Because EARP retains
its flexibility and informality under the Order-in-Council,
judicial notice of its recommendations is not required at
subsequent quasi-judicial hearings such as those of the
NEB. The combined effect is excessively costly, duplicative
and operates as a serious obstacle to economic development,
particularly for marginal projects.

Options

The Study Team recommends to the Task Force that the
government consider the following:

1. Increase the visibility of the EARP process before it
    reaches the panel stage to make the public aware that
    the environmental impacts have been assessed in all
    development projects in which the federal government
    has a "direct" interest.

2. Enact empowering legislation for the EARP process with
    a view to eliminating duplication and setting out
    specific parameters for review, requiring all
    subsequent reviews to be bound by the recommendations
    of the EARP process and compliance therewith.

3. Provide in enabling EARP legislation that reviews may
    take place only where the project will not be subject
    to any other comprehensive environmental impact
    assessment.

MIGRATORY BIRDS CONSERVATION PROGRAM - EC 97

Objective

To protect from indiscriminate slaughter and ensure the preservation of over 500 species of migratory birds that are either harmless or useful to man.

Authority

Migratory Birds Conservation Act (1917).
Canada Wildlife Act.

Description

The Migratory Birds Conservation Program provides for research on the listed species and their habitat, regulation of the numbers available for the hunt in each season, and the shared management and operation of Natural Wildlife Areas and Migratory Birds Sanctuaries. The program also involves cooperation with the provinces on Waterfowl Management Plans and the Crop Damage Prevention Agreement.

The program fulfils Canada's international obligations under the Migratory Birds Convention of 1917 and involves joint management and research programs to protect species shared by Latin American countries.

Resources

($000's)	82/83	83/84	84/85	85/86	86/87	87/88
Person-Years	235	241	240	256	256	256
Operating Expenses	13,210	13,530	13,827	16,279	16,279	16,279
- Salaries						
- O&M						
- Other Exp.						
Revenue	1,705	2,195	1,882	4,008	4,008	4,008
Subsidies						
Capital	672	1,074	979	663	663	663

Problem Identification

The program serves a useful objective in protecting migratory birds, and is not questioned in principle. However, several minor problems exist with respect to the program, including:

1. The federal review of hunting plans for migratory birds
    (eg. season) results in excessive delay and the
    requirement of a federal hunting licence for the
    migratory birds covered by the program duplicates
    provincial licensing schemes.

2. The list of species covered by the program dates from
    1916, and environmentalists assert that it excludes a
    number of species requiring protection.

Observations

In the view of the Study Team, Canada's efforts to
protect migratory birds require an equal commitment from
other host countries to be effective. Preservation of the
species is often not as high a priority with other
governments.

The Migratory Birds Conservation Program might serve as
a good model for the national protection of other endangered
species.

Options

The Study Team recommends to the Task Force that the
government consider the following:

1. Maintain the program as is.

2. Allow provinces to develop and administer a single
    hunting licence system and establish hunting
    regulations within a broad federal-provincial framework
    to eliminate duplication.

PARKS (LAND AND WILDLIFE REGULATIONS) - EC 901

Objective

To protect and conserve natural and cultural heritage resources and to provide for public safety in National Parks.

Authority

National Parks Act, Historic Sites and Monuments Act, National Battlefield Commission, Historic Sites and Monuments Board, UNESCO World Heritage Convention, International Council on Monuments and Sites (ICOMOS).

Description

Wildlife regulations prohibit hunting in all but one national park, except for aboriginal peoples in certain northern parks, and regulate fishing in the parks.

Parks Canada sets fees for its services including camping, park visitor vehicle entrance fees, fishing licences, etc., and regulates the delivery of visitor services, to control the amount and suitability of development within a park.

Parks Canada unilaterally carries out land-use planning and municipal-style zoning for five townsites within National Parks.

An A-base review was completed in 1983-84, and a comprehensive audit done by the Auditor-General in 1982-84.

Resources

($000's)	81/82	82/83	83/84	84/85	85/86	86/87
Person-Years	4,983	5,093	4,941	5,222	4,902	
Operating Expenses	162,000	186,000	198,000	209,000	213,000	
Capital	100	101	114	113	90	

These are the resources for the entire Parks Canada Branch, including National Parks, Historic Sites, Administration, Recreation and Conservation Agreements. Regulatory activities do not consume all these resources, but it is difficult to estimate what portion is ascribed to regulatory functions.

Problem Identification

The parks regulations present an insurmountable obstacle to economic development. This has been the intent of Parliament, as national parks were created in the first place to be areas precluded from economic development. The development of tourist and recreation facilities is severely curtailed resulting in significant loss of tourism revenues. Industry claims that it is restricted from developing vast tracts of northern land, with arbitrarily established boundaries, while these areas also remain largely inaccessible to Canadians wishing to enjoy their natural heritage. Park townsite dwellers have no input into local issues.

There is considerable polarization of views on national parks. Contrary to the "industry view" is a wide range of individuals and interest groups who stress the priority for preservation and restricted access, as well as for additional areas of park land to be set aside.

Parks officers are plagued by the ambiguity of their role: on the one hand education and on the other enforcement. When conducting enforcement activity, they are hampered by having no sanctions at their disposal short of criminal prosecution.

Observations

The National Parks policy does not appear responsive to any of the groups we consulted. Some environmentalists advocated enhanced preservation, while the majority of those consulted indicated that the parks should be more available for recreation.

Options

The Study Team recommends to the Task Force that the government consider the following:

1. Undertake a major review with public consultations of parks policy, addressing the issue of the purpose and use of National Parks: preservation, conservation, recreation, development.

2. Allow for resource exploration and development, and undertake consultation with industry before parks boundaries are established, to achieve optimal allocation of resources.

3.   Implement a multi-tier approach to National Parks (development/recreation/conservation/preservation) allowing for greater economic benefits, especially those arising out of tourism.

4.   Require greater cost recovery in National Parks.

5.   Develop and publish a compliance and enforcement policy to structure the discretion of Parks officers.

6.   Implement a ticketing scheme for minor offences.

WILDLIFE CONSERVATION PROGRAM - EC

Objective

To control the illegal export of game killed in one province and transported to or possessed in another province or territory.

Authority

Game Export Act.

Description

A permit must be obtained to export game from the province or territory in which it was killed. It is illegal to possess the game beyond the provincial boundary without a valid export permit obtained from the province of origin.

The definition of game for the purposes of this program includes the carcass, or any part thereof, including the skin of any wild animal, domestically-raised fur-bearing animal, wild fowl or wild bird.

The legislation was enacted at the request of the provinces, and is administered by the provinces and enforced by provincial officials, the RCMP and Customs officers. The sole role of the Canadian Wildlife Service is to respond to provincial requests for changes in the legislation.

Resources

The Act is administered entirely by the provinces and territories, with no resources allocated by the Canadian Wildlife Service for administration.

Problem Identification

While there are no problems with the existing Game Export Act, the program applies only to dead animals or parts thereof. A more important issue might be the transfer of live animals across provincial or territorial borders, and the potential effects of introducing these animals into new ecosystems.

Options

The Study Team recommends to the Task Force that the government consider the following:

1. Extend the legislation to cover the transportation of live animals across provincial and territorial borders.

2. Maintain the program as is.

OVERVIEW

IMMIGRATION

In the context of the high unemployment rates of recent years, immigration is increasingly an economic issue. Although there is recognition of the historical and traditional importance of immigration in Canadian society, there is also a growing apprehension about the effects of current policies on the competition for scarce jobs. In European countries, these concerns have led to stringent reactive measures including the repatriation of thousands of "guest-workers".

Several problems were identified with respect to recruitment and selection and, more particularly, enforcement:

- The abuse of refugee claims has clogged the processing and enquiry systems resulting in high public costs and unacceptable delays. The former government commissioned Rabbi G. Plaut to study these issues and the report's recommendations are being considered.

- The estimated 50,000 or more illegal immigrants attest to the difficulties and weaknesses involved in current enforcement procedures. These illegal aliens presumably use available social and medical services through illicit means and many hold jobs which could otherwise be available to Canadians.

- Current Unemployment Insurance and social assistance benefits make it difficult and even impossible for industries requiring seasonal workers (e.g. horticultural) to employ Canadians. As a result, foreign workers are given temporary permits to meet the labour requirements of seasonal enterprises.

- There are divergent views on current procedures applied to immigration for family reunion purposes. Some hold the view that this "non-contentious" area should be partially deregulated since its administration is needlessly complex and costly. Others maintain that current procedures are justified in terms of screening applicants who would potentially result in costly burdens on existing social and medical assistance programs. Thus, for example, they point to the importance of a medical examination as part of the clearance process.

While certain issues will remain sensitive, particularly with respect to family-reunification immigration, it may be desirable to increasingly and visibly include immigration policy as part of the broader framework of economic policy.

IMMIGRATION: RECRUITMENT AND SELECTION – EIC 901

Objective

To administer the admission into Canada of immigrants and visitors in accordance with Canada's economic, social and cultural interests.

Authority

Immigration Act (1976) and Regulations; Canada Employment and Immigration Reorganization Act (1977)

Description

This program regulates the volume and composition of immigrants and certain categories of visitors (e.g. foreign students, temporary workers) entering Canada in accordance with legislation, regulations and policy. Recruitment and selection activity abroad is carried out by the Department of External Affairs.

In 1983-84, 89,034 persons were admitted under this program of which the majority come under the category of family re-unification, and the rest of which are defined as follows:

- 8,961 refugees;
- 6,407 through a 1982 measure restricting the admission of selected workers to those with approved job offers;
- 12,524 entrepreneurs, self-employed persons, retirees and their families as well as those admitted for special humanitarian reasons.

In addition to processing immigrant applications and refugee claims, the program's workload also includes the issuance of over 200,000 authorizations and extensions annually to temporary foreign workers and foreign students.

Immigration levels are planned for a three year period in annual consultations with the provinces and interested private sector organizations, including labour. An approved three year plan is tabled in Parliament each year.

All observations for this program also apply to its operations abroad which are now under the responsibility of External Affairs.

Resources

($000's)	82/83	83/84	84/85	85/86	86/87	87/88
Person-Years	587	562	483	561		
Operating Exp.	16,590	17,683	14,763	19,373		
– Salaries	15,382	17,129	13,879	18,339		
– O&M	1,208	554	884	1,034		
– Other Exp.	–	–	–	–		
Subsidies	–	–	–	–		
Capital	16	22	22	22		

Problem Identification

Although the need for this program was not questioned, the groups contacted raised the following concerns:

1. Groups had widely-divergent views on whether current immigration levels constitute an obstacle to job creation. Some noted that, except for family reunions, immigrants compete directly for scarce jobs in a situation of high national unemployment. Others stated that immigrants create jobs (e.g. Toronto has low unemployment rate and highest ratio of persons not born in Canada) and that Canada is in a precarious labour market position with respect to its steadily declining population.

2. Recruitment and selection abroad (under External Affairs) should be streamlined: there are too many resources in European countries where emigration to Canada has declined in the past decade and too few in developing countries, which are increasingly the source of family reunification (the largest immigrant component).

3. Rules and application of selection criteria are inconsistent.

4. The legal requirement to obtain landed immigrant status outside of Canada has broken down; policy for individual cases has taken over resulting in perceived inequity and costly procedures, including the direct involvement of ministerial discretion. The statute and regulations should be amended to allow the least contentious groups (e.g. family reunification with aged parents and children) to obtain landed status in Canada.

5.   Foreign temporary workers should not be used when there is a high unemployment rate. Yet, they are needed because certain economic sectors (e.g. horticultural) cannot compete with the generous UI and welfare benefits which are too close to the minimum wage. Changes should be made to those systems, at least on a seasonal basis, in order to permit domestic employment of seasonal workers.

Observations

1.   It is understandable that in an area where immigration officers deal with individual human beings whose lives and futures can be determined by an administrative decision, certain discretionary actions and flexibility are required and results are inevitably subject to challenge.

2.   There is some inconsistency in implementation. For example, family reunification procedures in one country of origin can take three or four times longer than in another. Also, the Entrepreneur Program which has the potential of contributing to job creation, is easier to implement in countries of origin which do not restrict the export of capital than in those which do.

3.   At a time of high domestic unemployment, it is very difficult to support even the temporary employment of foreign seasonal workers.

Options

     The Study Team recommends to the Task Force that the government consider the following:

1.   The program clearly has to be maintained but streamlining and changes are required. The Standing Joint Parliamentary Committee on Regulations has made comments in recent years, including observations about the extent of Ministerial discretion and involvement which should be addressed. Consideration should be given to permitting landed status within Canada for certain non-contentious categories.

2.   Although such a measure could increase violations of entry rules, the difficult issue of foreign temporary workers should be addressed in terms of Canadian interests and would require a review of current

unemployment and welfare measures to promote seasonal employment in agriculture. The developing countries affected (principally in the Caribbean) could react adversely.

IMMIGRATION: ENFORCEMENT - EIC 902

Objective

To enforce legislation and regulations as related to the entry, stay and removal of persons from Canada, thereby protecting the health, safety and good order of Canadian society.

Authority

Immigration Act (1976) and its Regulations; Canada Employment and Immigration Reorganization Act (1977).

Description

Enforcement of the immigration statute, regulations, and policies is achieved through the examination of documents, the apprehension and detention of persons who do not have valid documents, the investigation of violations and representations at enquiries into violations or appeal procedures. In many ways, this is a policing function.

The primary inspection of the some 35 million persons entering Canada annually is provided by Customs Officers (Revenue Canada). The more careful secondary examination - 1.9 million were conducted in 1983-84 - are undertaken by Immigration Officers. They also carry out investigations of violations of the Act. In 1983-84, 71,000 investigations took place and 6,391 persons were deported as a result of these investigations.

Canada is a signatory to a UN program to aid the placement of refugees. Part of the enforcement problem arises from the continued increase of persons, principally from Third World countries, who claim refugee status after entry into Canada, often on visitor status. The recent introduction of visa requirements for certain countries which were producing high volumes of such claims should provide some degree of preventive enforcement though not without creating some other problems for the potential "refugee". The increase in costs, delays, as well as the abuse of the refugee component of the program by fraudulent claimants are issues which have been in a review commissioned from Rabbi G. Plaut.

The program is highly decentralized in 10 regional offices, with 106 Canadian Immigration Centres across the country. An automated Field Operational Support System (FOSS) provides an on-line data network containing status information and will be completed as a comprehensive registry in 1987-88.

Resources

($000's)	82/83	83/84	84/85	85/86	86/87	87/88
Person-Years	1078	1053	1167	1047		
Operating Exp.	41,785	46,945	47,599	42,566		
- Salaries	36,833	37,842	41,157	39,290		
- O&M	4,952	9,103	6,442	3,276		
- Other Exp.	-	-	-	-		
Revenue *	2,316	2,600	2,680	3,000		
Subsidies	-	-	-	-		
Capital	29	31	31	48		

*   Revenue largely from forfeited bonded deposits, and carrier penalties as well as cost-recovery fees.

Problem Identification

None of the groups contacted questioned the need for enforcement of the Act and its regulations, however, the following issues were raised:

1.   The number of persons illegally in Canada (the estimates start at 50,000 cumulative, according to a 1982 study) indicate the dimension of the enforcement problem.

2.   The abuse of refugee claims in recent years has led to a backlog in the enquiry system. Furthermore, the very recent Supreme Court decision giving those claiming refugee status the right to full hearings before the Immigration Appeal Board (previously the Board could render a decision based on a transcript of an examination by an officer) will further clog the system and aggravate the backlog problem (currently some 13,000 cases).

3.   The use of universal visa could be an effective preventive measure to reduce the cost of enforcement.

4.   There are too many legal and regulatory loopholes which encourage delay in the deportation process and which represent significant federal administrative costs.

In order to increase cost-recovery, the department will be proposing new or higher fees to Cabinet for various categories of documents.

Observations

1. In the Study Team's view, there is a serious cost/benefit issue in this program. With over 1,000 person-years and nearly $100 million expended yearly, there is still a significant negative perception about the effectiveness of enforcement.

2. Because of a recent Supreme Court decision regarding refugee determination, the department will clearly have to find more effective means of screening at ports of entry.

3. Consideration of using a universal visa system to more effectively screen entries requires an analysis of impact on reciprocity arrangements with other countries, particularly the U.S. Another important factor is the additional administrative burden, particularly in operations abroad (under External Affairs).

Options

The Study Team recommends to the Task Force that the government consider the following:

1. Although the program clearly needs to be maintained, more effective screening methods at ports of entry should be developed and implemented to reduce costs. Rabbi Plaut's recommendations regarding refugee status are under consideration and improved screening prior to entry could be the outcome of reform.

2. The option of allowing domestic requests for landed immigrant status for certain non-contentious categories (e.g. children, aged parents for family reunification) could be considered in the context of possible legislative change, although a prior assessment of possible negative effects, particularly in terms of increasing the number of illegal residents, would be desirable before any decision on change.

CITIZENSHIP REGISTRATION AND PROMOTION - SSI

Objective

To promote Canadian citizenship, provide services for the acquisition and proof of Canadian citizenship and provide other services mandated by legislation.

Authority

Citizenship Act.

Description

The Secretary of State program which administers the Act and its regulations, provides services for granting and establishing proof of Canadian citizenship. These services include promotional activities. In 1984-85, it processed 123,558 applications for grants of citizenship and 43,948 applications for proof of citizenship as well as 6,992 record searches. Decentralized services are provided through 29 Citizenship Courts and sub-courts, and through dual-site headquarters in the National Capital Region and in Sydney, Nova Scotia. Almost 40 per cent of all citizenship applications and processing occurs in Toronto.

Citizenship applications with supporting documents and fees are initially examined by a regionally-based officer, are forwarded to the Sydney office which arranges for RCMP criminal and security clearance, and are then sent to the appropriate Citizenship Court. The Citizenship judge, through verbal exchange, tests the applicant in accordance with requirements (e.g. knowledge of Canada), and approves the application. A certificate is subsequently prepared, followed by a second appearance before the judge for a presentation/oath-taking ceremony.

Changes in immigration legislation and policy impact on the program's operations and workload as do any increased requirements for proof of citizenship.

Resources

($000's)	82/83	83/84	84/85	85/86	86/87	87/88
Person-Years	390	429	330	330	330	330
Operating Exp.						
– Salaries	9,103	11,124	9,679	9,839	9,839	9,839
– O&M	*541	**791	1,973	1,596	1,896	1,896
– Other Exp.	137	146	192	146	146	146
Revenues	1,732	1,995	2,000	6,500	5,525	5,525
Subsidies			NIL			
Capital	45	184	38	28	28	28

*   Figures for overhead and Regional Operations not available.

**   Figures for overhead, Regional Operations and EDP costs not available.

NOTE: The above figures exclude resources related to the Citizenship Language Instruction and Language Textbook Agreements. They do, however, include resources related to promotional activities as these are an integral component of the process of acquisition of Canadian citizenship or proof of Canadian citizenship.

Problem Identification

No problems were identified from the regulatory point of view. However, the department noted that costs of the ceremonial aspects of the program could be reduced. In addition, a 1984 internal evaluation referred to the possibility of transferring promotional activities to voluntary associations which would be funded through seed money provided by the Secretary of State.

Observations

It is possible to reduce ceremonial costs and even enhance the significance of acquiring citizenship by having Members of Parliament perform a simplified granting ceremony. New citizens would come in direct contact with their elected representatives who also symbolize the fundamental institution of Canadian democracy.

Options

The Study Team recommends to the Task Force that the government consider the following:

1. <u>Simplify and transfer</u> the ceremonial aspects of the program from a Citizenship judge to a Member of Parliament. This would require all-party agreement and legislative change. Savings achieved would include the current costs for 34 Citizenship judges, some court support staff as well as related O&M expenditures.

2. <u>Eliminate</u> the ceremonial aspects and only require prospective citizens to take the oath, at their cost, before an officer of the court (e.g. notary); documents would be processed by officials and certificates would be issued by regional and district offices. Similar savings to those noted immediately above would be achieved.

3. <u>Maintain</u> the current ceremonial aspects of the program.

THE PASSPORT PROGRAM - EAC 1

Objective

To provide Canadian citizens and other eligible residents with the timely issuance of travel documents and to maintain their integrity.

Authority

Canadian Passport Order (Order-In-Council 1981-1472). Diplomatic & Special Passport Order (Order-in-Council 1956-1373).

Description

The Passport Program involves the issuance of passports to Canadian citizens and the issuance of certificates of identity to landed immigrants who are unable to obtain travel documents from their country of origin.

The issuance of passports is decentralized to 16 regional offices in Canada as well as two offices in the National Capital Region. Passports are also issued at 110 Canadian missions abroad.

Other services include extension of validity, addition of married name, addition and deletion of children and observations. Diplomatic and Special passports are issued in appropriate circumstances.

The Passport Office is also responsible for policy formulation and coordination, and for its own personnel, financial and administrative services.

The program operates under Treasury Board Revolving Fund Regulations and is financially self-sustaining. Consequently no departmental appropriations are used to support the program.

Resources

($000's)	82/83	83/84	84/85	85/86	86/87	87/88
Person-Years		339	353	351	351	351
Operating Exp.		15,545	16,495	18,146		
– Salaries						
– O&M						
– Other Exp.						
Revenue		17,819	19,451	19,451		
Subsidies	–	–	–	–	–	–
Capital		106	792	738		

Problem Identification

The program is not questioned in principle and Canadian passport services are generally held in high regard in Canada and enjoy a high reputation internationally.

Although the program operates on a basis that exceeds full cost recovery, the costs of issuing passports abroad are not fully recovered.

Observations

Passport services are highly visible and the risks associated with the issuance of passports containing errors or inaccurate information underline the importance of high quality performance.

In the view of the Study Team, both regional and Ottawa offices have attained acceptable levels of service to the public with passports being issued to personal applicants in three days and to applicants by mail in five to seven days plus mailing time.

Passport applications forms are available at some 8,000 post offices, 2,000 travel agents, the major air carriers and all passport offices.

Bilingual service is provided in all passport offices.

Options

The Study Team recommends to the Task Force that the government consider the following:

1. No change in view of the program's efficiency and strong cost recovery performance.

2.   Some costs might be cut by closing certain regional
     offices but this would reduce service to the public.

3.   The Department of External Affairs should review
     options for improving the cost recovery of passport
     issuance services at overseas posts.

OVERVIEW

ENERGY AND MINES

At the beginning of its work, the Regulatory Programs Team expected the energy sector to require a great deal of attention since the regulatory structure, then in place, was almost a textbook example of how the use of regulation to achieve non-economic policy objectives can have serious deleterious economic effects. However, the conclusion of the Western Accord halfway through the study offered many remedies for the major regulatory issues in this area.

There are certain significant issues not affected by the Accord which impact on atomic energy control. For example, particular concern is expressed about intergovernmental "falling between stools" that seems to exist with regard to regulation of low-level radioactive waste.

There are also federal regulatory programs which have an important but indirect effect on the mining sector. However, most direct regulation of mining south of 60° is done at the provincial level. A background paper outlines the mining industry's view of federal regulation. Related suggestions are listed below. They should be read in relation to the Team's work on Fisheries as well as Northern Development. They offer a very good example of how one important industry can have interests across a broad spectrum of the regulatory landscape.

The following suggestions for adjustments to regulatory processes could lead to a higher level of economic activity in the minerals sector:

-   Amend the Fisheries Act to recognize that some competing water uses may have higher priority than protection of fish habitat and introduce Regional Review Boards to resolve disputes.

-   Accelerate the process of project approval for the great majority of project proponents by granting automatic approval when regulatory authorities cannot demonstrate a need for compliance standards more stringent than existing legislation.

- Give project proponents the right to "debate" the need for specific terms and conditions of approval before these are cast in stone.

- Introduce a "single-window" coordinating body to facilitate project approvals North of 60°.

- Adopt policies of multiple land use North of 60°.

- Accept, in principle, the need for equitable public sharing in the costs of sulphur dioxide control.

- Continuously review the relevance of regulations in relation to technological advance and apply company-specific standards as appropriate.

ATOMIC ENERGY CONTROL BOARD - AECB 1

Objective

To control the development, application and use of atomic energy in Canada, and participate on behalf of Canada in international measures of control, in the interests of health and safety, and national objectives.

Authority

Atomic Energy Control Act, Nuclear Liability Act.

Description

The Atomic Energy Control Board performs the following functions:

1. Licenses and administers the siting construction operation and decomissioning of nuclear facilities.

2. Licenses the possession, use, sale, import, export of prescribed substances.

3. Administers Canada's obligations for the international control of atomic energy.

4. Administers Nuclear Liability Act including designation of nuclear installations and prescription of basic insurance for operators.

5. Sets standards for and certifies packaging for transport of radioactive materials.

6. Establishes and administers regulations for physical security of certain nuclear materials and facilities.

7. Conducts R&D in support of atomic energy regulatory requirements.

    The Board is composed of one full-time president and four part-time appointments.

Resources

($000's)	82/83	83/84	84/85	85/86	86/87	87/88
Person-Years	254	271	283	285	285	285
Operating Exp.						
- Salaries	10,270	11,791	13,792	15,069	15,071	15,071
- O&M	5,388	7,505	6,104	7,809	7,010	6,485
- Other Expenses						
Revenues	1,210					
Subsidies	18	38	24	481	504	711
Capital	227	1,357	245	291	307	379

Problem Identification

The Atomic Energy Control Board is generally considered to administer well an important regulatory program. However, criticism has emerged over the Board's composition of one full-time and four part-time representatives. It is contended that the Board members do not have the time to devote to Board issues, nor often do they have the expertise required to understand their complexities. The Board has also been criticized for not maintaining an arm's length relationship with industry, and for administering the regulations inconsistently.

A second problem was identified by the AECB administrators and concerns the disposal of low level radioactive waste. While waste management is a provincial responsibility (except for certain designated substances), the management of radioactive materials is a responsibility of the AECB. However, the AECB does not own or operate waste sites for the low level wastes which are produced throughout our society. There is no agreement on which jurisdiction should be responsible for these wastes, and they are being held in temporary facilities or are disposed of in normal dump sites. As low level waste increases, so too does the need for permanent disposal facilities.

Observations

The use of performance standards to achieve regulatory objectives often results in least-cost alternatives for the industry. AECB regulations are prescriptive for smaller companies which may not have the resources to devote to R&D. This combination of types of regulation appears optimal.

The incremental cost of increasingly stringent regulations is insignificant compared to the degree of safety achieved. The atomic energy regulations set a superior safety standard, and must be administered consistently to preserve public confidence in the energy industry.

The Study Team is of the view that AECB's regulatory program represents an undue burden on the uranium mining industry and intrudes more than necessary into provincial spheres of jurisdiction.

Options

The Study Team recommends to the Task Force that the government consider the following:

1. Review the structure of the Board and expand number of members to include more permanent members representing industry, labor and public interests.

2. Convene a task force of industry representatives, AECB members, and provincial government representatives to determine the appropriate jurisdiction for low level radioactive wastes and optimal disposal methods, within one year.

NATIONAL ENERGY PROGRAM REGULATIONS - EMR 2, 20, 21, 901

Objective

To contribute to increased Canadian ownership and control of the energy sector, promote energy self-sufficiency, and provide for a single "made-in-Canada" price.

Authority

Canadian Ownership and Control Determination.
Energy Administration Act.

Description

The NEP regulations included a broad range of activities, including:

1. Setting and collecting the Petroleum Compensation charge applied to crude oil flow to refineries in Canada.

2. Establishing and paying New Oil Reference Price for oil discovered after 1973 at a level higher than the Special Old Oil price for pre-1973 known reserves to stimulate the exploration and development of new oil sources.

3. Establishing rate and paying Oil Import Compensation to provide flat rate compensation to importers of crude oil and petroleum products to promote lowest cost imports and insulate from rapid changes in world oil price.

4. Paying compensation for exchanges of Canadian crude for foreign crude through Domestic Transfer and Crude Oil Exchange and, transportation costs for domestic crude to Atlantic refineries to promote utilization of domestic crude, limit shut-in and minimize imports and cost to consumer of imported oil.

5. Making rulings for Canadian Ownership Rate, and Control Status, to encourage Canadianization.

6. Administering Petroleum Incentives Program payments, covering up to 80 per cent of exploration costs on Canada Lands for eligible Canadian-owned and controlled firms.

7.   Establishing natural gas prices.

It should be noted that much of this Program has been overtaken by the Western Accord and the Atlantic Accord, while the government has indicated that it intends to substantially alter gas pricing regulations in the near future.

Resources

($000's)	82/83	83/84	84/85	85/86	86/87	87/88
Person-Years	118	149	145	145	145	145
Operating Expenses						
- Salaries	4,076	6,165	5,410	5,410	5,410	5,410
- O&M	2,220	2,593	2,733	2,733	2,733	2,733
- Other Expenses						
Revenue*	1,889	1,614	2,553	2,520	2,520	2,520
Capital	2	250	35	35	35	35

* from Petroleum Compensation Charge

Problem Identification

NEP regulations restrict development on an economic basis as follows:

1.   Entry into the market is restricted by Canadian ownership requirements and back-in provisions.

2.   Exploration decisions are distorted by PIP grants which may encourage exploration in less economic frontier areas.

3.   Production decisions may be based on optimization of revenues from artifically higher New Oil Reference Price (NORP) reserves, even where production from reserves valued at Special Old Oil Price (SOOP) might be lower cost.

4.   Oil Import Compensation program may skew optimal mix of imported and Canadian oil.

5.   Single artificial made-in-Canada price is onerous when world prices fall below Canadian prices.

6. Natural gas prices are significantly above world prices, making Canadian exports uncompetitive and resulting in little depletion of enormous shut-in reserves.

The cost of the Petroleum Gas Revenue Tax (PGRT) and oil prices artificially inflated above world levels probably outweighs the benefits derived from exploration in frontier areas and non-traditional reserves, particularly since much of these reserves can only be extracted and brought to market significantly over current world oil prices (and world oil prices in the foreseeable future).

The petroleum industry has indicated that while the PGRT and other taxes are levied on all producers, the major producers are almost exclusively the beneficiaries of PIP grants since they are the only ones capable of participating in high cost frontier projects.

Entrepreneurial initiative is stifled by prices in excess of world levels, and Canadian ownership requirements. There may be a considerable spillover effect on suppliers and services to the petroleum industry, including drillers and equipment manufacturers.

Observations

Most of the problems identified by the petroleum industry seem to have been addressed in the Western Accord.

Options

The Study Team recommends to the Task Force that the government consider undertaking a joint private sector/public sector review in three years of the Western and Atlantic Accords, and the new natural gas regulations as announced, using similar criteria to those of the Task Force's Study Team on Regulatory Program Review.

EMERGENCY MANDATORY ALLOCATION & RATIONING PROGRAM - EMR 12

Objective

To prepare contingency plans for programs of mandatory allocation and rationing to ensure the equitable distribution of available petroleum supplies during a national emergency. Upon declaration of a national emergency to implement and operate these programs.

Authority

Energy Supplies Emergency Act (1979).

Description

The Energy Supplies Emergency Act (1979) establishes the Energy Supplies Allocation Board (ESAB), consisting of a Chairman and up to six members, and makes provision for programs of mandatory allocation and rationing of petroleum products in the case of a national emergency. In the event of an emergency, very broad powers are assigned to the Board. The Board may make regulations to allocate supplies of controlled products, to assign suppliers to wholesale customers, to prescribe prices, to regulate imports and to deal wth any other aspect of a mandatory allocation program. If, in the opinion of the Governor in Council, a national emergency exists by reason of an actual or anticipated shortage of petroleum products, the Board is required to immediately implement a mandatory allocation program. This order must be placed before Parliament within seven days and must be confirmed by Parliament for it to continue in force.

ESAB will expand rapidly in an emergency. It will open offices in all provinces and territories and its personnel complement will rise to 170, when mandatory allocation is in effect, and to approximately 1,000 if rationing is implemented.

These programs are designed to meet Canada's commitments under the Agreement on an International Energy Program which was signed by Canada in 1974. ESAB is also responsible for liaison with the International Energy Agency (IEA) on emergency planning matters and provides Canadian representation on the IEA's Standing Group on Emergency

Questions (SEQ). ESAB is also the National Oil Board with respect to NATO petroleum planning activities. Staff provide Canadian representation on NATO's Petroleum Planning Committee and related bodies.

ESAB is assisted by two advisory committees established during 1979. These are the Petroleum Industry Advisory Committee (PIAC) and the Provincial Advisory Committee (PAC). Both Committees are chaired by the Chairman of ESAB.

Resources

($000's)	82/83	83/84	84/85	85/86	86/87	87/88
Person-Years	26	31	25	25	25	25
Operating Exp.	1,647	2,493	2,018	2,018	2,018	2,018
Revenue						
Subsidies						
Capital	14	18	8	9	9	10

Problem Identification

As this Program has never been implemented, no problems were evidenced.

Observations

The Emergency Mandatory Allocation and Rationing Program is necessary to fulfil Canada's international obligations and to prepare plans for a national energy emergency. However, it may not be necessary to have 25 people devoted to the continual review and reassessment of contingency plans for a potential, future disruption of oil supplies.

Options

The Study Team recommends to the Task Force that the government consider the following:

1. Maintain the Program as is.

2. Assign responsibility for the development of contingency plans to a central energy industry monitoring group (e.g. Energy Supply Branch, NEB).

3. Reduce the number of people devoted to the preparation and maintenance of contingency plans by developing one

set of viable plans subject to periodic (e.g. biannual) review by a joint industry/ESAB committee.

4. Close the program, integrate the responsibilities of ESAB in another departmental unit and absorb the resource costs.

PETROLEUM MONITORING AGENCY - EMR 30

Objective

To monitor and assess the condition of the petroleum industry, including production costs, profitability, capital expenditures, ownership and control.

Authority

Energy Monitoring Act.

Description

The Agency publishes the Canadian Petroleum Industry Monitoring Survey semi-annually, which assesses the industry's financial and economic performance. Petroleum companies are required to submit complete financial information to the Agency for inclusion in the report. The only exceptions to this reporting requirement are very small companies with less than $10 million in assets or revenues. Such companies are, however, required to submit similar but less detailed financial information to Statistics Canada, which supplies this information to the Petroleum Monitoring Agency.

Resources

($000's)	82/83	83/84	84/85	85/86	86/87	87/88
Person-Years	16	15	15	18	18	18
Operating Exp.	1,077	947	980	1,532	1,524	1,524
- Salaries						
- O&M						
- Other Exp.						
Revenue						
Subsidies						
Capital	4	4	20	20	20	20

Problem Identification

The private sector identified a number of problems with the Petroleum Monitoring Agency, including;

1. PMA duplicates information collected and available from other sources including Statistics Canada (although exchanges of information exist between the agencies), and provincial governments and agencies.

2. Some of the information collected is probably not necessary or useful for government or industry policy and decision-making processes.

3. The petroleum industry feels that it is unfairly singled out from Canadian industry for monitoring of financial performance, and objects to the additional costs associated with PMA reporting requirements

4. Privately-held companies are required to supply financial information that would not normally be subject to disclosure requirements.

5. The amount and complexity of information required by PMA is constantly increasing, while timeframes for compliance with requests may be unreasonable and unresponsive to a company's own accounting periods.

The program department asserts that PMA analyses are objective, comprehensive and timely, and that they improve petroleum market efficiency.

Observations

1. In recent years, the program has been kept significantly below budget levels, indicating efficient administration of the program.

2. It is not clearly demonstrated that the information assessed by the PMA is best collected independently of information relating to petroleum reserves, production plans, etc.

Options

The Study Team recommends to the Task Force that the government consider the following:

1. Eliminate PMA.

2. Conduct an internal review of all information collected by PMA, and eliminate that not fundamental to policy-making or available elsewhere.

3. Privatize PMA.

4. Subsume PMA into a departmental monitoring group mandated to consider all aspects of the energy industry including assessment of reserves, trade in petroleum products, emergency planning, etc.

EXPLOSIVES ACT ADMINISTRATION - EMR 114

Objective

To ensure public safety through compliance with the Canada Explosives Act and Regulations.

Authority

Canada Explosives Act and Regulations.

Description

The Explosives Branch nationally regulates the manufacture, importation, storage, sale and transportation by road of explosives by inspecting and licensing factories, magazines and road vehicles by testing and authorizing explosives, by providing technical advice to other government agencies (international, federal and provincial), and by providing training courses on explosives safety.

Intergovernmental liaison includes provincial mining and labour bodies, police departments, and foreign bodies such as the United Nations Committee on the Transport of Dangerous Goods. Within the federal government, the Explosives Branch must coordinate its regulatory activities with those of Transport Canada with respect to the Transport of Dangerous Goods Act.

The Explosives Branch conducts its regulatory work with a staff of 30, including 13 regional inspectors, and is complemented by the research activity of the Canadian Explosives Reserach Laboratory, CANMET, with its staff of 14. An A-Base Review of these functions, conducted in January, 1983, concluded that the separation of the two units within the Research and Technology Sectors was rational and should be maintained.

Resources

($000's)	82/83	83/84	84/85	85/86	86/87	87/88
Person-Years	41	41	44	44	44	44
Operating Expenses	1,871	1,960	1,772	1,847	1,847	1,847
Revenue	19	19	22	22	22	22
Subsidies						
Capital	72	65	55	50	52	54

Problem Identification

No significant problems were expressed by the private sector. Explosives Regulations appear to be administered effectively toward their objective, the protection of human life and public safety. The costs in achieving the desired benefits do not appear excessive.

Management of the Explosives Branch expressed the need to review the regulations on an ongoing basis to identify and eliminate specific irritants through routine Order-in-Council amendment. For example:

1. Load limits for truck transport of explosives in Canada are much lower then in the U.S., i.e. 10,000 lb. vs. 40,000 to 45,000 lb. The lower limit appears to cause inefficiency, and may in fact be conducive to greater risk: four trucks loaded with 10,000 lb. explosives may pose more risk than one with 40,000 lb.

2. All explosives are required by regulation to bear owner identification designation. This is in the interest of security and crime prevention. Certain explosives (eg. "alpha") are rarely, if ever, used illegally; thus the regulatory requirement appears unnecessary. Provincial and territorial governments are responsible for the end-use control of explosives, for example in mining and construction. This does not constitute overlap with the Explosives Act Administration.

Observations

Transport Canada's new responsibilities under the Transportation of Dangerous Goods Regulations include transport of explosives by any mode. These regulations have only recently been promulgated; thus, it is premature to judge whether there is overlap with the Explosives Regulations. To eliminate any potential for this, EMR and TC have drawn up a Memorandum of Understanding, defining respective responsibilities within the common field.

Options

government consider the following:

1. Continue with the status quo.

2.   Remove Transport Canada's jurisdiction in the transportation of explosives by consolidating it within EMR.

3.   The reverse of the above.

4.   Review the situation within two years to determine if there are any problems of overlap and concomitant inefficiency.

NATIONAL ENERGY BOARD - NEB 100

Objective

To regulate specific areas of the oil, gas and electrical energy industries and to provide advice to the government on energy matters.

Authority

National Energy Board Act, Energy Administration Act, Northern Pipeline Act.

Description

The NEB has the following responsibilities:

1. Licenses exports of energy after public review (with Governor in Council concurrence for major exports or by order for minor exports).

2. Recommends export pricing of energy to Minister.

3. Issues certificates of public convenience and necessity for major pipeline/power transmission lines after public review and authorizes minor construction of pipelines/power lines, including detailed routing approval.

4. Inspects construction, grants leave to open.

5. Inspects ongoing pipeline operations.

6. Sets tolls and tariffs for interprovincial pipelines, after public review conducts enquiries into accidents involving loss of life or serious impacts.

7. Audits accounts of regulated companies for compliance and to ensure that all costs are reasonable.

8. Collects data to determine current Canadian energy supply and demand.

9. Regulates price of natural gas in interprovincial and export trade.

10. Closes energy transmission operations.

The NEB is a quasi-judicial agency and has all the powers vested in a court of record. The Board consists of eleven members; an additional six temporary members may be appointed by the Governor in Council. Most hearings are conducted by three Board members, and most of the regulatory workload is divided among three-member Panels (including the Electrical, Financial Regulatory, Gas, Oil and Pipeline Panels) with reference to the full Board for major decisions.

The National Energy Board has been the object of several comprehensive reviews, including those conducted by the Special Committee of the Senate on the Northern Pipeline (March 1983), the V.L. Horte Task Force on pipeline construction costs (September 1983) and a comprehensive audit carried out by the Auditor-General (1984). A number of public recommendations for regulatory reform have been made; NEB response has been to act on most, but not all, of these (note Reforming the Regulatory Environment, statement by C.G. Edge, Chairman, National Energy Board, to the Senate Standing Committee on Energy and Natural Resources (May, 1984).

Resources

($000's)	82/83	83/84	84/85	85/86	86/87	87/88
Person-Years		462	458			
Operating Expenses						
- Salaries	17,160	19,747	20,686	21,865	21,811	21,811
- O&M	2,852	3,916	4,524	4,674	4,674	4,674
- Other Expenses						
Revenue	1,031	650	800			
Capital	294	243	51	510	169	214

Problem Identification

Since its establishment in July, 1959 as a quasi-judicial body intended to de-politicize energy matters, the NEB has acted, in part, as a public utility style regulator and, in part, a technical referee in the construction and operation of pipelines. In respect of these functions it has been non-controversial and effective. The NEB was also, however, set up as an adviser to the Minister of Energy, Mines and Resources. During the 1970's EMR's expanding energy policy role challenged NEB's function; in the 1980's we see both EMR and NEB carrying out similar functions with respect to petroleum resource monitoring, export/import forecasting, and policy advice to the Minister of EMR. During the period of severely strained federal-provincial relations in energy, the NEB was increasingly viewed by the provinces as a less-than-impartial policy arm of the federal Minister, and thus distrusted by the producing provinces.

There are a number of areas where NEB functions overlap or duplicate those performed elsewhere, including:

1. NEB/COGLA: the jurisdiction for approvals for offshore pipelines and development plans is contested by NEB and COGLA. Both appear to have a valid claim to jurisdiction, and a policy decision is required to allocate control to one agency.

2. NEB/EARP: Lengthy and expensive environmental assessment reviews undertaken early in the project development stage in the EARP process may be duplicated later in NEB hearings. The NEB must consider all factors in licensing and granting leave to open and as a court of record can only take judicial notice of EARP findings, but cannot be bound by them. Thus, the same environmental impact issues may be "re-reviewed".

3. NEB/Alberta Energy Resources Conservation Board/ Petroleum Monitoring Agency/Stats Canada: Many provincial and federal government agencies monitor various aspects of the petroleum industry, and may duplicate each other's information gathering and dissemination.

Observations

Although the Western Accord has removed much of the NEB's regulatory activities in oil and gas, certain remaining powers are viewed by some provinces and industries as unnecessary or duplicative irritants.

In discussions with the NEB, it was noted that Agency functions could be fully cost-recoverable.

Options

The Study Team recommends to the Task Force that the government consider the following:

1. Legislate policy to grant only one federal agency (NEB, COGLA, in a new agency) sole jurisdiction over offshore development.

2. Eliminate environmental and social impact factors for NEB consideration.

3. Require NEB to be bound by EARP findings on environmental issues.

BACKGROUND

A MINING PERSPECTIVE ON REGULATORY PROBLEMS*

1. ## PROBLEMS IN THE REGULATION OF MINING

No comprehensive study has been done on the extent of
regulations impacting on the mining industry or their
cost to individual companies. However, a strong
impression exists that the sector is heavily regulated.

Because of the nature of the industry, the effects of
government controls are felt most strongly during the
project approvals process, particularly with respect to
access to land and water. The most serious problems
result from the single-purpose nature of the Fisheries
Act, the application of single-purpose land use
policies North of 60°, and the complexity of the
approvals process itself that results from the number
of agencies and departments involved. These problems
impact disproportionately on smaller, as opposed to
large companies. Sulphur dioxide (the cause of acid
rain) control regulations also have important cost
implications for the industry and the increasing pace
of technological advance may create a requirement to
rethink the approach to regulation.

2. ## COMMENT

It is difficult to assess the costs of regulation on
the industry, largely because, once in place,
regulations quickly become standard operating
practice. This is the case with health and safety
legislation, for example, where it is unlikely that
industry would do things much differently if existing
regulations were dropped. Thus, a good portion of
government efforts to offset the negative cost
implications of regulations on the industry should
target on streamlining regulatory processes rather than
amending the regulations per se. This paper, is
therefore, mainly concerned with streamlining
regulatory processes and particularly those related to
project approvals. Discussion of the Fisheries Act is

---

*   This paper does not deal with regulatory problems North
    of 60°, with narrow regulatory issues on a subject
    basis (e.g. health and safety) or with general
    regulation of economic environment.

included because it contributes to many bottlenecks in current regulatory systems.

3. OPTIONS

a) The Fisheries Act

The narrow, single-purpose dimension of Section 33 of the Fisheries Act gives it unwarranted power, for it raises protection of fish habitat to a position of social priority above all other objectives.

i) Amend Section 33 of the Fisheries Act to explicitly recognize that industrial development may be allowed where it can be shown that:

- other economic uses of water have higher social value (including creation of jobs) than the absolute preservation of fish habitat; or

- rehabilitation (including natural processes) or other means can redress the potential for permanent harm to fish habitat that results from temporary disruption;

ii) Establish regional fisheries review boards, having final authority to adjudicate disputes when DFO has reached an impasse with either an industrial project proponent or provincial and/or territorial governments.

b) Complexity of project approvals processes

i) In a federal/provincial context, there is little need to establish a single-window for processing project approvals, particularly if the Fisheries Act and its administration, which are the main stumbling blocks to federal/provincial accord, are modified as suggested above.

ii) The project approvals process North of 60° is more complex than in any other jurisdiction, in part because of devolution of

administrative and political authority to the
territorial governments. Here, there is a
need for a single-window to act as a point of
first entry into the approvals process and to
provide comprehensive information on general
requirements, departmental responsibilities
and contacts.

Project proponents also need an opportunity
to discuss the rationale for specific terms
and conditions that must be met in order to
receive project approval, before these are
cast in stone by the bureaucracy. This
function could be coordinated by the
"single-window" authority.

Caution: In the Team's view, no attempt
should be made to give this coordinating body
more authority than basic departmental
legislation allows lest the "single-window"
add another layer of bureaucracy to the
process.

iii) Project approvals processes are designed to
catch the "worst case" projects and are
essentially set up to provide prior
assurances that companies will comply with
regulations. In effect, project proponents
are assumed to be "probably guilty" of
environmental damage and must prove their
innocence.

Reversing the onus so that regulators must
prove probable environmental damage in order
to require impact studies, public hearings,
etc., could result in significant
streamlining of the project approvals
process. There is little need for complex
approvals procedures to protect the public
interest for the vast majority of project
proposals.

Aside from one project in British Columbia
that has been held up by DFO, every other
mining proposal in the country has eventually
received the approval of regulatory
authorities. In the last few years, speedy
approval has been granted for several

projects. The reason is that the intelligent application of state-of-the-art environmental control technology means that projects can proceed with very little negative impact.

There is considerable scope for introducing a quick assessment of the potential for significant environmental disruption. If such potential cannot be demonstrated, then projects should be allowed to proceed subject only to their meeting existing environmental protection regulations. It should be clearly understood that industry will be held accountable for non-compliance once the project is operational. This proposal would have great significance in supporting economic renewal in the mining sector.

c)   Land use policy

Uncertainty over long-term access to land deflects investment in mineral exploration and development. The bureaucracy tends to look to land use planning to resolve this uncertainty. However, land use planning processes take time and defer decisions on land use for many years. In addition, they are based on two assumptions:

-   that it is possible to determine, at a particular point in time, maximum value land uses that will endure for all time, and

-   that mining is incompatible with some uses or that it results in permanent, irretrievable damage.

Both these assumptions are highly questionable. The industry is constantly adding to geological knowledge and improving the economics of resources extraction. Technological advance is also increasing the ability of the mining industry to live in harmony with nature. Thus, classification of maximum value land use is not possible in the case of mineral development until such time as mineral discoveries have been made and specifications for protective measures for a specific project proposal are evaluated in relation to the receiving environment.

The Team believes that multiple land use policies in the North and guarantees to the mining industry of their eventual "right to develop" are needed. The guarantees should be subject only to the requirement for site-specific terms and conditions when preliminary evaluation of development proposals suggests, as indicated above, that significant environmental damage might otherwise result. The prohibition of mining should only occur when dictated by the meaningful evaluation of competing land uses.

d)   Acid rain

Society bears the cost of pollution. Society also bears a portion of the costs of pollution control if a lower level of economic activity results.

In recognition of this fact, governments should accept, in principle, the need to share with industry the costs of sulphur dioxide abatement. The exact split must reflect the need to treat all companies on an equitable basis and take into account the circumstances of the industry throughout the period specified by governments for eventual compliance. The choice of control technologies should also be tempered by considerations of productivity, modernization and competitiveness.

e)   Implications of technological advance

New technologies and ways of doing things create a growing requirement for flexible regulatory structures. For example, as automated, remotely-controlled mining equipment is introduced underground, ventilation standards may not have to be as stringent as they now are to protect worker health. Other legislation (e.g. labour) may slow the rate of technological adaptation. Thus, flexible standards that differentiate between companies on the basis of their technological capability may be required to encourage innovation and to reap the full economic and productivity benefits from the use of new technologies.

267

REGULATION OF THE FISHERIES: TERMINAL CASE OF SCHIZOPHRENIA

A.   ISSUES

The existing regulatory framework governing the
fisheries is seen as a vast burden by all participants in
the sector. But various participants have different views
of whether more or less regulation is the solution. Not
surprisingly, the Department has tended to favour regulatory
solutions.

The degree of regulation can be appreciated when
considering that it takes $690 million (total expenditures
of the Department of Fisheries and Oceans in 1984-85) to
ultimately regulate an industry in which the landed value of
fish is almost $900 million and the value of derived
products is some $2 billion annually.

The objectives of fisheries policies and regulations
are schizophrenic, unclear and often contradictory. That is
to say, the Department of Fisheries and Oceans consciously
and unconsciously mixes its primary resource habitat
protection objectives with its socio-political objectives
and all of the above with its economic objectives. The
industry labours under over 1000 pages of regulations, yet
is chronically unstable and heavily reliant on government
assistance, factors which indicate that policies and
regulations may not be meeting any of their objectives
adequately. Certainly, they do not foster economic
viability in the sector. In fact, no one disputes that the
economic efficiency and viability of the sector is seriously
prejudiced by the web of fisheries and other federal and
provincial regulations aimed at job and income maintenance.
In other words, the unwritten objectives in fisheries
regulation and policy may have little to do with the overt
regulatory objectives making inefficiency chronic and
dependence nearly irreversible.

It also appears that, despite various consultative
mechanisms, the private sector has had only limited input in
the formulation of current federal management tools
(including regulations) which the Study Team found to be
highly interventionist and which ultimately shape the
industry.

B.   WHY REGULATE?

The fishery has traditionally been viewed as a common property resource. Unlike land, and land-based resources (e.g. timber), the fishery has not been alienated (sold or leased) to the private sector. In a common property resource, regulatory control is needed because the resource is prone to abuse; it can be damaged, depleted or even annihilated. Due to the absence of private property or marketable rights, there is no incentive to conserve the resource, thus the law and regulation become the arbitrator. Controls on inputs (vessels, fishermen, gear) are used to constrain the aggregate fishing effort and, ultimately, the number and kind of fish actually caught. Over the years, the regulatory objective of conservation has evolved to comprehensive socio-economic regulation, determining who has access to what portion of the resource, as well as how and where fishing activity is pursued.

C.   MAJOR PROBLEMS

1.   Legislative scope. Under the Constitution Act 1867 the federal government has paramount jurisdiction over the fisheries (commercial, sport and Indian fisheries). The Fisheries Act is comprehensive in its controls over a broad spectrum of activities. In the fisheries, it gives absolute ministerial discretion in certain areas (e.g. s.7 on licensing) and powers extend well beyond conservation measures to such issues as the export of fish (s.34) and detailed information requirements from processing plants (s.17). Land-based industry is also affected through the Act's broad environmental powers (s.33) which can restrict or control land-use and such economic activities as logging and mining which are constitutionally a provincial concern.

2.   Over-regulation. Both fisheries industry and employee groups agree about the overall tendency to regulate all aspects of the sector. The regulatory burden is partly due to detailed conservation measures and the department's tendency to incrementally layer or add-on regulations fairly regularly to close loop-holes or keep pace with new gear and technological

innovation. Over-regulation is also due to the pursuit of socio-economic benefits, namely, income maintenance for as many fishermen as the resource can bear. In fact, for many participants in the industry who live in small communities (particularly in the Atlantic region) which offer few, if any, alternative sources of employment, fishing combined with various government assistance programs (e.g. special Unemployment Insurance provisions, fleet support) provides only a marginal livelihood.

3. Over-crowding. There appear to be too many fishermen and fishing vessels in terms of the limited fishery resources available. The past decade saw a surge of increased participation in the sector, mainly due to the 200-mile territorial extension. In the Atlantic fishery, for example, between 1974-81, the number of fishermen increased by 45 per cent (from 34,500 to 53,500) and processing plants increased by 34 per cent during that time (from 519 to 700). Unemployment Insurance provisions available to fishermen encourage artificial seasonality and contribute to participant overcrowding in the sector. The regulatory framework, in fact, supports the crowding by restricting the use of efficient technology (ostensibly for conservation reasons) in order to support the large number of participants and by further limiting the catch (due to over-crowding) and therefore the revenue of each participant.

4. Diminishing returns. While fish are a renewable resource, stocks must be carefully managed to ensure replenishment. For this reason, the resource is seasonally and even cyclically limited or finite even though it is renewable. It is therefore subject to the same types of seasonal pressures in terms of potential harvesting as a non-renewable resource. Yet, the expansion of the 200-mile offshore zones of the sea coasts in 1977 led to a surge of optimism in the sector with respect to increased stocks. The incremental rapid growth which followed led to a "race" for the 200-mile expanded fishery (more participants accessing still controlled, and therefore limited, resources), and also led to over-capitalization

(bigger vessels). Increased catching capacity which has involved increased investment costs for fishermen was not, however, accompanied by increasing revenues since they continue to operate under total allowable catches and controlled catching capacity through a multitude of restrictions on gear, vessels, technology, etc.

5. Other Inefficiencies. Extensive regulatory restrictions and overcrowding which lead to dissipated economic rent are compounded by other difficulties. Export opportunities and potentially higher export revenues are foregone through restrictions aimed at promoting processing (e.g. changing consumer patterns are increasingly favouring frozen over canned salmon, yet the department continues to protect jobs in the processing industry by limiting frozen salmon exports). Also, the seasonal race for the fishery results in overloading the freezing/processing capacity which is largely under-utilized in off-season. Furthermore, inadequate product promotion and marketing strategies for which the department has assigned resources are also contributing factors to the failure of regulation to achieve efficient use of the economic potential of the fisheries.

6. Inadequate enforcement. As commissioned reports in recent years indicated, lack of adequate enforcement of conservation controls can damage the stock and therefore the industry. There are currently too many incentives to breach the law, and the number and complexity of regulations are difficult to enforce. Current penalty fees are not commensurate with the market value of one day's illegal catch of certain species and provisions for other sanctions (e.g. seizure of vessel) are rarely enforced.

D. THE NEED FOR REFORM

In the Study Team's view, greater clarity of policy objectives and a simplified, improved regulatory framework to support the objectives are required. If the priority is to be placed on promoting a more efficient, viable industry, many existing approaches and practices will have to be challenged and changed.

- The common property concept will have to be modified to permit quasi-property rights which are marketable in areas where this is feasible. There are a variety of options available to achieve this change and the department is currently experimenting with this concept on a limited basis. The advantages of quasi-property marketable rights is that they basically encourage efficiency, permit market incentives and could eventually reduce the need for certain forms of government assistance.

- Conservation regulation will have to be reduced, simplified and designed to be easier to enforce. Straightforward quotas on catch, as well as time and location restrictions, for example, where species and other circumstances make such simple control possible, should be considered in order to eliminate the intricate and numerous regulations on gear, vessel and technology.

- The damaging overcrowding in the sector has to be addressed. Alternative policy and regulatory instruments, some of them already implemented on a trial basis (e.g. buy-back schemes) must be further developed in order to substantively reduce the number of participants. The net effect will be fewer fishermen with potentially higher incomes. Alternative employment strategies will have to be developed for those adversely affected by these measures, since their impact would have serious consequences for small communities, particularly in the Atlantic region. In this regard, for instance, the Science Council recently issued a report in which it identifies the potential of aquaculture (fish-farming) as one viable option for jobs lost in the traditional fisheries (in Norway, for example, salmon ranches yield about $30,000 earnings per employee per year). This and other options obviously require further study and consultations with participants in the sector and with the coastal provincial governments.

- The general dissatisfaction with the existing regulatory framework in part reflects the fact that with a common property resource, it is the regulatory agency (the Department) which determines access to the resource and allocates it among competing users. Moreover, with its vast regulatory powers, the Department may undertake many initiatives for its convenience as regulator rather than for the benefit of the regulated. Serious consideration should be given to involving the private sector (management and labour), including tourism interests (in terms of sportfishing) in decisions involving access and resource allocation (much like the joint councils in the U.S.). The Department would continue to set overall quotas for each species for conservation purposes and would maintain its enforcement role.

E. CONCLUSIONS

1. The Study Team found that the regulatory priorities and objectives in the fisheries need to be more clearly articulated with the full participation of the private sector and provinces - the economic costs of the regulatory priorities must be faced up to and "fudged" no longer. To that end, the Department should undertake a detailed regulatory review and report to the Ministerial Task Force by early 1986.

2. There is an urgent need to reduce the regulatory burden and clarify functions and responsibilities as well as accountability in all aspects of economic regulation in the fisheries sector - in particular, there should be much greater reliance on industry self-regulation and on market solutions. Enterprise allocation concepts in particular need to be enlarged.

3. In carrying out a review, the Department should take into account the comments of the Standing Joint Committee of Parliament on Regulations and other Statutory Instruments prior to the implementation of changes.

4. Fewer simpler regulations, or indeed the pursuit of the efficiency option in the sector should clearly have to be accompanied or encouraged by a corresponding decrease of federal resources assigned to the fisheries.

5. There is an urgent need for strengthened penalties for violations under the relevant legislation.

6. Consideration should be given to further regulatory "pilot projects", including the formation on a trial basis of a regional fisheries council in which regulatory policy would be developed by industry representatives subject only to ministerial approval.

FISHERIES & OCEANS: LICENSING AND RESOURCE ALLOCATION

Objective

To manage the common property aspect of fisheries through licensing and resource allocation.

Authority

Fisheries Act, Coastal Fisheries Protection Act, Territorial Sea and Fishing Zones Act.

Description

The protection and conservation of fisheries stocks is entirely under federal jurisdiction. Access to stocks is controlled through licensing of fishermen in the Atlantic region and of vessels in the Pacific. Resource allocation is achieved through total allowable catches (TAC) assigned to domestic and foreign fleets (under bilateral international agreements in return for trade benefits to Canada). Recreational fisheries licensing is administered by provinces, but stock conservation norms are set by the federal government.

Both conservation measures and access restrictions are required in the fisheries, which is traditionally viewed as a common property resource. In contrast to land-based resources, neither individuals nor companies have exclusive proprietary or leasing rights. In this rather unique situation, greater efficiency and investment in catch capacity can result in lower returns. In order to address these types of common property problems which have emerged in recent years resulting in too great numbers of fishermen, excess fishing capacity and over-investment in the sector, the program has selectively initiated some limited licensing regimes (involving buy-back of licences) and introduced enterprise allocation schemes (allowing barter and sale of quotas, and choice of boat size and gear).

There are currently some 81,000 commercial fishermen (including part-time) and 42,000 federally-registered fishing vessels.

<u>Resources</u>   *

($000's)	82/83	83/84	84/85	85/86	86/87	87/88
Person-Years			176			
Operating Exp.						
- Salaries			6,701			
- O&M			5,762			
- Other Exp.						
Revenue						
Subsidies						
Capital			600			

*   As part of a major internal review, the department is
    restructuring its activities. The Department states it
    cannot provide reliable data for 1982-83 since it has
    changed its coding procedures. Also, final allocations
    have not been made for 1985-86, thus only aggregate
    data, adjusted for salaries (four per cent) is shown.
    Finally, for 1985-88 inclusive, no expenditure
    breakdowns were provided.

<u>Problem Identification</u>

The following major concerns were raised by industry
and labour groups contacted on both sea coasts and at the
national level:

1. Basically, government should decide whether fisheries
    policies are used to maintain jobs or to promote a
    viable, efficient industry. Until now, jobs have been
    the first priority to the detriment of those in the
    industry who could potentially increase their returns
    if regulations supported them.

2. There are too many participants for the stocks
    available, and consequently, efficiency is not only
    controlled but also discouraged, particularly with
    respect to the use of up-to-date technology.

3. There is too much socio-economic regulation
    (determining who can fish, how, what, where) and
    conservation regulation is sometimes unclear; quotas
    are sometimes seen as being set in terms of market
    capacity rather than resource availability.

4. There is extensive over-regulation of the fisheries;
    the view is that there is more government control than
    in any other sector.

5.   There are conflicting interests in the fisheries, e.g.
     there is encroachment of commercial fisheries
     activities through measures favouring sportfishing
     i.e. tourism; land-based industries threaten both
     commercial and sportfishing.

Observations

1.   The Study Team found that there are major regulatory
     problems in the fisheries and licensing is a principal
     focus of difficulties. The overview on the fisheries
     outlines the issues and some available options, some of
     which require further study. In the Study Team's view,
     clearly fundamental changes are required in the
     regulatory framework, and in the legislation as well.

2.   Although private sector advisory committees are in
     place to advise the Minister, both industry and labour
     have insufficient input to the decisions which
     ultimately determine the extent and nature of the
     fisheries.

Options

     The Study Team recommends to the Task Force that the
government consider the following:

1.   There is a need to clearly determine whether economic
     efficiency (substantively fewer fishermen, with larger
     quotas and the possibility of using updated on-vessel
     technology should be a priority (as suggested in the
     Kirby Report on Atlantic Fisheries) and whether the
     government should consequently focus on conservation
     rather than socio-economic regulation. The adverse
     impacts (e.g. loss of employment) related to such a
     change of thrust should be clearly identified and
     options for mitigating those impacts should be
     developed.

2.   If the current objective of providing employment is to
     be maintained, a major regulatory review is
     nevertheless required to simplify and clarify
     regulations. An extensive up-dating of the legislation
     periodically amended only on a piecemeal basis since
     Confederation is also required. The possibility of
     addressing Pacific and Atlantic fisheries which are
     very distinct and different through separate sections
     in the Act should be explored.

3.   Initiatives such as enterprise allocation (currently tried on a limited basis) should be expanded where appropriate since they promote efficiency and involve less regulation.

4.   A joint industry (including tourism representation) - labour resource allocation board (based on the U.S. model) could be established on a "pilot" experimental basis in a coastal region in order to directly involve the private sector in fisheries management. Conservation quotas would continue to be set and enforced by the department.

FISHERIES AND OCEANS: MONITORING, CONTROL AND SURVEILLANCE

(OFFSHORE, COASTAL, INLAND)

Objective

To ensure the conservation and protection of fisheries resources in offshore coastal and inland Canadian fisheries waters.

Authority

Fisheries Act, Coastal Fisheries Protection Act, Territorial Sea and Fishing Zones Act.

Description

This program is essentially focused on enforcement. It ensures compliance by both domestic and foreign fleets with measures designed to assure optimal use of fisheries stock in accordance with requirements for conservation. Inland fisheries enforcement is delegated to five provinces and is federally-administered in the other five and in the two Territories.

Fisheries, a common property resource, involves regulating harvesting through a total allowable catch in order to avoid depletion and promote conservation. Because stocks can be severely depleted through overfishing, the resource is considered to be finite and subject to seasonal restrictions. Enforcement is therefore essential to the maintenance and development of a viable fisheries industry.

Regulating the commercial fisheries involves such regulatory measures as the registration of some 42,000 fishing vessels, the licensing of vessels and fishermen, restrictions on gear and the management of open and closed areas as well as of fishing times. In addition, there are the numerous restrictions on the sport fishery which involves approximately six million anglers (including one million foreign visitors) who spend over $1.7 billion annually on sport fishing. Finally, the regulation of the commercial Indian fishery involves among other objectives, enforcing limits on fishing times and preventing the illegal sale of fish.

The enforcement program therefore involves often technical and complex compliance in a variety of circumstances covering large areas including the 200-mile offshore territorial zone. In addition, the economic incentive to fish illegally has risen dramatically in recent years since one day's illegal catch of certain species far outweighs the current penalty fees. Moreover, convictions on charges laid by Fishery Officers have been difficult to obtain. For example, in the Pacific region, in 1981, 1,014 charges were laid but only 492 convictions were obtained.

Resources   *

($000's)	82/83	83/84	84/85	85/86	86/87	87/88
Person-Years			1,319			
Operating Exp.						
- Salaries			47,527			
- O&M			26,685			
- Other Exp.						
Revenue						
Subsidies						
Capital			26,185			

*   As part of a major internal review, the department is restructuring its activities. The Department states it cannot provide reliable data for 1982-83 since it has changed its coding procedures. Also, final allocations have not been made for 1985-86, thus only aggregate data, adjusted for salaries (four per cent) is shown. Finally, for 1985-88 inclusive, no expenditure breakdowns were provided.

Problem Identification

Both fisheries industry and labour groups agreed on the need for adequate enforcement of laws and regulations aimed at protecting the resource and noted the following concerns:

1.   Enforcement is inadequate in terms of the vital need to protect the resource in order to ensure a viable industry.

2.   There are many competing interests which threaten the resource (e.g. land-based industrial development can damage habitats).

281

3. It is almost impossible to adequately police the 200-mile coastal territorial zones in terms of foreign fishing fleets with extensive technological catch capacity.

4. There is a perception of inconsistency and some arbitrariness in the way certain Fishery Officers carry out enforcement duties which includes a perceived bias favouring sportfishermen (and therefore tourism) over commercial fishermen.

The Department notes that the potential benefits for offenders far outweigh the current level of deterrence. In 1982, a Memorandum of Understanding with the RCMP was developed to designate their officers across Canada as Fishery Officers with enforcement powers under the Fisheries Act. The department further indicated that new surveillance technology could improve enforcement on a more cost-effective basis.

Observations

1. Due to the common resource property character of the sector, and the dangers of depletion, enforcement and deterrence measures are crucial elements of a viable fisheries industry.

2. According to the Pearse Task Force Report on the Pacific Fisheries, enforcement efforts and skills are insufficient.

3. While enforcement per se can be viewed as burdensome by some fishermen, most of them, including the industry appear to want assurance of tough policing and surveillance. A quota system only enjoys the confidence of fishermen and the industry when all are assured that violators do not profit from breaking the rules.

Options

The Study Team recommends to the Task Force that the government consider the following:

1. Combine the enforcement functions of the Department in the salt-water fishery with Coast Guard and any other federal marine resources offshore.

2. As an alternative to the above, adopt more of the major recommendations on enforcement proposed by the Pearse Report which could be equally applied to the Atlantic fisheries. Pearse points to the importance of setting examples for the purpose of deterrence. For example, the Report points out that although the Act empowers the Fishery Officer to seize vessels and equipment when laying a charge, in the majority of cases only the less valuable illegally-caught fish are seized. It would be preferable to make legislative provisions to enable the courts to virtually remove the offender's ability to pursue his livelihood for a certain period of time. Also, penalty fees should be substantially raised.

FISHERIES PRICES SUPPORT BOARD - F&O 1

Objective

To promote the financial stability and independence of fishermen and permit processors to continue operations by reducing the adverse effects of wide fluctuations in market prices.

Authority

Fisheries Prices Support Act

Description

Reporting to the Minister of Fisheries and Oceans, the Board's primary functions are essentially reactive in that it generally initiates action where needed to compensate for sudden price declines or other adverse events beyond the control of the industry. In this regard, it provides deficiency payments and inventory financing, thus ensuring the stability of earnings for the harvesting and processing sectors. In prescribing prices the Act stipulates that "the Board shall endeavour to secure a fair relationship between the returns from fisheries and those from other occupations" (S.9(2).

While the Board's main function is that of stabilizing prices and returns, it also purchases fishery products for which there are no buyers or which are stored for prolonged periods of time for purposes of resale to international food aid programs. For example this can involve resale to the Canadian International Development Agency to help meet its food fish requirements, a transaction which often results in cost-recovery for the Board.

284

Resources

($000's)	82/83	83/84	84/85	85/86	86/87	87/88
Person-Years	3	3	3	3	3	3
Operating Exp.						
– Salaries	107	126	131	131	131	131
– O&M	43	27	20	26	26	26
– Other Exp.						
Revenue						
Subsidies	91	3,100	3,235	*	*	*
Capital						

* Figures for subsequent years are not available as monies are provided when market fluctuations occur, on a case-by-case basis.

Problem Identification

The following issues were raised by the groups contacted:

1. While the function of the Board is generally viewed to be essential, its interventions should be restricted to times of severe hardship experienced by the industry as a whole. There is a view that the Board has unused potential, but that until now it has been largely reactive to sectoral issues in the industry, tending to favour certain specific interests over others.

2. One industry spokesperson suggested that the Board should be replaced with an agency akin to a merchant bank in order to reduce political involvement and ensure a cash flow (under stipulated conditions) to meet the urgent needs of industry as they arise. It was noted that industry experiences great difficulties in acquiring loans from chartered banks.

3. Another industry spokesperson at the national level emphasized the need to maintain the Board or a similar function as a much-needed "safety net" for the industry which, at times, is quite vulnerable. The spokesperson did not alter this position when asked whether a "safety net" would still be needed if the government were to decide to deregulate certain aspects of the fishery in order to promote greater efficiency and therefore greater returns in the industry.

In the Department's view this program is not regulatory, but rather, one of subsidization. It was nevertheless reviewed since it is an element of government intervention in the fisheries which should not be separated from the broader regulatory framework.

Observations

1. It appears there are two distinct views about what the Board's functions ought to be: one is that it should respond only to system-wide needs in the industry; the other is that it should meet the individual financing needs in industry, possibly as an independent merchant bank-like structure.

2. Certainly, the Board's operations could be more effective if it did not function on individual case-by-case policy decisions. Any considerations of a changed function of the Board or its elimination should be seen in relation to problems in the fisheries as a whole. Even if legislative and regulatory changes were to be undertaken in support of greater efficiency in the industry, it may well be that some form of cash flow assistance, possibly on a facilitated loan basis may be required. On the other hand, the review of the industry's experience, if and when such changes were to occur, could very well conclude that such assistance would no longer be appropriate.

Options

The Study Team recommends to the Task Force that the government consider the following:

1. Develop a clearer definition of the Board's objectives, defining in statute the parameters of its scope in order to better focus on systemic problems with respect to broad market fluctuations. The legislation which came into force in 1947 probably should be updated in any case, taking into account the approaches used to address unpredictable market fluctuations by other countries with an important fisheries industry.

2. Maintain the program until and if the government decides to make fundamental changes in the regulatory framework governing the fisheries. If such changes were to occur, further consultations with industry and employee groups may be appropriate prior to considering elimination or a redesigned program.

3. Transfer the function to a consolidated food
   commodities prices and incomes stabilization board
   reporting to the Minister of Finance.

NATIONAL FISH INSPECTION - F&O 7

Objective

To ensure that fish and fish products intended for domestic consumption (including imports) and for export meet Canadian and/or importing countries' standards for grade, handling, identity, processing, quality and safety.

Authority

Fish Inspection Act, Fisheries Act, sections of Food and Drug and Consumer Packaging and Labelling Regulations.

Description

Under this program, fish and fish products are inspected on-board vessels, at unloading sites, in transit and during processing and storage. Federal inspection is required for products traded interprovincially and internationally. Eight of the provinces (Quebec and Manitoba excepted) have complementary fish inspection legislation which is enforced by federal inspectors through agreements with the provinces.

Some 80 per cent of fish and fish products are exported with a value of $1.6 billion in 1983. There are 990 federally-registered fish processing plants and some 42,000 federally-registered fishing vessels.

In response to a relatively high rate of refusal and recall due to handling damage and quality problems, a national quality improvement program was initiated in 1980 and is still maintained. Many importing countries require certification on health, quality, identity and labelling specifications. The importance of high standards cannot be overemphasized given the export dominance in this sector.

Resources *

($000's)	82/83	83/84	84/85	85/86	86/87	87/88
Person-Years		454	499			
Operating Exp.						
- Salaries			18,180			
- O&M			4,019			
- Other Exp.						
Revenue						
Subsidies						
Capital			1,970			

* As part of a major internal review, the department is
restructuring its activities. The Department states it
cannot provide reliable data for 1982-83 since it has
changed its coding procedures. Also, final allocations
have not been made for 1985-86, thus only aggregate
data, adjusted for salaries (four per cent) is shown.
Finally, for 1985-88 inclusive, no expenditure
breakdowns were provided.

Problem Identification

The industry and labour groups contacted noted the
following concerns:

1. Industry recognizes the need for inspection,
   particularly with respect to importing countries'
   requirements, however, it feels that a hard-nosed
   approach is required for violators.

2. Several export markets require Health and Welfare
   inspection approval in addition to fisheries
   inspection; this indicates a certain lack of confidence
   in fisheries' inspection level of service.

3. While some do not envisage possibilities of
   self-regulation in inspection, others feel that quality
   should increasingly be controlled by industry and
   market forces.

The Department notes it consults with industry about
new standards and provides the opportunity to challenge
original inspection decisions through facilitating
re-inspection.

Observations

1. In the Team's view, the requirement of certain importing countries to have national certification (at times with Health and Welfare concurrence) of fisheries products makes it difficult to envisage self-regulation or even the transfer of fish inspection responsibilities to the provinces.

2. The industry, given its current instability and inefficiency in many areas, will be highly resistant to any cost-recovery initiative in inspection. However, should the government adopt economic viability as the first priority in fisheries, industry would be in a better position to pay for this "value-added" service.

3. The Pearse Report on the Pacific Fisheries pointed to the use of quality controls to restrict export trade. For example, in the interest of protecting jobs in local processing, certain policies restrict the export of frozen salmon. As the overview paper on the fisheries points out, there is a need to decide on conflicting socio-economic regulatory objectives; the current regulatory thrust to maintain jobs in the sector should be evaluated in terms of potentially higher returns from exports if market forces were increasingly allowed to operate.

Options

The Study Team recommends to the Task Force that the government consider the following:

1. Under a single food inspection agency, inspection powers and standards in the fisheries sector should not be different from those applying to the meat sector, for example. The current instability of the fisheries industry, however, would make it difficult to apply cost-recovery. Should the overall fisheries regulatory framework be reviewed in terms of promoting efficiency (as noted in the overview) cost-recovery would be feasible since the industry could bear the costs.

2. The current duplication of inspection involving Health and Welfare should be eliminated, possibly by transferring fish inspection responsibilities and resources to that department. Frequency of inspection norms should

be further developed according to past company compliance records.

3. Given that eight provinces have fish inspection legislation, the possibility of developing national handling, health/safety and for fish products processing standards should be explored in order to avoid the rather cumbersome and unclear current federal-provincial arrangements.

4. Export opportunities should be enhanced by permitting greater flexibility of response by industry to changing market opportunities (e.g. by opting to export fresh or frozen rather than processed products). Moreover, industry and Canada's international reputation would benefit from the application of stiffer penalties for poor quality and handling.

OVERVIEW

FINANCIAL SECTOR: REDUCED REGULATION NOT DEREGULATION

A. SYNOPSIS AND CONCLUSIONS

This section reviews federal regulatory programs directed to financial institutions - Inspector General of Banks, Department of Insurance, and Canada Deposit Insurance Corporation. Although the Bank of Canada has a regulatory dimension, it was not reviewed for the purposes of this study.

The failures of a number of federally and provincially regulated trust and insurance companies in recent years point to the inadequacy of the regulatory system for financial institutions in Canada. At the same time there are mounting international and domestic pressures to permit financial institutions a broader range of corporate powers. The balkanization of financial industry regulatory authority among the federal and provincial governments and the outdated nature of some federal regulatory legislation makes reform in this area of utmost importance.

The government's discussion paper on financial industry regulatory reform indicates that a high priority is being accorded to this critical area. Canada's economic future will be greatly affected by the decisions emerging from this overdue process. Rather than debating the issues now in the public domain, the Team suggests that:

1) Legislative amendments confirming decisions arising out of the process be tabled - uncertainty arising from the process of evaluation should be kept to the minimum.
2) The new policy should mitigate regulatory "overburden" where appropriate and possible.
3) The new policy should encourage a major diminution of federal-provincial regulatory "balkanization" - Canada is too small a market to allow the regulatory smorgasbord related to financial institutions that now prevails.
4) Urgent priority be given to cleaning up the policies and procedures of the deposit insurance framework.

B.   BACKGROUND

1.   The Principles of Regulation

The financial sector is an extensively supervised and regulated sector of the economy. This stems from its central place in the economy through its role in allocating credit, providing the core of the payments system and its unique position of trust in handling large amounts of funds belonging to the general public.

The prime regulatory rationale is solvency. This reflects concern for small savers whose funds are entrusted to these institutions. It also reflects concern for the stability of the financial system as bankruptcies could shake public confidence, leading to large-scale withdrawals of funds and a breakdown in the payments mechanism. The solvency issue has been reinforced since 1981 by the failure of four property and casualty insurance companies, not to mention the current difficulties afflicting the banking sector.

Self-dealing and conflicts of interest constitute a second rationale for regulation. While they are not problems unique to the financial sector, they are of greater concern than those in the non-financial sector. As intermediaries in the flow of funds from savings to investment, financial institutions influence the allocation of resources in the economy. Additionally, the amount of funds financial institutions borrow from or handle on behalf of the general public, far exceeds the equity investment of their shareholders. It is therefore critical that the financial system function fairly, protect consumers' interest and be seen to function fairly to maintain public trust.

Guarding against the abuses stemming from concentration in financial markets is a third reason for regulation of the financial sector. The latitude for existing firms to engage in non-competitive behaviour would depend on how easy or difficult it is for other firms to begin serving the same market. Thus, competition policy in the financial sector has historically been left to the institutional regulators, i.e. Minister of Finance.

In developing and implementing regulatory policy, government is also aware of the need for "competitive equity", or the fair treatment of different institutional groups. Currently, different institutional groups are subject to different regulations, even for some services that are similar. This has been the source of complaints and has led to demands that government provide a "level playing field" for the different institutional groups.

2.   Regulatory Jurisdictions

The financial sector in Canada is characterized by significant federal/provincial overlap and duplication of regulation. Banks lie exclusively within federal jurisdiction while securities underwriting and credit unions are provincial concerns. Trusts, insurance and pension funds can be either federal or provincial. However, even where federal chartering and regulation is the case, provinces through their fiduciary authority, contract powers and corporate governances may also regulate. There is a lack of uniformity in standards setting, enforcement and compliance among many of the provinces and between the provinces and the Federal Government.

3.   Regulatory Means

Observing standards of prudency is the basis of much of the governmental supervision of all major types of financial institutions. In the case of contractual savings institutions, such as pension funds and life insurers, this has been the only safeguard and is therefore crucially important. Disclosure requirements also play a major role in some supervisory activities as do ownership limitations which are often set in statute (e.g. banks, securities). A guarantee of savers' funds up to a maximum amount is employed by government to promote public trust in the financial system. Insurance protection offered to the saver through the institution should be extended by government only as a privilege in meeting prudent standards. Finally, administrative devices such as erecting a communications barrier between two functions within an institution (Chinese Wall), imposition of prohibition on activities, and redress to civil law are utilized to some extent by supervisory agencies.

The principles for regulating the financial sector are
not at issue. Nor does the Team consider it
appropriate to consider "deregulation" of the financial
industry. However, there is an urgent need for
improved regulation based on four main principles:

a)   more competition
b)   less federal-provincial balkanization
c)   minimum government regulation
d)   maximum industry self-regulation and
     accountability

4.   Pressures for Change

Canadian financial institutions are in the midst of
change. Traditional roles (banking, trusts, insurance,
securities underwriting, co-operative credit societies)
are being broken down by a variety of new
developments. Such trends and pressures include:

-    shifting markets which have caused institutions to
     be wary of narrow specialization and seek wider
     portfolio powers;

-    application of new technology which has altered
     the distribution of financial services and
     breaks down jurisdictional boundaries;

-    antiquated legislation and/or uneven legislative
     and regulatory change among each of the
     traditional financial "pillars";

-    the influence of changes in other countries (due
     to shifting markets and technology application)
     particularly the U.S., U.K., Australia, Japan;

-    the growing internationalization of financial
     services;

-    the rise of the conglomerate form of organization
     and ownership; and

-    recent failures of Canadian non-bank financial
     institutions.

The regulatory system is under pressure to adapt. The
exact exposure of institutions to risk in the modern
financial system is difficult to assess. The size of

outstanding obligations has increased and debtors and financial institutions tend to be more highly leveraged (i.e. little equity relative to assets). Financing arrangements have become increasingly complex and international in scope.

In response to these pressures, the Federal Government has issued a discussion paper "The Regulation of Canadian Financial Institutions - Proposals for Reform". Cross-ownership of financial institutions through a holding company framework is the major thrust. Individual institutions would be grouped by current classification (banks etc.) and remain subject to their specific acts and regulations. A "ruthless" ban would be placed on self-dealing amongst institutions in the holding company. Additionally, a number of administrative devices would be introduced, notably the Chinese Wall and a consumer protection agency. A private sector Ministerial-initiated task force is also to report on the deposit insurance framework.

The Ontario Government is considering the amendment of its Trust Company Act, has streamlined its regulatory bodies and awaits recommendations of a Task Force on financial institution reform. The Ontario Securities Commission is currently deciding on regulation and ownership of securities and underwriting firms within its jurisdiction. Quebec unilaterally amended its Insurance Act in 1984, and is in the process of amending its Trust Companies Act which together will allow direct integration of most non-bank activities without pursuing a corporate holding company framework.

CANADA DEPOSIT INSURANCE CORPORATION - CDIC

Objective

Ensure public confidence in the financial system. Provide for the benefit of a person having deposits in banks, trust companies and mortgage loan companies, insurance against loss of part or all of their deposits to a maximum of $60,000.

Authority

CDIC Act (Schedule "D"), Investment Companies Act, Cooperative Credit Associations Act.

Description

CDIC ensures the safety of the deposits of small investors. Insurance is mandatory for federally chartered banks, trust companies and mortgage loan companies. Provincially incorporated companies submit applications for coverage. Quebec has its own plan of deposit insurance applicable to non-federal deposit-taking institutions active in that province.

Deposit insurance applies to demand deposits and term deposits maturing in five years or less to a total of $60,000 per person (raised from $20,000 effective January 4, 1983). Deposits in foreign currency, deposits not payable in Canada and debt instruments payable to bearer are not covered. CDIC also functions as a lender of last resort to make loans to member institutions for liquidity purposes when such institutions do not have access to their normal sources of liquidity. The latter function also includes advances to Canadian controlled Sales Finance Companies, cooperative credit societies and to provincial credit union stabilization funds.

The Corporation relies on financial standards established by federal and provincial supervisory services. The monitoring of the financial position of member institutions is through financial reporting and reports of supervisory agencies (Department of Insurance, Inspector General of Banks) or contracted out as appropriate. Sanctions include termination or cancellation of deposit insurance or the placement of an insolvent company into liquidation.

The Corporation's lean staff functions primarily in financial administration of the Insurance Fund. The Board consists of a Chairman appointed by the Governor in Council, and officers of the Bank of Canada, Inspector General of Banks, Departments of Insurance and Finance. Activities are centralized in Ottawa.

The Corporation is charged with the obligation of operating on a self-sufficient basis. It is funded through member institutions by a flat-rate premium structure which is assessed against the insured deposits on hand as at April 30 each year. Presently, it is in a deficit position due to eight institutional failures since 1981.

Resources

($000's)	82	83	84
Person-Years	15	15	
Operating Exp.	981	53,580	
- Salaries	195	262	
- Interest on Borrowings	82	50,828	
- Inspection fees	514	1,683	
Revenue	25,903	78,528	
Provision for Loss	–	(650,000)	
Accumulated Net Earnings (Deficit) at year end	71,236	(565,096)	

NOTE: 1984 not available

Problem Identification

1. The program does not guard against the moral hazards of insurance, and the burden of its costs are placed on well managed financial institutions and the taxpayer.

2. "Winding-down" agreements, liquidity funding to faltering institutions, and permitted mergers effectively offer 100 per cent protection to depositors. This process artificially shelters institutions from the discipline of the marketplace and removes the incentive to avoid excessively risky behaviour.

3. Delegation of standards, supervisory and inspection powers to federal and provincial authorities raises concern for ultimate accountability. This is

aggravated by the lack of uniformity in standards setting, inspection and compliance enforcement among the governments. No minimum standards, reporting or compliance requirements exist. The majority of the institutional failures for which the program has accepted liability lie within provincial jurisdiction.

4. Relevancy is questioned in light of evolving trends in financial markets (e.g. availability of deposit substitutes, size of coverage, increased risks and supervisory capabilities due to integration, technology's impact on third party liability, etc.)

5. Reduction of the accumulated deficit.

Observations

1. CDIC is operated as a special government fund with a draw on the CRF to $1.5 billion. The corporation does not function as an insurance company (policy, standards, limitations on the policy-holder relative to risk, premium recoveries). The current deficit is reported to be somewhere between $650 million and $1.6 billion.

2. In the Study Team's view, to date the insurance program has failed to operate as an integral part of the regulatory framework.

3. A private sector committee appointed by the Minister of State for Finance is currently examining the present system of deposit insurance. The committee is expected to report in the near future and will likely recommend changes to the current legislation.

Options

The Study Team recommends to the Task Force that the government consider the following:

1. Consider as soon as it becomes available the private sector report on this program.

2. It is not desirable to maintain the status quo. Insurance must be incorporated into the regulatory framework as a privilege for maintaining established standards. The following are some suggestions:

a) Restructure and operate the corporation as an
    insurance company. Insurance protection could
    also include plans for insurance industry policy
    holders, securities underwriting, etc.

b) Roll the insurance operations into a single
    regulator of financial institutions. It would be
    an independent body similar in status to the Bank
    of Canada, with a Board comprised of industry
    representatives on fixed term and rotation.
    Provinces could contract out regulation,
    insurance, enforcement and compliance to the
    federal corporation or go it alone accepting the
    liability.

DEPARTMENT OF INSURANCE - DI 1

Objective

To ensure the confidence of the public in non-bank financial institutions and federally registered pension plans. Protect to the greatest extent possible the depositing and insuring public from failures of financial institutions.

Authority

Department of Insurance, Canadian and British Insurance Companies Act, Foreign Insurance Companies Act, Loan Companies Act, Trust Companies Act, Co-operative Credit Associations Act, Investment Companies Act, Pension Benefits Standards Act, (Under the Canada Deposit Insurance Corporations Act, the Superintendent of Insurance is required to conduct examinations on behalf of CDIC of trust companies and loan companies to which the Trust Companies Act or the Loan Companies Act applies).

Description

The stability of the financial system in Canada is of utmost importance to the socio-economic well-being of the country. The Department directly supervises all federally registered or licensed financial institutions (other than banks) and pension plans. Additionally, under agreement with certain provinces or the Canada Deposit Insurance Corporation, provincial registered financial institutions and pension plans are supervised. In total, 614 institutions (insurance, trusts, investment companies, some credit unions, fraternal benefit societies) and 655 pension plans are supervised.

The process of supervision varies according to the Acts governing specific financial functions. This includes certification of registry and licensing, direct examination (inspection) of books and records at the head offices of supervised institutions, compliance monitoring of standards established for capital adequacy, conflicts of interest, directors activities, investment activity, funding of pension plans, foreign ownership and mergers and amalgamations. The Superintendent may take control of the assets of a company upon determining the impropriety of management or insolvency.

The industry is assessed annually for the costs of administering part of the program that applies to it. The regulation-making and financial analysis is done in Ottawa while on-site examinations are undertaken through five district offices situated in centres where a significant number of financial institutions are located.

There is a large degree of federal-provincial overlap and duplication. Generally, the provinces have left the solvency regulation of federal companies to the Department but exercise supervision over these same companies in matters falling within exclusive provincial jurisdiction, such as contracts, licensing of agents, and fiduciary activities. Additionally, provinces directly supervise provincially chartered or licensed financial institutions. Pension plans are often subjected simultaneously to federal and provincial pension legislation.

Resources

($000's)	82/83	83/84	84/85	85/86	86/87	87/88
Person-Years	204	208	226	226	226	226
Operating Exp.						
- Salaries	7,671	8,860	9,589	10,132	10,132	10,132
- O&M	5,550	4,375	3,154	3,358	2,343	2,343
- Other Exp.	2	2	1	1	1	1
Revenue	10,829	13,490	12,998	12,831	12,430	11,430
Subsidies	-	-	-	-	-	-
Capital	29	213	21	15	15	16

Problem Identification

1. Federal-provincial entanglement. The lack of uniformity in standards, enforcement and compliance, and regulatory approaches among governments creates uncertainty, increases costs and generally leads to a "balkanization" of financial markets.

2. The Department of Insurance is overburdened and subject to enabling legislation which with respect to standards, enforcement and compliance is antiquated and fragmented where similar financial functions are performed.

3. Scope of surveillance at the federal level is too broad to allow for timely inspection of all institutions. Supervisory framework should be realigned in order to concentrate more effort on detection and resolution of

high risk problems before there are major ramifications to the financial community.

4. Separation of policy making, administration and regulation, and insurance protection at the federal level often results in a lack of clear focus on pressing financial issues, inconsistency in legislation and regulations, and lengthy response times. (Note – Federal Government participants include Department of Finance, Department of Insurance, Inspector General of Banks, Bank of Canada, Canada Deposit Insurance Corporation and Consumer and Corporate Affairs.)

5. Insurance, trust and pension legislation requires updating with specific references to asset and liability powers, corporate governances and supervisory activities.

Observations

1. The Department maintains close liaison with the provinces to bring uniformity to laws and standards governing financial institutions and pension plans. The more critical problem is the lack of uniformity in the application of standards and enforcement of sanctions among the governments.

2. The legislation under which financial institutions are regulated is currently subject to review at the federal level and in some provinces to reflect the new environment and the trend towards diversification. However, there is a diversity of approaches which could lead to a further tiering or conflict of financial regulation and inconsistency in the operations of financial institutions.

3. The Study Team found that the quality of federal regulation is considered good and is much superior (and preferred) by many to that of the provinces.

4. In the Study Team's view, the size and complexity of financial markets requires a strong federal presence and the establishment of a common safety net.

Options

The Study Team recommends to the Task Force that the government consider the following:

1. Redefine federal-provincial regulatory jurisdiction with respect to financial institutions.

2. Institute self-regulation by the industry in a manner similar to the U.K.

3. Streamline the surveillance function by shifting to oversight supervision of external audits combined with more detailed and timely (quarterly) reporting of operations. Prudent standards could be set and employed quarterly as a trigger mechanism for detailed and specific action.

4. Combine policy, administration, enforcement and compliance, and insurance protection into a single, independent body similar in status to the Bank of Canada.

5. Sunset all financial institution legislation every 10 years.

INSPECTOR GENERAL OF BANKS - FC 2

Objective

To ensure the confidence of the public in Canada and abroad, in the Canadian Banking System. Protect to the greatest extent possible depositors and shareholders from failures of chartered banks.

Authority

Bank Act (Part IX), Quebec Savings Banks Act (Section 56).

Description

The Office of the Inspector General of Banks was established in the Bank Act of 1924 following the failure of the Home Bank in 1923. It is responsible to the Minister of Finance but is administered independently of other Finance programs.

The Office is accountable for incorporation and licensing of domestic and foreign bank subsidiaries/ representative offices, standards and guidelines for prudent operating practices, and compliance auditing. Regulations are promulgated pursuant to the Acts and include: capital and liquidity adequacy evaluation and guidance; asset and earnings quality assessment; disclosure for consumer protection, shareholder information and supervisory purposes; and the prescribing of remedial action to correct unsatisfactory conditions. Compliance auditing consists of management oversight of banks' internal and external auditors and mandated quarterly detailed operational reports. Operational control of the banking organization is the ultimate sanction. The Office also responds to ad hoc public enquiries regarding banking matters and provides policy advice with respect to banks and the financial system in general.

Supervision encompasses 72 banks and 55 representative offices of foreign banks. Person years expended total 33. It is undertaken directly from a centralized location (Ottawa) with annual or more frequent on-site audit of each bank. Cost recovery is provided under the Bank Act from all banks operating in Canada. Recoveries are credited to the Consolidate Revenue Fund in the subsequent fiscal year and are not available for use by the program.

Constitutionally banks and banking are federal matters. However, provincial legislation impinges upon banks through their jurisdiction over contracts and securities law.

Resources

($000's)	82/83	83/84	84/85	85/86	86/87	87/88
Person-Years	26	33	35	42	42	42
Operating Exp.						
- Salaries	965	1,315	1,436	1,815	1,815	1,815
- O&M	154	179	234	250	250	250
- Other Exp.	126	171	178	254	254	254
Revenue	-	-	-	-	-	-
Subsidies						
Capital	-	-	-	-	-	-

Problem Identification

The operations of the banking regulation and supervision program is considered by the private sector to be as effective as possible within the existing resource and regulatory policy constraints. However, both private and public sector experts acknowledge the need for significant reforms of all aspects of financial regulation.

Observation

1. Programs of this nature are accepted world-wide as the most appropriate way of dealing with the special place of banks in a national economy.

2. The present form of supervision (management audit and moral suasion) is considered to be a reasonable form of government intervention which presents firms with the greatest discretion possible over their portfolio. Canada is relatively unencumbered from detailed banking/financial regulations as compared with the U.S.

3. Entry requirements are seen by some as a barrier which perpetuates elements of protection. However, the control of entry seeks to ensure to the greatest extent possible that only those applicants possessing the capital, expertise and management resources necessary to long-term success are admitted.

4. In the Study Team's view, the question of whether banks should be permitted to fail or be propped-up by tax

dollars is not related to the functioning of this program but is a broader government policy issue.

5. The program as presently constituted and operational could require radical change depending upon the Government's course of action with respect to financial services integration. Some new approaches could result in a greater reliance on detailed inspection, less moral suasion, the adoption of detailed regulatory guidelines and appeal processes.

Options

The Study Team recommends to the Task Force that the government consider the concept of a single financial institution regulatory body with specific and expanded powers as the response to financial integration and solvency-threatening situations are clarified. With respect to the latter, a strengthening of the Inspector General's legal authority may be required.

INTEREST ACT - FC 901

Objective

To make transparent to the borrowing public, interest charges, fines and general payment conditions of all loans, and provide for interest on judgement debt as applied to certain provinces.

Authority

Interest Act

Description

There are no regulations to the current Interest Act. The Act is self-enforcing through direct legal action by affected parties.

Amendments to the Interest Act were tabled in the last Parliament but died on the Order Paper. The Amendments focussed on the right of individuals to prepay mortgages without undue penalty, imposed ceilings on prepayment charges, standardized calculation of prepayment and generally improved disclosure of terms and conditions of borrowing. The self-enforcing nature of the current Act was to be retained. Regulations, prepared jointly by the Departments of Finance and Consumer and Corporate Affairs, would establish a formula to standardize calculation of interest prepayment, explain use of the formula, define financial terms and provide rules of disclosure.

Provincial governments have similar but not identical powers exercised through their contract and fiduciary authority, and financial institutions chartering and regulation.

Resource

No resources allocated.

Problem Identification

The regulatory program receives a "no problem" classification. However, the Study Team observed repeated concern about the possible introduction of Amendments. These focused upon:

1. Federal/provincial entanglement - lack of uniformity across 11 governments with respect to credit-granting rules and cost of borrowing disclosure;

2. Definitions, rules, calculations promulgated in regulation as opposed to statutory inclusion; and

3. Provincial concern for the undermining of their authority by regulations promulgated subject to a Federal Act.

Observations

1. In the Team's view, all governments should cooperate to ensure consistent credit-granting and disclosure rules. Alberta has just issued a new draft Credit Transaction Act which has acknowledged the industry's concern and is patterned on the federal Bank Act disclosure regulations. This could serve as a model for federal/provincial/industry harmonization.

2. Should amendments be introduced, the Finance Department is considering the introduction of statutorily defined financial terms and calculation formulas;

3. The financial system in Canada is subject to a high degree of federal/provincial overlap and duplication. In this case, jurisdiction over "interest" is a federal matter but "contracts" is considered to be provincial. While it is laudable to "harmonize" activities, the present blurring of institutional boundaries and the trend towards internationalization suggests a rethink of the jurisdictional bases for financial institution regulation in Canada.

Option

The Study Team recommends to the Task Force that the government consider amending the present Act with due consideration for consistent credit granting and disclosure rules presented in statutory frameworks.

OVERVIEW

HEALTH AND WELFARE: REGULATORY DEMANDS EXCEEDING REGULATORY RESOURCES

Social regulation affecting human health and safety is the main focus of the programs reviewed in this Department. The principal objective is risk-reduction through a variety of regulatory methods (e.g. product inspection, analysis, recall). Traditionally, governments err on the side of caution in this regulatory area where the consumer feels personally vulnerable and has articulated demands for protection.

The programs reviewed fall into two categories:

1.   mandatory health services (HWC 17, 18, 22) provided as part of broader regulatory objectives (e.g. civil aviation medicine as part of safe air transport); and

2.   controls (HWC 100, 101, 102) related to the potential health hazards in basic goods such as foods and drugs and in the environment (e.g. drinking water). Major problems were identified in this category.

The following issues were identified by the Study Team in the regulation of food, drugs and environmental factors affecting human health:

1.   There is a serious backlog/delay problem, particularly in drug and medical devices control activities which is costly to industry. In part, this is due to more stringent Canadian standards than those applied in other jurisdictions (e.g. chronic toxicity testing requirement in the U.K. takes six months, in the U.S. 12 and in Canada 18).

2.   In the case of drugs, HWC does not sufficiently recognize the validity of results (when available) from foreign regulatory agencies (e.g. U.S. Food and Drug Administration), maintaining that medical practices and Canadian health characteristics are sufficiently different to warrant full domestic

assessment. (The Thalidomide issue is often raised as an example of how Canadian assessment proved to be more effective than that of the U.S. and the U.K.). Moreover, it investigates testing results obtained from Canadian clinical experts (about $100 million a year is spent on Canadian R & D) rather than ensuring the validity of results at the outset of testing (e.g. through certification or "bonding" of testing experts and greater clarity in setting requirements). The overall effect is perceived waste and delay.

3. With respect to regulating food, industry currently has to deal with four departments: HWC, AGR, F&O and CCA. The single food inspection agency concept is appealing to some, while others have doubts about its feasibility or desirability. In addition, HWC develops new regulatory measures in areas which are considered low-risk (e.g. labelling requirements) and does not sufficiently address the potential for greater self-regulation in these areas. There are concerns that such new initiatives would aggravate the backlog problem.

4. With respect to environmental hazards, there are indications (from a recent evaluation) that there is a problem of inadequacy where potentially high risks are involved. For example, with its current resources, HWC is not able to sufficiently assess drinking water in populated regions.

5. The stringency of certain regulations place some industries, particularly in the food sector, at a disadvantage with respect to competitive imports.

CIVIL AVIATION MEDICINE - HWC 17

Objective

To provide medical assistance and advice to Department of Transport in setting standards for civil aviation personnel; to advise on medical and human factors of aviation safety; to support government and the aviation industry with relevant civil aviation medicine research and development in Canada.

Authority

Aeronautics Act, International Civil Aviation Organization Standards and Recommended Practices Annex 1 to the Chicago Convention, 1944, National Health and Welfare Act Order in Council PC 4515,1946.

Description

As part of legislated requirements and international agreements, the program oversees the mandatory medical examinations of civil aviation personnel. In 1983, there were 81,602 civil aviation licenses and permits requiring medical examinations under the program's responsibility. Actual examinations are conducted by Canadian physicians designated by the Department and fees are paid by those examined since the service is not covered by Medicare. Designated physicians are those who, through seminars and information provided by the Department, are specialized in civil aviation medicine. Their findings are reviewed by the Department which further reviews any cases which point to the need for more detailed examination.

Under the program, mandatory basic aeromedical training is provided to pilots as part of their overall training in response to the Dubin Commission on Aviation Safety's recommendation in this regard. The program also provides advice to the recently-established Aviation Safety Board and conducts research in civil aviation medicine. In fact, the program's medical officials are the repository of this medical specialization in the country.

Resources

($000's)	82/83	83/84	84/85	85/86 *	86/87 *	87/88 *
Person-Years	48	48	48	457	476	476
Operating Exp.	2,210	2,439	2,494	22,042	22,142	22,142
– Salaries	–	–	–	16,484	16,614	16,614
– O&M	–	–	–	3,152	3,205	3,205
– Other Exp.	–	–		2,405	2,323	2,323
Revenue	–	–	–	–	–	–
Subsidies	–	–	–	–	–	–
Capital	271	75	421	1,082	1,204	1,108

* Until 1984-85 this activity corresponded exactly to
  Civil Aviation Medicine. Starting in 1985-86, a new
  structure resulted in this activity being part of a
  broader activity called "Health Assessment and Advisory
  Services" under the 1985-86 Fall Update approved
  reference levels.

Problem Identification

No problems from the regulatory point of view have been
identified. An interdepartmental Task Force (with Transport
and the Canadian Aviation Safety Board) is currently
reviewing medical services requirements and it will be
making recommendations to the government in the coming
months.

Observations

1. With 48 person-years, it appears this program achieves
   its objectives efficiently. Together with the
   Department of Transport, it is establishing a
   computerized medical screening system which should
   enhance and expedite services to clients, including
   industry. The current program should probably be
   maintained, pending the findings of the
   interdepartmental Task Force.

Options

Nil

QUARANTINE - HWC 18

Objective

To promote the health of Canadians through the prevention of the importation of diseases into Canada in accordance with national and international requirements.

Authority

Quarantine Act, International Health Regulations (World Health Organization), Potable Water Regulations for common carriers.

Description

The function is to examine, inspect and apply quarantine measures where required, with respect to international aircrafts, foreign vessels and international passengers (including Canadians re-entering Canada from abroad); and apply mandatory immunization where necessary.

Through a formal arrangement with Customs and Excise, customs officers provide primary inspection and health officials usually get involved only where documents are not valid. Flight kitchens and potable water supplies in carriers (including interprovincial aircraft, trains and buses) are examined as required.

Resource

($000's)	82/83	83/84	84/85	85/86	86/87	87/88
Person-Years	9	9	9	457*	476	476
Operating Exp.	1,719	1,966	2,020	22,042	22,142	22,142
- Salaries	-	-	-	16,484	16,614	16,614
- O&M	-	-	-	3,152	3,205	3,205
- Other Exp.	-	-	-	2,406	2,323	2,323
Revenue	-	-	-	-	-	-
Subsidies	-	-	-	-	-	-
Capital	9	-	9	1,082	1,204	1,108

* Starting in 1985-86 a new structure resulted in this activity being part of broader activity called "Health Assessment and Advisory Services." 1985-86 Fall Update approved reference levels.

Problem Identification

No problems from a regulatory point of view have been identified. The Department notes that cost-recovery for inspection services is not possible since International Health Regulations under the World Health Organization stipulate that free services be provided.

Observations

1. The 9.3 person-years and related costs together with those of Customs primary inspection are modest in terms of the preventive health protection provided. However, only random inspections of flight kitchens and vessel facilities are possible with such limited resources.

Options

Nil

BACKGROUND

CIVIL AVIATION MEDICINE AND QUARANTINE

RESOURCE PROFILES

-   From 1985-86 onward, the resources indicate the
    regrouping of medical services programs of which the
    major component - 75 per cent - is dedicated to
    providing medical services to the federal public
    service. In addition, emergency and prosthetic
    services are also included.

-   With one exception, there are no substantive changes in
    the specific programs' projected resources for 1985 to
    1988 inclusive from the data shown for 1984-85 other
    than four per cent inflation increase. The exception
    is Immigration Medicine which is reduced from 51
    person-years in 1984-85 to 28 person-years in 1985-86
    as the final phase of transfer of resources operating
    abroad to External Affairs. In other words, aside from
    this reduction, all columns subsequent to 1984-85
    should be identical to the 1984-85 column with four per
    cent added each year.

IMMIGRATION MEDICAL SERVICES - HWC 22

Objective

To ensure that prospective immigrants, certain categories of visitors, students and workers meet medical requirements/standards with a view to protecting Canadian interests.

Authority

Immigration Act, National Health and Welfare Act.

Description

The Immigration Act requires that prospective immigrants and other categories of persons who enter Canada in order to temporarily reside in the country must pass a medical examination. The health assessment evaluates whether a condition poses: a) a danger to the health of Canadians; b) a potential excessive demand on health or social services; c) the risk of ill individuals not being able to support themselves. Such an examination is conducted in the country of origin by physicians who are approved by the medical officials (who are also physicians) of this Health and Welfare program which in 1983-84 processed nearly 139,000 assessments.

Program delivery is decentralized. Medical assessments for persons examined in all countries except the U.S.A. and Canada (except Quebec) are processed in 14 posts abroad. In those foreign posts, the program's representative also serves as in-house physician to other federal officials. Applicants in Canada, and in the U.S. are largely processed by headquarters in Ottawa. The Quebec region processes applicants (e.g. foreign students) within the province, and liaises with the provincial government which is closely involved in immigration issues.

The program provides the Canadian Employment and Immigration Commission (CEIC) with medical assessments. It also pays for certain medical expenses for persons identified by CEIC as eligible for assistance.

Resources

($000's)	82/83	83/84	84/85	85/86 *	86/87 *	87/88 *
Person-Years	70	47**	51	457	476	476
Operating Exp.	4,206	4,632	6,240	22,042	22,142	22,142
- Salaries	-	-	-	16,484	16,614	16,614
- O&M	-	-	-	3,152	3,205	3,205
- Other Exp.	-	-	-	2,406	2,323	2,323
Revenue	-	-	-	-	-	-
Subsidies	-	-	-	-	-	-
Capital	36	-	142	1,082	1,204	1,108

*   Starting in 1985-86, a new structure resulted in this
    activity being part of a broader activity called
    "Health Assessment and Advisory Services".
    1985-86 Fall Update approved reference levels.

**   23 person-years transferred to External Affairs
    (services abroad).

Problem Identification

No problems were identified from a regulatory point of
view. According to the Department, the current health
criteria for admissibility could be jeopardized if local
foreign physicians in the applicants' countries of origin
were to be given the final say on medical standards. It is
felt that the potential for bias favouring applicants by
foreign physicians is too great in terms of adequately
protecting Canadian interests.

Observations

1.   It would be difficult to remove this Canadian medical
    control from the process of admission or rejection of
    persons entering Canada as immigrants, visitors or
    temporary workers. To limit it to foreign physicians
    alone is to relinquish an important element of entry
    criteria which is a prerogative of the admitting state.

2.   The program has just centralized its assessment
    functions from regional offices in Canada to
    headquarters in Ottawa, except for the Quebec region.
    As a result, person-years were reduced by 5.5. The
    relatively limited remaining resources appear to be
    cost-beneficial in terms of protecting Canadian

interests, particularly in screening persons in terms of their potential financial burden on Canadian health and social services.

Options

Nil

BACKGROUND

IMMIGRATION MEDICAL SERVICES

- Foreign local physicians assessing prospective immigrants are not subject to assessments themselves. The current procedure is that HWC has a roster of some 1,000 designated local foreign physicians who are given guidelines (a handbook) by Canadian medical officers. The only performance leverage used is to remove a foreign physician from the roster if he or she repeatedly submits reports of poor quality which do not meet requirements. On occasion, Canadian officials request further assessment and reporting from a physician if the initial report is suspect.

- It should be noted that often there is a lengthy period of time between a medical assessment of a prospective immigrant and the granting of permission to enter Canada with landed status. That gap, which can be several months, is not covered by medical examination. For example, a person can become seriously ill or permanently handicapped during that time, and could subsequently represent a cost burden on Canadian medical and social services. No mechanism is currently in place to prevent such a situation.

FOOD SAFETY, QUALITY AND NUTRITION - HWC 100

Objective

To ensure a high standard of health for Canadians through the prevention of exposure to controllable health hazards in the food supply.

Authority

Food and Drugs Act (1952-53, amend. 1970, 76), National Health and Welfare Act (advises on Fisheries Act, Canada Agricultural Products Standards Act, Meat Inspection Act, Fish Inspection Act).

Description

Through research, evaluation and inspection, this program regulates the dangers associated with microbiological and chemical hazards in the food supply. It also oversees the nutritional quality of foods, particularly those which are highly processed and special dietary foods (e.g. infant formula). In 1983-84, some 38,000 analyses were carried out, over 2,000 inspections were conducted, 63 food products were recalled, 13 were seized and six prosecutions were undertaken. The program costs $30.9 million to regulate the food and beverage industry with an approximate value of $35 billion.

The Department consults extensively with industry. Private sector advisory committees are regularly used and information letters regarding proposed new or revised regulations are issued to 2,451 recipients who then receive summarized industry responses to departmental initiatives.

Since resources are inadequate to allow all manufacturers and products to be assessed, the program encourages compliance through the development, with industry, of codes of good manufacturing practice, a pre-marketing alternative to after-the-fact food testing which can also provide options for meeting regulatory requirements.

Memoranda of Understanding concerning the regulation of the food supply have been signed with eight provinces and informal arrangements exist with the other two provinces. The purpose of these is to prevent overlap and duplication and facilitate cooperation in inspections, product recalls and investigation of food poisonings. The growing trend toward the export of finished food products to Canada has prompted the program to undertake bilateral discussions with foreign regulatory agencies to communicate Canadian requirements to exporting countries. Under an agreement with Customs, imported foods can be detained until examined.

Resources

($000's)	82/83	83/84	84/85	85/86	86/87	87/88
Person-Years	577	575	589	591	591	591
Operating Exp.	24,099	26,092	27,147	27,925	27,968	27,968
- Salaries	17,569	18,647	20,120	20,589	20,589	20,589
- O&M	3,998	4,697	4,457	4,445	4,488	4,488
- Other Exp.	2,532	2,748	2,570	2,891	2,891	2,891
Revenue	-	-	-	-	-	-
Subsidies*	15	15	55	15	15	15
Capital	2,453	3,727	3,452	2,974	3,113	2,776

*   The program is authorized to make grants and contributions but does not pay subsidies.

Problem Identification

Recognizing the high potential of risk requiring government regulation of the food supply, private sector groups nevertheless expressed a number of concerns regarding the program:

1.   The industry has to deal with three departments: HWC, AGR and CCA. Sometimes compliance with regulations of one department contravene those of another. This leads some groups to favour a single-window food inspection agency while others favour HWC supremacy and have doubts about the single agency concept.

2.   On-shelf inspection should be avoided as being too costly to industry in terms of total investment already made should recall or seizure occur.

3.   The Food and Drugs Act is currently too restrictive (e.g. compositional standards for processed foods such as ketchup which ensure consistent quality); there is a need to modernize/streamline the legislation.

4.   Food processing plants have three levels of inspection (federal, provincial, municipal): then is a need for

Canada-wide national standards to avoid the extra costs of diverse compliance requirements.

5.   There are currently hundreds of imported finished products which do not meet the same packaging and labelling requirements which Canadian producers must meet; this constitutes unfair competition. Greater efforts should be made to stop products not meeting standards at border points of entry.

6.   Industry is opposed to cost-recovery measures regarding inspection.

In the Department's view, the public is highly supportive of this program's protective regulation which also enhances Canada's international reputation for good food products and which reduces illness and related costs.

Observations

1.   Although all agree on the clear need to regulate in this area, there are indications that regulatory review, including legislative updating are required. Greater self-regulation by industry should be promoted in certain types of quality controls (e.g. compositional standards) where no risks or health hazards are involved.

2.   Although from several points of view, a single control agency is appealing, the Team is of the view that further consultation with industry regarding a single food inspection agency will be required, given some of their current misgivings. Also, lead responsibility will have to be assigned, probably to HWC which has the expertise to control the highest-risk function of food regulation.

Options

The Study Team recommends to the Task Force that the government consider the following:

1.   Create a single food inspection agency giving lead responsibility to HWC. Functions would include those currently under Agriculture and Fisheries and Oceans, as well as those deemed still to be required from CCA. The responsibilities would include inspection of

imported processed/packaged food at entry, or at least, before distribution.

2. Update the Food and Drug Act (1952) and regulations (last amendment 1976) with emphasis on maintaining controls in risk/hazard to health areas. Voluntary standards should be developed for current areas which focus on product quality and do not involve risk or health hazard such as compositional or "recipe" requirements for certain products.

3. In order to address overlapping inspections from three levels of government, national standards for handling and processing facilities for foods and beverages could eventually be developed to reduce both public administrative costs and compliance costs for industry, particularly those with operations in more than one province.

DRUG SAFETY, QUALITY AND EFFICIENCY - HWC 101

Objective

Identify and control dangers to health from drugs, cosmetics and veterinary drugs, prevent their improper use or diversion from legal to illicit markets.

Authority

Food and Drugs Act 1952-53, amend. 1970, 76), Narcotic Control Act, Consumer Packaging and Labelling Act, Broadcasting Act.

Description

Through pre-marketing controls and approval of drug advertising/labelling, this program minimizes hazards and promotes the judicious use of drugs, including veterinary drugs and their impact on foods and therefore on human ingestion. Both Canadian and international control requirements, including licensing and import/export permits, govern dangerous drugs, including narcotics. Enforcement through seizure, recalls or prosecutions, is included in the program's objectives. Analyses and advice regarding dangerous drugs are provided to law enforcement agencies.

Regulatory requirements in this program, where the risk factor is high are fairly intricate and involve lengthy and costly procedures for manufacturers which must submit clinical research evidence of safety, efficacy and quality. Even where voluntary compliance is achieved (manufacturer has met all testing and information requirements satisfactorily), manufacturers are subsequently required to meet rigorous criteria (a process which can take considerable time) regarding claims which they can make about their drugs in advertising and labelling. Such claims must be strictly supported by clinical findings.

In 1983-84, 790 notices of compliance were issued for new drugs, 533 inspections were undertaken, 43 drug products were recalled, 75 were seized, 45,000 illicit drug samples were analysed and three prosecutions were undertaken. Regulatory, self-imposed time-limits for certain control procedures have been temporarily suspended by HWC in order to deal with backlogs. Findings of the Eastman Commission of Enquiry on the Pharmaceutical Industry to be made public within the next few months address the backlog issue as

well as concerns in the industry arising from the Patent Act
under Consumer and Corporate Affairs responsibility.

Resources

($000's)	82/83	83/84	84/85	85/86	86/87	87/88
Person-Years	656	656	678	672	673	673
Operating Exp.	32,403	34,795	39,183	39,745	39,767	39,767
- Salaries	19,497	21,476	24,011	24,331	24,330	24,330
- O&M	9,978	10,155	12,185	11,999	12,022	12,022
- Other Exp.	2,928	3,164	2,987	3,415	3,415	3,415
Revenue	5,345	5,339	5,261	5,261	5,261	5,261
Subsidies*	-	-	-	-	-	-
Capital	2,031	2,264	2,347	1,459	2,620	2,717

* The program is authorized to make grants and
   contributions but does not pay subsidies.

Problem Identification

While recognizing the clear need to regulate drugs,
industry groups expressed the following concerns:

1. The backlog in HWC controls and processing of
   submissions is costly to industry; there has been court
   action on grounds of "unreasonable delay". Industry
   notes that similar review and clearance in other
   countries (e.g. U.S., U.K.) take far less time than in
   Canada. (Please refer to the attached background note
   for explanation of controls and concerns.)

2. There are cases of inconsistent application of rules
   e.g. certain companies' products are recalled while the
   same product for other companies are left on the
   market.

3. The costs of proposed new security measures for
   narcotics (e.g. vaults) as part of the legalization of
   heroin will be too high for many retail pharmacists.

4. Industry spends some $100 million annually on Canadian
   clinical research, yet HWC often questions the findings
   of such research.

The Department acknowledges the backlog problem. It
feels it should investigate research findings; in the U.S.
there is a 10 per cent fraud rate in laboratory results. To
avoid delays due to inadequate submission of evidence, HWC

is now requiring that summarized data be certified by company chief executive officers.

Observations

1. The findings of the Eastman Commission which addresses the backlog issue will undoubtedly require further consultation with the industry.

2. In the Team's view, given the backlog situation, certain proposed new initiatives in areas where experience has not indicated serious risks or hazards (e.g. extension of regulation to certain minerals, vitamin, health foods substances) do not make good management sense.

Options

In light of the findings of the Eastman Report, consideration should be given to such measures as:

1. The reintroduction of time-limits in regulations (suspended due to the backlog) to strengthen accountability and provide greater certainty to the industry.

2. Forego new regulatory initiatives in lower risk areas such as "natural" health products.

3. Move towards industry self-regulation in advertising through the development of transitional self-regulatory standards to be administered by private sector organizations (e.g. Pharmaceutical Advisory Board for prescription drugs, Canadian Advertising Board for non-prescription) and monitored or audited by HWC. Stiffer liability measures would be required under full self-regulation.

4. Proposed security measures for narcotics should be reconsidered in light of the performance of current measures governing narcotics in retail pharmaceutical outlets. Retail pharmacists who have to contend with narcotics-related crimes (e.g. hold-ups, robberies) have devised ways acceptable to them to secure narcotics which they currently sell.

BACKGROUND

DRUG SAFETY, QUALITY AND EFFICIENCY

1. The pharmaceutical prescription drug industry in Canada is centred around manufacturers of two types: innovative and generic. Innovative manufacturers (representing some 90 per cent or over $1 billion in annual prescription drug sales) are required to invest extensively in the discovery and development of new products. Generic manufacturers, however, simply copy the discovery developed by innovative firms at much lower cost (through Patent Act provisions which are addressed under CCA programs), and are therefore able to offer lower prices to the consumer.

2. The regulatory burden is more onerous and more costly for the innovative drug industry because of the lengthy (up to eight years) preclinical and clinical research required by Food and Drug Act regulations. The time factor is due to the need to study long-term effects on animals and humans. In terms of industry's investment, such research and testing often follows lengthy and costly in-house chemical research which results in the invention of the new drug. The results of all testing and research as well as proposed labelling are presented to HWC as a new drug submission. After analysis and sometimes lengthy consultations on labelling, the Department issues a Notice of Compliance which clears the new drug for sale in Canada. Labelling and accompanying information/advertisement brochures destined for use by retail pharmacists and physicians often cause delays because HWC must ensure that curative claims are backed by research and testing results and that possible side-effects are clearly, accurately defined.

3. The generic industry, on the other hand, is subject to fewer controls since it does not have to undertake lengthy preclinical and clinical research already undertaken by the inventor firm. Its product is assessed only in terms of content, manufacturing procedures, but is also subjected to labelling and advertising clearance.

4. The innovative drug industry recognizes the need to carefully regulate this potentially high-risk area. Yet, it has concerns about recovering its costs as

329

quickly as possible once research and testing are complete. It feels strongly that the backlog in HWC impinges on its cost-recovery, particularly since it has only a limited time to sell its product before a generic competitor can copy it and sell it at a lower price. Therefore, the innovative industry would like to see changes to the Patent Act to prolong its non-competitive position in the marketplace when a new drug is introduced, and more resources in HWC to speed up the regulatory process.

5. The industry is also of the view that certain regulatory testing requirements are too stringent, for example, chronic toxicity testing are required for new drugs in the U.K. is six months, in the U.S. 12 months and in Canada 18 months. Moreover, the backlog problem is compounded by the deluge, in recent years, of submissions to HWC for the review of generic drugs, which are essentially approved drugs already available on the market. These submissions, the industry claims, currently take up about 40 per cent of total HWC regulatory review time. HWC, on the other hand, maintains that even generic drugs, albeit copies of approved drugs, must nevertheless be assessed since they are chemically composed and manufactured under distinct conditions and, therefore, their safety as well as quality must be carefully evaluated prior to release.

6. The non-prescription (proprietary) drug industry (annual sales of about $1 billion) confirm the complaints of the other industries in the sector with respect to delays due to backlogs in HWC. The focus of its concerns, however, is on controls over labelling and advertisement which are viewed as overly restrictive.

ENVIRONMENTAL QUALITY AND HAZARDS - HWC 102

Objective

To ensure a high standard of health for Canadians through the prevention of exposure to controllable health hazards.

Authority

Radiation Emitting Devices Act, Environmental Contaminants Act, Canada Labour Code (Part IV), Pest Control Products Act, Clean Air Act, Transport of Dangerous Goods Act, Food and Drugs Act.

Description

Through such methods as inspection, enforcement, evaluation of information supplied, this program regulates medical devices (e.g. pacemakers, anaesthetic equipment), radiation emitting devices (e.g. X-ray). It also assesses, monitors and sets standards for exposure to chemical hazards (e.g. pesticides, asbestos). In concert with the provinces, the program also develops, on an ongoing basis, national guidelines for drinking water contaminants which it assesses.

Through assessments of environmental contaminants in the workplace, the program provides advisory services to Labour Canada's Occupational Safety and Health program in accordance with an interdepartmental agreement. In order to coordinate standards and related activities, a federal-provincial Advisory Committee on Environmental and Occupational Health meets and reports to Deputy Ministers of respective jurisdictions. The program also provides Agriculture Canada with assessments on the acceptability and conditions for marketing pesticides.

In 1983-84, regulations for 16 classes of radiation-emitting devices were enforced, corrective action was taken for 146 devices and 103 products were recalled. It is expected that in the current fiscal year, 100 hazardous medical devices will be removed form the market. A national radiation service is provided on a cost-recovery basis to monitor radiation exposure for some 107,000 workers a year.

Resources

($000's)	82/83	83/84	84/85	85/86	86/87	87/88
Person-Years	263	280	274	276	279	281
Operating Exp.	13,055	15,167	16,484	16,144	16,289	16,433
- Salaries	7,924	8,784	9,346	9,688	9,796	9,881
- O&M	4,041	5,088	5,976	5,101	5,113	5,160
- Other Exp.	1,090	1,295	1,162	1,355	1,380	1,392
Revenue	792	858	1,000	1,000	1,000	1,000
Subsidies*	965	807	847	55	55	55
Capital	1,119	1,944	1,693	1,575	1,314	3,710

* The program is authorized to make grants and contributions, for example, to international organizations whose research and findings are used to achieve mandated objectives.

Problem Identification

The national industry group contacted with respect to this program identified backlog as a serious problem. Over 90 per cent of medical devices are imported from the U.S. Devices range from implanted pacemakers to anaesthetic equipment. There are instances where Canadian companies have to wait a year or more for HWC approval of a device, which represents high costs in foregone revenues. It was noted that HWC does not have sufficient resources to regulate medical devices and that one solution to the backlog problem is to issue temporary clearance for sale based on approval by the U.S. federal regulatory agency.

The Department notes that in respect of medical devices, there are sufficient recalls of those which have been approved in the U.S. to warrant full application of regulations. It maintains that there are cases of "dumping" devices which are outdated or which have not performed well in the U.S. into the Canadian market. However, the department also points to recent initiatives to de-regulate certain devices (e.g. dental) which pose only limited risk as a way of redefining priorities and reducing the workload.

Observations

1. An internal departmental evaluation completed in August 1984 notes that in many cases, the program does not have the resources to adequately assess and control hazards under its mandate. For example, the number of chemicals being discovered in drinking water is increasing much faster than the program's ability to

assess them; the frequency of inspection of X-ray facilities was found to be too low in terms of potential risk.

2.   In the control of medical devices, there is no evidence that there is monitoring of the entry of devices (90 per cent imported) which may be of marginal quality or safety and which should probably be rejected at entry point to avoid unnecessary regulatory costs for the importer.

Options

The Study Team recommends to the Task Force that the government consider the following:

1.   The resources allocated to this program appear inadequate. The Team supports the provision of additional resources to it, and also a readjustment of its priorities. The program should expand the regulatory review initiatives it has undertaken and develop better, new ways of promoting voluntary compliance. While its intervention in industry depends on compliance record and not firm size, it should provide better assistance in meeting regulatory requirements to smaller firms.

2.   In addition, with respect to radiation-emitting and medical equipment/devices, there should be greater use of non-government sources in the development of performance and safety standards (e.g. Canadian Standards Association), thereby permitting the program to better focus on rapidly emerging health issues.

OVERVIEW

NORTHERN AFFAIRS REGULATION: A REGULATORY NIGHTMARE

INTRODUCTION

The policy and administrative setting of Northern
Canada has undergone a number of significant changes during
this century, in which periods of consolidation of
responsibility and authority under centralized agencies have
been interrupted by policies for more widely distributed
authority and organization. The period of the 1970's to the
present has been characterized by the latter trend, which
will undoubtedly accelerate through the 1980's with
devolution or transfer of program responsibility and
statutory authority from DIAND to the territorial
governments. Such devolution, accompanied by the settlement
of comprehensive native claims, will have very significant
effects on policies and programs for resource management
and, concomitantly, the complexion of regulation.
Obviously, regulatory reform should be coordinated with the
ongoing devolution of federal programs and responsibilities
to the territorial governments.

This overview briefly describes the policy context for
the management of natural resources in Northern Canada,
highlights the principal issues or problems, and sets out
possible directions for change. While some of the issues
relate mainly to the form and substance of regulation, the
more fundamental issues are those of a political or policy
nature: what objectives are being sought for these
resources, who is accountable for their management, who are
the principal beneficiaries, is an adequate balance and
stability being reached, and are the returns commensurate
with the costs?

AUTHORITY FOR RESOURCE MANAGEMENT IN THE NORTH

The Department of Indian Affairs and Northern
Development (DIAND) was formerly established by statute in
1966, but its roots extend back to Confederation. In
various forms, such as the Department of the Interior
(1873), Department of Mines (1907), Department of Northern
Affairs and Natural Resources (1953) and DIAND, the federal
government has performed in the territories the resource
management functions normally conferred to the provinces
under the constitution. The DIAND Act provides for (a) the
coordination of activities in the NWT and Yukon of federal

departments and agencies; (b) promoting economic and political development in the territories; (c) fostering, through science and technology, knowledge of the North in order to pursue further development. The Act also specifically gives the Minister responsibility for the control, management and administration of all lands in the territories, save certain exceptions. This all-embracing authority is further consolidated by a number of specific acts and regulations for the management of land, water, oil and gas, minerals, and the environment. The most important of these acts and regulations are:

1. Land: Territorial Lands Act and Regulations.

2. Water: Northern Inland Waters Act and Regulations, Arctic Waters Pollution Prevention Act and Regulations.

3. Oil and Gas: Canada Oil and Gas Act and Regulations, Oil and Gas Production and Conservation Act.

4. Minerals: Yukon Quartz Mining Act; Yukon Placer Mining Act; Canada Mining Regulations.

5. Environment: Most of the above plus Fisheries Act, Ocean Dumping Control Act; and the Environmental Assessment and Review Process (EARP) (a policy instrument only).

Most, but not all, of these statutory authorities and subordinate legislation are the responsibility of the Northern Affairs Program (NAP), DIAND. The important exceptions are the Canada Oil and Gas Act (Canada Oil and Gas Lands Administration), the Ocean Dumping Control Act (Environment Canada) and the Fisheries Act (Fisheries and Oceans Canada). In addition, comprehensive native claim settlements, enshrined in new legislation (e.g. the Inuvialuit Settlement Act), confer certain resource management functions on native organizations.

Paralleling the federal and native initiatives have been those of the territorial governments. Both YTG and GNWT have moved to occupy areas that were once the exclusive domain of DIAND. Both governments have established departments of economic development which are expanding into non-renewable as well as renewable resources functions.

Responsibility for socio-economic matters is claimed by the territorial governments, yet federal departments retain major programming (e.g. CEIC, DRIE, Indian and Inuit Affairs Program of DIAND). The territorial governments have moved into the regulatory or quasi-regulatory field as well, e.g. the GNWT's resource development policy and its Development Impact Zone Groups. Both territories control wildlife regulation (but not wildlife habitat). Insofar as socio-economic matters, wildlife management, and the physical environment are interrelated, the federal and territorial division of responsibility is artificial and is leading to increasing tension and inefficiencies in resource management.

In sum, there is a myriad of statutes and regulations for resource management in Northern Canada. However, the reality is that "integrated resource management", "comprehensive land use planning", or "a holistic approach to conservation and development" remain abstract concepts, much discussed and advocated, but difficult if not impossible to practise. This is due to fragmented authority, duplication and overlap, lack of clear policy, and the rather unwieldy character of the federal government and its bureaucracy in dealing with local and regional issues.

CHANGING FEDERAL-TERRITORIAL RELATIONS

Administration of the territories was carried out, until recently, by the federally-appointed Commissioner who presided over fully or partially elected Councils. Political development in the Yukon since the late 1970's has essentially brought responsible government along political party lines, and has relieved the Commissioner of administrative authority. In the case of the NWT, administration was transferred from Ottawa to Yellowknife in 1966; political development subsequently has brought a fully elected legislative assembly, not aligned along political parties as in Yukon, and employing a consensual decision making process, unique in Canada. The Commissioner no longer presides over the legislative assembly but he does retain chairmanship of the Executive Council (cabinet).

While there has been a steady trend toward fostering responsible government and the autonomy of the territorial governments, the federal government has retained tight control over the ownership and control of all natural resources. Administratively, this management function is conducted for the most part by the Northern Affairs Program of DIAND. (The Canada Oil and Gas Lands Administration (COGLA) is an important exception.) Organizationally NAP is decentralized with two regional offices (Yellowknife and Whitehorse) and some 16 district offices. However, NAP's policy functions are decidedly centralized at Headquarters; therefore, regional administrators of the resource management functions have been given little latitude to respond flexibly to changing demands and political environments in the North. This has led to considerable federal-territorial tension and frustration on the part of the territorial governments, federal regional officials and the general public, who feel that rigid control from distant Ottawa is anachronistic.

PRIORITIES AND ISSUES

The longest standing Northern priority has been "development", usually in the sense of "opening up the frontier" and pushing forward with industrial projects - mining, oil and gas. Roads and hydroelectric development have been big-ticket infrastructure items within the Northern Affairs Program in pursuit of or sometimes in anticipation of these developments.

In the early 1970's, the federal government reoriented its priorities to a focus on improving social conditions, enhancing the environment, and stimulating renewable resource development. These were clearly ranked above non-renewable resource development, which was consistent with the prevailing values for a clean environment and better lifestyles. Several major pieces of legislation and policy pursued these priorities: NIWA, AWPPA, Territorial Land Use Regulations, EARP, to note examples. DFO and DOE expanded operations and policies for the North. The Northern Pipeline Agency was created, and exerted a major regulatory presence in the path of the proposed Alaska Highway Gas Pipeline. DIAND expanded significantly, both in the regions and in Headquarters, primarily in the administration of renewable resources and environmental protection. EARP Panels flourished, the Water Boards became proactive, moratoriums on land allocations were proclaimed, special enquiries such as Lysyk and Berger gained national attention, and many environmental interest groups were established. Finally, native organizations were founded to advance the cause of aboriginal claims, many of which were based in land, wildlife and the general environment.

In summary, federal northern policy during the 1970's and up to 1984 rested on these priorities: social development (emphasis on native people), environmental protection, renewable resource development, native claim negotiations and settlement, political development (which stopped well short of devolution or provincial status). Alongside these objectives, but never really acknowledged as a priority, was the continuing thrust of mining, oil and gas exploration and production, and pipeline construction. While deferring to major concerns for socio-economic and environmental matters, DIAND never quite lost sight of its "development" role, although it was often alleged to have. The keynote was "balanced development", a laudable objective, but in reality resulting in dissatisfaction on all sides: developers, environmentalists, natives, the territorial governments, the general public.

There has been a fairly recent, heightened awareness of the need for reducing federal/provincial/territorial tensions and for job creation and economic development generally. Further, there arose a priority on the native claim negotiation process so that settlements could be arrived at and the numerous moratoria on development could be lifted. On the political development front, devolution leading to eventual provincial status, assumed a greater priority. So too does division of the NWT to create a new territory (Nunavut) in the Eastern Arctic. Environmental concerns are not necessarily denigrated, but there is a growing awareness of the need to rationalize environmental and socio-economic programs and regulation, which will involve consolidation and/or devolution. Thus, Northern priorities for the latter half of the 1980's appear to the Team to embrace:

1.   Economic development, with emphasis on reviving the collapsed mining industry of the Yukon, encouraging hydrocarbon developments in the NWT, rebuilding the northern radar line, implementing the economic development agreements. A joint industry-government approach to development appears to be the keynote.

2.   Devolution: land transfers to the Yukon government, forestry to the government of NWT, possibly mineral resource administration in whole or in part, inland waters, non-anadromous fish. There are various combinations in the resource transfer, and may be applied differently in each territory, e.g. a geographic system of block transfers in Yukon, a

functional transfer in NWT (e.g. forestry but not necessarily land).

3. Division of the NWT; creation of Nunavut; amendments to the Yukon Act; changing role of Commissioner to Lieutenant Governor (Yukon).

4. Settlement of remaining native claims - Tungavik Federation of Nunavut (TFN), Council for Yukon Indians (CYI), Dene-Metis of Mackenzie Valley.

5. Regulatory reform, streamlining, fast-tracking of approvals. Involves devolution, may result in establishment of powerful single authority regulatory boards in each territory.

6. Resource revenue sharing: a complicated and problematical issue, bound up in native claim provisions, the policy governing federal contributions to the territorial governments, the tax effort in the North (relatively low), and federal-provincial precedent (e.g. Canada-Nova Scotia agreement). Tentative steps on resource revenue sharing are being taken, i.e. Panarctic's Bent Horn, NWT, project.

7. Tourism and small business: the tourism potential is enormous and in this as well as other economic sectors, growth will depend to a large extent on the small business entrepreneurs.

CONCLUSION

This overview has attempted to describe salient features of the political and policy environment of Northern Canada. Rapid political, economic and social change over the past 15 years has rendered old institutional frameworks and authorities, housed mainly in the Northern Affairs Program, less than adequate to deal with the difficult issues of the 1980's. The private sector, which drives the critically important primary industries of the North, requires stability and clarification of government policy, programming and regulation.

The Minister of Indian Affairs and Northern Development is responsible for a wide range of both horizontal and vertical policies and programming. In the Team's view he is faced with two basic options: (1) reconsolidate power and leverage within DIAND as an integrative federal agency of development, management and regulation; (2) devolve as much as is practical of DIAND's traditional quasi-provincial responsibilities for resources to the territorial governments, phased in an orderly fashion, and reorient the federal department to a role with concerns only for broad national interests in the North. A third option, discussed frequently over the years, has been to disperse DIAND's responsibilities among other federal departments, such as EMR, DOE, DRIE, CEIC, etc. Most analysts, and Northerners, have not been enthusiastic about such proposals, as they are perceived to splinter jurisdiction further, detract from the need for integration and coordination, and politically weaken the North's voice in Ottawa.

NORTHERN LAND USE PLANNING - INAC 58

Objective

To establish and operate a land use planning process in both the Yukon Territory and the Northwest Territories, designed to guide and direct land use and resource planning and management decisions, so as to avoid conflict and to optimize resource usage.

Authority

Territorial Lands Act, DIAND Act, Yukon Planning Act, Inuvialuit Settlement Act

Description

Northern Land Use Planning (NLUP) was initiated by the federal government in 1981; since then DIAND has attempted to reach formal agreements with the governments of each territory to carry out a joint land use planning program. This has been achieved in NWT but not in Yukon. Plans are to be developed on the basis of policies, goals and objectives of the federal and territorial governments in consultation with native organizations, industry, committees, and the general public.

Particular activities include identification of information requirements; preparing technical, policy and position statements on planning areas and activities, coordinating federal government policy, planning and technical activities in support of land use planning, providing financial support to federal departments, territorial governments, and native organizations in support of land use planning.

There is no specific legislation to authorize land use planning, except for the Inuvialuit Settlement Act which provides for it on COPE lands. The Yukon's Planning Act provides for planning on the Commissioner's Lands in Yukon. Thus the Northern Land Use Planning Program (NLUP) is based in policy rather than in regulation.

NLUP is intended as a process funded jointly by the federal and territorial governments, who are to provide staff for planning operations. Although plans would be approved by Ministers of both levels of government, an independent Land Use Planning Commission would be established in each territory to set goals and priorities, to conduct the public process, and to guide planning operations. In this function the Commission would be somewhat analogous to the Water Boards, but would not have quasi-judicial authority.

Implementation of plans is intended to be voluntary in nature. Departments, agencies, etc. would be expected to adjust programs to conform with plans approved in each territory.

Resources

($000's)	82/83	83/84	84/85	85/86	86/87	87/88
Person-Years	--	11	26	23	N/A	N/A
Operating Expenses	--	1,214	1,801	1,752	N/A	N/A
Revenues	--	--	--	--	--	--
Subsidies	--	--	--	--	--	--
Capital	--	13	10	10	N/A	N/A

Problem Identification

As described in other profiles, the North is rife with land use conflicts, controversy over the timing and pace of development, lack of agreement on priorities for development, conservation and protection, controversy over native claims, and a confused, fractious regulatory process. This confused and uncertain situation is in perception and in reality a constraint to economic development and contributes as well to destabilizing traditional lifestyles. The objective of NLUP is to resolve these conflicts in order to facilitate development and orderly resource management.

The main problem with NLUP is that, after four years of discussion, consultation and negotiation, it is still not operational. Part of the reason for this is that NLUP has been bound up in the larger issues of federal-territorial land transfers, devolution, political developments and native claim negotiations. As a result, a formal agreement has only just been reached in NWT, while in Yukon, the situation remains deadlocked.

Judging from industry statements in forums like the Beaufort Sea Environmental Assessment and Review, and the Task Force on Northern Conservation, the private sector supports an effective land use planning process and methods of integrated resource management. However, some opinion opposes NLUP in the belief that it would occasion further delay in development and serve to promote land withdrawals for single-purpose conservation ends.

Regardless of how strong the rationale and support for NLUP, it may have difficulties owing to the lack of a federal statutory base and its reliance on suasion.

Observations

In the Team's view, at the "grass-roots" level, NLUP should reflect local and regional needs and priorities. As these can be determined most effectively by the territorial and local levels of government, the primary responsibility of NLUP should reside with those levels of government. Insofar as the federal minister is party to approval of plans, national planning concerns and priorities are ensured of adequate consideration.

When NLUP is operational, it must be rationalized with EARP and other public processes (eg. Water Board hearings, NEB hearings) for environmental/socio-economic planning and impact assessment. It must also integrate provisions of native claim settlements for planning and environmental assessment. These were among the conclusions and recommendations of the recent Task Force on Northern Conservation Policy (January, 1985), a joint government-industry-interest group enterprise.

Options

The Study Team recommends to the Task Force that the government consider the following:

1.   Terminate NLUP.

2.   Defer attempts to implement NLUP until native claims and devolution questions are resolved.

3.   Continue efforts to establish a territorial-federal cooperative agreement to carry out NLUP; facilitate involvement of native groups.

4.   As devolution proceeds, pass responsibility for land use planning to the territorial government; encourage specific legislative authority (already exists in Yukon).

5.   Introduce federal legislation to give planning authority to DIAND over federal programs and activities in the North.

YUKON AND NORTHWEST TERRITORIES MINING - INAC 79, 180, 225

Objective

To regulate mineral exploration activities in each territory through disposition and recording of rights and claims inspection; to collect mineral royalties; to conduct geological studies and reviews; to regulate mine safety (Yukon); to develop and implement Northern mineral policy.

Authority

INAC 79 (Yukon): Yukon Placer Mining Act; Yukon Quartz Mining Act, Territorial Lands Act (Territorial Coal Regulations, Territorial Quarrying Regulations); Yukon Blasting Ordinance; Mining Safety Ordinance.

INAC 80 (NWT): Territorial Lands Act (Canada Mining Regulations, Territorial Land Use Regulations, Territorial Dredging Regulations, Territorial Quarrying Regulations), Public Lands Grants Act.

INAC 225 (Headquarters): YQMA, CMR, DIAND Act

Description

Although different mining acts apply in the Yukon and NWT, all provide for a system of mineral rights acquisition, recording, maintenance of tenure, and collection of fees and royalties. They also provide for methods of resolving disputes and for sanctions for non-compliance. Yukon mineral rights are conferred and controlled only through Statute (YPMA (1906), and YQMA (1924)). In NWT, the Canada Mining Regulations apply a regulatory regime. All these are responsibilities of DIAND.

Regulatory activities in both territories are integrated with geological surveys, assessment analysis and reporting and mineral resource advice and information to the private sector. These activities are discretionary, not regulatory.

In Yukon, the federal government still carries out regulatory activities on behalf of the Yukon government for mine health and safety and blasting. In NWT, these functions have been transferred to GNWT.

Headquarters activity is oriented toward mineral policy, revisions of legislation, subsidies or financial assistance to mining, economic analysis of mining projects and associated infrastructure; HQ continues to levy and collect fees and royalties under the YQMA and CMR.

Resources

($000's)	82/83	83/84	84/85	85/86	86/87	87/88
Person-Years - Yukon	36	37	36	36	36	36
- NWT	25	26	24	22	22	22
- HQ*	10	9	8	8	8	8
Total	71	72	68	66	66	66
Oper. Exp.- Yukon	1,702	1,754	2,097	2,088	2,088	2,088
- NWT	1,368	1,485	1,596	1,610	1,610	1,610
- HQ*	481	534	663	560	560	560

(* Includes "operations" only; excludes "policy" (7 PY's and O&M 1985/86))

	82/83	83/84	84/85	85/86	86/87	87/88
Revenue - Yukon	941	813	760	765	765	765
- NWT	382	459	575	575	575	575
- HQ	2,073	607	3,300	1,360	N/A	N/A
Subsidies - HQ	107	116	136	49	49	49
Capital - Yukon	100	217	205	231	231	231
- NWT	95	252	205	145	145	145
- HQ						

Problem Identification

The Canada Mining Regulations, applied only in the NWT, are generally satisfactory to the mining industry. Certain minor "housekeeping" or administrative changes are required; these can be routinely handled and warrant no elaboration here.

The two Yukon mining acts are very outdated. The 80-year-old Placer Mining Act essentially reflects nineteenth-century technology, economics and resource management values. The Quartz Mining Act (which governs hardrock mining) has been amended recently to accommodate modern exploration practice. The Yukon mining industry, characterized by many individual prospectors and small mining operators, has long resisted government attempts to replace the old acts with a modern Yukon mining bill that would be geared to provide regulation (thus ministerial discretion) and environmental provisions. The industry is prepared to keep on living with archaic administrative provisions and awkward staking and tenure provisions, rather than exposing the old acts to omnibus amendment and reform.

The pressure to replace the old acts with modern ones comes mainly from government and officials who desire more efficient administration and a greater return from royalties and taxes. Some of the larger mining companies also prefer a revised system, to conform more closely with provincial regimes.

To conclude, in the view of the mining industry, the real regulatory problems to contend with are those that impose burdensome environmental or socio-economic terms and conditions in obtaining a water licence, infrastructure support, or project approval. The industry strongly objects to land withdrawals that would abrogate access to lands for exploration (eg. environmental uses and native claims). These problems are described in other profiles.

Observations

In the view of the Study Team, a priority policy issue that will affect any mining regulatory regime is whether to devolve any of the mineral resource bases of the territories to the territorial governments. Public, private sector and government thinking on this issue is quite divided:

1. In Yukon, the Yukon Chamber of Mines strongly urges devolution and territorial control. Large companies, represented by other associations (e.g.: B.C. & Yukon Chamber of Mines, Mining Association of Canada) are more cautious, and favour retaining federal jurisdiction for the time being. The Yukon Government would like to control mining revenues, and ultimately the resources.

2. In NWT devolution of mineral resources is less a concern than is obtaining an agreement for resource revenue sharing. The large companies that operate there prefer keeping federal jurisdiction, perceiving it to be stable.

3. As in other resources, the transfer of minerals to control of native claimants remains a controversial issue. Such transfers will likely become the norm, in various degrees of ownership, sharing and control.

Options

The Study Team recommends to the Task Force that the government consider the following:

1. Repeal and reform the Yukon mining legislation with new federal legislation.

2. Revise existing legislation only as absolutely necessary pending resolution of broader issues on devolution (this is basically the status quo).

3. Encourage each territorial government to establish and build a modern, competent department of mines and phase transfer of DIAND responsibilities for mining.

YUKON AND NORTHWEST TERRITORIES
LAND, FOREST, AND WATER MANAGEMENT - INAC 201

Objective

To inspect, license or permit the use, conservation and protection of lands, forests and water; to monitor and enforce compliance with guidelines and regulations; to provide adequate information to the Minister and public.

Authority

Land: Territorial Lands Act and Regulations; Land Titles Act; Public Lands Grants Act; Canada Land Surveys Act.

Water: Northern Inland Waters Act and Regulations; Arctic Waters Pollution Prevention Act and Regulations.

Forests: Territorial Lands Act; Territorial Transfer Regulations; Forest Protection Ordinance; Commissioner's Land Ordinance.

General: Department of Indian Affairs and Northern Development Act; Yukon Act; Northwest Territories Act.

Description

This broad program of renewable resource management is carried out by the Northern Affairs Program of DIAND under the Northern Renewable Resources and Environmental Protection Planning Element. This is organized under a headquarters policy branch, the Yukon Region with 10 district offices, and the Northwest Territories Region with six district offices.

The overall function is to develop and implement policies, legislation, regulation, plans and programs for the conservation and utilization of land, forest and water resources. It includes the development and maintenance of an effective, comprehensive environmental management regime and for the development and management of renewable resources in Yukon, NWT and adjacent offshore areas.

While this is wholly a DIAND responsibility, Environment Canada, Fisheries and Oceans, and each of the territorial governments have important responsibilities

350

for environmental/renewable resource management: DOE for environmental habitat protection and conservation; DFO for fish resource management; YTG and GNWT for fish and game regulation. Note also that native claim organizations have assumed or may assume certain such responsibilities under aboriginal claim legislation (e.g. Inuvialuit Settlement Act (COPE - Committee for Original People's Entitlement)).

In addition to land, forest and water management, Land Use Planning, Environmental Assessment and Review, and Environmental Research are carried out. These programs are covered in other regulatory program profiles.

Resources

($000's)	82/83	83/84	84/85	85/86	86/87	87/88
Person-Years	321	355	340	340	340	340
Operating Expenses	32,853	34,330	32,180	31,109	31,109	31,109
Revenues	N/A	382	391	396	N/A	N/A
Subsidies/Grants/ Contributions	N/A	89	82	116	N/A	N/A
Capital	2,568	3,220	3,601	3,601	3,224	3,224

Problem Identification

Since the early 1970's, when several pieces of Northern environmental legislation were passed, DIAND has been criticized frequently by the private sector (particularly the mining and oil and gas industries) as having an environmental bias and levying an oppressive regulatory regime that unduly raises costs and delays decision-making on development projects. The private sector has perceived the Department as devoting the preponderance of its budget to "the environment" as opposed to "development". The attached schematic and the breakdown of NAP's 1985-86 budget illustrate the actual allocations. Numbers, as always, can be misleading; while the renewable resources and environmental protection function comprises the largest budgetary element, a substantial proportion of this is devoted to fire management, renewable resource development, field operations and information services, all in support of the private sector or economic development.

There are other views, perceptions and opinions; environmental groups have long contended that DIAND has a pro-development bias (historically that was indeed its role) and that environmental regulatory programs are inadequate.

Water, land use, habitat protection generally are especially seen to be weakly protected.

Finally, native groups and the territorial governments have been very critical of this function. Land is an especially contentious item. The territorial governments see DIAND's resource management role as properly their responsibility, as it is in the provinces.

Observations

Within this complex and fractious political environment, several major issues have been identified by the Study Team with respect to land, forest and water management (and environmental management generally):

1. Devolution: what to transfer, how fast, integrated or not integrated? The priority for transfer in Yukon is land; in the NWT it is forestry.

2. Legislative and regulatory reform: the existing base is labyrinthine and stands in great contrast to the regimes of the provinces. A major priority.

3. Native claim negotiations and settlement: a major priority, not handled by Northern Affairs (though there is close liaison); native claim provisions permeate the interests and responsibilities of NAP, other federal departments, and the territorial governments.

4. The need for an integrated, holistic approach to development, resource management, and environmental protection and conservation.

Options

The Study Team recommends to the Task Force that the government consider the following:

1. Devolve responsibility for land, forest and water management to the governments of Yukon and Northwest Territories, taking into account their priorities and timeframes for transfer, as well as the emerging provisions in native claims.

2. Consolidate environmental management responsibility in the North, (that is, from DIAND (NAP), DIAND (COGLA), DOE, DFO, territorial government) by having:

a) in one federal department, eg. DIAND or DOE,
b) in the territorial government, or
c) a federal-territorial agency or board.

3. Encourage territorial governments to enact legislation in anticipation of transfer.

YUKON AND NORTHWEST TERRITORIES LANDS MANAGEMENT
INAC 201-1

Objective

To provide, authorize and regulate the sale, lease or other disposition of territorial lands, including grants of rights-of-way under specified terms and conditions; to regulate use of land and certain resources on territorial lands.

Authority

Territorial Lands Act
Territorial Lands Regulations
Territorial Land Use Regulations
Territorial Quarrying Regulations
Territorial Dredging Regulations
Lands Titles Act, Public Lands Grants Act, Canada Lands Surveys Act

Description

There are several components to this program:

1. The sale, lease or other disposition of territorial lands. (Note that "territorial lands" are those vested in the Crown in right of the Minister of Indian and Northern Affairs, in other words "federal lands" or, in terms of oil and gas North of 60°, "Canada Lands". Apart from this are certain areas under the control of the territorial governments termed "Commissioner's Lands"; these land areas comprise less than two per cent of Crown lands North of 60°. Land disposition for territorial lands is controlled through DIAND regional offices in Yellowknife and Whitehorse. The territorial governments have similar administrations for disposition of Commissioner's lands. Federal land policy for many years has been to alienate land through lease, issued for a specific period of time (e.g. five to 30 years) and for different uses of land surface (e.g. recreational, commercial, agricultural, residential). The leases do not confer title or subsurface rights to land. Only under very restricted circumstances are lands sold in fee simple by the federal government; in contrast, this is the usual practice of the territorial governments.

Applications for territorial (federal) lands are processed by the Federal-Territorial Lands Advisory Committee (FTLAC) for clearance by both levels of government. The approved lease or permit includes conditions which specify the nature and extent of land use, including the annual rent.

2. The regulation of land use through the Territorial Land Use Regulations. Most uses of territorial (federal) lands require a Class A or Class B Land Use Permit; Class A permits are required for all significantly large operations and any operations in areas of interest to one or more communities. These must be issued within 42 days. Class B permits are needed for small operations, and must be issued within 10 days. Activities exempted from Land Use Permits include all those on quartz or placer mining claims in Yukon, resident hunting, fishing and trapping, prospecting or locating a mineral claim, or operations on lands where the federal government has transferred or granted surface rights to another party (e.g. another federal department). Operating terms and conditions, designed mainly to safeguard the physical environment, are contained in land use permits, and are inspected and enforced by land use inspectors of DIAND.

3. The regulation of NWT mining, forestry, quarrying, dredging; these activities are covered in other Regulatory Program Profiles.

Resources

($000's)	82/83	83/84	84/85	85/86	86/87	87/88
Person-Years	50	52	42	46	46	46
O&M	3,498	2,142	3,129	3,418	3,418	3,418
Capital	133	71	66	66	66	66

Problem Identification

1. Land Disposition: the fundamental problems here are policy and political in nature, not regulatory. These policy problems have been extremely acrimonious, straining relations between the federal and territorial governments (especially Yukon) to a severe degree. These have been mitigated, but not yet resolved, since the new government came to power. While varied and complex, the problems can be summarized thus:

a) The withdrawal of substantial areas of land by unilateral action of the federal government for purposes of environmental protection: national park reserves (e.g. Northern Yukon, East Arm Great Slave Lake), International Biological Sites (IBP Sites), wildlife and bird sanctuaries, etc. Private sector reaction to these withdrawals, if done without prior assessment of resource development potential (especially minerals), has been hostile. The policy has been deemed to have constrained economic growth.

b) Moratoriums placed on land disposition for various reasons: native claims, agricultural use, rural residential, etc. These are perceived to constrain private initiative (e.g. homesteaders, farming, tourist operations) and frustrate individuals' desire to settle or use the land. Moratoriums have contributed greatly to problems of illegal occupancy of lands (squatting) both on territorial (federal) and Commissioner's lands.

c) Lease vs. freehold tenure: private citizens frequently express their preference to own rather than lease land. Among other problems, leasehold confers little or no collateral with lending institutions.

d) Balanced against the foregoing are the interests of native groups, whose aboriginal claims are pending, and of some (but not all) environmental/ conservation groups.

e) The entire process of land disposition is not public.

2. Land Use: The land use permitting system, provided in detailed regulation and guidelines, has certain strengths, e.g. the fixed time limits for issuance, and the specificity of conditions. The system draws considerable support from those concerned with environmental management, and native groups. However, many problems, mainly of policy and process, remain:

a) The mining industry and, to some extent, the petroleum industry operating on land areas (e.g. Petro-Canada) criticize the TLU Regulations as unduly onerous, costly to comply with, and

356

inflexible. In the NWT the requirements for
consultation (with local groups, communities,
natives) as a condition of permit are becoming
very cumbersome and time-consuming.

b)   Land Use permits are issued annually rather than
over the life of the project.

c)   There is an inadequate means of integrating land
use permitting with other resource management
functions, e.g. water use, socio-economic impact
assessment. The permits specifically exclude
socio-economic concerns, which are often more
dominant than the strictly biophysical. This was
one of the principal findings of the Task Force on
Northern Conservation Policy (January, 1985).

d)   There is no specified avenue for appeal, the
process of granting land use permits is not public
(although the consultative needs are onerous).

e)   Land use permits are not required for mining
exploration or production in Yukon, having been
exempted by law. Thus, any environmental benefits
of the TLU Regulations in the Yukon may have a
patchwork quality. Note that the mining industry
strongly favours this arrangement, and would
resist vigorously any legislative attempt to
extend TLU Regulations to mining lands, as is the
case in NWT.

Observations

The system of land management and regulation in the
North is a fundamental source of federal-territorial
discord, and has been perceived since the early 1970's as a
major constraint on economic growth and the realization of
individual freedom of expression.

Options

The Study Team recommends to the Task Force that the
government consider the following:

1.   Devolve responsibility for land management North of
60° to the Yukon and NWT governments.

2.   Adopt the recommendations of the Northern Conservation
Task Force (January, 1985).

YUKON AND NORTHWEST TERRITORIES FOREST MANAGEMENT
INAC 201-2

Objective

    To regulate the cutting of timber on Crown land; to provide for fire protection.

Authority

    Territorial Lands Act; Territorial Timber Regulations; Forest Protection Ordinance (Yukon, NWT); Commissioner's Land Ordinance.

Description

    Forest management in Northern Canada is carried out by the Northern Affairs Program of Indian and Northern Affairs Canada, largely through its regional and district offices in Yukon and NWT. Forest management has three components, only one of which is regulatory:

1) Timber harvesting (regulated by the Territorial Timber Regulations);

2) Forest fire protection or "fire management", carried out by DIAND under territorial ordinances;

3) Inventory, sylviculture, mapping, studies, etc. (no clear statutory authority).

    As a group, these activities consume a substantial proportion of NAP's budget.

    The cutting of timber on Crown land requires a permit for all commercial operations. Citizens and non-profit institutions may cut trees for private use. Hunters, trappers, prospectors and scientists in the field do not require timber permits. Three types of permits are issued by district forestry officers of DIAND:

i) special permit, available to residents at no charge to harvest 25 cords or less for personal use;

ii) commercial domestic permits, required for volumes greater than 25 cords for domestic use, with fee commensurate with quality of timber harvested;

iii) commercial resale permits, required for commercial harvesting operations, fee based on quality of timber harvested.

On very infrequent occasions the Minister of INAC has entered into formal Forest Agreements with a forest company, in which case the Minister issues a multi-year licence stipulating stumpage, rates of harvest, and other conditions.

Fire management is not regulatory and will not be described in detail. Forested areas in Yukon and NWT are divided into priority zones which govern whether a forest fire is attacked immediately, monitored, or ignored.

Forest inventory, mapping, sylvicultural studies, etc. are discretionary expenditures in NAP's regional operations. They are supportive of the regulatory function.

Resources

($000's)	82/83	83/84	84/85	85/86	86/87	87/88
Person-Years	186	179	152	123	123	123
Operating Exp.						
O&M	22,274	22,473	17,226	17,561	18,076	18,076
Capital	1,189	1,375	3,206	2,806	2,806	2,806

Problem Identification

As a component of land, forest and water management, timber regulation poses relatively minor problems, in that commercial forestry in the North is a very small sector in the economy. An evaluation of NAP's forest management function was carried out by J.S. MacTavish and Dendron Resource Surveys Ltd. (May 1982). The report is excerpted as follows:

"The present situation is wasteful of government resources. It does not satisfy the needs of industry, nor does it respond to requirements of other departmental programs, including land use planning and native claims settlements." (Page 109)

"The DIAND Act provides a broad mandate for forest management in the North but it has not been used as a basis for policy development. The specific forest management mandate of the Department of Indian Affairs and Northern Development is narrowly restricted to the regulation of timber harvesting. It is silent on important issues of forest inventory and management planning. It is inadequate with respect to timber allocation policy. It is virtually useless for the regulation of timber harvesting, having been poorly drafted...Regulatory powers over timber harvesting in the North are very weak in comparison to those used in British Columbia and Alberta." (pp. 111-112).

DIAND has developed a draft discussion paper to respond, inter alia, to the inadequacies raised in the evaluation and is developing a policy paper for consideration by Cabinet seeking policy approval and authority to prepare the necessary legislative amendments and incremental resources to improve forest management.

Far more serious problems exist in respect of fire management, especially in the NWT which suffered several successive seasons of widespread fire in the past six years. Fire control is very costly, thus only priority fires (e.g. for protection of life and property) are attacked. In NWT, fire has destroyed large areas valued by native peoples for hunting and trapping. Considerable criticism of the federal government by native leaders and the government of NWT has led to negotiations to transfer the fire management function to GNWT and to give native organizations a greater involvement in forest fire control.

Observations

The primary policy decision is whether and how to devolve forests and forest management to the territorial governments. If this is done without transfers of the land (surface and sub-surface) an awkward resource management system could result.

Options

The Study Team recommends to the Task Force that the government consider the following:

1. Pass a new federal Northern forest management act, embracing modern resource management concepts.

2. Transfer forests to YTG and GNWT and urge new territorial acts for forest management.

3. Integrate forest management with land, water, wildlife and other renewable resource planning and management programs.

360

YUKON AND NWT WATER RESOURCES MANAGEMENT (INLAND)
INAC 201-3-1

Objective

To provide for the conservation, development and use of the inland water resources of the Yukon and Northwest Territories through the Water Boards in each territory to license water use and waste disposal.

Authority

Northern Inland Waters Act (1970) and Regulations

Description

The Northern Inland Waters Act and Regulations are administered in part by the Northern Affairs Program (NAP) of Indian and Northern Affairs Canada and, insofar as water licensing is concerned, by the Water Boards, established in each territory. The Minister of INAC is responsible for the Water Boards.

NAP headquarters is responsible for general policy for northern water management. NAP regional offices in Whitehorse and Yellowknife administer minor uses of water and carry out inspection of water use and enforcement of licence provisions for major water uses. Since 1984, all major water uses must be licensed by the Territory Water Board; licences have a term of from one to 25 years, and they must be approved, or rejected, by the Minister, who does not have authority to alter licence conditions. The attached diagram illustrates schematically the licensing process.

The Northern water management system is unique in Canada because:

1. It integrates the functions of water quality (waste discharge) and water quantity (allocation) under one statute (NIWA) and is administered by the independent NAP - Water Board arrangement. This is not the case in the provinces, which separate the allocative and water quality functions.

2. The regulatory process, under the quasi-judicial Water Board provisions and rules, is public; this is also in contrast to the provinces. The process also provides for appeal.

361

There are other Acts and regulations that impinge on water use and habitat protection in the North, and these must be taken into consideration by NAP and the Water Boards. The most significant of these is the Fisheries Act, s.33, which is the responsibility of the Environmental Protection Service of Environment Canada, but is enforced by Fishery Officers of DFO.

Resources

($000's)	82/83	83/84	84/85	85/86	86/87	87/88
Person-Years	41	45	39	44	45	45
Operating Exp. O&M	3,807	3,787	4,351	4,967	5,054	5,054
Capital	468	406	447	446	446	446

Problem Identification

Water management in the Canadian North, as provided under NIWA, is characterized positively by its unique regulatory process, governed by the quasi-judicial Water Boards. However, there remain a number of serious problems of a policy and regulatory nature. These include:

1. The absence of standards for water quality, or effluent quality, except where provided under other legislation, e.g. the Fisheries Act. The absence of such standards bring the categorical authority of DFO into conflict with NIWA. The conflict as manifested in the placer mining industry in Yukon, has been acrimonious and has not yet been resolved in law.

2. The failure to set priorities among the classes of use of water, as provided under S.26(d) of NIWA. Such priorities include the non-consumptive uses (e.g. for fish, tourism, transportation) as well as consumptive uses (eg. mining, domestic supply, hydroelectric, municipal sewage disposal). The absence of a policy framework which establishes priorities and identifies trade-offs has made the work of the Water Boards, in setting conditions on licences, very difficult.

3. Related to the above, water management and regulation has not been integrated into the Northern Land Use Planning Process (which itself is a problem program), and the Water Boards are in a nebulous state as to their role in water management policy vs. a strict licensing function.

4. A major problem arises with respect to compensation. The Act states that lower priority licences are entitled to compensation but, without a priority framework, this is meaningless. The Act puts the onus for proving "adverse effect" on the injured party, but does not say how this is to be measured. Further, the Act does not provide for rights of compensation to non-licensed water users; this is an important matter to native water users, whose lifestyle or livelihood could be adversely affected by industrial uses of water.

5. As a result of a Federal Court decision in 1984 (the Dene Nation vs. The Queen), the powers of NAP to control minor uses of water (which formerly included most placer miners) were ruled ultra vires. This has led to uncertainty among minor water users and to a greatly increased workload for the Water Boards. Considerable administrative adjustment has been required.

6. There are other problems too numerous to detail here. Note that the Pearse Commission (Inquiry on Federal Water Policy), which had heard considerable testimony on a wide range of Northern water management issues, will undoubtedly contribute to the broader discussion on Northern resources.

Observations

Water management in the North, despite the basic strength of the legislation, has divided the interests of government, the private sector, the native community, and environmental/conservation groups. All parties have called for reform, beginning with a fundamental policy review, and the establishment of an effective process for setting water management objectives, water quality standards, water use priorities, and detailed guidelines for determining water licence terms and conditions.

Major legislative adjustment must be made between NIWA and the Fisheries Act in order to resolve certain intractable problems such as those besetting Yukon placer mining.

Options

The Study Team recommends to the Task Force that the government consider the following:

1. Give priority to follow-up to the Pearse Inquiry on water policy.

2. Give Water Boards clear role in water management and planning. Establish mirror legislation for water management by the territorial government and phase

3. devolution of responsibility from the federal government to the territorial governments.

4. Integrate water management and land use planning processes.

5. With respect to waste deposition and fish habitat provisions, amendments should be introduced to give precedence to NIWA over s.33 of the Fisheries Act.

YUKON AND NORTHWEST TERRITORIES WATER MANAGEMENT
(OFFSHORE) - INAC 201-3-2

Objective

To prevent pollution of offshore (marine) waters by regulating development and shipping activity in Arctic waters.

Authority

Arctic Waters Pollution Prevention Act
Arctic Waters Pollution Prevention Regulations (DIAND)
Arctic Shipping Pollution Prevention Regulations (TC)

Description

The Act provides for the regulation of industrial development and shipping activity in Arctic waters, i.e. waters adjacent to the mainland and islands of the Canadian Arctic. The Act prescribes limits of liability for unauthorized deposits of waste, design requirements for vessels operating in Arctic waters, and provides for the establishment of Shipping Safety Control Zones.

The administering agencies are Transport Canada in respect of Arctic shipping, Indian and Northern Affairs Canada in respect of non-shipping activities, and Energy, Mines & Resources re non-shipping activities in Hudson Bay and Hudson Strait.

Coordination with related legislation is achieved through the Arctic Waters Advisory Committee (AWAC), chaired by DIAND (Yellowknife), re AWPP Regulations. AWAC is closely associated with the Regional Ocean Dumping Committee (RODAC), chaired by Environment Canada to advise on Dumping Permit issuance under the Ocean Dumping Control Act.

AWAC is not a licensing body, nor are any non-shipping permits, licences, etc. issued under the authority of AWPPA. AWAC provides advice and reviews applications for licences, leases to dredge, or construct ice or artificial islands, under other legislation. AWAC provides information to Transport Canada for its administration of the Navigable Waters Protection Act, and it advises on subsurface lands management, e.g. construction of artificial islands, under the Public Lands Grants Act.

Under the Arctic Waters Shipping Pollution Regulations, Transport Canada seeks to curtail shipping pollution in a 100-mile zone offshore. The means are:

1) prohibition of all waste disposal from ships (two exceptions allowed);
2) establishment of 16 shipping safety zones wherein 14 classes of vessel are restricted in movement according to ice thickness and construction design;
3) requirements for special equipment and manning.

Resources

Not Available.

Problem Identification

1. Non-shipping: The main problem for the private sector developer is that DIAND has broad discretionary powers and works without guidelines; the result is uncertainty. AWAC can advise the Governor in Council to require modification or to prohibit the carrying out of construction or alteration. Oil and gas activity is the most prominent development in the offshore Arctic. In respect of that, the industry is involved with COGLA for purposes of oil and gas drilling, with AWAC, and with RODAC, all of which have powers to prevent or mitigate environmental impacts. DFO, with the Fisheries Act, looks over the shoulder of all three parties and in its own right can, and sometimes does, advocate negatively in industrial activity (example: Pan Arctic's Bent Horn project). Legally, DFO has overriding powers under s.33.1 of the Fisheries Act, and the Minister of Fisheries could modify, restrict or prevent any work or undertaking if deemed likely to deposit deleterious substances into water, or likely to alter or destroy fish habitat.

   A legal uncertainty exists in the definition of inland waters covered under the Northern Inland Waters Act and under the authority of the Territory Water Board. Certain configurations of land and coastal water, bound by headland-to-headland baselines, give rise to uncertainty or to whether the water is inland or part of the territorial sea, covered by AWPPA.

366

2. Shipping (Note: this is an area covered by another
    team): Transport Canada's problem here is opposite
    those experienced by DIAND, in that regulations are
    very specific; discretionary powers and open-endedness
    are not a problem. Rather, TC's challenge is to keep
    abreast of technological change and innovation, and to
    translate these quickly into regulatory provision. The
    private sector is usually much ahead of the government
    and thus can be expected to challenge the regulatory
    regime continuously.

    It should be noted that TC also administers the Canada
    Shipping Act, which regulates Arctic shipping pollution
    between 100 and 200 miles offshore, by dint of covering
    all 200-mile fishing zones in Canada. The Shipping Act
    has less stringent pollution requirements than AWPPA in
    that it allows pollution until excepted, and does not
    provide for regulation on crewing, equipping and
    designing of vessels.

Observations

As illustrated in Annex 1 and in the foregoing
description, there is a legislative, regulatory and
administrative maze. The private sector is understandably
confused (no doubt, so is the government). Reform through
legislative streamlining is warranted in the view of the
Study Team.

A very real problem, especially as the aboriginal
claims of the Eastern Arctic are settled, and if division of
the NWT proceeds as expected, is to provide for more local
levels of offshore jurisdiction. Offshore waters are as
important, or even more so, than land areas to Inuit
claimants; environmental controls embraced in settlement
acts must be rationalized with the existing federal legal
base, a task that will be exceedingly difficult.

Options

The Study Team recommends to the Task Force that the
government consider the following:

1. Clarify and rationalize environmental provisions of
    AWPPA, ODCA, Fisheries Act, Canada Oil & Gas Act, Oil &
    Gas Production and Conservation Act, NIWA, and Canada
    Shipping Act.

2.   House all environmental jurisdiction in one
      department/agency; consolidate environmental
      responsibilities of DIAND-NAP, DIAND-DOE, DFO, MOT,
      COGLA, GNWT, native claim organizations.

3.   Leave as is, but eliminate overlap, especially between
      Fisheries Act and the rest.

ANNEX 1

NORTHERN WATER MANAGEMENT: LEGISLATION & REGULATIONS

Legislation/Program	Authority/Standard	Responsible Department/Agency	Committees, Bonds, etc.
1. Northern Inland Waters Act			
Northern Inland Waters Regulations	Water licence	DIAND – Territorial Water Board	Yukon Territory Water Board Northwest Territories Water Board Regional Environmental Review Comm. (DIAND) NWT Water Board Technical Advisory Committee
2. Arctic Waters Pollution Prevention Act			
Arctic Shipping Pollution Prevention Regulations	Controls waste disposition by ships and ship navigation in arctic waters, standards for ship design, construction, machinery, equipment and operation	Transport Canada – Canadian Coast Guard	Arctic Waters Advisory Comm. (DIAND) Environmental Advisory Comm. (DOE) Arctic Shipping Control Auth. (TC)
Arctic Waters Pollution Prevention Regulations	Review and approve plans and specifications for installations that could be a source of pollution of arctic waters	DIAND – Regional Manager of Water Resources EMR – Hudson Bay & Strait	
Shipping Safety Control Zones Order		Transport Canada	
3. Fisheries Act			
Regulations: – Beluga Protection Regulations – Fish Health Protection – Fishways Obstruction Removal – Metal Mining Liquid Effluent – Narwhal Protection – Northwest Territories Fisheries Regulations – Walrus Protection – Yukon Territory Fisheries Regulations – Yukon Territory Gravel Removal Order	**Fisheries permit** Reviews and approves plans and specifications for works that would harm fish or damage fish habitat	Fisheries and Oceans Canada – Freshwater Institute (Winnipeg) for NWT – Pacific Region, DFO, for Yukon	Territorial Water Boards Arctic Waters Advisory Comm. (DIAND) Regional Ocean Dumping Advisory Committee (DOE) Regional Environmental Review Comm. (DIAND) Environmental Advisory Committee on Arctic Marine Transportation (DOE)

369

	Legislation/Program	Authority/Standard	Responsible Department/Agency	Committees, Boards, etc.
4.	Ocean Dumping Control Act Ocean Dumping Control Regulations	Ocean Dumping Permits	Environment Canada – Environmental Protection Service	Reg. Ocean Dumping Advisory Comm. (DOE) AWAC Territorial Water Boards
5.	Canada Shipping Act Oil Pollution Prevention Regulations Pollutant Substances Regulations	Ship-shore loading, unloading standards; mandatory updating of spills Prohibit discharge of materials toxic and bio-accumulative to marine life; mandatory reporting of discharges	Transport Canada	
6.	Canada Water Act	Gives advice or approval of company contingency plans; co-operation with industry in combatting spills	Transport Canada	
7.	Dominion Water Power Act Dominion Water Power Regulations	Applies to hydro developments on federal Crown lands North of 60 no longer in force for new developments see (NIWA)	DIAND	
8.	Canada Oil and Gas Act Canada Oil and Gas Drilling Regulations	Set out requirements for drilling program approvals and authority to drill a well; regulate environmental requirements, etc.	DIAND – Canada Oil and Gas lands Administration (COGLA) (North of 60)	COGLA Policy Review Comm. (COGLA) C-MIRB Northern Benefits Committee
	Canada Oil and Gas Production Regulations	Set out conservation, environmental, operational and safety requirements, etc.		
	Canada Oil and Gas Geophysical Regulations Canada Oil and Gas Pipelines Regulations Canada Oil and Gas Structures Regulations	Set out regulations for building and operating pipelines		
	Canada Oil and Gas Regulations – Diving Canada Oil and Gas Interests Regulations	Govern diving operations		

Legislation/Program	Authority/Standard	Responsible Department/Agency	Committees, Boards, etc.
Canada Oil and Gas Operations Regulations	Provides for reporting oil spills, etc.		
Environmental Studies Revolving Funds Regulations	Govern ESRF funding and administration		ESRF Advisory Board(s)
9. Canada Oil and Gas Production and Conservation Act	Licences and authorizations for the exploration, development and management of oil and gas production on Canada lands; governs processing and transportation, and off-shore pollution	DIAND (COGLA) (North of 60)	Senior Policy Committee on Northern Resource Development (DIAND) Committee on Mega project Industrial and Regional Benefits (DRIE) COGLA Policy Review Comm. (COGLA) Interdepartmental Environmental Rev. Committee (DIAND)
10. Territorial Lands Act	Reserves to the Crown beds of lakes, rivers and streams, and a 100-foot strip on each side of navigable stream, lakes and coasts	DIAND	Northern Benefits Committee (DIAND) Land Use Advisory Committee (DIAND)
Territorial Dredging Regulations	Dredging Lease	DIAND	Territorial Water Board Northern Benefits Committee (DIAND) NCPC - re supply of power
11. Government Harbours and Piers Act	Regulates control and management of public harbours and piers	Transport Canada	TERMPOL Coordinating Committee
12. National Transportation Act	Controls and licenses 'for hire' carriers on water	Canadian Transport Commission	
13. Navigable Waters Protection Act Navigable Waters Bridges Regulations Navigable Waters Works Regulations Ferry Cable Regulations	Regulates approval and works constructed in navigable waters	Transport Canada	Territorial Water Board RERC RODAC TERMPOL Coordinating Committee
14. Northern Canada Power Commission Act NCPC Regulations	Provides for generation of hydro-electric power in Yukon and NWT	NCPC	Yukon Territory Water Board NWT Water Board IERC RERC

371

Legislation/Program	Authority/Standard	Responsible Department/Agency	Committees, Boards, etc.
15. National Energy Board Act	Regulates transportation of hydro-carbons	NEB	
16. Yukon Placer Mining Act	Administers mining rights, collection of royalties, work performance and licence requirements in respect of placer gold in YT Water provisions subsumed by NIWA, 1970	DIAND	Yukon Territory Water Board Joint Committee on Placer Mining R&D
17. Public Lands Grants Act Public Lands Leasing and Licensing Regulations	Off-shore tenure land agreements	DIAND	
Public Lands Mineral Regulations	Licenses to dredge off-shore	DIAND	

CANADA OIL & GAS LANDS ADMINISTRATION (COGLA) - INAC 226

Objective

To negotiate, dispose and manage oil and gas rights on Canada Lands, and to regulate exploration, development, production, oil spill contingencies and benefit plans, in the interest of safety, environmental protection, resource conservation, economic and social developments; to act as a focal point for industry in Canada Lands.

Authority

Canada Oil and Gas Act (nine sets of Regulations), Oil and Gas Production and Conservation Act, Canada-Nova Scotia Oil and Gas Act

Description

The Canada Oil and Gas Lands Administration was established in 1981 under a Memorandum of Understanding between the Ministers of Indian Affairs and Northern Development and Energy, Mines & Resources, followed by a Letter of Agreement between the Deputy Ministers of those departments. (The significance of this is that COGLA, as an organization, is not contained in any statute.) By this arrangement the oil and gas functions of the two departments were pooled in COGLA and thus it is an integral part of both departments. However, both DIAND and EMR retained a capacity and staff to carry out oil and gas policy formulation.

COGLA's creation was a direct consequence of the government's priorities under the National Energy Program for Canadianization, self-sufficiency and "need to know" objectives, and has a particular association with the Petroleum Incentives Program (PIP).

COGLA's detailed functions and organization are described in the background paper. It is important to note that the Administrator of COGLA reports to the DM's of DIAND and EMR. He also is increasingly associated with provincial governments (ie. Nova Scotia and Newfoundland) by formal agreement.

Activities of the oil and gas industry in Canada Lands are managed by COGLA through a multi-phased approval system. Exploration agreements are negotiated to establish

the area where companies will explore. Within a fixed term
(less than five years) companies agree to carry out a
minimum of exploration work (seismic, drilling,
environmental); COGLA monitors this program and gives
technical approvals. COGLA regulations also provide for
return of lands to the Crown and for land reserved to the
Crown.

COGLA regulates "Canada benefits", by which a company
must submit a plan satisfactory to the Minister before work
is undertaken. COGLA also regulates environmental impact
assessment and contingency plans, as well as one half of the
Environmental Studies Revolving Fund (ESRF) (eight PYs; $1.2
million, 1985-86).

Resources

($000's)	82/83	83/84	84/85	85/86	86/87	87/88
Person-Years	146	196	230	246	246	246
Operating Exp.						
Salaries	4,600	7,000	8,580	10,007	10,088	10,008
O&M	3,400	3,900	5,486	7,382	7,732	8,040
Other Expenses						
Contributions*				50,000	50,000	50,000
Revenue	5,200	8,400	9,100	8,900	9,700	10,200
Capital	160	162	342	106	111	115

* Canada-Nova Scotia Offshore Oil and Gas Agreement

Problem Identification

Although scarcely four years old, COGLA is a powerful
regulatory agency, exercising broad technical, economic,
environmental and socio-economic roles over the oil and gas
industry on the 10.2 million-square-kilometre Canada Lands.
COGLA's creation and operations have posed numerous
problems, some due to start-up, others due to its
fundamental policy base, which is the National Energy
Program.

Like the NEP itself, COGLA's role and performance is
viewed by the private sector (oil and gas) in differing
ways; for example, the multi-nationals are more opposed to
its interventionist regulations than are the Canadian-owned
companies, which can benefit from the "farm-in" provisions
of PIP. Among the other things, COGLA was intended to be
the main operational contact for the industry working on
Canada Lands, i.e. a single window. Owing to the fact that

many policy and regulatory overlaps remain, industry (and, for that matter, government) does not see the single-window role of COGLA as effective.

Much of the private sector (again the bigger companies, especially the multi-nationals which predominate on Canada Lands) sees COGLA's regulatory powers as interventionist and a constraint to cost-effective exploration and development. In particular, the industry is very critical of:

1. The "work bonus" as compared to the "cash bonus" system of securing lands for exploration;

2. The requirement for compulsory relinquishment of lands under exploration agreements;

3. The "Canada Benefits" or "Northern Benefits" requirement, which give the Minister powerful intervention in the contracting of goods, services and personnel;

4. The Environmental Studies Revolving Funds (ESRF), the administration of which is divided between COGLA for the offshore Atlantic and Pacific, and DIAND for the North, and accused of detracting from efficient research effort by the industry itself;

5. The process and content of detailed regulations, which are voluminous borrowings from Norway or other jurisdictions, and not particularly appropriate to Canada; performance standards and general codes of conduct are preferred.

Other interests, e.g. environmental, native, are critical as well of COGLA's role, which is fundamentally to induce industrial development on the Canada Lands. The environmental provisions of COGLA and its Regulations will always be subordinate to the development thrust.

There are some serious overlap problems:

1. COGLA and Northern Affairs Program, DIAND, re approval of major projects;

2. COGLA-NEB, e.g. regulation of offshore pipelines;

3. COGLA-GNWT-DIAND re Northern Benefits;

4.   COGLA-NEB-FEARO (EARP)-GNWT-DOE-DFO-DIAND re
      environmental assessment/regulation.

Observations

COGLA's future direction is unclear. The factors that
obscure the direction include:

1.   The phasing out of PIP;

2.   Weakening foreign investment controls and the
      Canadianization objective;

3.   The re-emergence of the multi-nationals and the
      Canadian Petroleum Association in influencing
      government policy;

4.   The Atlantic Accord, which possibly may spread to
      subsume the Canada-Nova Scotia Agreement;

5.   Northern devolution policy and native claims.

Options

The Study Team recommends to the Task Force that the
government consider the following:

1.   Abolish COGLA immediately.

2.   Phase out COGLA. Revert oil and gas management to
      DIAND for northern Canada Lands.

3.   Keep COGLA but relieve it of environmental and Canada
      Benefits functions.

4.   Privatize ESRF.

BACKGROUND

CANADA OIL AND GAS LANDS ADMINISTRATION (COGLA)

THE FUNCTIONS AND ORGANIZATION OF COGLA

The Canada Oil and Gas Lands Administration (COGLA) was established in 1981 by a Memorandum of Understanding between the Ministers of Energy, Mines and Resources and Indian Affairs and Northern Development to support the achievement of mutually compatible energy and northern policy goals.

COGLA is responsible for the management of federal oil and gas interests on the Canada Lands, more than 10 million square kilometers which encompass onshore areas in the Territories and the Arctic, and offshore areas in Hudson Bay, and seaward from the Atlantic and Pacific coasts. COGLA is also responsible for the management of federal non-fuel mineral interests in the Atlantic, Pacific and Hudson Bay offshore areas and oil and gas and other minerals on federal public lands in the provinces.

The Administration serves as the principal point of contact between the federal government and the petroleum industry in all oil and gas activities on the Canada Lands. COGLA reports through the respective Deputy Minister to the Minister of Energy, Mines and Resources (for areas seaward of provincial boundaries) and the Minister of Indian Affairs and Northern Development (for Territories and areas seaward of the coast). Internal policy guidance is provided by the Policy Review Committee, which consists of the Administrator of COGLA and senior personnel from each parent department; the committee ensure that COGLA's policy directions are consistent with the policy requirements of each department.

The organization comprises six branches at headquarters and three regional offices:

1. The Land Management Branch is responsible for the administration of exploration and production rights under the Canada Oil and Gas Act. The branch negotiates exploration agreements, monitors interest owner performance and collects royalties and other revenues. It is also responsible for the issuance and administration of oil and gas rights in federal Public Lands within the provinces.

2.   The Engineering Branch is responsible for the
      regulation and monitoring of exploration, development
      and production under the Oil and Gas Production and
      Conservation Act. Authorization to undertake drilling
      activity is issued subject to environmental clearance
      procedures and safety inspections of equipment used by
      the industry.

3.   The Resource Evaluation Branch assesses the resource
      potential of the Canada Lands, authorizes geophysical
      and geological programs, analyzes geological factors
      and hazards in drilling programs, and monitors data and
      results from all oil and gas activity on the Canada
      Lands.

      The Administration, through its Resource Evaluation and
      Engineering Branches, issues the work program approvals
      and specific well approvals which operators have to
      obtain before they can begin work. As well as
      insisting on prior approval of operators' plans, COGLA
      inspectors regularly visit work sites to ensure
      activities are carried on safely.

      COGLA engineers also approve floating and fixed
      structures used by the industry, assess oil and gas
      reservoirs, and monitor management and development.
      Petroleum processing and production systems and
      pipeline systems within production fields are also
      licensed and inspected.

4.   The Environmental Protection Branch scrutinizes
      operators' plans and regulates their activities to
      ensure that the highest standards of environmental
      protection are maintained. This planning complements
      recommendations for environmental studies designed to
      assess the impact of resource development. It assesses
      the effect of oceanographic, meteorological and ice
      conditions on human safety and protection; identifies
      the impact of drilling operations on marine and coastal
      biota, shorelines and fisheries; and evaluates the
      validity and effectiveness of contingency plans and
      compensation schemes.

5.   The Canada Benefits Branch evaluates and monitors
      companies' plans to ensure that Canadian workers and
      businesses are given full and fair access to the
      opportunities provided by oil and gas activity.
      Benefits packages are negotiated with oil and gas

companies as part of exploration agreements and development plans. Working with other agencies of government, e.g. DRIE, CEIC, the branch advises companies on the preparation of acceptable Canada Benefits packages. The Minister ultimately must approve all proposals.

6. The <u>Policy Analysis and Coordination Branch</u> is responsible for the analysis, development, interpretation and implementation of policy for the management of oil and gas activity in the Canada Lands. The branch liaises with other policy groups within Energy, Mines and Resources and Indian and Northern Affairs, coordinates policy-related work of the COGLA Branches and provides secretarial support to the Policy Review Committee and to the Canada-Nova Scotia Offshore Oil and Gas Board. The branch is also responsible for coordination between COGLA and other federal departments and provincial government bodies.

Regional Offices

COGLA maintains regional offices in Yellowknife, Halifax and St.John's, which have operational responsibility for the North, the Nova Scotia offshore and offshore Newfoundland and Labrador, respectively.

Responsibilities include the issuing of Authorities to Drill a Well, authorization to undertake geophysical and geological programs, and conducting rig inspections and monitoring engineering, geological, environmental and Canada Benefits aspects of all industry operations. The regional offices also advise on policies, procedures and regulations from a regional perspective and undertake an important liaison role with provincial and federal departments.

COGLA also has a field office in Inuvik and an information office in Calgary.

Regulatory Process

The regulatory process normally begins under the Canada Oil and Gas Act with public invitations to bid for oil and gas rights on blocks of land through Calls for Proposals. Companies submit proposals for exploration agreements for the right to explore for oil and gas. The Minister, through COGLA, then negotiates exploration agreements with the successful bidding companies based upon their proposals.

Operators are also required to submit a Canada Benefits Plan satisfactory to the Minister.

An operator's work program is assessed in terms of its environmental and operational acceptability. Before drilling activity can commence, an operator must receive Drilling Program Approval and Authority to Drill a Well, both granted under the Canada Oil and Gas Drilling Regulations. COGLA inspects and monitors all exploration activities.

An operator making a commercial discovery may apply for a production license, provided Canadian ownership of the license is 50 per cent or more. Ministerial approval of a development plan is required before production begins. The operator supplies relevant technical and environmental information in the development plan, and a proposal on benefits to Canada.

CANADA BENEFITS

The objective of the Canada Benefits process is to ensure full and fair access for Canadians to the industrial, social and economic opportunities from petroleum activity on the Canada Lands.

The Process

Before the actual commencement of any work program, a benefits plan is approved outlining the benefits expected for Canada and for the specific province or territory where the activity will take place. Subsequently an annual benefits report is submitted for each calendar year during the term of the plan outlining the year's accomplishments and updating planned activities.

The plans include full and fair opportunity for Canadians to supply goods and services and to receive the employment and training opportunities related to petroleum projects. They also contain an assessment of other socio-economic implications of proposed activities on regions and local communities. In addition, affected community groups are consulted concerning the work program, the implications of the activity, and the plans or programs to enhance the benefits. Companies are also encouraged to develop special measures to enhance the participation of disadvantanged individuals.

Many interested federal departments and agencies, provincial and territorial governments, and community groups are involved with COGLA in the review of benefits plans. The information is used to assist in planning complementary programs in support of operations and to provide an indication of possible market and employment opportunities.

ENVIRONMENTAL STUDIES REVOLVING FUNDS

The rationale for the ESRF is:

1. To provide a national mechanism for equitably distributing the costs of necessary broad scale environmental and social studies throughout the oil and gas industry active on Canada Lands.

2. To ensure that an adequate level (quantity and quality) of environmental and social studies are carried out with minimum duplication.

3. To ensure that the results of environmental and social studies are readily available and open to scrutiny immediately after their completion.

Some 36 study agreements sponsored by the Environmental Studies Revolving Funds were initiated in 1984, for a total value of $5.4 million. This was in addition to 37 agreements that were signed in 1983. The results of 18 studies are now in draft report form and two have been published.

Administered jointly by COGLA and the Northern Affairs Program of the Department of Indian Affairs and Northern Development, the studies are financed by means of levies on the oil and gas industry ($1.2 million over 30 months, 1984-86). They cover a broad range of scientific disciplines in the physical, biological and social sciences. The major field studies that commenced or took place in 1984 included:

- An investigation into the measurement of bottom sediment transport on the Scotian Shelf.

- A study of the phenomenon of sea bottom ice scouring in the Beaufort Sea, caused by ice keels within drifting pack ice. At a cost of approximately $760,000 (including charter of a survey vessel), the study will provide data of crucial importance to design criteria for undersea pipelines.

- Two field studies of the remote sensing of icebergs on the Grand Banks, each of which involved a budget of approximately $350,000. The first, carried out in the spring of 1984, assessed the capability of rig-borne radar to detect small ice masses under a wide range of sea states and the second evaluated the capability of two different types of airborne radar to detect icebergs in variable sea conditions.

- A study dealing with the behaviour and fate of hydrocarbons in the marine environment and the variety of oil spill countermeasures.

- An investigation into the difficult problem of recovering spilled oil from ice-infested waters, including tank testing of a specially built oil-skimming ship bow.

- The monitoring of effects e.g. on marine mammals, of the operation of the oil and gas industry offshore.

- Other studies, including one to identify priorities that will serve as a guide for the ESRF social studies program for the next several years, another aimed at improving communication among governments, the oil and gas and fishing industries, and a third to assist in the designing of more appropriate Northern socio-economic studies in the future.

The present ESRF structure is shown on the following page. It is comprised of two advisory boards (the same industry and government members but with different chairmen - meeting concurrently), two management offices and ten industry-government expert Committees called Program Study Committees (PSC).

Current ESRF Structure

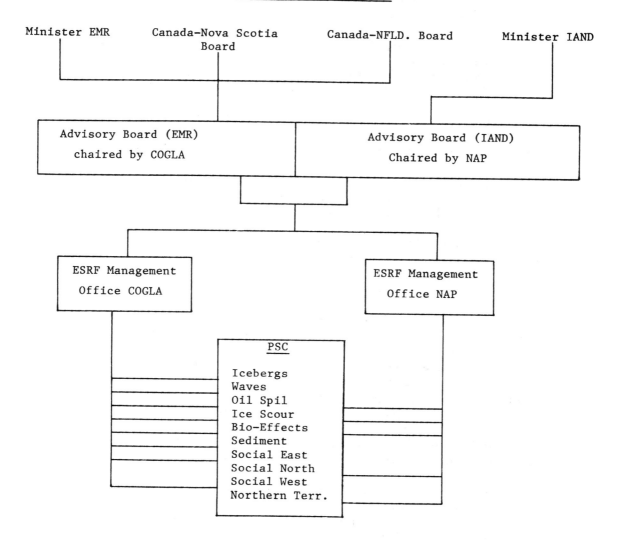

NORTHERN CANADA POWER COMMISSION – NCPC 1

Objective

To develop and manage electrical generation, transmission and distribution facilities in Yukon, Northwest Territories (NWT) and Field, B.C.

Authority

Northern Canada Power Commission Act; Dominion Waters Act.

Description

The Northern Canada Power Commission (NCPC) is a federal Crown corporation established in 1948. The NCPC Act requires the recovery of all costs in utility rates on an annual basis and that its projects be financed entirely by loans from Canada; these now amount to $247 million. Rates charged must provide sufficient revenue to cover the interest on investment, repayment of principal over the estimated lifetime of the project, operating, maintenance and administrative expenses and a contingency reserve. Although rate changes must be approved by the Treasury Board, effective regulatory mechanisms such as those that exist south of 60° do not exist.

NCPC has been experiencing financial and management problems for several years, and was the subject of a study by a sub-committee of the Standing Committee on Indian & Northern Affairs in 1981-82 (the "Penner Report"), and the subject of a public enquiry held by the National Energy Board (reported August, 1983). The NEB has just concluded a series of public hearings into Northern power rates, held in the Yukon and Northwest Territories. The expected output from the NEB panel hearings are:

1. Rate Design, i.e. diesel/hydro zones, equalized rates, rising or declining block rates, cross-subsidization, etc.;

2. Rate Levels, i.e. actual levels of rates within each rate zone (constrained by four per cent during 1985-86);

3. Rate Base, i.e. value of assets, depreciation methods and rates, proposed plant additions;

4.	Revenue Requirements and Cost Allocation;

5.	Capital Structure, ie. debt/equity ratio, rate of return, etc.

6.	Implications to the Direct Energy Subsidies.

Resources

($000's)	82/83	83/84	84/85	85/86	86/87	87/88
Person-Years	331	329				
Operating Expenses	72,005	76,063				
Revenues	79,257	81,919				
Subsidies*	N/A	N/A	4	5	5	6
Grants/Contribut.	41	20	6	4	2	2
(Loans)						
Capital						

*	Federal (DIAND) Energy Subsidies (Federal Power Support, Commercial Power Rate Relief, Home Heating Oil Subsidy)

Problem Identification/Observations

With a debt to Canada of $247 million, and having been subjected to the six per cent and five per cent Administered Prices Policy, NCPC is in a financial straitjacket. To comply with the NCPC Act, in the absence of compensatory government action NCPC must raise electric rates by 80 per cent in Yukon (none required in NWT), owing to the need to recover revenue to service the $61 million debt for the Whitehorse No. 4 hydro facility. Owing to the decline of the mining industry in Yukon, the Whitehorse No. 4 facility is now surplus to Yukon's current needs.

A variety of subsidies to consumers has been established in the North. As these were to expire March 31, 1985, Cabinet has been asked to decide on whether they should be continued.

Observations

With respect to rate setting, there is no provision for formal regulation of NCPC rates. Because NCPC has a monopoly on electricity generation in many parts of the North, a convincing case can be made to have a normal regulatory process for NCPC. This will require amendment of the NCPC Act. In the interim, an advisory role could be played by either the Territorial Public Utilities Boards (PUB's) or by the National Energy Board. Assignment of regulatory powers to the PUB's is preferred by Northerners and is consistent with the government's policy of devolution.

Cabinet has been asked to decide on the privatization or transfer to the territorial governments of NCPC.

Options

The Study Team recommends to the Task Force that the government consider the following:

1. Defer any action pending direction from Cabinet.

2. Review forthcoming rate recommendations of the NEB to ensure consistency with accepted regulatory practice.

3. Reinforce the need for privatization or divestiture from the federal government of NCPC and of regulatory authority over Northern power production and consumption. Note that this action would need to be considered with a like decision regarding continuation of federal subsidies.

NORTHERN PIPELINE AGENCY CANADA - NPAC 1

Objective

To oversee the planning and construction of the Canadian portion of the Alaska Highway Gas Pipeline project by the Foothills Group of Companies.

Authority

Northern Pipeline Act

Description

The Northern Pipeline Agency was created in 1978 to oversee the planning and construction of the Canadian portion of the Alaska Highway Gas Pipeline project by the Foothills Group of Companies. The Agency was designed to function as a "single window" to streamline and expedite the approval process. As a single regulatory authority, the agency administered the many federal acts which apply to the planning and monitoring of construction of the pipeline in Canada. This includes the full delegated authority of the National Energy Board.

NPA's mandate required that the project be carried forward in a way that will yield the maximum economic, energy and industrial benefit for Canadians with the least possible social and environmental disruption. Although NPA represents a "single window" approach to planning, possessing a strong degree of authority in law, Parliament authorized two committees to maintain surveillance of the Act and its implementation, that is, the House Standing Committee on Northern Pipelines and the Senate Special Committee on Northern Pipelines.

On May 1, 1982 the sponsoring companies in the United States and Canada announced their decision to delay completion of the pipeline to 1989. The "pre-build" portions, designed to feed Alberta natural gas to the Western United States, were completed and have been in use since 1981. The Northern Pipeline Agency has been phasing out its offices and personnel over the past three years, and will close completely in fiscal year 1985-86. Statutory authority to resume its activities exists if it is decided to resume construction of the northern sections of the pipeline in 1989 or subsequently.

All costs of the NPA are recoverable from Foothills Pipelines (Yukon) Ltd.

Resources

($000's)	82/83	83/84	84/85	85/86	86/87	87/88
Person-Years	134	63	30	11	8*	112*
Operating Expenses	6,642	5,414	3,789	1,442	775*	8,779*
Revenue	7,504	5,710	2,981	2,263	N/A	N/A
Subsidies						
Capital	48	19	1			

* Contingent on decision to resume construction.

Problem Identification

The private sector, particularly those initiating energy and other resource development projects, have frequently called for government to establish a "single-window" through which the proponent can obtain all necessary approvals required by regulation. As a concept, the "single-window" or "one-stop shopping" idea makes sense; in reality it has posed many problems for the proponent and government alike. These issues are elaborated upon in the background paper following this section.

The Northern Pipeline Agency, as a single-window, possessed the strongest degree of authority over regulatory activities. Furthermore, it was, and is, empowered to involve itself in a wide range of matters, including technical plans and specifications, socio-economic and environmental terms and conditions such as local business opportunities, equal opportunity to employment, native and women training, compensation to landholders, environmental mitigation, and protection of traditional native lifestyles. Thus, the NPA was far more intrusive into the private sector than was customary for pipeline construction, which is fairly routine in the settled portions of the country.

The private sector, generally speaking, has been critical of the NPA version of the single window experiment, saying it amounted to regulatory overkill in routine pipeline practice. The industry has acknowledged, however, that the North, with its special physical, cultural and economic challenges, probably warranted special care; notwithstanding, the private sector would not wish a replication of the NPA experience even for major Northern projects such as the proposed Polar Gas Pipeline.

Observations

The total costs since inception of the NPA, recovered largely from Foothills, will exceed $37 million. The Team agrees that this is considered to be grossly excessive, especially since most of the pipeline was not built and those segments that were built (Alberta, Saskatchewan, S.E. B.C.,) could have been regulated at a fraction of this cost.

Notwithstanding the complexity of issues and the inherent challenges of such a mega-project, if the Alaska Highway Gas Pipeline project is resumed a less powerful regulatory instrument than NPA would probably be appropriate.

Options

1. As the NPA is for all intents wound down, take no further action.

2. Repeal the Northern Pipeline Act so that the NPA cannot commence operations again in the future.

3. Consider weaker "by exception" coordinating mechanisms to project regulation and monitoring.

4. Abandon further "one-window" attempts; allow all federal, provincial and territorial agencies to exercise normal jurisdiction.

BACKGROUND

THE "SINGLE-WINDOW" CONCEPT OF REGULATION

INTRODUCTION

Of all the proposals and recommendations made to come to grips with regulatory overlap duplication, and jurisdictional confusion, the "single-window" idea has been raised frequently and with enthusiasm. Its apparent logic and simplicity appeals to industry or other "regulatees" who, for justifiable reasons of efficiency and cost, would prefer to deal with one agency for approval rather than many. The single-window idea <u>may</u> strike favour with regulators in government, who also have efficiency and cost-effectiveness as an objective. (Few bureaucratic organizations, however, willingly give up their regulatory powers for transfer to another.) Finally, public and public interest groups are rather divided on the issue.

This paper gives a general sketch of some of the strengths and weaknesses of the much-advocated "single-window" approach to regulation. If many of the examples are drawn from the Northern Canada experience of project approval and regulation, it is due to the fact that there the concept has been most frequently invoked.

SOME INDUSTRY EXPRESSION

Industry has frequently expressed the need for a single-window to regulation:

> "...It would be desirable to have a single-window approach to deal with the regulations; we believe COGLA has been a step in the right direction and could be used as a model for streamlining the entire regulatory process."

Before numerous panels, committees and other public and private means, industry has expressed its frustration with having to seek multiple approvals for project development and being subject to different squads of monitors and inspectors afterward. Industry views as unnecessary, duplicative and extremely costly the public process of assessment and review if there is more than one authority calling for voluminous information and conducting separate public reviews. An example of this during the 1980's was the Norman Wells oilfield expansion and oil pipeline

390

construction which occasioned separate reviews by an Environmental Assessment and Review Panel, the National Energy Board, and the Northwest Territories Water Board.

Smaller project developments, even if they do not have to go through a formal public review process, may have multiple hurdles to clear. For example, a mining company wishing to develop a property in the Northwest Territories may have to gain specific approvals from several federal and territorial departments, and to undergo reviews or assessments by a variety of co-ordinating or advisory committees before having the necessary permits and licenses in hand. A recent trend has been to layer upon these reviews, additional requirements to consult with local communities, native organizations or individual bands. Large and small companies alike have found these non-regulatory requirements to be as costly and time-consuming as the strictly regulatory hurdles.

GOVERNMENT RESPONSE

The federal government has long recognized the need for expeditious means of coordination, approval and monitoring of projects or activities that cut across jurisdiction. Many processes and structures have been tried, ranging from informal ones without legal authority to powerful, full-authority agencies like the Northern Pipeline Agency.

At the informal end of the scale, the usual mechanism has been the "advisory committee". In the case of Northern Canada, these abound: the Regional Environmental Review Committee, the Arctic Waters Advisory Committee, Land Use Advisory Committee, Regional Ocean Dumping Advisory Committee, Interdepartmental Environmental Review Committee, Policy Advisory Committee of COGLA, Senior Policy Committee on Northern Resource Projects, and the now-defunct Advisory Committee on Northern Development. These and a considerable number of others have similar aims: to get the federal and territorial "act" together and to have a common information base upon which to assess and permit operations. They comprise people at various ranks in the bureaucracy, from middle level managers to Deputy Ministers. A deficiency in a lot of advisory committees has been the phenomenon of downward delegation, especially as senior bureaucrats find more pressing and exciting priorities to deal with, and advisory committees thus wind down into relative insignificance (but never quite die).

Another government response has been to set up an office of coordinator. The Special Committee of the Senate on the Northern Pipeline (Hastings Committee) recommended in 1983 "that the appointment of a federal coordinator to each major energy project, responsible to a designated Minister, be tried on a pilot basis to test its suitability. An earlier attempt with a Beaufort Sea Office failed as it lacked the necessary authority. In the case of the Norman Wells Project a senior official was appointed to coordinate and facilitate activities of the federal and territorial governments with those of the project sponsors (Imperial Oil and Interprovincial Pipelines). Operating on a "by exception" basis (as distinct from an across-the-board approach), the Norman Wells coordination experiment has been partially successful. Its limitations lay in its weak level of authority, its lateness in being established (after the project approval stage), and its having to compete or coexist with other "one-window" mechanisms set up by the territorial government (i.e. the Development Impact Zone Group).

The Beaufort Sea Environment Assessment and Review Panel in its 1984 final report recommended a more senior Beaufort Sea-Mackenzie Delta Coordinator's Office, with the coordinator having a rank of Deputy Minister and accessible to (but not having regulatory authority over) the federal, territorial, local and industry groups involved in development projects. The BEARP recommendations have yet to be acted upon, but they recognize the need to elevate authority if a one-window is to be effective.

The ultimate level of authority is statutory and this was the approach used to regulate the planning and construction of the Alaska Highway Gas Pipeline by the Northern Pipeline Agency. This "solution" had its origins in the Mackenzie Valley Pipeline Inquiry (Berger Commission) and the unhappy experience of the Americans in building the Trans-Alaska Oil Pipeline. The NPA was indeed a powerful single-window, extending far beyond plans and engineering to socio-economic, environmental and political concerns of communities and regions. By its statute, the NPA abrogated the regulatory powers of all federal departments and agencies that had jurisdiction over pipeline construction, including the National Energy Board. As it turned out, the NPA got the job done but at a considerable cost to the project sponsor. The NPA experiment generally has been regarded by the private sector as an unnecessarily heavy intervention in an industrial sector that routinely operates (at least in Southern Canada) without such regulatory overkill. The desirability of replication of the NPA in other mega-projects would appear questionable.

Mention must be made of the Canada Oil and Gas Lands Administration (COGLA) as a single-window. Created not by statute but by policy and a Memorandum of Understanding in 1981, COGLA was intended to be a federal single-window to the oil and gas industry, operating in Canada Lands, for purposes of resource allocation, production and conservation, environmental and regional socio-economic matters. While space does not permit here an elaboration of the advantages and problems of COGLA, COGLA does not appear to have fulfilled its intended role. While it does carry considerable authority under the Canada Oil and Gas Act, Regulations and other statutory instruments, COGLA did not subsume the existing authorities of other departments, for example DIAND, DFO and DOE. COGLA was simply added to the list of actors that the industry must deal with.

To conclude this section, government has made a number of attempts to create and make workable the single-window concept. With the notable exception of the NPA, all have fallen short of the goal of one-stop regulatory shopping. But in the one "workable" case, the NPA, the one-window solution appears to have been less than fully satisfactory, at least in the view of the industry.

PUBLIC INTEREST EXPRESSION

Insofar as the interests of the public may be represented by various groups or associations, views seem to be divided on the desirability and practicality of single-window agencies. The Canadian Arctic Resources Committee, to cite one such interest group, shares the industry concern that "the public decision-making process for environmental assessment and regulation is unwieldly, expensive, inconclusive and long" (CARC, Northern Perspectives 12(1):3). A single-window, if one were to exist, would at least simplify the procedure and reduce the costs of lobbying for particular changes and objectives. On the other hand, if the single window is peceived to be an agency to promote or facilitate a particular end, e.g. development (which is COGLA's overall purpose), then it may be seen as desirable not to override the authority of other departments or agencies (like FEARO, DOE, DFO, native organizations, the territorial government). Balance of advocacy and power may thus be better achieved through diversity of authority and organization than through a single-window.

TEAM'S FINDINGS

1. To hold the "single-window concept" up as the panacea to regulatory problems is simplistic. It deserves considerable analysis as to its aims, authorities, counterbalances and costs/benefits.

2. There is a direct correlation between the level of authority of a single-window and its effectiveness.

3. Acts and regulations have been promulgated as a direct response to specific development proposals. Problems experienced by developers, and by government agencies, with both the projects and existing regulation have led to the creation of yet more regulation. The resulting jumble of acts and regulations cannot be succesfully traversed by setting up a single-window agency; a fundamental reform of the legislation and regulation is first required.

4. Single-windows can have different dimensions:

   a) project-specific, e.g. gas pipeline

   b) area-specific (Beaufort Sea)

   c) function-specific (environment, energy, (e.g. NEB),
      socio-economic, etc.)

   Function-specific windows may offer promise for reform.

   Example: make one agency accountable for all environmental regulation, even though there may be several players in the field.

OVERVIEW

JUSTICE PROGRAMS

The Team reviewed the following five programs under this section:

LRC-1	Law Reform Commission
Justice/ALR	Administrative Law Reform Project
PCOJ	Privy Council Office (Justice)
JUST 18	Statute Revision Committee
JUST/FDCE	Federal Offences Decriminalization and Compliance Enhancement Project.

While the five programs do not involve "regulating" per se, they each have an important function to play in maintaining and/or improving the quality of law, regulations and the overall regulatory system. Each raises its own special issues as indicated in the respective profiles. However, there are some common threads: many appear to be involved in partially overlapping activities, there are delay and/or productivity problems, and there is little evidence of effective coordination among the units or their work plans. On the other hand, each is characterized by the fundamental value or necessity of its function and one is left with the impression that many of the problems could be resolved with more effective coordination and, in some cases, better management.

It is not an easy matter to measure productivity among researchers - especially legal researchers - but the Team suggests that steps be taken to develop performance indicators to better measure (and spur) productivity in some of these programs.

In reviewing these programs and certain activities of the Solicitor General's department, the Team was struck forcefully by a problem it had not anticipated: serious ambiguity, and overlap and some confusion between the policy-making functions of Justice and Solicitor General. It is not entirely clear to the Team where the policy function of one department begins and the other ends. The result inevitably is direct duplication, non-compliance and waste. (e.g. The Ministry of the Solicitor General has a project known as Federal Law Enforcement Under Review - FLEUR - which seems very close to JUST/FDCE. FLEUR was unknown to the Team until it was too late to conduct a thorough review, but there seems to be a clear sign that the overlap problem in Justice may extend to the interdepartmental level also.)

In light of these observations: the Team suggests that a review be initiated of the respective policy functions of the departments of Justice and Solicitor General to find ways of rationalizing and consolidating policy-making functions in the federal justice system.

LAW REFORM COMMISSION - LRC 1

Objective

To review on a continuing basis the federal laws of Canada and make recommendations for their improvement, modernization and reform.

Authority

Law Reform Commission Act.

Description

The Law Reform Commission conducts legal research, surveys, discussions and hearings for the purpose of consulting with interested groups and individuals. Departments, branches and agencies of the government are required to make available to the Commission any information, advice and assistance it needs to discharge its functions properly.

Legal research at the Commission is divided into four areas:

1. Substantive Criminal Law

The project's main objective is the production of a new code of substantive criminal law for Canada.

2. Criminal Procedure Project

The project's long-term goal is the preparation of a comprehensive code of criminal procedure which will deal with four major aspects of criminal procedure: classification of offences; police powers; pretrial procedures; and trial and appeal procedures.

3. Protection of Life Project

The main objective of the project is to determine the existing strengths and weaknesses of the criminal law tool in combatting pollution in relation to the environment, the workplace and consumer products.

4. Administrative Law Project

To promote a better understanding of the relationship between law and administration. The Commission is

presently concentrating its efforts in three main
areas: independent administrative agencies; compliance
with administrative programs; and the special status of
the federal Crown.

Resources

($000's)	82/83	83/84	84/85	85/86	86/87	87/88
Person-Years	44	45	44	47		
Operating Exp.						
- Salaries	1,445	1,573	1,677	1,777		
- O & M	2,600	3,173	3,317	3,205		
- Other Exp.						
Cost Recovery						
Subsidies						
Capital	28	31	14	67		

Problem Identification

It is difficult to estimate the time required to
complete research projects causing problems in the forecast
and estimate of budgets.

Private Sector

- the LRC has done valuable work, particularly in
  criminal law in recent years.
- too much time spent on studying trivial aspects of
  a problem.
- in the past, many reports not released and
  Commission threatened by authors with law suits.
  By the time reports were released, they were
  out-of-date.
- too much time spent on Working Paper 25 (since
  1978).
- quality of work and costs do not always justify
  the production of some of the reports.
- researchers are inefficient; need pressure and
  deadlines or sanctions to increase productivity.
- should consult work of provincial law reform
  commissions.
- should consult with all sectors affected by
  studies and not just solicit views from the
  academic community.
- Justice works in the criminal law area; the two
  groups have the same objective, and consult the
  same groups of people.

Observations

An audit prepared by Supply and Services in 1982 reported the following observations:

1. Research plans have not set out measurable goals and objectives making it difficult to ascertain if expectations are being met or if changes in the scope or intent of research have occurred or are required.

2. Specific goals are not set for individual researchers for the ongoing planning of future resource requirements.

3. Usefulness of the reports to "recipients" is not measurable.

4. Needs formal goal-setting procedure for all levels with appropriate reporting and feedback system.

5. In 1983, the LRC published four Reports to Parliament, five Working Papers and two study papers. In its 14 years of existence, the Commission has produced for publication 24 Reports to Parliament, 39 Working Papers and 67 study papers - not high productivity relative to cost.

6. Despite recommendations made by the Audit Services Bureau to set detailed operating plans including measurable goals and milestone dates for all research projects, efficiency in this area does not seem to have increased.

7. Apparent overlap in research efforts between projects within the LRC (Administration Law and Protection of Life) and between LRC and the Administrative Law Reform Project and the Federal Statutes Compliance Project, which is also within the Department of Justice. All three groups undertake studies involving administrative/regulatory agencies and compliance. The lack of coordination and cooperation in the exchange of research information has impeded efficient and effective law reform.

Options

The Study Team recommends to the Task Force that the government consider the following:

1. Maintain the LRC.

2. Eliminate the LRC.

3. Introduce reforms designed to improve productivity and reduce duplication with other government activities.

4. Privatize - i.e. provide research grants to academics and others in the private sector.

5. Plan the LRC work program in direct relation to the requirements of government.

ADMINISTRATIVE LAW REFORM - JUSTICE/ALR

Objective

To develop and promote administrative law reform and regulatory reform within the federal department of Justice.

Authority

Statutory Instruments Act
Crown Liability Act
Federal Court Act

Description

The Administrative Law Reform Project is designed to carry out the following five initiatives:

1. Improve ways in which statutory instruments are made and reviewed, both in terms of government and private sector relations, and relations among branches of the government.

2. Streamline administrative appeals mechanisms, using as a pilot project a study examining ways to rationalize social benefits appeals tribunals in both the civilian and veterans affairs sectors.

3. Study the present status of the federal Crown with respect to its liabilities, powers, privileges and remaining royal prerogatives and to correct deficiencies in the laws defining relationships between the Crown and the citizen.

4. Develop uniform minimum guidelines or legislation on administrative procedure for federal administrative authorities.

5. Study the desirability of establishing an advisory body on administration or some coordination mechanism within the government to assist and encourage officials, on a continuing basis, in carrying out legal reforms concerning administrative institutions, practices and procedures.

<u>Resources</u>

	83-84	84-85	85-86
Person-Years	3	1	1
Operating Expenses	324,981	279,752	177,273

<u>Observations</u>

1. The project will terminate in March, 1986 and some of its functions will be carried out under the departmental Public Law Group.

2. The Administrative Law Project within the Law Reform Commission of Canada is also engaged in studies in the following areas:

    a) Advisory Council on Administration.
    b) Administrative agencies and programs.
    c) Status of the Crown.

    Although channels do exist for informal exchange of research information between the ALRP and the LRC, it is uncertain as to whether responsibilities of the two groups have been divided clearly to reduce overlap and duplication. Better coordination of research efforts can only enhance the efficiency and expediency of law reform.

<u>Options</u>

    The Study Team recommends to the Task Force that the government consider the following:

1. Disband and transfer remaining responsibilities to Public Law section of Justice which should absorb costs within existing resource levels.

2. Transfer responsibilities to LRC.

3. Maintain "as is" until termination of project in March, 1986.

PRIVY COUNCIL OFFICE (JUSTICE)- PCOJ

Objective

1. To carry out duties of the Deputy Minister of Justice under the Statutory Instruments Act.

2. To serve as legal advisors to officers of the Privy Council Office.

3. To prepare proclamations, commissions and other instruments issued under the Great Seal, including those for the appointment of judges.

Description

Responsible for carrying out the duties of the Deputy Minister of Justice under the Statutory Instruments Act, which requires that all proposed regulations be examined to ensure that they meet the criteria set out in that legislation. Advice is provided on rectifying legal difficulties and ambiguities, inconsistencies and technical errors in the proposed regulations.

Also responsible for ensuring that regulations do not contravene the Canadian Charter of Rights and Freedoms and the International Convention on Human Rights, and examines all statutory instruments required to be published in Part II of the Canada Gazette.

Counsel in this Section serve as legal advisors to officers of the Privy Council Office, particularly to the Assistant Clerk of the Privy Council. The Section prepares proclamation, as well as commissions and other instruments issued under the Great Seal, including those for the appointment of judges.

Resources

	82/83	83/84	84/85	85/86	86/87	87/88
Person-Years	21	22	26			
Operating Exp.						
- Salaries	189,000	710,000	794,000			
- O & M	7,000	30,000	90,000			
- Other Exp.						
Cost Recovery						
Subsidies						
Capital						

Problem Identification

Private Sector

1. Output too slow, lacks specialization.

Other Departments

1. There are serious criticisms of delays and inadequate service by a relatively inexperienced staff.

2. The delays sometimes result in departments and agencies resorting to administrative measures to achieve objectives which should normally be carried out by regulation.

3. The office represents a major bottleneck in the federal regulatory system.

Observations

The Deputy Minister of Justice has been interested in developing a major initiative to reform procedures and overcome the chronic delays in this office. An action plan has been developed and is at an advanced stage of progress. A critical issue is the unit's requirement for additional resources and improved accommodation.

Options

The Study Team recommends to the Task Force that the government consider the following:

1. Disband and transfer full examination responsibility under SIA to departmental legal counsel.

2. Maintain "as is" but report on progress of internal reforms.

3. Integrate this function into a newly constituted regulatory affairs unit with responsibility for legal as well as economic, social and other dimensions of regulatory system management under the authority of a specially designated minister.

STATUTE REVISION COMMISSION - JUST 18

Objective

To ensure that on a periodic basis, the public general statute and regulations are revised and/or consolidated in accordance with the requirement of the Statute Revision Act.

Authority

Statute Revision Act.

Description

A revision of the statutes is currently underway. The statutes are divided into categories by subject matter for revision and/or consolidation. All changes or corrections are made by in-house lawyers and editors and then circulated to the members of the Commission and/or departmental legal services for comments. The revised version is then finalized and sent to the Canadian Law Information Council for indexation.

Resources

($000's)	82/83	83/84	84/85	85/86	86/87	87/88
PYs	13.8	13.7	14.5			
Operating Expanses						
- Salaries	470	478	544	644	369	369
- O&M	6	177	625	1,513*	327	4
- Other Expenses						
Revenue						
Subsidies						
Capital						

* The increase in O&M is due to indexation and printing costs.

Problem Identification

1. The Department ascribes delays in revision mainly to computerization of the system.

2. The process is behind schedule. There has been no consolidation of federal statutes since 1970 and a 15-year interval reflects either bad planning or poor productivity.

Observations

1. This is an essential program since up-dated consolidations of laws and regulations are needed to ensure that the public has a reasonable opportunity to avoid being "ignorant of the law".

2. This program is grinding steadily to a conclusion but, in view of its importance, the Team questions why such a long interval has been allowed between consolidations. Is it a matter of inadequate resources, poor planning or bad management?

Options

The Study Team recommends to the Task Force that the government consider the following:

1. There is no option in the short term but to conclude the consolidation exercise as quickly as possible.

2. Consideration should be given to making consolidation an ongoing program to avoid delay in the next consolidation.

FEDERAL OFFENCES DECRIMINALIZATION
AND COMPLIANCE ENHANCEMENT PROJECT - JUST/FOCE

Objective

Less costly, more effective and better compliance
policies in the federal government, and appropriate and
extensive decriminalization of offences in federal statutes.

Authority

Justice Act.

Description

In August, 1982, the Government of Canada published a
statement of its criminal law policy entitled "The Criminal
Law in Canadian Society". A central theme of the policy
statement was that criminal law should be used with more
restraint. Cabinet subsequently authorized the Minister of
Justice in June, 1982, to prepare a workplan for the
coordination and comprehensive examination of the
offence-creating, sanction and enforcement provisions found
in federal statutes.

In June, 1983, Cabinet approved a workplan consisting
of two phases. The workplan provides for a
multi-disciplinary group to undertake a series of pilot and
research studies and operational tasks over a 15 to 18 month
period. By seeking to apply the law as a modern instrument
of public policy, the workplan is aimed expressly at
furthering government policies on reform of the criminal law
and regulatory reform. The principal output of Phase I will
be guidance on compliance enhancement (efficiency,
effectiveness and fairness) and on decriminalization
criteria and procedures. Phase II of the workplan,
scheduled to commence in October 1985, will involve the
comprehensive examination of existing statutes and of
proposals for new statutes. A budget for the latter will
have to be approved prior to commencement.

Phase I work is on target. The pilot study of the
Canada Labour Code, Part IV is completed and studies are now
underway of the Atomic Energy Control Act, the Fisheries Act
and the Canada Water Act. A draft code of procedure is now
being developed and, as part of the code, a ticketing scheme
has been finalized. As well, voluntary guidelines on
procedure are being prepared. An inventory of measures to

promote compliance has been finalized and a survey of every federal department has been made to determine what use they are making of these compliance techniques. Two studies are underway with respect to compliance psychology and a model for the evaluation of compliance systems is being developed.

A Phase II is anticipated subject to ministerial approval. It would involve the examination of existing statutes with a view to formulating recommendations for decriminalization within five years.

Resources

($000's)	82/83	83/84	84/85	85/86	86/87	87/88
Person-Years			7.75	3.5*		
Operating Expenses						
- Salaries			315,000	140,000		
- O&M			485,000	110,000		
- Other Expenses						
Revenue						
Subsidies						
Capital						

* In addition, other personnel will be assigned to the project as needed from the Department of Justice.

Problem Identification

No problems have been identified with the project to date. Indeed, two of the participants in the pilot studies made glowing recommendations on the work of the project.

Observations

1. The project seems to have a substantial regulatory reform component with a certain amount of potential duplication or overlap with the Office of Regulatory Reform. However, unlike the latter, the project assumes government intervention as a given factor and its focus is on the compliance and enforcement end of the regulatory spectrum. To the degree that it retains that focus, there is no significant duplication.

2. The proposed Phase II of the project would involve substantial apparent overlap with the Office of Regulatory Reform.

408

3.   The project appears to have the capacity to make
     significant changes to compliance systems which, in the
     long run, should generate cost-savings to the federal
     government.

Options

     The Study Team recommends to the Task Force that the
government consider the following:

1.   Continue project as is with a view to going on with
     Phase II.

2.   Terminate the project after Phase I.

3.   Integrate plans for Phase II into overall program of
     regulatory reform and management as decided in the
     light of the results of the Ministerial Task Force.

PRIVATE SECTOR COMMENTS

On programs in which public-service members of the Regulatory Programs Review Team might be perceived as having a conflict of interest, the practice was to invite comments only from the private-sector members.

The following are their comments on programs in this section:

The six private-sector members of the Regulatory Program Review Team, representing consumer, labour, small and large business interests, comment as follows:

Law Reform Commission

Administrative Law Project

- Concur with problem identification and observations -- considerable evidence of serious time delays, inefficiencies and lack of focus.

- Suggestions

   These two projects should be rationalized with all other law reform research projects housed in departments into one Law Reform Group reporting through Justice.

   Demonstrate such a consolidation, as well as the establishment of firm goals and deadlines, within one year.

Privy Council Office (Justice)

- Observations and Suggestions

   PCOJ is apparently redrafting all regulations from departments, with lengthy delays being experienced.

   Delays must be reduced on a priority basis.

Federal Offences Decriminalization and Compliance Enhancement Program

- ### Comments

    The public-sector members were horrified to learn that there are 97,000 criminal offences in federal statutes, <u>excluding</u> as much as five times that number in federal regulations, and that there is considerable discretion in the enforcement of these offences.

    This is a serious assault on good citizenship, as well as one's sense of fair play and the soundness of the judicial system.

- ### Suggestions

    Enhance and augment the pace and focus of this program, to clear objectives and aim at reducing the number of Federal criminal offences in Statutes by 50 per cent in five years.

411

OVERVIEW

LABOUR CANADA

Although labour legislation is primarily a provincial responsibility, the federal government has constitutionally based authority to enact labour legislation within its exclusive jurisdiction (e.g. transportation and communication). The Canada Labour Code currently applies to some 600,000 employees, 3,500 employers and amendments to Part IV will extend its jurisdiction to federal public servants with respect to occupational health and safety provisions.

Three Labour Canada programs were reviewed:

1. Conditions of Work (LC4) which oversees minimum labour standards (e.g. minimum wage) in the federal jurisdiction;

2. Conciliation, Mediation, Arbitration which provides services to maintain stable labour relations in federally-regulated undertakings;

3. Occupational Safety and Health (LC6) which oversees the workplace under federal jurisdiction with a view to preventing injuries and accidents.

In the Team's view, the main problematic issues emerged from the Occupational Safety and Health (OSH) program. The costs of workplace injury and disease are normally part of the costs of production, as are preventive training programs promoted by employers. In the absence of OSH regulations, such costs would be borne mainly by injured workers or by the public through medical and worker compensation programs. The Economic Council found that employer liability systems and the traditional legal rights of employees are not sufficient substitutes for OSH regulations. It also found that there is unequal sharing of the incentive to reduce risks of workplace injury or disease since these do not pose the same financial threat to employers as do work stoppages.

Some of the specific issues in the federal OSH program include:

1. The perceived overlap resulting from the numerous departments and agencies which deal with OSH issues.

Health and Welfare provides input on risk/hazard factors involving exposure to certain conditions (e.g. ureaformaldehyde insulation in the workplace). The Canadian Transport Commission oversees operational safety issues. In a railway accident for example, both Labour Canada and Canadian Transport Commission officials are involved in on-site investigation; the first because of OSH issues arising from accident conditions affecting those employed in clean-up procedures; the second to determine operational safety matters. Although amendments to the Code include giving Labour Canada lead responsibility in OSH, federally-regulated employers and employees will have to continue to deal with the various agencies involved.

2.   Certain Code amendments will involve additional compliance costs. For instance, the requirement for joint labour-management OSH committees for small groupings of employees will be difficult to implement, especially for larger enterprises with small operations scattered throughout remote regions (e.g. Bell Canada, railway maintenance or repair crews).

3.   Certain OSH provisions have already been challenged in the courts as contravening the Canadian Human Rights Act (e.g. the Sikh who for religious reasons cannot wear a hard-hat). Such conflicting thrusts in federal statutes which can involve litigation costs should obviously be avoided, either through provision for exemptions or through other, appropriate mechanisms.

The 1983 Auditor General's report was critical about the level of inspection and enforcement of the program noting that the high injury and fatality rate (in 1981, 82,000 workers were injured and there were 18 job-related fatalities) indicated clear inadequacy. Since then, the program has developed a compliance enhancement project with the Department of Justice in order to focus its efforts on hazardous workplaces (such as mining and longshoring).

Until 1979, federal inspection was contracted to provincial OSH officers since every province has OSH legislation. Budgetary restraints cancelled this arrangement and federal inspectors have since been used.

However, savings could undoubtedly be achieved if national OSH standards could be developed. These could be administered by the provinces who would inspect and enforce standards in workplaces under federal jurisdiction. If on the other hand direct federal administration were to be maintained, it would be more efficient to consolidate all OSH functions under one administering department as the Economic Council recommended.

MEDIATION, CONCILIATION, ARBITRATION - LC

Objective

To promote stable industrial relations in the work place in federal agencies legislated by the Parliament of Canada and in federally regulated industries (excluding the federal public service).

Authority

Canada Labour Code Part V.

Description

The Canada Labour Code applies to approximately 600,000 employees who work for a federal work undertaking or private business which includes interprovincial/international transportation, telecommunications, banks, certain Crown corporations, enterprises of national interest (e.g. uranimum mining) and those in the Yukon and the Northwest Territories.

The program fulfills the statutory responsibility for the provision of conciliation, mediation and arbitration assistance for dispute resolution in the federal private sector. Where direct negotiations have failed to settle differences, the program provides conciliation and/or mediation services where required to resolve differences, or to permit the legal right to strike/lockout, as the circumstances dictate. Discretionary powers of the Minister regulate behaviour of the parties e.g. delay strike action by continuing involvement of the mediator or imposing a cooling-off period. Where differences arise during the life of the agreement over the interpretation or application of any of the contract provisions, the program provides the parties with outside arbitrators for which the costs are borne by the parties involved.

In 1983-84 the program's operations resolved 90 per cent of all disputes handled without any stoppage of work. It dealt with 297 collective bargaining disputes and appointed adjudicators in 140 cases in that year. During the same period, the Minister received 115 requests for arbitration and appointments were made in 78 cases.

Resources

($000's)	82/83	83/84	84/85	85/86	86/87	87/88
Person-Years	67	69	69	69	69	69
Operating Exp.						
– Salaries	2,570	2,555	2,932	3,103	3,103	3,103
– O & M	647	683	885	933	933	933
– Other Exp.	0	0	0	0	0	0
Revenue			N/A			
Subsidies			N/A			
Capital	3	4	4	4	4	4
TOTAL	3,220	3,242	3,821	4,040	4,040	4,040

Problem Identification

No problems were identified from a regulatory point of view. Both labour and management groups contacted had praise for the program's performance and agreed its functions are necessary in promoting stable industrial relations.

The department notes that if the function were transferred to private practioners, the costs would be considerably higher. Also, the discretionary powers of the Minister provides flexibility in areas such as national transportation networks where stable industrial relations are vital. Such flexibility is also advantageous.

Observations

1. There appear to be no problems with this program and there is consensus that it should be maintained as a vital, positive function in promoting stable industrial relations in crucial sectors of the Canadian economy.

Options

Nil

CONDITIONS OF WORK - LC 4

Objective

To develop, administer and enforce comprehensive minimum labour standards (e.g., hours or work, minimum wage, unjust dismissal) to protect employees from unfair treatment, and to improve employees' conditions of employment in federal agencies legislated by the Parliament of Canada and in federally regulated industries (excluding the federal public service).

Authority

Canada Labour Code, Part III; Fair Wages and Hours of Labour Act.

Description

The Canada Labour Code applies to approximately 600,000 employees who work for a federal work undertaking or private business which includes interprovincial/international transportation, telecommunications, banks, certain Crown corporations, enterprises of national interest (e.g. uranium mining) and those in the Yukon and the Northwest Territories.

This Labour Canada program administers the Code's provisions regarding hours of work, wages, vacations and holidays with a view to ensuring minimum standards. Its operations include inspections, investigations of complaints and accidents as well as technical survey of the work environment. Federally-regulated industries, principally in the transportation, telecommunications and banking sectors as well as certain Crown corporations comprising some 600,000 employees are regulated through this program.

Resource

($000's)	82/83	83/84	84/85	85/86	86/87	87/88
Person-Years	87	88	100	105	105	105
Operating Exp.						
- Salaries	3,139	3,170	3,602	4,318	4,318	4,318
- O & M	278	399.5	280	310	310	310
- Other Exp.	-	-	-	-	-	-
Revenue	-	-	-	-	-	-
Subsidies	-	-	-	-	-	-
Capital	-	-	-	10	10	10

Problem Identification

No problems of a regulatory nature were identified by the business and unions groups contacted. However, a labour group pointed to the need to better inform employees about their rights and redress, as well as appeal, mechanisms.

A 1983 evaluation conducted by private sector consultants concluded that there is a demonstrable, ongoing need for minimum labour standards. Such standards, according to the department, contribute to an improved climate and stability in industrial relations. Federal and provincial jurisdictions are well defined and each province has legislation governing labour standards and minimum wages.

Although the department acknowledges a differential impact on large and small enterprises, it noted that large enterprises also have responsibilities entailing greater costs such as compensation for group termination of employment.

Observations

1. The Team found that, although there are relatively few small enterprises which are federally-regulated, they must nevertheless experience certain difficulties in implementing the program's objectives.

2. Since minimum wages are part of this program's responsibilities, the governments's recently-announced measures to implement recommendations of the Royal Commission on Equality in Employment with respect to equal pay for work of equal value will involve difficulties, particularly for smaller enterprises. This is despite the fact that enterprises with 100 employees or less have been exempted from these measures. The real difficulties with respect to this issue may emerge in the Canadian Human Rights Commission's complaints/investigations operations, although the costs of compliance for enterprises and the complexities of defining "work of equal value" also constitute problems.

3. The program should ensure through appropriate feedback mechanisms possibly including increased union consultations, that employees are better informed about their rights.

Options

The Study Team recommends to the Task Force that the government consider the following:

1. The program should find equitable ways of increasing its responsiveness to the compliance difficulties experienced by smaller enterprises. This is not an easy task since the program aims at ensuring minimum standards and differentiated treatment of enterprises based on size could be perceived as inequitable by employees.

OCCUPATIONAL SAFETY AND HEALTH - LC 6

Objective

To prevent accidents and injury to health in the work place for some 600,000 employees in federal agencies and in federally regulated private sector enterprises (e.g. telecommunications, interprovincial and international transportation, banks).

Authority

Canada Labour Code, Part IV.

Description

The regulatory activities of this program include the inspection, monitoring, certification and information requirements pertaining to occupational safety and health (OSH) as well as the investigation of complaints and accidents in the work place under federal jurisdiction. As in other labour legislation, the primary constitutional responsibility rests with the provinces, all of which have (OSH) legislation and regulations. However the federal government also has authority under the Constitution Act 1867 to enact labour legislation affecting matters under its exclusive jurisdiction.

Under the amendments of the Canada Labour Code's Part IV there is a consolidation of previously fragmented legislative powers for work health and safety, as well as an extension of jurisdiction (not applicable in the rest of the Code) to include employees in the federal public service. Currently, this part of the Code applies to 3,700 employers.

Of particular significance are those amendments to Part IV of the Code which essentially affect: the right of an employee to refuse to work if there is "danger" in the work place (previously the provision stipulated "imminent danger", now the term is much broader); and the requirement to establish joint management labour safety and health committees for establishments with 20 or more employees, and health/safety representatives for those with five to 19 employees. The amended provisions give the Minister of Labour the lead responsibility in OSH and it is the intention of the department to develop Memoranda of Understanding with the other federal departments and agencies involved (e.g. Canadian Transport Commission, Health and Welfare) to clearly delineate responsibilities.

Labour Canada is decentralized with five regional offices and 25 district offices. Until 1979, OSH inspection was contracted to provincial officers. In 1981, approximately 82,000 workers were injured and 18 died in on-the-job accidents under the Code's current jurisdiction (excluding the public service). Among the sectors with highest accident rates are mining and longshoring; among the lowest are banking and communications.

Resources

($000's)	82/83	83/84	84/85	85/86	86/87	87/88
Person-Years	121	122	140	149	147	147
Operating Exp.						
– Salaries	4,335	4,395	5,043	6,045	5,961	5,961
– O & M	2,774	981	2,081	2,160	1,604	1,561
– Other Exp.	–	–	–	–	–	–
Revenue	–	–	–	–	–	–
Subsidies	26	26	26	26	26	26
Capital	142	75	50	160	160	190

Problem Identification

Labour and management groups contacted have the following concerns:

1. While industry indicates LC leans excessively to social issues (not scientific evidence), labour insists on the need for a stronger visible lead role to be assumed by LC.

2. The amended version of the provision regarding danger in the work place giving the employee the right to leave a dangerous work place will be costly to enterprises and difficult to enforce.

3. The implementation of the requirement for joint OSH committees will be costly and difficult to implement, particularly in smaller, more remote work situations.

4. There is a perceived lack of clarity of roles: Canadian Transport Commission (CTC) has OSH functions, also Health and Welfare has responsibilities under Part IV of the Code relating to dangerous substances.

The department regularly develops Socio-Economic Impact Assessments (SEIA) of their regulations as required by Treasury Board policy. In response to the 1983 Auditor General's critical comments about level of service and high injury rates under the program, LC is developing alternative methods of delivery including greater self-regulation.

Observations

1. Statistics indicate that the injury and fatality rates in the workplace under federal jurisdiction warrant a continued need for preventive measures and regulation. While there are substantive costs of compliance, higher injuries/illness rates would probably be costlier, as would the sole existence of stiffer employer liability and accompanying litigation.

2. In terms of overall public administration costs, having 11 separate pieces of legislation on OSH hardly seems justified. The Economic Council has already recommended the development of national OSH standards.

3. If direct federal involvement in OSH were to be maintained, maximum efficiency would not necessarily be achieved through the proposed Memoranda of Understanding delineating the respective responsibilities of the agencies involved (LC, CTC, H&W). The Economic Council recommended consolidation of functions under one administering department.

4. The concerns of federally regulated industry about amendments pertaining to grounds for employee refusal to work do not appear to be supported by the experience regarding similar rights provided under provincial jurisdictions.

Options

The Study Team recommends to the Task Force that the government consider the following:

1. Develop national OSH standards and a single legislative framework. This would require the consent of all provinces and past, similar efforts have not been successful. Savings for the federal government could result by delegating administration of provisions to provinces or, where appropriate, by contracting inspection/investigation to provincially or

federally certified private agencies: the program would
be reduced to overseeing such delegation.

2. Centralize within one department the responsibilities
    and expertise for OSH, thereby eliminating the need for
    Memoranda of Understanding.

3. Maintain the "status quo" but require that the
    essential features of Memoranda of Understanding be
    communicated expeditiously to regulated industries and
    unions affected.

BACKGROUND

CANADA LABOUR RELATIONS BOARD

Labour relations legislation and regulations attempt to provide for the settling or adjudication of issues without resort to the courts. Under federal jurisdiction, where the maintenance of national transportation and communications networks and other services (e.g. banking) are vital, the speedy resolution of cases which can potentially lead to labour relations disruptions is particularly important. The CLRB has been established to provide a less formal, more flexible, and expedient mechanism for settling labour relations issues than is available through litigation in the courts.

The CLRB, which until 1973 was representational (including labour and management members), is now composed of labour relations practitioners and lawyers. The problems identified by the Study Team are delay and backlogs, combined with increasingly "legalistic", complex procedures. While the CLRB has implemented several of the recommendations made in a 1980 Law Reform Commission study of its functions, it has not provided follow-up to some of the key ones which address the procedural burden (e.g. the Law Reform Commission recommended public input in CLRB regulation-making). Moreover, although it has clearly identified case-load management problems, it is exempted from the program evaluation requirements of the Comptroller General and does not appear to use outside review expertise to address management problems. Given that speed in problem resolution and ready access by interested parties are decisive factors in the efficient and effective functioning of the CLRB, serious consideration should be given to the outstanding, unresolved issues raised by the Law Reform Commission study.

CANADA LABOUR RELATIONS BOARD - CLRB

Objective

To promote stable industrial relations through independent administrative and quasi-judicial functions, having the power to determine the rights of employers and employees under federal jurisdiction and to issue binding orders.

Authority

Canada Labour Code, Part V.

Description

The Canada Labour Code applies to approximately 600,000 employees who work for a federal work, undertaking or business which includes interprovincial/international transportation, telecommunications, banks, certain Crown corporations, enterprises of national interest (e.g. uranium mining) and undertakings or work in the Yukon and the Northwest Territories. Part V of the Code provides for the settling or adjudication of issues without resort to the courts. In the federal jurisdiction where vital national transportation and communications networks are involved, it is especially important that industrial relations be stable and orderly.

The Canada Labour Relations Board (CLRB) is a quasi-judicial body, with statutory and regulatory powers. It has 10 provincial counterparts which deal with provincial labour laws. In general, the CLRB interprets the statutory provisions which protect or circumscribe freedom of association in industrial relations. It does not, however, assist parties in collective bargaining, a function of the Minister of Labour provided through Labour Canada. It operates independently from the department, submits an Annual Report to the Minister which is tabled in Parliament and is exempted from program evaluation requirements of the Comptroller General.

Until 1973, the Board's functions were carried out by a tripartite tribunal which included part-time labour and management members. Since 1973, full-time appointees are non-representational (largely industrial relations practitioners and some lawyers) and are prohibited by law from holding any other office. Its functions in industrial relations include: powers relating to bargaining rights and their structure (e.g. certification of a union as bargaining agent); investigation and adjudication of complaints alleging contraventions of the Code (e.g. unfair labour practices) and the exercise of cease and desist powers in cases of unlawful strike or lockout.

Because speed and ready access to remedies are essential in industrial relations, the Board has five regional offices (Vancouver, Winnipeg, Toronto, Montreal and Dartmouth) which investigates complaints and responds to unlawful strikes or lockouts, and the Board travels extensively to hear parties on-site. In 1983-84, the Board received 771 new cases and settled 56 per cent of cases (including previous year's) outside of hearings. It is developing an automated case management/information retrieval system (to be operational by the summer of 1985) which should expedite the processing of cases as well as provide a jurisprudential data base with potential for sharing on a Canada-wide basis.

Resources

($000's)	82/83	83/84	84/85	85/86	86/87	87/88
Person-Years	96	99	104	104	103	103
Operating Exp.						
- Salaries	3,150	3,532	3,852	4,018	3,979	3,979
- O & M	1,184	1,412	1,299	1,370	1,368	1,368
- Other Exp.*	483	502	682	562	557	557
Revenue	-	-	-	-	-	-
Subsidies	-	-	-	-	-	-
Capital	6	6	149	31	6	6

*   This amount includes Statutory Items

Problem Identification

While both industry and labour groups contacted agreed on the need for this program, the following concerns were raised:

1.   Delays in certain areas and procedural burdens represent considerable costs to both management and labour. Lengthy procedures which are often too legalistic tend, at times, to aggravate industrial relations and can have the net effect of perceived denial of justice.

2.   A major industry and a labour group both indicated a need to make the Board more representational in order to emphasize practicality rather than the current legalistic/procedural context.

3.   A major labour group notes that the Board impinges on the right of association by imposing policy prerequisites tantamount to constraints on the certification process.

When advised of the current program review, the Board noted its position that it is not a regulatory, but rather a quasi-judicial function with statutory and regulatory powers. At its request, the Law Reform Commission (LRC) undertook a study of the Board's functions which was published in 1980 and which included 22 recommendations, some of which have been implemented by the Board.

Observations

1.   The rate of applications for judicial review by the Federal Court of Appeal as compared with total caseload is one indication of performance. Between 1973-81, the average was seven per cent, an acceptable rate. However, in at least one Supreme Court decision, a Justice expressed the view that the Board had gone beyond its jurisdiction.

2.   In the Team's view, delay, which can be detrimental to industrial relations, is a very real factor in the Board's operations when considering the number of carry-over cases from one year to the next (in 1979-80, 287 carry-over cases; in 1980-81, 334).

3.   The Board's principal "raison d'être" is to avoid lengthy, costly court litigation and industrial relations disruptions through more pragmatic and flexible adjudication of issues, yet excessive, costly, "legalism" is perceived as a problem.

4.   Although the LRC study recommended public input in rule-making (regulations), there has been no follow-up on this matter by the Board.

Options

The Study Team recommends to the Task Force that the government consider the following:

1. The Board should be maintained with the following
    suggested changes. Part-time members should be
    representative of management and labour, with the
    Chairman assigning them to cases. The LRC Study
    recommended a fully representational Board: the Board
    rejected this option. An independent (e.g. private
    sector consultant) management review should be
    undertaken to formulate ways to streamline procedures
    to reduce backlogs and delays including proposals for
    amendments and simplification of procedural regulations
    where required.

2. The Board's non-representational character could be
    maintained, however, the independent review as proposed
    above should be implemented. In addition, extensive
    efforts should be made to explore viable, equitable
    ways of resolving issues with less "legalism",
    particuarly with respect to certification agreed upon
    by parties involved (another LRC recommendation), and
    cases involving individuals unrepresented by counsel (a
    further LRC recommendation).

OVERVIEW

REVENUE CANADA CUSTOMS AND EXCISE

This section specifically highlights four bonding or licensing programs as part of the customs revenue control system, the duty refund/remission/drawback program and the excise duty.

Generally, the fundamental issues common to Customs programs are paper burden, red tape and delay. Import documentation is often cited by business, both large and small, as its overall concern. The lack of uniform and consistent interpretation and application of the Acts or regulations also frustrates the private sector. The complexity of the Customs System applied across-the-board at all entry ports demands a knowledge base which is not always evident at the field officer level. Too many departments are involved in the policy-setting and central administration of the Acts (Finance, Justice, DRIE, Privy Council) which adds to delay and confusion when dealing with government offices.

There are no major problems with the system but a general streamlining of procedures is required. In the view of the Study Team, amendments to the Customs Act deserve some priority. The private sector has requested that alternative import documentation procedures be formulated and presented for consultation with the affected industry. In this regard, the private sector suggests that electronic transmission and the establishment of "control ports" would expedite transactions and allow for greater and more specialized attention to problem areas. Consideration should be given also to focussing policy and administration in one department. Generally, the concept of "duty-free" ports received low marks since the private sector generally favours an efficient system, administered uniformly across Canada and in harmony with trading partners.

BONDED CARRIERS - RCCE 2

Objective

To ensure the collection of duty, control the importation of prohibited goods and substances, and facilitate international trade by providing for inland movement of goods on a timely basis.

Authority

Customs Act, Customs Tariff Act.

Description

The program serves an economic purpose and is part of the customs revenue control system. The declaration process is the first step in controlling and ensuring the payment of duty on imported goods. This consists of work associated with clearing goods from their entry into Canada to the presentation of documentation of brokers or importers requesting their release.

Certain major highway carriers are granted the status of "post-audit carriers", enabling them to transport goods into the country without examination at the border. These carriers must be licensed, meet standards and report regularly to ensure coverage of liabilities to the Crown resulting from the movement of non-duty, paid goods in Canada. The post-entry clearance consists of audits of the carrier's records and spot checks of the loads at the inland warehouse. Because of such procedures, fewer examinations are undertaken on these carriers than on others.

Resources

($000's)	82/83	83/84	84/85	85/86	86/87	87/88
Person-Years	433.6	413.6	434.6	434.6	434.6	434.6
Operating Exp.						
- Salaries	9,407	9,683	10,820	10,820	10,831	10,843
- O & M	357	375	425	425	426	426
- Other Exp.	1,317	1,356	1,513	1,515	1,516	1,518
Revenues						
Subsidies						
Capital						

Problem Identification

There are no discernible problems with this program.

Observations

1. The costs of the program are considered small compared to the collection of duties and detection of fraud or dumping.

2. The cost-effectiveness of the program could be improved as a result of a complete re-design of the Customs Commercial Clearance System currently in process.

3. Increasing deployment of EDP is an attempt to offset operating costs which primarily reflect salaries.

Options

The Study Team recommends to the Task Force that the government consider implementing cost-recovery by increasing the bonding fee and/or introducing an 'ad valorem' charge on the value of goods shipped.

BONDED WAREHOUSES — RCCE 3

Objective

To provide duty and tax deferral for imported goods in storage, ensure eventual payment to the Crown, and control prohibited goods and substances.

Authority

Customs Act, Customs Tariff Act.

Description

The program serves an economic purpose and is part of the customs revenue control system.

Importers may, under certain prescribed circumstances, bring goods into Canada under bond and pay the applicable duties and taxes as the goods leave the warehouse for domestic consumption, rather than at the time of import. Maximum time deferral is three years from date of first entry and warehousing thereof. The program extends to ships' stores and the disposal of unclaimed goods at customs offices.

Revenue Canada has allowed the establishment of approximately 1,200 bonded warehouses operated by the private sector which it inspects (audits) to enforce appropriate storage, and documentation to ensure eventual payment of the applicable duties and taxes.

Warehouse operators charge a licensing fee to importers as partial recovery of expenses incurred by Revenue Canada in administration of this program.

Resources

($000's)	82/83	83/84	84/85	85/86	86/87	87/88
Person-Years*	63.0	67.5	61.5	30.5	30.5	30.5
Operating Exp.						
- Salaries	1,408	1,612	1,565	749	750	752
- O & M	51	59	58	24	24	24
- Other Exp.	197	226	219	105	105	105
Revenue						
Subsidies						
Capital						

* Assumes passage of revised Customs Act in 1985/86. Projections for 85/86 to 87/88 include the elimination of 30 person-years from the base as a result of recent government decisions.

Problem Identification

1. No problems are identified.

2. Minor irritation with documentation paper burden, particularly export declarations.

Observations

1. The program provides significant savings directly to business by the deferment of duties and taxes, and indirectly through the ability to bulk purchase, ship and inventory.

2. The paper burden irritant has recently been addressed by Orders-in-Council (March 28, 1985) which remove the requirement for export declarations.

3. The costs of the program are small compared to the collection of duties and taxes, and the cash flow benefits to business.

4. In an effort to cut operating costs, the Government Expenditure and Program Review (November 1984) suggested restrictions on the program which would have resulted in a 75 per cent reduction in bonded warehouses. Business responded by agreement to full cost-recovery through an increase in licensing fees charged by warehouse operators. This was undertaken by an Order-in-Council (March 28, 1985).

Options

Nil.

435

CUSTOMS DUTY -- REFUND, REMISSION, DRAWBACK - RCCE 14

Objective

Allows for the waiver or return of duty and tax on imported goods to assist Canadian industry to compete in domestic and export markets and promote industrial growth in Canada.

Authority

Customs Act, Excise Tax Act, Customs Tariff Act, Financial Administration Act (sec. 17).

Description

The refund program returns duty and/or taxes paid, under certain conditions such as inferior goods, damaged goods, clerical error or overpayment. Under trade stimulus programs, drawbacks (recovery of duty paid) and remissions (forgiveness of duties otherwise payable) provide relief from the full impact of Canadian taxing statutes, without affecting Canada's right to maintain the levels of protection under the General Agreement on Tariffs and Trade. Specifically, duties and taxes are recovered or waived for commodities unavailable in Canada, and to which there will be significant Canadian value-added in the production process.

This is an adjunct of tax policy. Policy is set by the Department of Finance and involves major economic development initiatives. Administrative procedures and systems for compliance and enforcement are the responsibility of Revenue Canada. Administrative accountability for specific trade stimulus programs are often shared with the Department of Regional Industrial Expansion.

The process involves claim verification, supervisory review of source data supporting claims, auditing companies on refunds, drawback and remission programs, and the promulgation of regulations on document control and compliance auditing. The regulation-making apparatus is carried out centrally in Ottawa and delivered through regional units.

($000's)	82/83	83/84	84/85	85/86	86/87	87/88
Person-Years	360	357	354.4	353.5	353.5	353.5
Operating Exp.						
– Salaries	9,882	10,599	12,933	12,903	12,903	12,903
– O & M	538	569	595	595	595	595
– Other Exp.	1,383	1,484	1,811	1,806	1,806	1,806
Revenue						
Subsidies						
Capital						

Problem Identification

1. Paper burden and administrative costs to industry are excessive.

2. The process has resulted in a backlog of claims and remission applications which increase the direct costs to government and provides for a lengthy response time to business.

3. Failure to comply with the detailed administrative requirements often leads to disputes of an adverserial nature between claimants and government, even though the programs are designed to assist claimants.

4. Large corporations tend to lobby more and receive special treatment or concessions than does small business.

5. Remissions to specific companies or individuals under section 17 of the Financial Administration Act are not transparent. The "rules" under which these remissions are granted are not published.

6. The efficiency of the programs as trade or industrial growth stimuli is questionable. The burdensome red tape, lengthy turnaround time, often non-transparent nature and shifts in government fiscal and economic development policy are unlikely to result in major and lasting job creation.

Observations

1. Remission and drawback programs have promoted industrial growth and jobs but the costs-vs-benefits are not clear. Improvements and alternatives are sought.

2. The need for such programs often arises from industry lobby and are assessed and approved on an interdepartmental basis between the Department of Finance, Regional Industrial Expansion and Revenue Canada - Customs and Excise. The procedures framework is usually developed on a consultative basis between the control body responsible for regulatory development and the bodies responsible for program delivery.

3. Direct administrative costs to government and to the end-users of the program are sometimes not fully explored before the program is initiated.

4. The programs are accused of being highly discretionary but they do provide flexibility as economic conditions warrant.

5. The Study Team notes that paper burden, red tape, and delays in the marketplace do affect small and medium-size business to a proportionately greater extent than they do large business.

6. A movement to "freer trade" and/or major reduction in duties will render the program less adequate over time.

Options

The Study Team recommends to the Task Force that the government consider investigating ways to reduce paperburden and administrative costs to the private sector associated with this program and to improve transparency of decision-making.

EXCISE DUTY - RCCE 29

Objective

To ensure proper payment of excise duty and effect control over the manufacture, storage and transporation of exciseable goods.

Authority

Excise Act, Financial Administration Act, Importation of Intoxicating Liquors Act, Food and Drug Regulations.

Description

The program is both fiscal and regulatory in that it produces significant revenues, controls the production of goods to verify quantities produced and ensures products meet government standards. The commodities affected are tobacco and alcohol (distilleries, breweries, wineries, pharmaceutical and chemical producers).

The degree of tax is established by the Department of Finance as part of tax policy. Revenue Canada is responsible for administration, enforcement and compliance. Control is effected through the issuance of regulations and compliance audit. Regulations are both Ministerial and informal memoranda to industry detailing instructions of an administrative nature (e.g. types of books and records to be kept). Compliance is a mixture of on-site surveillance (distilleries), post-audit (tobacco, breweries) and voluntary bonding and reporting (pharmaceutical, chemicals). Delivery of the program is decentralized and executed in the regions.

Both federal and provincial governments apply duties/taxes to tobacco and alcoholic products. Both levels of government exercise controls over the movement and/or marketing of these products.

Resources

($000's)	82/83	83/84	84/85	85/86	86/87	87/88
Person-Years			81	81	81	46
Operating Exp.						
- Salaries			2,960	2,988	2,988	1,868
- O & M			288	289	289	289
- Other Exp.						
Revenue						
Subsidies						
Capital					2	2

Problem Identification

1. Federal-provincial entanglement; too many regulators; cost of final product reflects a layering of duties; paperburden is excessive; complicates marketing activities interprovincially.

2. Taxing and effective control of production and marketing is the outgrowth of social/moral concerns. Fiscal considerations at two layers of government have through the years pushed economic costs far above market-determined levels. This leads to distortion (e.g. price competition with imports, barriers to entry, media advertising). The social and fiscal elements of the program should be disentangled.

3. Duty structure is considered by some to be inequitable and the rationale non-transparent across the alcoholic beverage product spectrum.

4. Cost-effectiveness and appropriateness of on-site surveillance activity is questioned. However, some distilleries see federal government surveillance as providing a marketing advantage to their product lables in international competition. Generally, alternative, less costly means are sought to ensure that government standards are met.

Observations

1. The dutiable base is not all federal, the largest duty/tax is applied at the provincial level. All governments see the program as essentially fiscal and significant revenues are raised.

2.   The Federal Government is gradually moving away from
     on-site surveillance to post-audit procedures.

Options

The Study Team recommends to the Task Force that the
government consider the following:

1.   Institute a program of industry self-regulation coupled
     with mandated reporting to government, and supervisory
     oversight by government of external audits.

2.   Proceed as proposed with the reduction in the Duty
     Program through the elimination of all surveillance
     activities over distilleries, breweries, tobacco
     manufacturers and bonded manufacturers effective April
     1987.

LICENSING OF CUSTOMS HOUSE BROKERS - RCCE 4

Objective

To ensure that persons who act on behalf of importers in dealing with Customs have knowledge of the Acts, regulations, enforcement and administration, and are generally qualified to do so.

Authority

Customs Act, Customs House Brokers Licensing Regulations.

Description

The customs broker is a professional who provides both a specialized service to the importing public and facilitates entry processing which reduces detailed inspection by government.

Through Revenue Canada (Customs and Excise) examinations, an individual may become qualified to act as a customs broker, i.e. work for a brokerage firm. To date, there are about 2,000 qualified individuals. To obtain a brokerage licence, applications must be made to a government board, the Licence Advisory Committee which, relative to criteria, subjects the applicant to both departmental and RCMP investigations. Credit worthiness and personal background are critical elements of the process as well as knowledge requirements.

Licences are renewed annually by the Licence Advisory Committee based upon input from the department's regional collector. Licence revocation is difficult, requiring in effect, a legal case being made. There are about 350 licensed firms. It is a national licensing program administered centrally, with receipt of applications, renewals, and day-to-day interface with brokers carried out locally.

Resources

($000's)	82/83	83/84	84/85	85/86	86/87	87/88
Person-Years	4.0	4.0	4.0	3.0	3.0	3.0
Operating Exp.						
- Salaries	120.0	120.0	120.0	90.0	90.0	90.0
- O & M	5.0	5.0	5.0	5.0	5.0	5.0
- Other Exp.	16.8	16.8	16.8	12.6	12.6	12.6
Revenue*	105.0	105.0	110.0	110.0	135.0	135.0
Subsidies						
Capital						

*   Licence Fees

Problem Identification

1.   No performance standards exist for licence renewal. The subjective views of the department's regional collector constitute the basis for renewal with rubber stamping by the Licence Advisory Committee.

2.   There is consensus by both the public and private sectors that licence revocation is at best difficult and that government at times has not been tough enough in enforcing licence renewal.

3.   The government sees a twofold risk in certification of individuals and licensing of firms:

    a)   signaling effective control over the brokerage industry when none exists; and,

    b)   financial liability to the importing public in the event of errors made by the broker.

4.   Enabling legislation and regulations require updating to accommodate information technology which affects purchasing, warehousing, shipping and inventory. Informatics also enables individuals to offer customs brokerage functions without being qualified or licensed as brokers.

Observations

1.   The present Customs Act revisions will address the need to update legislation in conformity with changes in the industry, notably arising from the impact of information technology.

2.   In the view of the Study Team, complete elimination of the licensing program would be unacceptable to both importers and government as brokers provide a much needed expertise and the alternative of dealing directly with government would create delays and add to administrative costs.

3.   The Licence Advisory Committee includes only one industry representative who has been a member for the past 15 years. The Committee essentially performs a "rubber-stamp" function.

4.   In the public interest, there is a desire to enhance the professional image of the Customs Broker.

Options

The Study Team recommends to the Task Force that the government consider the following:

1.   Self-regulation. A Society of Customs Brokers could be established to qualify and license.

2.   Enhance the role of the Licence Advisory Committee through:

   a)   equal industry representation on fixed term and rotational basis;

   b)   broaden requirements for qualification and licensing;

   c)   set and monitor measurable performance standards; and,

   d)   establish a policy advisory function to Revenue Canada on issues relating to the business of importation.

3.   Full cost-recovery if the option of self-regulation is not chosen.

REGISTRATION AND LICENSING OF VESSELS – RCCE 34

Objective

Identification of vessel ownership.

Authority

Canada Shipping Act.

Description

Revenue Canada's mandate to control the international movement of goods also gives it an administrative or enforcement role for legislation that is primarily the responsibility of other government departments. The above program constitutes an administrative function carried out on behalf of the Department of Transport.

Small vessels are licensed to provide legal owner identification and meet basic safety standards much in the same manner as vehicular registration. Because small vessel licensing is voluntary compliance program, it has no organized enforcement.

Registration of ships serves the same purpose as the Land Titles Office – it identifies owners, protects the interests of owners and licence-holders, and ensures that safety standards are met at the time of registration. Sanctions employed are the failure to obtain a license or registration, and detention of the ship if not properly registered.

Licensing and registration is undertaken through regional offices and customs ports of entry.

Resources

($000's)	82/83	83/84	84/85	85/86	86/87	87/88
Person-Years	24.0	18.65	19.5	19.5	19.5	19.5
Operating Exp.						
– Salaries	590.0	448.0	535.0	535.0	535.0	535.0
– O & M	29.0	21.0	24.0	24.0	24.0	24.0
– Other Exp.	82.6	62.7	74.9	74.9	74.9	74.9
Revenue						
Subsidies						
Capital						

Problem Identification

1. There are no regulatory problems in this program.

2. Despite small operating costs, Revenue Canada questioned the overall efficiency and appropriateness of administering the program outside the mandate of the Department of Transport.

Observations

1. There is consensus that licensing and registration is required for legal identification of property and adherence to safety standards.

2. The costs may be small but the benefits of the program are not clearly recognizable from a Revenue Canada perspective.

3. The mandate for ship/vessel standards-setting (including safety standards) lies with the Department of Transport and, logically, licensing and registration could be more closely tied to compliance and enforcement activity within that department.

Options

The Study Team recommends to the Task Force that the government consider the following:

1. Licensing of small vessels (pleasure boats) could be turned over to the provinces.

2. Ship registration could be centralized with greater reliance on EDP and handled through the Department of Transport.

3. Implement full cost-recovery through increases in licence and registration fees.

OVERVIEW

TRANSPORTATION PROGRAMS

The next five sections deal with various aspects of the transportation sector in Canada. The programs, which were examined prior to the release of the Minister of Transport's discussion paper "Freedom to Move", range from direct economic regulation to the provision of infrastructure and basic transportation services. This wide range of programs was covered because of tight inter-relationships between regulatory and regulatory-related programs.

This section examines general transportation programs, those that are multi-modal in nature. It also contains a background paper on transportation safety and one on the respective roles of Transport Canada and the Canadian Transport Commission in developing national transport policy.

The next two sections deal with highway transport and the current and proposed responsibilities of the federal government in this transportation mode, as well as the regulatory programs in the marine industry, the mode with the longest history of regulation. Finally, programs regulating the aviation industry, the most highly regulated of the modes and some of the rail regulatory programs as well as grain transportation and handling are reviewed. This latter section concisely develops the pivotal role of grain transport policies and programs in determining the current structure and performance of the rail and western transportation systems.

The programs analyzed are administered by Transport Canada, the Canadian Transport Commission, the Canadian Grains Commission and the Canadian Wheat Board. The examination of the latter body represents one of the few independent commentaries on that uniquely isolated regulatory agency.

The issues described in this overview are multi-modal in nature or are sufficiently general that they pertain to more than one of the regulatory programs.

The transportation of dangerous goods regulations call for the implementation of a comprehensive national program on July 1, 1985. The details of the program have not been finalized as of (April, 1985) and many companies are unaware

447

of their obligations under the Act. The trucking industry will be regulated in this regard for the first time and faces a massive employee training requirement. Most industries affected complain of inadequate consultation, the absence of sound cost-benefit analysis, a system designed to produce large numbers of convictions for non-compliance, the significant differences between U.S. and Canadian regulations and generally inadequate planning for program administration. In the Team's view, the program implementation date should be postponed by a few months and a private and public sector study team should work together to modify the program using cost-benefit and risk analysis when appropriate. Reciprocity with the U.S. should be negotiated and educational efforts by TC should be increased substantially. However, all these considered conclusions must be analyzed in light of the new situation created by the recent PCB leak incident in Ontario.

Transportation accident investigation and safety policy development are functions that should be separated from the day-to-day enforcement and regulation-making functions since there is an inherent conflict of interest between the two. The creation of the Canadian Aviation Safety Board and the use of commissions of inquiry to investigate major accidents reflect this situation. However, the other modes have not fully separated the functions. Canada should study the feasibility of creating a multi-modal transportation safety agency that would conduct all accident investigations, provide independent safety policy advice and perform a safety ombudsman role. (See background paper.)

The roles of the CTC and TC in developing transportation policy should be clarified. Unlike a government department, at this time the Air Transport Committee (ATC) of the CTC has the power to make regulations without the requirement to publish them in the Canada Gazette and have them cleared by the Department of Justice legal group within the Privy Council Office. In addition, the President of the CTC has at times issued reports or made speeches that have varied or contradicted the minister's policy stance and the minister has had on occasion to use his power to vary or rescind ATC decisions in order to enforce the policy established by the government. It follows that consideration should be given to removing the CTC's policy-making function, leaving it a quasi-judicial agency that simply implements government policy. (See background paper.)

The final general issue concerns the <u>hearings process</u> used by the CTC. Criticism was forthcoming from numerous private sector sources that CTC hearings were overly time-consuming, legalistic, complex and expensive for participants. The hearings have become politicized and Commissioners appear to hold hearings, in some cases, just to ensure that the CTC is seen to be functioning in all parts of the country. It is ironic that on the one hand serious participants find it necessary to retain legal counsel to represent them at the hearings and at the same time the openness of the hearings allows them to become a platform for eccentrics. Procedural reforms should be undertaken on a priority basis.

TRANSPORTATION OF DANGEROUS GOODS - TC 93

Objective

To prevent avoidable transportation accidents involving dangerous goods through better handling, packaging and transporting of such goods; and to minimize the risk and consequences to the population and property whenever such accidents occur.

Authority

Transportation of Dangerous Goods Act.

Description

The program develops and implements a comprehensive national regulatory program for the transport of dangerous goods by all modes and applicable to all phases of the commercial cycle. It also provides timely and accurate emergency response information in the event of accidents.

Resources

($000's)	82/83	83/84	84/85	85/86	86/87	87/88
Person-Years	43	50	60	86	103	112
Operating Exp.						
- Salaries	1,266	1,583	2,941	3,947	4,702	5,081
- O&M	404	537	3,954	3,347	3,586	3,893
- Other Expenses						
Revenues						
Capital	-	-	40	50	65	37

Comments (e.g. estimation and projection assumptions, sources) TDG regulations have recently been promulgated.

Resources in 1985-86 to 1987-88 include a base of 60 PYs and $5,457,000. Incremental resources shown in the table were obtained from a draft TB submission seeking resources to implement the new regulations. Since the submission has not been analysed by TBS and has not received TB approval, actual resources for future years might be different from those shown.

Problem Identification

Private Sector:

This program was the subject of the largest number of critical comments. The reason for this, at least in part, is that the regulations are to come into force on July 1, 1985. The trucking industry will be regulated in this regard for the first time and faces a massive employee training requirement. This burden will be particularly onerous for small trucking operations. The new regulations are multi-modal and based on UN systems. Reciprocity regarding transborder shipments has not yet been negotiated with the U.S. The cost of the implementation schedule is likely greater than the associated benefits. The cost of compliance, e.g. placards costing 10 times as much as those required by U.S. regulations, was another issue raised and whose associated benefits were questioned.

Extensive consultations with TC officials were held, but often they led to no change in the draft regulations or changes in an unanticipated direction. The chemical and trucking industries will be dramatically affected and the latter feels it was inadequately consulted. Problems in transborder trucking will likely occur, with Canadian truckers likely to be charged for non-compliance with US regulations when driving in that country, if reciprocity is not negotiated quickly.

Program Department:

The legislation and regulations have been the subject of intensive federal, provincial and industry negotiations for nearly a decade and underwent lengthy scrutiny in Parliament before passage of the legislation. The program has support from the industry in that it has eliminated duplicative and often conflicting regulations of several federal and provincial bodies.

Intergovernmental

The program is a joint federal/provincial initiative and the roles and responsibilities of all parties have been clearly delineated; the provinces are responsible for enforcement in the highway mode and federal authorities for other modes. The federal government is also responsible for packaging and handling regulations, except in Alberta.

Observations

Of all the programs reviewed by the Team, this was perhaps the subject of the most consistent anger by the private sector. The process of developing the regulations was totally "inadequate", consultation was "superficial", advance warning was "ludicrous", the implementation lead-time "laughable if it were not serious".

The Team believes that the government's regulatory "image" will suffer greatly if nothing is done to address this private sector concern.

Adjustment to the regulations appears to be the most difficult and costly in the trucking area. Indications by TC officials that there will be little enforcement activity and much educational activity in the months following July 1 does not relieve the industry of their concerns, nor of their liability under the law. An earlier implementation plan called for a 12-month period for trucking and six months for the other modes.

Fifteen areas of specific concern identified by the Canadian Manufacturers' Association are attached.

It appears that the regulations have not been fully developed and, despite this, are being implemented on a very tight schedule. This risks bringing federal regulatory administration into serious disrepute.

Of course, the recent PCB spill in Kenora severely limits the government's options to remedy the situation created by these regulations. At the same time, the PCB accident should not be used to "railroad" through hundreds of pages of regulations which will have severe economic effects on many levels of the economy.

Options

The Study Team recommends to the Task Force that the government consider the following:

1. Initiate immediate steps to form or activate a senior level, public/private sector committee whose mandate should be to develop an action plan which would (a) delay implementation of non-critical elements of the regulations and (b) reconsider and reevaluate the elements of the regulations identified by the CMA as needing further consideration.

2. A comprehensive cost-benefit analysis should be a major component of the work performed by the proposed senior-level committee.

3. Efforts to negotiate reciprocity with the U.S. should be assigned the highest priority, as this is a major concern of transborder shippers and truckers.

4. Educational efforts should be increased, reflecting the large number of employees who must become knowledgeable of those parts of the regulations with which they will be dealing.

BACKGROUND

TRANSPORTATION OF DANGEROUS GOODS

The Canadian Manufacturers' Association
List of Major Problems with the Transportation of
Dangerous Goods Regulations

1. The July 1, 1985 implementation date will not be met by most manufacturers and so, as of that date, they will be breaking the law. CMA understands this will also be true in the non-manufacturing sectors that are regulated, such as the carriers. At least a year is required for implementation. During that time major substantive problems with the regulations will also need to be resolved to make the regulations workable.

2. A total exemption for consumer commodities and limited quantities is required. The present regulations provide such a very limited and qualified exemption that it is not really an exemption at all and is of little use. If some limited number of specific substances that are consumer commodities or are in limited quantities do need to be regulated, these should be specifically listed and thereby excluded from what should otherwise be a total and comprehensive exemption. Such an approach will cleanse the regulations of a number of contradictory and complex provisions that only serve to confuse users and do not ensure adequate levels of public safety.

3. The shipping documentation requirements are unworkable and require substantial revisions that will take considerable work and time. The main problem is the inflexibility of the requirements as to how information must be conveyed, resulting in overly detailed, lengthy, difficult-to-read documents that will do little to achieve public safety.

4. It is claimed that the regulations are a consolidation and unification of existing regulations for air, water and rail transport with road regulation added. Yet requirements are different for different modes of transportation. A simplified approach is required for intermodal shipments. Compromises and considerable work will be required to develop a solution.

   We tentatively suggest two possible approaches. One, develop truly uniform requirements covering all modes of transportation. Two (our preference), if different modes of transport are used for a shipment, you should be able to choose to use only the regulatory requirements for the most critical mode. We do not think either approach will lessen public safety and we know either approach will decrease paper burden.

5.   The emergency response requirements are unrealistic and unworkable and may jeopardize voluntary arrangements that are currently working well. It will be particularly difficult for small manufacturers to comply and it is questionable whether public safety will be enhanced despite the increased expense.

6.   A better in-plant exemption is required so the legislation starts and stops at the loading and unloading dock and leaves in-plant activity to be regulated by provincial occupational health and safety legislation.

7.   Returns and rejects that are shipped back to the supplier need to be treated differently and much less onerously than shipping products that are sold. Cost/benefit considerations require this. Considerable work will be required to develop a solution.

8.   Requirements that foreign vendors shipping into Canada must have Canadian agents may facilitate enforcement, but we believe the resulting increased costs and the associated inteference with commercial relations will far outweigh any benefits and will not result in any higher standard of public safety.

9.   Certification requirements for training should be eliminated. They are another example of supposed benefits (i.e. easier enforcement) being outweighed by the cost of paper burden.

10. Classification, particularly for products not listed in the schedules, is a very complicated procedure particularly for smaller companies. As a minimum, worrying about classification should only be an obligation of the suppliers. To achieve this, restricting classification obligations to shippers only will not work as the shipper can be either the purchaser or the supplier depending on the contractual arrangements as to when title passes. (A purchaser fits the definition of a shipper if goods are bought from a supplier FOB the supplier's works, which

455

means that title is taken at the point before actual carriage of the goods begins.)

11. Waste shipments that do not cross provincial boundaries should not be covered by the regulations until federal and provincial governments formally agree on a uniform format for waste manifests that would have three parts: one for the consignor, one for the carrier and one for the consignee. To do otherwise creates increased paperburden in provinces that do not have a three-part system.

12. Provisions creating liability for employees may assist in enforcement of the regulations, but will create significant labour relations problems and we doubt the benefits justify the costs. At least at this initial stage, liability should rest on the employer alone until it is shown that another approach is needed for public safety.

13. Shipments from the United States complying with the U.S. equivalent to Transportation of Dangerous Goods Regulations should be totally exempted from the Canadian TDG regulations. Qualifications to such an exemption that are currently provided in the regulations should be eliminated unless the benefits the qualifications achieve are shown to outweigh the costs they will impose.

14. A satisfactory cost/benefit analysis of the regulations is required. This will need to address many of the above listed major problems and technical problems as well (e.g. the mandatory use of retroflective placards). The WHMIS Cost-Benefit Analysis should be used as a model, particularly for: the size of the sample, real cooperation with industry to obtain a high response rate and meaningful results, and the need for the analysis to be undertaken by someone who is independent of the government department sponsoring the regulations.

15. The registration requirements are not of any value as they do nothing to improve public safety. These only increase paper burden and should be eliminated.

NOTE: This list of major problems with the Transportation of Dangerous Goods Regulations is as of April 12, 1985 and can be expected to be expanded as more problems are brought to CMA's attention by CMA members as they become more familiar with the regulations and attempt to apply them to their operations.

April, 1985.

INSPECTOR GENERAL – TRANSPORTATION SAFETY – TC 500

Objectives

To act as the auditor of departmental safety policy, practices and procedures and to play an ombudsman role as a contact point for the public with safety-related complaints.

Authority

N.A.

Description

The Inspector General reviews and comments on major transportation safety policy proposals, provides a point of contact for the public, studies safety issues as requested by the Minister or Deputy, alerts the Minister to emerging transportation safety issues and reviews major accident reports for the Minister.

Resources*

($000's)	82/83	83/84	84/85	85/86	86/87	87/88
Person-Years	--	--	6	7	7	7
Operating Exp.						
- Salaries	--	--	330	391	391	391
- O&M	--	--	128	103	103	103
- Other Exp.						
Revenue						
Subsidies						
Capital						

*   Resources for 86/87 and beyond are indicated on the assumption that the department can provide justification for the continuation of this activity in the context of the 1985 MYOP.

Problem Identification

Private Sector:

This program was not identified as a problem by private sector contacts. The private sector is generally unaware of the program. Limited quantitative assessment data reported the program as neutral.

Program Department:

TC considers the benefits of the program to exceed the costs and that it has fulfilled its first objective during the short period of its existence. The ombudsman objective has not been achieved because the necessary public relations and promotional efforts have not been undertaken. The need for an independent review body is necessary to the efficient and effective implementation of public policy concerning transportation safety.

Intergovernmental:

No similar programs have been implemented by subordinate levels of government.

Observations

The Office of the Inspector General - Transportation Safety (IGTS) was created at the request of the previous Minister of Transport to counter a growing public perception of lack of attention by Transport Canada to near-accidents and to the apparent conflict of interest when government departments and agencies with safety regulatory responsibilities are also responsible for prevention and/or investigation of accidents.

The role of the IGTS is, therefore, one of ombudsman or auditor of departmental safety policies, practices and administration. The IGTS does not have any regulatory role whatsoever but acts as a contact point for members of the general public who have safety-related complaints and who might feel dissatisfied with responses provided by transport regulators. It also performs an advisory role for the Deputy Minister and Minister of Transport on safety matters.

The IGTS has been providing a corporate advisory service to the Minister and Deputy during the 13 months of its existence and has developed a very limited public profile.

Options

The Study Team recommends to the Task Force that the government consider the following:

1. The IGTS and its functions should be incorporated into the proposed multi-modal transportation safety agency. (See attached overview paper.)

BACKGROUND

TRANSPORTATION SAFETY IN CANADA

INTRODUCTION

Transportation safety is one of the major concerns of the Canadian public. A recent survey conducted for Transport Canada found that transportation safety was ranked the third most serious national concern, after unemployment and inflation. This is due at least in part to the spectacular nature of transportation accidents and the great media attention paid to them.

Historically, the federal government has had total responsibility for safety in the air, marine and rail modes. The motor vehicle mode has been jointly administered by the federal and provincial governments, with the former responsible for vehicle equipment standards and the latter for operating safety.

Another feature of the administration of transportation safety in Canada has been the use of the Commission of Inquiry as a means of investigating major accidents. Such commissions are usually directed by a judge and are characterized by formal hearings and testimony given under oath. The basic reason why the commission approach is taken is to assure the public that an objective, impartial and comprehensive investigation takes place.

ISSUES

The first major issue was alluded to in the preceding paragraph, namely that the accident investigation function be separated from the safety regulation-making and enforcement function. The potential conflict of interest between these two functions is clear and is recognized by most interested parties. Even in the absence of a conscious attempt to influence the results of an accident investigation, an individual's general orientation developed during regulation making or enforcement would likely mould his way of approaching the issue and thereby bias his investigative work. This is one reason why the Canadian Aviation Safety Board (CASB) was established and why the marine accident investigation group was moved from the Coast Guard to a corporate policy organization within the Marine Administration. The recent creation of the office of the Inspector General, Transportation Safety with a mandate to audit transportation safety policies and programs, and to act as an ombudsman is yet another manifestation of the perceived importance of separating the safety rule-making and accident-investigation functions.

The second major issue involves consultation both during the regulation-making process and the subsequent enforcement periods. Recent interviews with private sector sources raised the lack of meaningful consultation as a major problem and one with significant cost implications for the industries involved. This criticism was raised not only by those in the trucking, rail and marine transport industries but also by representatives of manufacturing industries. These people believed that they had alternative ways and means of achieving the objectives of the safety programs, but that they were rejected out-of-hand by the regulatory authorities.

The third and most recently developed issue is the accident-investigation function of the Occupational Safety & Health (OSH) unit of Labour Canada. This group conducts its investigation from an employee-and-work-conditions perspective. Currently, there is a mixture of delegation and direct administration of its responsibilities.

PROPOSAL

One proposal to address the three issues described above would be to take the accident-investigation functions from TC, the CTC and Labour Canada, and unite them in a multi-modal transportation safety agency. The proposed agency would be independent of TC and would report directly to Parliament. It would unite existing modal accident investigation and recommendation activities, and constitute an alternative source of safety policy advice for the government. It would also perform the audit and ombudsman role of the Inspector General Transportation Safety.

The agency would replace the use of commissions of inquiry and would conduct investigations into all accidents, regardless of their magnitude and mode of transportation. Agency staff would be supplemented, when necessary, by consultants and other sources of expertise (e.g. problem experts from private companies).

AN EXAMINATION OF THE CURRENT SYSTEM AND THE PROPOSED ALTERNATIVE

The conflict of interest and inadequate consultation issues that have been raised apparently have not been adequately handled by the current system. The creation of the CASB is a testament to this. The TC accident investigation functions are still susceptible to the conflict of interest criticism as they continue to remain within the department. The CTC rail accident investigation function is even more susceptible to such criticism. The new multi-modal agency would provide a solution to this policy problem.

At present, the sole conduit for consultation other than is the responsible department or agency is the Inspector-General Transportation Safety. That organization is sufficiently new, small and fragile that it cannot exert significant influence over the safety programs of the modal administrations. A meaningful and successful consultation process is more likely to be established if a strong and independent agency is in place.

The Commission of Inquiry approach to major accident investigations has some serious shortcomings that have been identified over the years. First, there is the problem of persons with little technical expertise in transportation safety examining technically complex issues. If the Commissioner is a judge, the person will have certain approaches to dealing with the problems that may lead to a certain way of thinking about the issues and towards certain kinds of policy instruments, namely, legislation and regulation. Second, the procedures of such bodies are overly legalistic, formal and time-consuming. Third, the hearing process can become politicized because the hearings are usually the focus of much media attention and the Commissioner becomes sensitized to the concerns of the various interested parties. Fourth, open public hearings attract a variety of concerned individuals and run the risk of becoming a platform for eccentrics.

The advantages of a multi-modal accident investigation agency are numerous. First, there would be no conflict of interest since the agency would perform only the investigation functions. Second, it would have a permanent base of resident expertise and thus be able to quickly and efficiently complete investigations that would be, and be seen to be, objective, high-quality and practicable.

Third, in the case of a major investigation, the agency would have an inventory of the various centres of excellence in transport safety and people with expert knowledge of the topics of concern. It could use this resource to quickly recruit and create special study teams to carry out these major investigations. Fourth, the agency could develop expertise in multi-modal transport safety issues, and be prepared to develop more comprehensive safety policies than organizations oriented along modal lines. One of the emergency transport safety policy problems is how to deal with the multi-modal issue studies. Fifth, other economically developed countries have agencies and their experience could be studied and used in designing a Canadian agency.

CONCLUSIONS

In the view of the Study Team, the reasoning presented above clearly supports the serious consideration of creating a multi-modal transportation safety agency. This proposal should become the subject of a comprehensive study performed by an independent joint study team.

BACKGROUND

THE CANADIAN TRANSPORT COMMISSION
AND NATIONAL TRANSPORTATION POLICY

Since its inception in 1967, the CTC has been the
subject of almost continuous criticism, ranging from
administrative inefficiency to interference with the
development and initiation of innovative transportation
policy. Criticisms, both specific to the CTC and general to
the problems affecting regulatory agencies in Canada, may be
found in reports by the Law Reform Commission (1978), the
Economic Council of Canada (1981/82), the Privy Council
Office (1982/83), the Lambert Commission, etc. This list,
of course, ignores academic output by authors such as
Stanbury and Reschenthaler, as well as provincial views on
the agency. In short, the CTC as a badly functioning agency
has been studied 'ad nauseam' by economists, lawyers, public
administration specialists, consumer advocates, industry
lobbyists and other bureaucrats.

A great deal of this analysis misses the essential
point about the CTC: changing or reforming the CTC will have
a minimal effect on the transportation system, economic
efficiency or anything else until there is a clear
government view about transportation policy in general. It
is obvious that the future of the CTC is inextricably
related to the directions that regulatory policy may take in
Canada, and it is equally obvious that a regulatory agency
can influence policy direction. The more important
questions are how the government wishes to use the CTC to
communicate its policy direction to the transportation
sector, if at all; whether there are legitimate and
"constant" functions for such an agency in a rapidly
changing environment; or, whether the best use of the CTC is
an arms-length forum for the expression of shipper, carrier
and general public concerns.

Viewed logically, it is clear that any government has
at its command a wide range of instruments with which to
control and/or influence the behavior of regulatory
agencies, and to maintain its political control over
important policy matters. As noted by the Economic Council,
the problem is not really whether a government can get its
own way with statutory agencies; rather, it is a question of
the way in which it will proceed to achieve its objective.

On the basis of the foregoing, one can assume that the manner in which the CTC has operated since 1967 reflects a series of compromises, and very possibly confusion, about the direction of government policy with respect to transportation. There is little doubt that some of the recent suggestions about improving policy direction to the CTC, or ensuring the Minister of Transport has greater policy control, will improve the efficiency of the agency but the question remains as to its effectiveness. For example, the recent CTC hearings on whether to extend the recommendation for confidential contract rates from transborder movements to domestic rail traffic -- a move which seems unavoidable since many shippers to the U.S. also ship within Canada and significant rate differentials could not be tolerated -- means that the CTC's rate-filing function is no longer required. This also means that issues such as branch-line abandonment could be removed from the CTC. Its remaining functions would be to provide a forum for complaints by "captive shippers" and possibly to monitor rail safety issues.

However, before looking at the role that the CTC might play, it is useful to review the trends in transportation policy since 1967 which have contributed to the confusion about the appropriate role for it.

THE CTC AND MANAGEMENT OF NATIONAL TRANSPORTATION POLICY

The Royal Commission on Transportation (commonly known as the MacPherson Commission) reported its findings in 1961. Established in 1959 to resolve the most recent in a series of railway crises, the Committee quickly moved beyond its ostensible mandate to comment on the changing nature of transportation in Canada. In particular, it noted that monopoly-based regulation was inappropriate in light of the actual and potential competition in the transportation sector, and it recommended that the level of freight rates should be determined by competition among the various modes.

In 1967, the National Transportation Act (NTA) was passed which, it is argued, reflects the views of the MacPherson Commission. The NTA stressed the need for an "economic, efficient, and adequate transportation system". The Act continued by stating that these objectives are most likely to be realized in a transportation environment where the modes compete against each other according to their respective characteristics and strengths. While the NTA provided a new framework for transportation policy, numerous modal acts and regulations were left intact, while others (like the Railway Act) were modified.

As is well known, the CTC was established, with the passage of the NTA, as a single body to regulate all modes under federal jurisdiction. Since its inception, the CTC has been attacked for being both too rigid and too flexible; for confusing national transportation policy and turning it in new and possibly undesirable directions; of being unduly judicial in its outlook and of pushing through solutions with unseemly haste, etc. In many respects the ambivalence towards the CTC reflects both the dissatisfaction of it as a regulatory agency and the confusion about what a national transportation policy is all about.

This confusion was apparent a mere seven years after the passage of the NTA. While its critics noted that act was "schizophrenic" by advocating inter-modal competition while each mode was still regulated, the government in 1975 felt that it had gone too far in the direction of competition. In 1974, Mr. Marchand noted that "transportation policy is a mess" and that the "fundamental principal (i.e. competition among the modes of transport) is wrong in Canada". In June, 1975 a long-awaited transportation policy statement reinforced Mr. Marchand's views. It argued that due to significant changes in the social and economic environment of the world since 1967, competition could not be viable in some segments of the transportation system, and should not be a primary factor in transportation regulation generally.

While the amendments never passed, the government, in effect, was prepared to reverse and modify the adjectives concerning policy in the NTA. The objective was an accessible, equitable and efficient system, rather than an economic, equitable and adequate one. In short, by 1975 the government was prepared once again to use transportation as an instrument of policy -- more regulation -- to achieve social and development goals (given the energy crisis).

Barely two years later, this led to the Cabinet-directed creation of the Interdepartmental Committee on Transportation Competition and Regulation (comprised of CTC, CCA and Transport Canada officials) to resolve differences between the proposed changes to the NTA and the Combines Investigation Act which advocated sweeping competitive reform, and would include regulated industries under its mandate. The following year (1978) this committee was overshadowed by the Regulation Reference of the Economic Council of Canada (ECC). While the ECC reported in 1981, the Interdepartmental Committee never reported back to Cabinet as was its original instruction.

It is important to note that at the time the Canadian government was prepared to alter the "competitive focus" of the NTA towards essentially more regulation, President Ford's Program of Regulatory Reform was taking hold and would lead to concrete deregulation initiatives under the Carter Administration. From 1975 to 1980, the U.S. air cargo, air passenger, rail and truck industries were deregulated. It was precisely at this time that the Interdepartmental Committee and the Economic Council were engaged in their analyses with experts who often tended to discount the emerging U.S. experience as being irrelevant to Canada. As will be discussed below, in less than a few years the impact of U.S. deregulation on Canada would be felt in very tangible ways as U.S. carriers captured more U.S.-bound traffic from Canadian firms.

Throughout the period in question (1967-1980), but more particularly during 1975-1980, the CTC attempted to regulate transportation in a rapidly-changing environment. There can be little doubt that it influenced national transportation policy, both in its decisions and its analytical contributions to the examination of regulation being undertaken by the Economic Council and the Interdepartmental Committee. Indeed, in order to satisfy CTC, the Interdepartmental Committee had to tone-down many of its pro-competitive recommendations in order to allow for completion of the research. (The final reports were delayed for over a year, despite the CTC announcements that it was not involved in policy.) Matters were further complicated by CCA proceeding with anti-combines cases against trucking firms and thus raising the possibility that committee-inspired CTC research could be used to demonstrate "Crown inconsistency" with respect to condoning such anti-competitive behavior.

There is no need to dwell on these matters other than to note the CTC did become actively involved in policy formulation and direction. To say the CTC was inefficient, ineffectual, or that it distorted economic decisions by regulation, borders on a truism. The more important question is how did the CTC receive and incorporate (inconsistent) policy direction into its regulatory processes.

DEFINING A NEW ROLE FOR THE CTC

The relationship between the Minister of Transport and the President of the CTC has been "informal" with respect to policy formulation. CTC staff monitor ministerial speeches and pronouncements in order to detect shifts in policy direction, which can be further supplemented by conversations to clarify the directions in which the government may wish to move. The power of the Governor-in-Council to override the decisions (or ministerial appeal in the case of air licensing decisions) of CTC offers the most direct route of indicating the policy direction. While such actions allow for political control over sensitive issues, they also tend to downplay the status of the CTC.

The balance between having clear and enforceable rules and the need to maintain political control over sensitive issues is a delicate one indeed. Overlaying this problem is the important effect U.S. deregulation was (and is) having in Canada. It is clear that U.S. economic and legal extra-territorial impacts are adding an international competitive dimension to the transportation system which is beyond the ability of the Canadian government to control events. The matter is further complicated by the differential impact by mode and by regulatory jurisdiction -- air bilaterals extend beyond the U.S., while trucking regulation is in the hands of the provinces, and rail and marine regulation are in the hands of the federal government.

Without going into detail, the CTC is still attempting to regulate in a way that is inimical to carriers' current interests on the basis of legislation such as the Railway Act which is inadequate to promote effective regulation, or flexible enough to deal with changing circumstances. Every piece of transportation legislation -- the NTA, the Transport Act, the Aeronautics Act, the Canada Shipping Act, the Motor Vehicle Transport Act, etc. needs revision or is in the process of being revised within the context of the existing policy framework as evolved since 1967. Moreover, the government's intentions for Crown corporations (which tend to major players in every transportation sub-sector) introduces additional uncertainty.

As a first step in resolving these difficulties, the government may consider announcing its own "Transportation Policy", either confirming or altering the current framework. Second, all transportation legislation should be viewed as a "total package" and planning policy priorities laid down as the various acts proceed to revision. Third, the government may consider clarifying its stance on Crown corporations and their roles in the transportation system. Finally, the Study Team suggested that the government review the need for an agency below the CTC as part of a consultative and non-economic regulatory agency.

With regard to the latter point, it is clear that even in the deregulated U.S. environment some regulations are maintained. For example, after rail deregulation, the Americans realized that an arm's-length mechanism was necessary to protect "captive (i.e. generally resource) shippers", and in fact closely examined the long-standing but generally ineffective Canadian provisions. Similarly, selected safety and accident-reporting provisions were necessary as well.

Rather than focus on rate-making and rate-behavior, the CTC could provide a quasi-judicial arena for the discussion of these sensitive issues; issues which are best removed from policy makers on a day-to-day basis. Review provisions regarding mergers or anti-competitive behavior (Section 27 of the NTA) could be maintained within the CTC. While some research expertise would be necessary to provide Commissioners with up-to-date information, this would emerge through the hearing process or from experts. It is clear that a large research staff, publishing self-serving studies on the merits of regulation, would not be required. Section 23 cases, which allow for CTC hearings on any matter of public interest are generally ineffective or result in stalling and should be replaced by clear guidelines.

Many of these issues are inter-related and not susceptible to easy separation. For example, it could be argued that the CTC maintains safety through regulations on the type of equipment and where it may be used, while it could also be argued that its concern should be to establish appropriate procedures for the use of any equipment. In short, there is no easy way to prevent overlap in functions or influence. To the extent that regulation will always be subject to interpretation, the question arises as to the need for adequate policy direction. This topic has come up before with respect to Privy Council Office proposals. However, a new and clearer statement of Transportation Policy, including proposals to amend the various pieces of legislation, would go a long way to correcting the situation. Also, appeals should not go to the Minister; rather all appeals should be to the Governor-in-Council.

OVERVIEW

ROAD REGULATION

SYNOPSIS

The Team is dissatisfied with the pace of reduced regulation implemented so far by most provinces. Provincial regulation remains an obstacle to efficiency and growth. It risks becoming an irritant in Canada's relations with the U.S. where trucking has been deregulated for some time to the advantage of Canadian trucking companies. The Team suggests that action be taken to speed up trucking deregulation in Canada.

DETAILS

The regulation of the trucking industry in Canada has historically been administered by provincial governments. The federal government delegated its authority over extra-provincial trucking (interprovincial and transborder) to the provinces by passing the Motor Vehicle Transportation Act in 1954. The decisions of provincial trucking regulation agencies have resulted in a diversity of administrative, operational, safety and economic regulations that have been demonstrably costly for the trucking industry, have distorted its structure, and have made it vulnerable to the revitalized deregulated U.S. trucking industry. The implications of this for transborder trade are very significant, particularly in the current trade liberalization environment.

Efforts at rationalizing and reforming the trucking regulatory regimes have been attempted by the Canadian Conference of Motor Transport Administrators (CCMTA). These have been largely unsuccessful, despite the best of intentions. Consequently, the changes in trucking regulation needed by the Canadian industry, and being forced on it by the deregulated U.S. industry, requires federal action. The Team suggests that the current regulatory coordination role of Transport Canada be transformed into a leadership role, that the necessary changes to federal legislation be made and that economic regulatory reform for extra-provincial trucking be implemented. This would lead the way for the provincial governments to introduce regulatory reform for intraprovincial operations and to allow the industry to respond to market forces.

The role of the federal government in road safety and motor vehicle regulation, on the other hand, has been developed to an extent that is larger than is appropriate. In the Team's view, specifically, the implementation of the safety and performance standards program should be carried out by the private sector with policy direction being provided by TC. The current program involves duplication of testing activities by motor vehicle producers and the federal government. The federal testing centre should be privatized and the testing done by TC should be delegated to the industry and the provincial governments. Finally, the Team is of the opinion that the new emission standards should not be implemented. This initiative, in the Team's view, was poorly conceived and had imperceptible effect on bilateral Canada-U.S. negotiations. From an environmental point of view, it has been empirically documented that there are more cost-effective alternative methods of dealing with the acid rain problem. These should be implemented before the emission standards.

ROAD SAFETY AND MOTOR VEHICLE REGULATION - TC 275

Objectives

To contribute to the reduction of deaths, injuries and property damage resulting from motor vehicle use through improved safety of motor vehicles.

To contribute to a reduction in health impairment by reducing noise and exhaust emission levels of new motor vehicles.

To contribute to energy conservation by reducing the average fuel consumption of motor vehicles.

Authority

Motor Vehicle Safety Act.
Motor Vehicle Tire Safety Act.
Motor Vehicle Fuel Consumption Standards Act (not yet proclaimed).

Description

The Road Safety Directorate is comprised of four elements, Traffic Safety Standards and Research, Vehicle Safety and Energy Operations, Motor Vehicle Test Centre, and Planning and Regional Operations. The Directorate develops and enacts safety and emission standards for motor vehicles, and enforces compliance with these standards through an audit and test program. Revenue is generated through the recovery of costs of industrial and other government users of the Test Centre and the return of test motor vehicles to Crown Assets.

Resources

($000's)	82/83	83/84	84/85	85/86	86/87	87/88
Person-Years	131	135	136	136	133	133
Operating Exp.						
- Salaries	4,322	4,765	4,954	5,156	5,042	5,042
- O&M	4,420	6,027	6,452	6,269	6,223	6,223
- Other Exp.						
Capital	1,464	1,502	1,608	1,972	1,972	1,972
Revenue	117	101	135	135	135	135

Problem Identification

Private Sector:

Private sector contacts provided two major criticisms. The first concerns the recently announced vehicle emission standards and the universally accepted empirical analysis that they will cost $2B to $4B over 10 years and reduce acid rain by only 2 per cent. If $4B were invested in pollution control equipment in the industries contributing 94 per cent of the acid rain, there would be a 40 per cent reduction.

The second is more general and involves questioning the role of the federal government in areas of provincial jurisdiction and/or areas that should be self-regulated, specifically, the motor vehicle test centre and its operation, vehicle safety and energy operations, and traffic safety standards and research. There is a duplication of both facilities and testing operations.

Program Department:

The decision to adopt the U.S. emission standards was taken at the political level and TC officials had no influence over it. The rationale supporting the decision was based on considerations involving Canada's acid rain negotiations with the U.S.

Regarding the second point, TC states that since the establishment of this program, the number of highway fatalities has dropped by 30 per cent, exhaust emissions have decreased by 70 per cent and fuel consumption has decreased by 50 per cent. They contend that it is doubtful, based on historic evidence, that these sorts of improvement could have been achieved in the absence of government regulation. The current costs of motor vehicle accidents in Canada are about $5B annually.

Intergovernmental:

The activities of this program and those of provincial governments are coordinated by the Council of Transport Ministers and the Canadian Conference of Motor Transport Administrators.

Observations

In the Team's view, the empirical case against adopting the U.S. motor vehicle emission standards is most convincing and comprises a strong argument for retaining the present standards.

The decreases in fatalities, fuel consumption and, to a lesser extent, emissions were likely as much the result of economic pressures and market forces as the result of federal regulations. Since the motor vehicle industry is truly international, it is difficult to believe that Canadian regulations have had the impact on safety performance and fuel efficiency that has been claimed.

The provinces carry out safety programs concerning vehicle operation and, therefore, must be given some credit for their contribution to decreased fatalities.

The Team finds that developing motor vehicle standards that respond to Canadian needs and requirements does not require ownership of a testing centre since the use of privately owned centres, as required, is a viable possibility.

Options

The Study Team recommends to the Task Force that the government consider the following:

1. The emission standards should not be implemented at the present time without further consideration of economic and other factors.

2. The TC test centre should be privatized and sold to a consortium of other users. The testing that TC does could be delegated to the industry and the provinces, as appropriate.

MOTOR VEHICLE TRANSPORT REGULATION - CTC 30

Objective

To regulate the development and operation of interprovincial and international truck and bus services in order to protect the interests of the users of transportation, to maintain the economic well-being and growth of Canada, and to coordinate and harmonize the operations of transport carriers.

Authority

National Transportation Act.
Transport Act.
Motor Vehicle Transport Act.
Lord's Day Act.

Description

Trucking regulatory authority has largely been delegated to the provinces. Federal activity includes trucking company mergers or acquisitions; trucking on Sundays; CN Roadcruiser tariffs and levels of service in Newfoundland.

Resources

($000's)	82/83	83/84	84/85	85/86	86/87	87/88
Person-Years	4	4	4	4	4	4
Operating Exp.						
- Salaries	140	150	172	177	177	177
- O&M	30	35	55	55	55	55
- Other Exp.						
Revenue						
Subsidies						
Capital			2	2	2	2

Problem Identification

Private Sector:

The profile of this program is so low that little was said about it in private sector interviews. The Lord's Day Act provisions were viewed as an amusing anachronism. In practical terms, Sunday trucking is avoided by the industry because of the high overtime costs for employees.

Program Agency:

The CTC must administer those pieces of legislation for which it is responsible. At the time of drafting this report, it is thought that the Lord's Day Act may be ruled obsolete by the Supreme Court in a case before it. Section 27 of the NTA regarding mergers and acquisitions in trucking and hearings as to whether they are in the public interest and/or restrict competition is a worthwhile activity that yields net benefits to Canadians.

Intergovernmental:

As mentioned above, most responsibility for the regulation of trucking has been delegated to the provinces and therefore there are no competing or duplicative programs administered by other levels of government.

Observations

The CTC is playing a minimal role in trucking, just enough not to be seen to completely abdicate the field to the provinces. The program therefore appears to be appropriate, given the history of trucking policy decisions by the federal government.

Options

The Study Team recommends to the Task Force that the government consider the following:

1. Trucking operations should be exempted from the provisions of the Lord's Day Act for reasons of economic efficiency.

2. The Motor Vehicle Transport Committee should be disbanded and its remaining functions transferred to the Rail Committee.

MOTOR CARRIER REGULATION COORDINATION - TC 999

Objective

To facilitate reform in the trucking regulatory regimes that are administered by the provincial and territorial governments.

Authority

National Transportation Act
Motor Vehicle Transport Act
(These provide for delegation of authority to provinces.)

Description

The program develops policy concerning trucking and motor coach operation both in the federal jurisdiction and in coordination with provincial jurisdictions. The Motor Carrier Branch is <u>not</u> a regulatory agency. The Branch also administers contribution, demonstration and research and development programs concerning the trucking or bus industries.

Resources

($000's)	82/83	83/84	84/85	85/86	86/87	87/88
Person-Years	9	9	8	8	8	8
Operating Exp.						
- Salaries	292	329	315	344	344	344
- O&M	425	417	905	879	508	508
- Other Expenses						
Capital		198				
Subsidies	236	300				

Problem Identification

Private Sector:

Private sector contactors, particularly shippers, have criticized the variability of trucking regulations from province to province. These regulatory regimes have created barriers to interprovincial trade, induced inefficiencies in trucking routes and operations, created economic rents which have been captured in part by unionized labour and contributed to the growth of both private truck fleets and the quasi-legal owner-operators. The trucking associations and labour organizations do not perceive the market distortions created by the different regulatory regimes to be as serious as shippers do, and call for caution to be exercised if regulatory change is made.

Program Department:

Provincial governments have authority to regulate intra-provincial trucking and the Motor Vehicle Transport Act (MVTA) delegates to them the authority to regulate extra-provincial (inter-provincial and transborder) trucking. The federal role is limited to promoting uniform provincial regulations which do not impede efficient and effective inter-provincial and international trucking and bus operations. The Canadian Conference of Motor Transport Administrators (CCMTA) is the mechanism through which the coordination role is carried out.

Intergovernmental:

Because trucking transport is important to many sectors of the economy there are a number of federal departments concerned with both domestic and transborder trucking. Because both TC and the CTC have policy roles there is a potential for conflict and duplication. Because extra-provincial trucking regulation has been delegated to the provinces, there is considerable duplication (and sometimes conflict) between provinces over a given bus or trucking undertaking. Finally, because the federal government is responsible for international trade there is duplication with regard to transborder trucking.

Observations

The Canadian trucking industry has long been identified as a prime example of the distortions that regulatory regimes can create. Alberta has no economic regulation over intraprovincial trucking and the benefits of low rates and efficient operations are obvious. The cartel-like powers of tariff bureaux, the exorbitant values of route authorities (licences) and the complex, time-consuming and costly procedures involved in obtaining licences reflect the costs of regulations in other provinces.

Options

The Study Team recommends to the Task Force that the government consider the following:

1. Continue to attempt to coordinate reform through the CCMTA; some modest advances have been made, particularly in the technical and operational areas.

2. Repatriate federal authority over extra-provincial trucking (including the intra-provincial trucking operations of those companies engaged in extra-provincial undertakings). This would then allow TC to make the final moves to establish uniform national technical regulations (the provinces have largely achieved this now). More importantly, TC could then eliminate the entry, exit and tariff controls that have led to market distortions and inefficiencies.

OVERVIEW

MARINE REGULATION

The problems raised in the marine mode are well defined and long standing, probably a reflection that marine transport has the longest history of regulation and has experienced a relatively slow rate of technological change.

The duplication of hull and machinery inspections by both TC and Classification Societies such as Lloyd's Register of Shipping and the American Bureau of Shipping is an issue that has been debated for 80 years in Canada. In the Team's view, as no other maritime country requires government inspection and the Classification Society inspection is required to obtain insurance, Canada should conform with international practice and require TC inspection only when a vessel's condition is in question.

The Pilotage Act establishes the four pilotage authorities as crown corporations and requires compulsory pilotage in specified bodies of water, regardless of ship's masters' and officers' knowledge of those waters. The Act should be changed to exempt masters and deck watch officers who have the required knowledge of local waters and whose vessels meet navigation equipment standards. Furthermore, the Study Team has found that the pilotage authorities should be privatized as a means of increasing their efficiency and there should be enhanced liability for marine accidents.

TC currently provides vessel traffic services (VTS) consisting of information, advice, instruction and emergency coordination. There is concern on the part of ships' owners, masters and pilots that VTS will evolve from an information service to a traffic control system and they are opposed to the navigation of their ships being controlled by land-based bureaucrats. Amendments to the Canada Shipping Act which, among other things, provide authority for a national VTS program were recently approved by the government. The Study Team is of the view that these plans should be put on hold, pending an independent assessment of the need for VTS, a cost-benefit analysis including an examination of the possibilities of cost-recovery and a study of how a Canadian VTS program will operate in contiguous water in the absence of a complementary U.S. program.

WATER TRANSPORT – CTC 12

Objective

To ensure efficient, economic and adequate water transportation services in those areas subject to economic regulation, i.e. shipping conferences, coasting trades and water carriers on the MacKenzie River and in the Western Arctic.

Authority

National Transportation Act.
Transport Act.
Canada Shipping Act.
Shipping Conferences Exemption Act.
Pilotage Act.

Description

The licensing of water carriers in designated areas; the examination and acceptance of tariffs; the review of acquisitions and mergers involving water carriers; investigations of tariffs proposed by Pilotage Authorities; the provision of advice to the Minister of National Revenue on applications of foreign vessels being considered for engagement in the coasting trade; economic analysis and advice on water transport matters; and the monitoring of international maritime and multimodal transportation matters.

Resources

($000's)	82/83	83/84	84/85	85/86	86/87	87/88
Person-Years		33	33	33	33	33
Operating Exp.						
- Salaries		1,305	1,357	1,383	1,383	1,383
- O & M		227	217	227	227	227
- Other Exp.						
Revenue						
Subsidies						
Capital		3	4	4	4	4

Problem Identification

Private Sector:

Private sector contacts raised the issues of the Shipping Conferences Exemption Act (SCEA) and the formulae used to calculate pilotage tariffs. The SCEA permits conference members to fix the rates charged for ocean liner services. Not only is this arrangement (which creates higher than market determined rates) contrary to economic efficiency, but it also involves significant transfers of income abroad (since there are no Canadian conference members). Canadian shippers would benefit from the abolition of the SCEA to the extent that they could negotiate lower rates from ocean vessels.

The pilotage tariff formulae have been criticized by vessel owners as being unnecessarily complicated and excessive.

Program Agency:

The CTC has no discretion over the SCEA policy and is responsible only for its administration.

This is also true of the pilotage tariffs except in the event that a tariff is appealed to the CTC.

Intergovernmental:

The federal mandate is clear and there are no competing or duplicative programs administered by other levels of government.

Observations

The two issues raised by the private sector comprise only a portion of the CTC's Water Transport Program.

The SCEA has been extended for one year beginning April 1, 1985. It is difficult to estimate the cost of the SCEA to Canadian shippers or the extent to which they could negotiate lower rates if the SCEA was not extended. Some observers contend that ocean vessel service would be withdrawn by conference members if Canada did not extend the SCEA. Others suggest that non-conference vessel owners would provide the service.

The more general issue of compulsory pilotage and the need for their services is assessed under another program review. This is considered to be a major problem program.

Options

The Study Team recommends to the Task Force that the government consider reviewing the option of not extending the SCEA.

MARINE AIDS TO NAVIGATION - TC 47

Objective

To facilitate the safe and efficient movement of marine traffic in Canadian and adjacent waters.

Authority

British North America Act - Section 91.
Canada Shipping Act - Parts X, XI.

Description

TC provides a network of fixed and floating aids such as buoys, lightstations, range marks and radio positioning systems. There are no regulatory requirements associated with the use of these aids.

There are private buoy regulations that assure they conform with the Canadian standards and that they are not damaged by individuals.

The Sable Island regulations restrict access to this hazardous and environmentally sensitive site.

Resources

($000's)	82/83	83/84	84/85	85/86	86/87	87/88
Person-Years		2,698*	2,808	2,818	2,802	2,788
Operating Exp.						
- Salaries		86,674*	92,292	99,530	98,799	68,799
- O & M		49,432	59,019	61,698	60,464	61,222
- Other Exp.						
Revenue		1,757*	2,164*	2,173	2,173	2,173
Subsidies		62	57	7	7	7
Capital		84,253*	273,044*	184,772	56,227	109,610

*   Resource information updated.

N.B.:   These resources cover the total Marine Aids to Navigation Program, only a small portion of which applies to the regulatory aspects of the program as described under "Regulatory Objectives".

Problem Identification

Private Sector:

This program was not identified as a problem.

Program Department:

The 1983 Auditor General Report identified ways in which program delivery and efficiency might be improved and the Coast Guard is addressing these issues. Technological advances are being introduced to the program over time.

Intergovernmental:

The federal mandate for this program is clear and there are no competing or duplicative programs.

Observations

In the Team's view, this program is a service provided by the Coast Guard and meets the established objectives at reasonable costs.

Options

The Study Team recommends to the Task Force that the government consider the following:

1. This program might be privatized although the economics of scope that the Coast Guard may enjoy would probably not be realized by a private company.

POLLUTION REGULATION (MARINE) — TC 57

Objective

To protect the marine environment from shipping pollution and to limit the risks to the public and to the environment from the marine transport of hazardous or polluting cargoes.

Authority

Canada Shipping Act.
Arctic Waters Pollution Prevention.

Description

The program involves developing and enforcing regulations, standards and guidelines for the prevention of pollution from shipping, including the development of guidelines on risk assessment procedures for use in building new ship terminals to transport potentially hazardous or polluting bulk cargoes.

Resources

($000's)	82/83	83/84	84/85	85/86	86/87	87/88
Person-Years		10	15	15	15	15
Operating Exp.						
- Salaries		411	671	679	679	679
- O & M		380	275	280	280	280
- Other Exp.						
Revenue						
Subsidies						
Capital						

Problem Identification

Private Sector:

There was some concern expressed on the part of ship owners that pollution regulations were sometimes enforced inconsistently. On balance, however, the regulations were not viewed as a problem. Another issue that was raised involved the cost impact of changes to regulations that required equipment alteration or replacement.

Program Department:

The success of this marine pollution prevention program is essential to the economic health of such industries as fisheries, tourism and water resource usage. The pollution regulation program is moving towards conformity with international standards.

Intergovernmental:

The federal government has authority over shipping and related pollution regulation. The Province of Ontario currently regulates the control of pleasure craft sewage in its waters, an area which the federal authorities had not regulated.

Observations

Pollution prevention is critical to economic growth and job creation in tourism and fisheries, two important industries in Canada. There are proposed amendments to the Canada Shipping Act to strengthen pollution regulations and to bring Canada into conformity with the Marine Pollution Convention (MARPOL). This would assure financial compensation for Canadians in the event of a pollution accident and the right of direct action against the insurers. The amendments have received Cabinet approval.

Options

The Study Team recommends to the Task Force that the government consider the following:

1. Although the course of action that Canada is pursuing is in line with that of other developed countries, it might be desirable to further increase the liability of ships polluting Canadian waters. This course of action could prove to be complicated since ultimate ship ownership is sometimes difficult to trace.

MARINE CASUALTY INVESTIGATION - TC 61

Objective

To investigate shipping casualties and accidents for the purpose of formulating recommendations to prevent a recurrence.

Authority

Canada Shipping Act.

Description

The greater part of the service provided by this program involves the public disclosure of the causes of marine accidents, the administration of public hearings and the production of annual statistics. It is regulatory related in that its recommendations may lead to new or modified regulations.

Resources

($000's)	82/83	83/84	84/85	85/86	86/87	87/88
Person-Years		40*	41	44	50	50
Operating Exp.						
- Salaries		1,362*	2,130*	2,378	2,530	2,530
- O & M		216*	224*	228	263	264
- Other Exp.						
Revenue						
Subsidies						
Capital		-*	180	142	148	154

*   Resource information updated.

N.B.:   These resources cover the total Marine Casualty Investigation Program, only a small portion of which applies to the regulatory aspects of the program as described under "General Description".

Problem Identification

Private Sector:

This program was not identified as a problem by private sector contacts. It was viewed as a necessary role, adequately administered by the Coast Guard.

Program Department:

The program has recently been examined in a review of the Marine Administration by the Auditor General and a ministerial study by Mr. B. Deshenes. Both found the program to be run in a cost-effective manner, but recommended that it become independent of the Coast Guard.

Intergovernmental:

The federal mandate for the program is clear and there exist no competing or duplicative programs.

Observations

The program is performing the traditional government accident investigation and prevention role and to that extent it is providing a public good. The Canadian marine safety record is quite good. However, in the Study Team's view, its relation to safety activities in other modes, the CTC and in Labour Canada might be further studied. It currently reports to the Marine Administrator but could become more independent of TC.

Option

The Study Team recommends to the Task Force that the government consider the following:

1. There is a very real possibility that the program could be incorporated within a multi-modal transport safety commission. This would follow the models established in other advanced countries.

VESSEL TRAFFIC SERVICES/TRAFFIC MANAGEMENT - TC 67

Objective

To develop, provide, maintain and ensure the efficient operation of vessel traffic services (VTS) facilities and other systems to facilitate the safe and expeditious movement of marine traffic in Canadian and adjacent waters.

Authority

Canada Shipping Act.

Description

The program provides vessel traffic information, advice, instruction and emergency coordination on a 24 hour, seven day a week basis. The service is provided through nine systems using 12 vessel traffic centres. The majority of these systems are responsible for interactive traffic management.

Resources

($000's)	82/83	83/84	84/85	85/86	86/87	87/88
Person-Years		476	479	414	411	411
Operating Exp.						
- Salaries		17,772	19,682	17,296	17,092	17,092
- O & M		4,264	7,060	7,060	7,060	7,060
- Other Exp.						
Revenue		94	116	116	116	116
Subsidies						
Capital		1,417	4,129	6,524	12,136	12,500

Problem Identification

Private Sector:

The primary concern of both ships' owners and officers is that VTS remain an information service and not a traffic control system. There are fears that the initial information system will develop into a control system. This is particularly the case in the St. Lawrence/Great Lakes system. Ships' pilots are concerned that VTS will reduce the demand for their services. Some interested parties see VTS as the newest empire building effort in TC with the installation of radar communications and plotting

490

systems employing the latest computer technology and
equipment.

Program Department:

TC perceives the program as a response to developments
in the marine industry. In terms of the coastal
systems, incoming vessels must supply basic information
that is used to assess them as a safety or pollution
risk, with appropriate direction then given by the
Coast Guard. The St. Lawrence/Great Lakes systems
provide traffic information and advice services in one
of the busiest waterways in the world.

Intergovernmental:

The federal mandate is clear and there are no competing
or duplicative programs administered by other levels of
government.

VTS in the Strait of Juan de Fuca and in the St. Clair
and Detroit rivers operates in concert with the U.S.
Coast Guard.

Observations

This is a controversial issue and is linked with the
compulsory pilotage issue, another major problem. Ships'
owners and masters do not want the navigation of their ships
to be controlled by land-based bureaucrats. The same
technological advances that permit the introduction of VTS
have also been incorporated into a vessel navigation and
communictions system. There is the potential for costly
duplication of systems. Ships' owners consider the volume
of traffic in eastern Canada to be too low to merit VTS
control. It is also not clear if VTS operates solely in
the Canadian half of contiguous waters and what control
Canadian VTS officials have over foreign vessels and those
that refuse to communicate with it. The U.S. has no such
system for the Great Lakes; it has VTS covering only three
bodies of water; those in and around the harbours of New
York, Galveston and San Francisco.

Amendments to the Canada Shipping Act which, among
other things, provide authority for a national VTS program
were recently approved by the government.

Options

The Study Team recommends to the Task Force that the government consider the following:

1. The approved plans for a national VTS program should be put on hold, pending an independent assessment of the need for VTS. A full cost-benefit analysis should be performed and consultations with all those affected should be carried out. The assessment should examine the viability of operating the program on a cost-recovery basis, on the costs to ships' owners, and on the ability of a Canadian VTS program to operate in contiguous waters without a complementary U.S. program.

PERSONNEL REGULATION (MARINE) - TC 315

Objective

To contribute to marine safety and the prevention of pollution by ensuring that ships are properly manned by officers and crews who have been trained and certified to meet standards established by the program.

Authority

Canada Shipping Act.

Description

The program establishes policies, regulations and standards for the certification of marine officers and crews; it provides a mechanism for conforming with the standards set by the International Maritime Organization and the International Labor Organization.

Resources

($000's)	82/83	83/84	84/85	85/86	86/87	87/88
Person-Years		49	50	50	50	50
Operating Exp.						
- Salaries		2,014	2,238	2,265	2,265	2,265
- O&M		187	366	372	372	372
- Other Exp.						
Revenue		488	502	1,050	1,080	1,110
Subsidies		14	14	14	14	14
Capital		20	91	100	104	108

Problem Identification

Private Sector:

While this program was not identified as a problem, there were certain technical aspects of certification-granting that required some personnel to use special permits in order to qualify for their duty. Moreover, the inconsistency of current standards in Canada and in international conventions did not facilitate the movement of Canadian personnel to employment in the south during the winter months.

493

Program Department:

TC assesses this program as one of ongoing occupational certification that is necessary to the safe and efficient operation of Canadian shipping. It is similar to the certification that is carried out in the other transport modes.

Intergovernmental:

The federal mandate for this program is clear and there exist no competing or duplicative programs.

Observations

The proposed amendments to the Canada Shipping Act include provisions for the training and certification of staff, and bringing Canadian standards into conformity with international standards.

Options

The Study Team recommends to the Task Force that the government consider the following:

1. The certification of personnel could be performed by an industry organization with an audit function performed by TC. It is not clear if this would meet the requirements of relevant international organizations.

SHIP REGULATION – TC 320

Objectives

To ensure the safety of persons and the seaworthiness of ships and oil drilling rigs in Canadian waters.

Authority

Canada Shipping Act.
Arctic Waters Pollution Prevention Act.

Description

This program involves the development and promulgation of regulations and standards; the inspection of ships and ships' equipment, oil-drilling rigs and cargoes to ensure seaworthiness; and the registration of ships and licensing of vessels. It also monitors the marine safety training program, and examines and certifies officers and crews to ensure that ships are manned with competent personnel.

Resources

(000's)	82/83	83/84	84/85	85/86	86/87	87/88
Person-Years		316	333	336	326	326
Operating Exp.						
- Salaries		10,806*	14,993	15,315	15,073	15,073
- O&M		3,867	2,264	2,301	2,196	2,196
- Other Expenses						
Revenue		1,489	1,342	2,650	2,720	2,790
Subsidies		1	15	15	15	15
Capital		806	631	958	724	753

* Resource information updated

Problem Identification

Private Sector:

The primary concern raised regarding this program was the duplication of hull and machinery inspections by TC and by classification societies such as Lloyd's Register of Shipping and the American Bureau of Shipping. In the majority of the maritime nations, there is only one inspection by the classification societies; this is required by insurance companies. TC carries out the inspection on a cost-recovery basis and the fees have increased recently, thus increasing the costs of operating Canadian ships. There is also considerable cost in the duplication of documents and records and taking ships out of revenue service to allow for the inspection. Ship owners don't question TC's other safety and environmental pollution regulation enforcement activities.

TC has established a very formal and highly structured consultation process for its ship safety and other regulatory programs. It has been criticized as being all form and no content. Ship owners have stated that the consultations do not influence the decisions of the bureaucrats writing the regulations or enforcing the program.

Program Department:

TC points out that Canada does not have a national classification society and therefore does not obtain the same quality of inspection as countries with national societies. Moreover, classification societies operate solely in the interests of the ship owners and this is not always consistent with the public interest or that of the crew. Canada has a good safety record and this is in large part due to the ship safety program, which includes hull and machinery inspection. The debate on this issue has been continuing for 80 years.

Intergovernmental:

The federal mandate is clear and there are no competing or duplicative programs administered by other levels of government.

Observations

In the Study Team's view, Canada does appear to have adopted a policy different from those of other countries both the U.S. and the U.K. use classification societies. Australia, a country with no national society, does not require a second inspection. The standards enforced in the US are apparently less stringent than those in Canada. The Glassco Commission report in 1961 recommended that the statute be amended "to permit acceptance by the Board of Steamship Inspection of survey reports issued by approved Classification Societies".

Inspection and certification of a vessel by a classification society increases its resale value since it receives an internationally accepted endorsement.

Options

The Study Team recommends to the Task Force that the government consider the following:

1. Canada should conform with the practice of other maritime countries and delegate hull and machinery inspection on insured vessels to classification societies. This would not prevent a TC inspector from investigating any vessel and requiring supplementary inspection if the vessel's condition were in question.

SHIP RADIO INSPECTION REGULATIONS - TC 325

Objectives

To ensure the safety of persons and the seaworthiness of ships and oil rigs in Canadian waters by regulating their radio and electronic equipment.

Authority

Canada Shipping Act
Arctic Waters Pollution Prevention Act

Description

The Coast Guard provides standards and regulations for radio and electronic equipment carried by ships for safety, communications and navigation purposes; carries out inspections of equipment and issues certification to ships in compliance with the regulations.

Resources

($000's)	82/83	83/84	84/85	85/86	86/87	87/88
Person-Years		2	2	2	2	2
Operating Exp.						
- Salaries		82	90	91	91	91
- O&M		579	688	700	703	703
- Other Exp.						
Revenue				300	700	700
Subsidies						
Capital						

Problem Identification

Private Sector:

This program was not identified by the private sector contacts as being a problem. It was viewed as being one component of a general marine safety program.

Program Department:

This is a small, but specialized component of the overall ship safety program. TC feels that without their activities, vessels would maintain a lower level of shipboard radio and electronic capability and would thereby constitute a greater accident risk.

<u>Intergovernmental</u>:

The federal mandate is clear and there exist no competing or duplicate programs.

<u>Observations</u>

The program is carried out in conjunction with Department of Communications staff (9 PYs). Full cost-recovery has been approved beginning in 1986/87.

With the movement towards full cost-recovery and the accompanying pressures on program efficiency, it appears that a reform initiative has commenced.

NAVIGABLE WATERS PROTECTION - TC 330

Objective

To protect the public right of navigation by ensuring the review, analysis and approval of works constructed in navigable waters.

Authority

Navigable Waters Protection Act
Canada Shipping Act
Railway Act
National Energy Board Act

Description

The works approved include bridges, dams, wharves, and overhead and submarine cables constructed in navigable waters. There is also responsibility for the removal and disposal of wrecked vessels to ensure the public right of navigation.

Resources

($000's)	82/83	83/84	84/85	85/86	86/87	87/88
Person-Years		31	28	28	28	28
Operating Exp.						
- Salaries		1,274	1,253	1,420	1,420	1,420
- O & M		156	478	486	486	486
- Other Exp.						
Revenue						
Subsidies						
Capital						

Problem Identification

Private Sector:

This program was not identified as a problem by the private sector contacts. It is a long established activity and has been complied with for an extended period of time.

Program Department:

This program protects the historic rights of all Canadians with respect to marine transport and provides a quasi-judicial function in dealing with the different players involved in construction in Canada's waterways.

Intergovernmental:

The federal mandate is clear, but there exists some misunderstanding about the overlap with provincial responsibilities for water management and environmental conservation. Construction of works in or over water courses usually requires approvals from agencies in both levels of government.

Observations

The program has evolved over the years and has seen such adjustments as the granting of interim approvals to avoid delays and reduced documentation for private applications for minor works.

Options

The Study Team recommends to the Task Force that the government consider the following:

1. The possibilities of increased cooperation and coordination between federal and provincial agencies might be investigated and the "single window" approach might be considered, i.e. all applications are submitted to one agency which also coordinates the approval process.

FOUR PILOTAGE AUTHORITIES - TC 610

Objectives

To establish, operate, maintain and administer, in the interest of safety, an efficient pilotage service within their respective regions and to prescribe tariffs of pilotage charges that are fair and reasonable, and that provide sufficient revenue to permit the authority to be financially self-sustaining.

Authority

Canada Shipping Act
Pilotage Act

Description

The federal government supports four pilotage authorities: Atlantic Pilotage Authority, Great Lakes Pilotage Authority, Laurentian Pilotage Authority and Pacific Pilotage Authority. All are corporations specified in Schedule C1 of the Financial Administration Act and, with one exception, are owned directly by the government. The Great Lakes Pilotage Authority is a wholly-owned subsidiary of the St. Lawrence Seaway Authority.

Resources

The Pilotage Authorities are Crown corporations and the government does not have the same type of financial data concerning their operations as other programs. However, federal appropriations are made to cover the cash shortfall between expenditures and revenues. These are given below:

Pilotage Authority	82/83	83/84	84/85	85/86
Atlantic	527		150	109
Great Lakes		250	432	
Laurentian		966	1,400	1,084
Pacific				
Total	527	1,216	1,982	1,193

Problem Identification

Private Sector:

Canadian ship owners view compulsory pilotage as a costly and unnecessary burden to the industry in cases where the ship's master or deck watch officer is familiar with the waters. In these cases, which would comprise the vast majority of Canadian owned ships, the benefits of a pilot's services are negligible while the costs are substantial. In 1984 the operators of Canadian flag vessels paid $9.2M for compulsory pilotage in Canadian waters, while total payments to pilots was $47.7M. An undetermined amount of the total is paid by ships whose officers are unfamiliar with Canadian waters and they clearly receive some value for their payments.

Program Department:

TC views compulsory pilotage for ships whose masters and officers have knowledge of local waters to be a questionable allocation of resources. There are provisions within the regulations for masters and officers to obtain pilot certificates, but they have not chosen to submit to the required oral and written examinations.

Intergovernmental:

The federal mandate is clear and there are no competing or duplicative programs administered by other levels of government.

Observations

There appears to be a consensus, except among the beneficiaries of the scheme, that many of the services provided by the pilots are not required and that the incomes of pilots may exceed the value of the services they provide. This is particularly so given the recent advances in electronic navigation and communications systems used in these vessels.

The CTC will hold hearings regarding the proposed tariff increases in May, 1985. The increases were planned to achieve the total cost-recovery objective established for the Pilotage Authorities and will thereby place an increasing cost burden on ships owners. In the Study Team's view, paying the full cost of a service that they do not require is the ultimate in over-regulation.

Options

The Study Team recommends to the Task Force that the government consider the following:

1. The Pilotage Act should be changed to provide exemptions for masters and deck watch officers who have the required certificates and knowledge of local waters and whose vessels meet the standards regarding electronic navigation equipment.

2. The masters and officers should also be encouraged to submit to the examinations required for certification as a pilot.

3. The provision of pilotage services should be transferred to the private sector and there should be enhanced liability for marine accidents.

OVERVIEW

AIR REGULATION

The activities of the federal government in the air
mode can be divided into three areas: (1) the provision and
operation of the infrastructure (airports, etc.), (2) the
safety regulation and (3) economic regulation. Only the
latter two activities fell within the purview of the
regulatory program review. However, there is considerable
overlap between the first two (e.g. air traffic control,
aviation information services). Moreover, this type of
overlap is accentuated by divisions of responsibility
between Transport Canada and the CTC.

The implementation of air safety programs was generally
given positive assessments in terms of effectiveness. Their
efficiency is difficult to assess as there are few alternate
programs upon which to base comparative analysis. However,
the recent TC "A-base" review has addressed the efficiency
issue directly and is expected to yield substantive
recommendations regarding both resource allocation and
organizational structure that will improve the efficiency of
air administration operations. A current review of the air
administration by the Auditor General will probably produce
a similar analysis in the near future. The recommendations
of both reviews should be consolidated and acted upon
without delay.

The issue of cost-recovery in the air transport
administration was not raised by any of the private sector
contacts. However, it was raised by members of the Study
Team. The difficulty in addressing this concern stems from
the point raised above -- the overlap between airport
administration and the delivery of safety regulation
programs. TC has identified nine major airports as
self-supporting and is implementing some efficiency
improvement measures. Both the "A-base" review and the
Auditor General's report contain recommendations for further
action in this regard.

There is a comprehensive review of all transportation
policy currently being conducted by TC. This includes all
modes, safety and economic regulations and the roles of TC
and the CTC. Nonetheless, the issue of the economic
regulation of air transport was examined by the Team since
major concerns were raised in its private sector contacts
about the problems and uncertainty associated with the
current policy. A further relaxation of economic regulation
is suggested by the Study Team: two options are outlined,

505

and a simulation of their impact on the structure and performance of the air industry is presented in a background paper.

A specific course of action is not offered, but the simulation results show that full deregulation (with appropriate safety nets) will yield greater efficiency gains but will be accompanied by significant structural adjustments. The more moderate reform policy will produce fewer efficiency gains and less structural adjustment. Whatever policy is chosen, in the view of the Study Team, the Aeronautics Act should be amended to change the requirement that entry and exit decisions satisfy the public convenience and necessity test. This change is required to provide a legislative base for the existing policy which was announced in May 1984 and to provide formal direction to the CTC to carry out the policy.

The Study Team has found that the safety nets that accompany policy reforms should include labour relocation and retraining programs and air transport subsidies to provide service that is deemed to be "essential". These programs should be developed as a part of the total regulatory reform package and should be designed as interim adjustment programs with appropriate sunset provisions. The existing subsidy programs should be eliminated as they make little economic sense and are not in concert with current regulatory policy.

DOMESTIC AIR CARRIER SUBSIDIES - CTC 2

Objectives

To administer subsidies under the Regional Air Carrier Policy, or as requested by the Minister of Transport, for the operation of commercial air services in the public interest.

Authority

National Transportation Act.

Description

The program involves administering and paying subsidies to Quebecair and EPA under the Regional Air Carrier Policy, and providing administrative services to Transport Canada for the Prairie and St. Leonard Air Services subsidies.

Resources

($000's)	82/83	83/84	84/85	85/86	86/87	87/88
Person-Years	0.5	0.5	0.5	0	0	0
Operating Expenses						
- Salaries						
- O&M						
- Other Exp.						
Revenue						
Subsidies*	1,500	1,500	1,500	0	0	0
Capital						

*   Amounts do not include subsidies for Prairie Air Services and St. Leonard which are funded by Transport Canada.

Problem Identification

Private Sector:

All private sector contacts commenting on this program recommended its abolition. Air carrier subsidies were considered unnecessary and a waste of taxpayers' money. The administration of the subsidies by the CTC was not criticized. The economic and policy environment that created the subsidy program has changed; this is clearly illustrated by the fact that the Magdalen Islands route now sees a subsidized carrier competing with a non-subsidized carrier.

Program Agency:

The CTC is implementing government policy and is carrying out its administrative role in an efficient and effective fashion. CTC audits show that the carriers have lost more than the subsidy payment to them in 1983. TC has recommended that the subsidies be extended for one year to provide time for a comprehensive review of the need for direct operating subsidies.

Intergovernmental:

Ontario has a program that provides capital equipment (aircraft) to level 3 carriers to provide service on low density routes, as well as an operating subsidy to cover losses incurred by the carriers.

Quebec has a program on the Sept-Iles/Blanc Sablon route which involves financial assistance in equipment acquisition and subsidizes operating losses.

Newfoundland subsidizes operating costs of carriers serving communities on the coast of Labrador to ensure frequency (three times a week) and level of service.

Observations

The federal program is purported to serve economic development and job creation purposes but, in the Team's view, the unrepresentative allocation of the subsidies suggests that they were developed and continued on an ad hoc basis. It is difficult to understand, for example, why there are no subsidies paid to carriers in the North. It is also difficult to understand why the program is continuing after the Regional Air Carrier Policy was abolished by the Minister in 1984. There is a need to review this subsidy program along with those being funded directly by TC.

Options

The Study Team recommends to the Task Force that the government consider the following:

1. The specific subsidies covered by this program should be eliminated, either forthwith or by attrition when each individual agreement expires on its renewal date. The issue of whether or not air carrier subsidies are to be necessary in principle should be considered in the context of the proposed further reform of air regulatory policy.

AIR CARRIER OPERATING CERTIFICATES - TC 4

Objective

To assure the safe and efficient movement of civil aircraft in Canadian and adjacent international airspace.

Authority

Aeronautics Act.

Description

Transport Canada issues operating certificates and operating specifications for domestic and foreign commercial air carriers with consideration given to safety criteria and is responsible for issuance of amendments, cancellations and suspensions.

Resources

($000's)	82/83	83/84	84/85	85/86	86/87	87/88
Person-Years	10	10	10	10	10	10
Operating Exp.						
- Salaries	351	369	402	402	402	402
- O&M	64	67	71	71	71	74
- Other Exp.						
Revenue	19	20.9	22	22	22	22
Subsidies						
Capital						

Problem Identification

Private Sector:

Some concern was mentioned regarding the shared responsibility of the CTC and TC in issuing operating certificates: the CTC makes licensing decisions based on economic criteria; TC then rules on those decisions with regard to safety criteria and issues operating specifications. While the issuance of certificates is currently quite rapid, there may be a potential future problem in having the two authorities reside in separate organizations.

Program Department:

TC views this activity as a smoothly running operation that is an integral part of the air traffic management system. Since the new economic air policy was introduced, the workload has increased and this has led to the streamlining of procedures and use of new equipment. Further increases in workload may require additional PYs. These issues will be considered in the action plan following the "A-base" review.

Intergovernmental:

The federal mandate for this program is clear and there exist no competing or duplicative programs.

Observations

CTC requires TC documentation attesting to facility requirements and operational feasibility of the proposed service before granting licenses. Resource shortages in TC sometimes result in inadequate information being provided to the CTC. This administrative problem has been identified by the TC "A-base" review and will be addressed as part of that exercise.

Options for this small program cannot be considered in isolation and must be included in the review of the total program.

AIR TRANSPORT REGULATION – CTC 20

Objectives

To promote, through economic regulation, an economic, efficient and adequate air transportation system at the lowest total cost to protect the interests of the users of transportation and to maintain the economic well being and growth of Canada. To ensure that the suppliers of air transportation services are appropriately established through financial commitment to provide reasonably stable supply and to ensure that economic regulation is for the benefit of the Canadian travelling public including the handicapped and those required to travel for compassionate reasons.

Authority

National Transportation Act.
Aeronautics Act.

Description

The Air Transport Committee of the Canadian Transport Commission administers the government's domestic and international air transport policies through promulgation of the Air Carrier Regulations made pursuant to the National Transportation Act and the Aeronautics Act and through Decisions and Orders issued on a daily basis.

Resource

($000's)	82/83	83/84	84/85	85/86	86/87	87/88
Person Years	132	132	133	150	130*	130*
Operating Expenses						
– Salaries	5,000	5,131	5,136	6,014	5,295*	5,295
– O & M	1,000	1,202	1,551	1,577	1,192*	1,192
– Other Expenses						
Cost Recovery						
Subsidies						
Capital		66	10	15	10	10

* In March 1984, Treasury Board approved an allocation of 15 PYs and $705,200 for 1984/85 and 20 PYs and $922,700 for 1985/86 to implement a national enforcement program. Continuation of funding for the program was dependent on the development of adequate statement of objectives and

linkages and results statements in order to establish an appropriate level of resources for 1986/87 and beyond. As staffing action could not be completed during the first year, a program evaluation to establish the need for a continuing allocation of resources was postponed one year. It is proposed in the 1986/87 MYOP that the resources for the enforcement program approved for 1985/86 be extended through 1986/87.

Problem Identification

Private Sector:

The various air carriers that were contacted complained that the CTC pricing regulations for scheduled carriers were too rigid relative to those for charter carriers. This has encouraged an uneconomic shift of the former regional carriers' output from scheduled to charter service and therefore decreased their efficiency. The current entry regulations and licence consolidation provisions are a confusing mix of the old and the new regulatory schemes. The relaxation of entry regulations without parallel action regarding exit regulations inhibits taking advantage of the former.

TC's administrative control over airport facilities, gateways and landing and take-off slots has not reflected the changing dynamics of the air transport market. Thus, Air Canada's "preferred carrier" status has continued in this regard, despite the new economic policy that has eliminated that role for the Crown corporation.

Unions fear that regulatory reform will lead to changes in wage packages and work rules.

Program Agency:

The CTC views itself as fulfilling the mandate established in the National Transportation Act and responding to the policies articulated by the current government. It is responding to the May, 1984 policy of relaxed regulation, as confirmed by the present government. The CTC is contemplating further regulatory reform and is working to further reduce the regulatory burden.

<u>Intergovernmental</u>:

> The federal mandate is clear and there are no competing or duplicative programs administered by other levels of government, except the domestic air carrier subsidies.

<u>Observations</u>

The past regulatory regime has rigidly regulated the Air Transport industry and has determined entry exit route structures, aircraft used, prices and levels of service. As a result, economic rents were created and captured by capital and labour. Regulatory reforms, of the nature identified above, will increase competition, output and total employment. In addition, regulatory reform will likely see major carriers leaving regional and local routes and expanding into international routes.

If the current north/south split in Canada of full regulation and relaxed regulation is to be continued, some agency will be required to administer regulation in the north. The staff requirements of the CTC, in this case, would be greatly reduced.

<u>Options</u>

The Study Team recommends to the Task Force that the government consider the following:

1. A further relaxation of economic regulation is suggested: two options are outlined and a simulation of their impact on the structure and performance of the air industry is presented in the attached background paper. The simulation results show that full deregulation (with appropriate safety nets) will yield greater efficiency gains but will be accompanied by significant structural adjustments. More moderate reform policy will produce fewer efficiency gains and less structural adjustment.

2. Whatever policy is chosen, the <u>Aeronautics Act</u> should be amended to change the requirement that entry and exit decisions satisfy the public convenience and necessity test. This change is required to provide a legislative base for the current policy which was announced in May 1984 and to provide formal direction to the CTC to carry out the policy.

BACKGROUND

ALTERNATE POLICY SCENARIOS FOR
THE ECONOMIC REGULATION OF AIR TRANSPORT IN CANADA

This paper will provide a simplified report on some very recent research carried out for the federal government's Office of Regulatory Reform that simulates industry costs under alternative regulatory policy regimes. The vehicle for the simulations is a state-of-the-art "translogarithmic" cost function consistent with widely held principles of neoclassical microeconomics. The quantitative results provide the output, input and operational characteristics that would be associated with the different policy scenarios.

Since the cost models were estimated from historical data (1964-1981), the simulated costs would reflect only the cost efficiencies that can be achieved through changes in the level and mix of outputs, network variables, and input prices. Production technology is held constant. In other words, the simulated costs would not reflect the gains in cost efficiency due to fundamental changes in airline production technology. An example of a change would be relaxation of overly restrictive work rules in union contracts. Thus, these simulations do not provide a means of assessing how the cost relation might shift under deregulation and thus the simulations represent conservative estimates of the industry and carrier adjustments under different scenarios.

The models are simulating the costs of only the two transcontinental and four regional carriers which existed in 1981. The simulation results do not include the gains in cost efficiency by other carriers (Wardair and local service carriers) which one would expect to participate more vigorously in the transcontinental and regional routes under a regulatory relaxation scenario.

Four policy scenarios will be presented: the pre-May 10, 1984 status quo, the May 10, 1984 policy, advanced relaxation and deregulation. The essential features of each policy will be described and the industry and carrier adjustment to each will be analyzed.

REGULATORY POLICY 1: STATUS QUO (PRE MAY 10, 1984 POLICY)

The regulatory policy which existed prior to the New Canadian Air Policy of May 10, 1984 may be summarized as follows:

1. Entry and exit were regulated and carriers were required to meet PCN (public convenience and necessity) criterion for any change.
2. The Regional Carrier Policy confined the Regionals to their respective geographical regions, and discouraged competition between the Regionals and the transcontinental carriers.
3. For many route licences, capacity, type of aircraft, stop-over conditions and frequency of service were stipulated.
4. CTC approval was required for any fare changes, including discount fares. For regular fares, Air Canada's distance-based fare formula was accepted by the CTC and other carriers.

By confining the Regional carriers primarily to short haul, medium to low density routes, the policy encouraged the Regionals to overexpand in charter markets, far beyond the efficient mix between scheduled and charter services. It also helped maintain Air Canada's and CP Air's monopoly power on transcontinental routes. Labour input prices were kept high at least in the sense that some inefficient work rules were tolerated. The equipment the Regionals acquired to provide charter service was not appropriate to their scheduled service and thus their operations were much less efficient than otherwise would have been the case.

For simulation purposes, all variables are given actual 1981 values. Since the pre-May 10 regulatory policy (status quo) forms the reference point for the other policies of our cost simulations. Table 1 summarizes by categories the 1981 output levels and average revenue per RTK (revenue tonne kilometre) for each of the six transcontinental and regional carriers. From the table, it is clear that the two transcontinental carriers produced relatively small proportions of their total outputs from charter services, compared to the regional carriers (except EPA). Charter services accounted for about 28 per cent of total outputs for the regionals.

TABLE 1

1981 Output and Average Revenue by Output Type
(Revenue Shares in parenthesis)

Carrier	Scheduled Passenger		Schedule Freight		Charter		Total RTK and average revenue per RTK
	output in million RTK	average revenue per RTK	output in million RTK	average revenue per RTK	output in million RTK	average revenue per RTK	
AC	2044 (76%)	$0.892	569 (21%)	$0.431	68 (3%)	$0.679	2681 $0.789/RTK
CP	877 (73%)	$0.727	224 (19%)	$0.384	96 (8%)	$0.703	1197 $0.661/RTK
PWA	151 (59%)	$1,494	23 (9%)	$1.048	80 (32%)	$0.65	254
QA	23 (56%)	$1.586	2. (5%)	$1.495	16 (39%)	$2.54* (1980:1.04)	41
EPA	60 (85%)	$1.218	7 (10%)	$1.382	4 (6%)	$0.714	71
NA	58 (50%)	$1.251	24 (20%)	$0.782	35 (30%)	$0.902	117
Total for Regional Carriers	292 (60%)	$1.396	56 (12%)	$0.992	135 (28%)	$0.763	483 1.17/RTK
Total Industry	3213 (74%)	$0.893	849 (20%)	$0.456	299 (7%)	$0.725	4361 $0.796/RTK

Because Statistics Canada changes its reporting statistics in 1981, it was not possible to determine average revenue per RTK precisely for Quebecair. This figure is approximated using past trends of all available statistics. For this reason, we used the 1980 average revenue $1.04/RTK in computing the industry and the regional carrier means.

POLICY 2: MAY 10 LIBERALIZATION

The Minister of Transport announced the new Canadian Air Policy on May 10, 1984. It was an intermediate policy in that it provided some specific short-term policy instructions to the CTC and referred longer term issues, including legislative change, to the Standing Committee on Transport. The new policy received the full blessing of Cabinet. The essential features of the policy are as follows:

1. The merits of competition should be given a heavier weight in judging PCN for entry licensing;
2. The Regional carrier policy is abolished -- regionals may apply for licences for routes outside their traditional regions;
3. Removal of all restrictions on route licences -- carriers are encouraged to apply for consolidation of their licences;
4. Eventually (within two years) CTC control on decreases in air fares are to be ended -- fare increases are to be restricted to within the growth of an input price index which excludes labour input.

Although it is impossible to precisely pinpoint without a fully developed Canadian demand model, effects of the May 10 policy on the key variables included in the airline cost function, the model attempts to put some numbers on them, relative to what actually happened to the carriers if the May 10 policy were effective in 1981. A demand model has not yet been constructed for the Canadian industry because the necessary data are not publicly available.

The May 10 policy has had little impact on Air Canada, largely because the policy has provided it with little opportunity for dropping communities. The policy would exert no significant pressure for the carrier to lower its labour costs, although the new financial funding requirements would induce Air Canada to reduce its capital stock by 10 per cent. CP Air would experience a small increase in output and obtain a 5 per cent reduction in its labour bill. As CP Air is relatively efficient with regard to capital utilization, no adjustment is expected in its capital stock. With the removal of licence restrictions, the Regionals would increase output and stage length by 10 per cent and reduce charter output by 10 per cent. This more efficient output mix would be accompanied by a 5 per cent reduction in capital.

Table 2

Variables used in the May 10 Policy Simulation
(Relative to the Base Case)

	Air Canada	CP Air	Regionals
Total output	no change	3% increase	10% increase
No. of points	no change	no change	no change
Output mix: Passenger	no change	no change	balance to make 10% increase in total output
Charter	no change	no change	10% absolute reduction
Freight	no change	no change	no change in absolute level
Stage length	no change	no change	10% increase
Load factor	no change	no change	no change
Labour prices	no change	5% reduction	no change
Capital	10% reduction	no change	5% reduction

POLICY 3:   ADVANCED RELAXATION

This policy is characterized by the following additions to the May 10, 1984 policy:

-   the benefits of competition are to be given greater weight in determinations of exit petitions in specific markets;
-   carriers operating aircraft with 36 or fewer seats are exempted from all forms of route and pricing regulation;
-   carriers are to be given freedom to raise fares 30 per cent above a reference fare level in markets less than 500 kilometres and 15 per cent in markets between 500 and 1,000 kilometres.
-   carriers will be allowed unlimited freedom to enter one way charter markets;
-   northern Canada is subject to the same policies as southern Canada (specifically northern Canada loses its protection from entry, exit and pricing regulation);
-   a small and isolated community subsidy program is to be instituted.

Under the Advanced Relaxation Policy, new third level carriers using small aircraft would exert considerable pressure on the regional carriers. As a result, the regionals would have to streamline labour input prices, reduce their charter services and excess capacity, and participate selectively in some medium to long haul high density routes. This policy would in turn put the regionals in a very vulnerable situation. The competitive response of the Regionals would create some additional pressures on Air Canada and CP Air, forcing them to reduce somewhat their input prices and excess capacity. The best estimates as to what would have happened to the key variables in 1981 are summarized in Table 3.

There is some opportunity under this policy for Air Canada to drop service at some small communities, being replaced by regional or third level carriers. The regionals in turn are likely to drop their smallest points being replaced by third level carriers. This drop by Air Canada and the Regionals of their smallest communities is likely to increase the stage length of each. CP Air, with relatively less service at smaller communities, is likely to have no net change.

Regionals would realign their networks in order to enter more dense markets increasing their stage lengths and realizing some density economies. Both moves result in cost reductions and productivity increases. Exit would occur in short haul markets which third level carriers will enter. Entry could occur in trunk or transcontinental routes traditionally served by Air Canada. The extent to which this would occur would depend on whether the CTC followed the philosophy of not interpreting PCN as the continuity of Air Canada in its present form and size. There is not likely to be new jet air carriers on major routes as PCN is still applied. However, there may be third level carriers entering regional routes and short-haul dense routes. One can expect that Air Canada will have a reduced proportion of the total Canadian domestic market as its ability to compete is still constrained as in the May 10 Policy. This will give it an incentive to seek gains in the international sector, possibly at CP Air's expense. Relative to the previous two policy scenarios, advanced liberalization gives potential for significant cost decreases, particularly for the Regionals. These performance improvements can be effected by the CTC depending upon its use and interpretation of PCN.

Table 3
Variables Used in the Advanced Relaxation Policy Simulation

	Air Canada	CP Air	Regionals
Total output	5% reduction	no change	10% increase
No. of points	10% reduction	no change	10% reduction
Output mix: Charter	no change	no change	20 % absolute reduction
Freight			same in absolute
Passenger			whatever is necessary to make 10% increase in total output
Stage length	10% increase	no change	15% increase
Load factor	no change	no change	no change
Labour prices	5% reduction	10% reduction	10% reduction
Capital Stock	10% reduction	no change	10% reduction

POLICY 4: COMPLETE DEREGULATION

The final regulatory policy is complete deregulation. Here carriers have unlimited freedom to enter and exit markets and unlimited freedom to raise and lower fares. To achieve this, legislation is required to remove the public convenience and necessity criterion of the Aeronautics Act. In its place one would propose a fit, willing and able criterion as in the U.S. Carriers would be continually monitored to ensure that they maintain high safety standards and financial qualifications.

Complete deregulation is characterized by the following points:

- replacement of "public convenience and necessity" with a "fit, willing and able" criterion in awards of licences;
- continue regulation "into the industry" (as opposed to "onto" routes) using the "fit, willing and able" criterion;
- no regulation of entry or exit from routes;
- no regulation of fare increases or decreases;
- no regulations on conditions of service such as number of stops, frequency of service, aircraft type or capacity;
- no north/south distinction;
- small and isolated community subsidy program;
- introduction of an airline employee dislocation retraining program;
- a statement of what constitutes predatory behaviour in a market, a mechanism for enforcement and provision of effective penalties to defer such behaviour;
- a public information program concerning buying ticket insurance in case of carrier bankruptcy.

The complete deregulation policy removes all economic constraints on carriers' choice and performance in air transport markets in Canada. The small and isolated community subsidy program is retained, recognizing that Canada will continue to have a goal of maintaining service, possibly unprofitable, to such communities.

Under deregulation, there could be major changes in the structure of the industry, route and network structures of carriers, and input prices. Air Canada is expected to contract its domestic services considerably, to seek opportunities internationally, and to streamline their

523

labour input prices and excess capacity. Under deregulation, the Regionals, by channelling their existing feed traffic onto new long haul routes, are expected to gain most. CP Air is expected to gain a little as well due to its earlier reductions in costs. Wardair and a new jet carrier or two, if they choose markets to enter, could achieve some gains as well. Table 4 summarizes the simulated impact of deregulation on the variables in the cost model. Traffic is expected to increase significantly as fares decrease and service quality and range increase. Moves to hub and spoke patterns will increase density and stage lengths will increase. Air Canada will reduce its domestic operations in the face of competition on short-haul dense routes. Third-level specialized carriers will develop to serve local markets and feed Regionals. Air Canada's domestic operations will serve fewer points as it is replaced by Regionals. Fares will generally fall as costs decline with increased operating efficiency.

Table 4

Variables in the Deregulation Policy Simulation

	Air Canada	CP Air	Regionals
Total output	15% reduction	10% increase	30% increase
No. of points	15% reduction	no change	10% decrease
Output mix: Charter	no change	change	change 5% of output
Freight		no change	same in absolute
Passenger		balance to make total output grow by 10%	balance to make total output grow by 30%
Stage length	30% increase	10% increase	30% increase
Load factor	no change	no change	no change
Labour prices	15% reduction	15% reduction	20% reduction
Capital stock	35% reduction	10% reduction	15% reduction

RESULTS OF REGULATORY POLICY COST SIMULATIONS

The variable cost model was used to simulate the total cost of each carrier under the four alternative regulatory policies outlined above. The results are summarized in Table 5.

In order to interpret the simulation results appropriately, it is necessary to take into account the fact that each carrier's total output and output mix (passenger, freight and charter) vary with the regulatory policy. Since consumers value the three outputs differently, the changes in output mix should be viewed as changes in the quality of the output. Average revenue per RTK was used as an indicator of quality of output. By normalizing the average revenue per RTK around the value for the status quo (pre-May 10) regulatory policy, the output quality index listed in the table is obtained.

For the purpose of comparing the cost efficiencies of alternative policies, a quality adjusted unit cost reduction factor was computed. Table 5 can be summarized as follows;

1. <u>May 10 Liberalization Policy</u>: Cost efficiency of the industry would improve by 4.4 per cent as compared to the status quo. Under this policy, the cost efficiency of Air Canada, CP Air and the regional carriers is expected to increase 4.3 per cent, 2.5 per cent and 6.3 per cent respectively. Costs fall for Air Canada. CP Air and the Regionals are expected to experience cost increases, but these are more than offset by output increases. Total industry output is expected to increase roughly 2 per cent under the May 10 policy.

2. <u>Advanced Relaxation Policy</u>: Cost efficiency is expected to increase to 6.5 per cent compared to the status quo. This is an improvement of 2.1 per cent over the May 10 policy. Air Canada, CP Air and the Regionals are expected to increase their efficiency by 5.5 per cent, 3 per cent and 15 per cent respectively. Total industry output falls by 2 per cent since Air Canada's output falls by 5 per cent. Increases are expected for third level carriers and Wardair such that net output for all Canadian air carriers goes up by 6.2 per cent.

3. <u>Deregulation</u>: This policy is expected to increase cost efficiency by about 8.8 per cent compared to the status quo. This is an improvement of 4.4 per cent over the May 10 policy and 2.3 per cent over advanced

deregulation. Air Canada, CP Air, and the Regionals would improve their cost efficiency by 9.2 per cent, 5.0 per cent and 12.5 per cent respectively. Output for the 6 air carriers falls by 3.2 per cent, due to Air Canada's drop of 15 per cent. While substantial gains are made by CP Air and the Regionals, they do not offset the drop of Air Canada. Net output for all Canadian air carriers is expected to increase by 7.7 per cent. The difference will be captured by third level carriers, perhaps Wardair and perhaps a new jet air carrier or two.

In these simulations the status of Air Canada has been maintained as it is today. Specifically, under the May 10, 1984 policy, Air Canada has been constrained in its ability to act competitively in Canadian airline markets. Thus other carriers will be able to grow at the expense of the crown carriers. A more complete analysis would involve simulating results of changes in Air Canada's status.

Table 5
Cost Simulation Results for Alternative Regulatory Policies

Regulatory Policy	Industry	Air Canada	CP Air	Regionals
(A) Status Quo (Pre—May 10)				
Total cost	$3493	$2138	$ 779	% 576
Output (RTK)	4360	2680	1200	480
passenger	74%	76%	73%	60%
freight	20%	21%	19%	12%
charter	7%	3%	8%	28%
average revenue	$0.80/RTK	$0.79/RTK	‐ $0.66/RTK	$1.17/RTK
output quality index	1.0	1.0	1.0	1.0
(B) May 10 Liberalization				
total cost	$3468	$2069	$ 783	$ 616
(% change)	−0.8%	−4.3%	0.5%	6.9%
output (RTK)	4443	2680	1236	527
(% change)	2.3%	0%	3%	10%
passenger	74%	76%	73%	66%
freight	19%	21%	19%	11%
charter	7%	3%	8%	23%
average revenue	$0.80/RTK	$0.79/RTK	$0.66/RTK	$1.21/RTK
output quality index	1.003	1.0	1.0	1.032
quality-adjusted unit cost reduction	4.4%	4.3%	2.5%	6.3%

528

Table 5

Cost Simulation Results for Alternative Regulatory Policies

Regulatory Policy	Industry	Air Canada	CP Air	Regionals
(C) Advanced Liberalization				
total cost	$3242	$1912	$ 756	$ 574
(% change)	-7.2%	-10.5%	-3%	-0.4%
output (RTK):	4273	2546	1200	527
(% change)	-1.4%	-5%	0%	10%
passenger	75%	76%	73%	69%
freight	19%	21%	19%	11%
charter	6%	3%	8%	21%
average revenue	$0.80/RTK	$0.79/RTK	$0.66/RTK	$1.22/RTK
output quality index	1.004	1.0	1.0	1.046
quality-adjusted unit cost reduction	6.5%	5.5%	3%	15%
(D) Deregulation				
total cost	$3196	$1621	$ 819	$ 756
(% change)	-8.6%	-24.2%	5.1%	31%
output (RTK):	4221	2278	1320	623
(% change)	-2.0%	-15%	10%	30%
passenger	78%	76%	77%	86%
freight	19%	21%	19%	9%
charter	3%	3%	4%	5%
average revenue	$0.805/RTK	$0.79/RTK	$0.66/RTK	$1.33/RTK
output quality index	1.017	1.0	1.001	1.135
quality-adjusted unit cost reduction	8.8%	9.2%	5%	12.5%

AIRWORTHINESS/AIRCRAFT – TC 27

Objective

To ensure the quality and safety of aeronautical products, including their manufacture and maintenance.

Authority

Aeronautics Act

Description

The program is responsible for developing standards and type approving aeronautical products and their manufacture and maintenance. The function comprises approvals, surveillance and continuing airworthiness. It includes the flight testing of aircraft, issuing directives to correct for problems, occupational certification of maintenance engineers, issuing flight authorities affecting the flight safety of an aircraft, approval of training courses for maintenance engineers, approval of maintenance programs for air carriers and developing international agreements relating to airworthiness.

Resources

($000's)	82/83	83/84	84/85	85/86	86/87	87/88
Person-Years		217	272	273	273	273
Operating Exp.						
- Salaries		7,818	11,878	11,926	11,926	11,926
- O&M		1,585	2,136	2,152	2,152	2,152
- Other Exp.						
Revenue		84	84	84	84	84
Subsidies						
Capital		13		177	177	177

Problem Identification

Private Sector:

Air carriers generally are satisfied with the program, although there is some concern over the slow response time during periods of peak demand. Some sources suggested the delegation of inspection and approval activities to the private sector. However, other sources did not see the benefits of such adjustments.

Program Department:

TC provided little information regarding the assessment of this program and apparently anticipates little change from the current situation. TC claims that any delays in providing service to industry are the result of the limited capacity of the responsible branch.

Intergovernmental:

The federal mandate for this program is clear and there exists no competing or duplicative programs.

Observations

The Federal Aviation Administration (FAA) in the U.S. has delegated much of airworthiness inspection and approval activities to the private sector and ensures safety by auditing private sector work. The benefits of private sector efficiency has been realized without a diminution in safety levels. The appropriateness of the current activity organization and resource allocation levels in the Air Administration is being assessed as part of the TC "A-base" review.

Options

The Study Team recommends to the Task Force that the government consider the following:

1. The privatization alternatives might be further examined through a study of the FAA experience. This could be a part of the current general review of transport policy.

AIR CUSHION VEHICLE REGULATION - TC 310

Objective

To ensure the safety, seaworthiness and proper use of Air Cushion Vehicles (ACVs).

Authority

Aeronautics Act.

Description

This program generally regulates the design, manufacture and use of ACVs.

Resources

($000's)	82/83	83/84	84/85	85/86	86/87	87/88
Person-Years		1	2	2	2	2
Operating Exp.						
- Salaries		41	90	91	91	91
- O & M		35	108	110	110	110
- Other Exp.						
Revenue						
Subsidies						
Capital						

Problem Identification

Private Sector:

This program was not raised as a problem by any of the private sector contacts.

Program Department:

TC intends that ACVs are designed, constructed and operated so that they provide levels of safety at least equal to those of other modes of transport and that they conform to the provisions of an international code.

Intergovernmental:

This program is confined to Canadian waters within federal jurisdiction. The overland use of ACVs is subject to provincial/municipal authority.

Observations

When this program was first introduced, there were great expectations about the extent of use of ACVs in Canada. That potential was never met and control over a rapidly growing transport mode failed to become a government priority.

Proposed amendments to the Canada Shipping Act will shift authority over ACVs from the Aeronautics Act to the former.

Options

Nil

AIRCRAFT REGISTRATION - TC 405

Objective

   To contribute to the safe and efficient movement of
civil aircraft in Canadian and adjacent international
airspace.

Authority

   Aeronautics Act.
   Air Regulations.

Description

   Air Regulation 200 requires aircraft to be registered.
The program advises the public as to what is required to
import aircraft and register them in Canada. The program
compiles and maintains the Canadian Civil Aircraft Register.

Resources

($000's)	82/83	83/84	84/85	85/86	86/87	87/88
Person-Years		13	13	13	13	13
Operating Exp.						
- Salaries		367	367	367	367	367
- O & M						
- Other Exp.						
Revenue						
Subsidies						
Capital						

Problem Identification

   Private Sector:

      This program was not identified as a problem by
      the private sector contacts.

   Program Department:

      The program is viewed as a routine registration
      and information service that is provided to the
      public across Canada. This program is being
      examined as part of the TC "A-Base" review and
      administrative changes or resource reallocations
      may result.

<u>Intergovernmental</u>:

The federal mandate is clear and there are no competing or duplicative programs.

Observations

The program constitutes a small element within the total Air Navigational Activity and would be subsumed to a decision regarding the overall activity.

Options

Nil.

AIR TRAFFIC SERVICES - TC 420

Objective

To assure the safe and efficient movement of civil aircraft in Canadian and adjacent international airspace.

Authority

Aeronautics Act.

Description

The program comprises one of the two main functions of the Air Navigational Activity. It consists mainly of the personnel required to operate the various air traffic control facilities and flight service stations. A network of seven area control centres, nine terminal control units and 61 airport control towers exist to provide en route, arrival and departure air traffic control Some 114 flight service stations provide a variety of flight information to pilots.

Resources

($000's)	82/83	83/84	84/85	85/86	86/87	87/88
Person-Years	3,845	3,700	3,724	3,724	3,724	3,724
Operating Exp.						
- Salaries	169,854	152,333	184,164	184,164	184,164	184,164
- O&M	17,757	18,995	20,087	20,087	20,087	20,087
- Other Exp.						
Revenue	89,397	91,296	100,342	72,475	79,689	93,395
Capital	610	2,070	12,766	10,800	15,500	17,700

Problem Identification

Private Sector:

Private sector contacts reported that the air traffic services program was providing an acceptable level of service, given the capital equipment being employed. There were suggestions that state-of-the-art equipment be acquired. There was one comment that the PY allocation in air traffic control was being shifted, over time, from operational to supervisory positions, which effectively is reducing the operational capacity of the program.

Program Department:

The program is integral to the safe movement of aircraft within Canadian airspace. The safety record of air traffic services argues that its benefits exceed its costs. The recently completed "A-base" review may result in some reorganization and resource reallocation. There are efforts underway or in planning to upgrade equipment and improve service levels. Planning is also underway to develop specifications to allow use of a 1,000 foot vertical separation between aircraft operating above 29,000. This would yield annual fuel savings of $40M.

Intergovernmental:

The federal mandate for the program is clear. However, some provincial governments, (e.g. Alberta, and municipal or private airports) provide air navigation aids; these conform to the TC standards.

Observations

This program comprises a fundamental service that the federal government supplies to the Canadian air transport industry. Changes in this program of a substantive nature could only occur if certain other major changes occurred, e.g. selling airports to private companies. If air traffic services were privatized, a monitoring and auditing role would remain.

Options

The Study Team recommends to the Task Force that the government consider the following:

1. The complementary role that provincial, municipal and private airports are playing in traffic management might be expanded in the future. However, the great majority of service is being provided by TC, much of it on a subsidized basis; only the major airports would provide the revenues necessary to privatize the program.

AIR NAVIGATION AIDS – TC 425

Objective

To ensure the safe and efficient movement of civil aircraft in Canada and adjacent international airspace.

Authority

Aeronautics Act
National Transportation Act

Description

The program comprises the personnel, goods and services needed to develop and maintain the flight information services and navigational aids services. There are several hundred navigational aids which assist pilots in determining their location and direction while enroute between airports and to help them land and take off safely.

Resources

($000's)	82/83	83/84	84/85	85/86	86/87	87/88
Person-Years		1,887	1,867	1,867	1,867	1,867
Operating Exp.						
– Salaries		65,931	84,767	84,767	84,767	84,767
– O&M		36,525	38,289	38,289	38,289	38,289
– Other Exp.						
Revenue		33,735	44,522	44,522	44,522	44,522
Subsidies						
Capital		42,500	96,334	--	--	--

N.B. As Main Estimates for 1984/85 and previous years were prepared by Activity rather than Planning Element, these figures are estimates only. Year-to-year have not been adjusted to reflect organizational changes.

Problem Identification

Private Sector:

This program was assessed by private sector contacts as providing a system that allows aircraft to enjoy conflict-free and fuel-efficient flight profiles. This positive assessment was made subject to the criticism of the out-dated equipment (the same as that regarding Air Traffic Services). Efficiency and productivity levels could be raised if new equipment were introduced.

Program Department:

The program comprises the centre of technical expertise and is responsible for the integrity of all national air navigational technical systems. It has succeeded in minimizing the risk of equipment-related aviation incidents and accidents. The implementation of the Cnadian Airspace Systems Plan over the next decade will modernize air traffic facilities and equipment.

The TC "A-Base" review has included this program and may result in organization restructuring and/or resource reallocation.

Intergovernmental:

The few provincial, municipal and private airports provide navigational aids in conformity with TC standards. The federal mandate in this area is clear.

Observations

This program comprises a fundamental service that the federal government supplies to the Canadian air transport industry. Changes in this program of a substantive nature could only occur if certain other major changes occurred, e.g. selling airports to private companies. If air navigation aids were privatized, a monitoring and auditing role would remain.

Options

The Study Team recommends to the Task Force that the government consider the following:

1. The non-federal airports may provide a model for the privatization of air navigational aids service, although there are likely only a few large airports where private businesses could make a profit.

AVIATION SERVICES - TC 430

Objective

To ensure the safe and efficient movement of civil aircraft in Canada and adjacent international airspace.

Authority

Aeronautics Act.
National Transportation Act.

Description

The program involves the development of standards for air navigation services and facilities, and the inspection of navigation aids to ensure they meet operating standards.

Resources*

($000's)	82/83	83/84	84/85	85/86	86/87	87/88
Person-Years	168	173	172	172	172	172
Operating Exp.						
- Salaries	5,796	5,796	7,122	7,122	7,122	7,122
- O&M	6,279	6,474	7,621	7,621	7,621	7,621
- Expenses						
Revenue		19	20	20	20	20
Subsidies						
Capital						

* (estimates and assumptions)

Problem Indentification

Private Sector:

This program was largely indistinguishable from Air Traffic Services and Air Navigation Aids for the majority of private sector contacts. Accordingly, it received the same qualified positive assessment as those two programs.

Program Department:

The program is viewed as an integral component of the air traffic management system. TC states that the degree of specialization is such that the work

cannot be carried out at less cost. The program
has recently been reviewed and is being
centralized with substantial long term savings
(estimated at 27 PYs).

Intergovernmental:

The federal mandate is clear and there exist no
competing or duplicative programs.

Observations

TC is apparently making advances in improving the
efficiency of this program. It is a component of one
general service air traffic control and air navigation
systems that the majority of knowledgeable parties feel
should be provided by a government body.

Options

The Study Team recommends to the Task Force that the
government consider the following:

1. The options for change are limited since a government
   body should probably retain the authority to establish
   and maintain standards for air navigation services and
   facilities. A tripartite organization is one possible
   option, particularly since many of the standards are
   developed by international bodies.

AVIATION SAFETY AND ENFORCEMENT – TC 435

Objective

To assure the safe and efficient movement of civil aircraft in Canadian airspace and of Canadian civil aircraft abroad.

Authority

Aeronautics Act
Air Regulations
Air Navigation Orders

Description

This program involves responding to the Canadian Aviation Safety Board (CASB) recommendations, promoting aviation safety and enforcing air safety regulations in respect of all civil aviation in Canada. These activities are complementary to the CASB.

Resources

($000's)	82/83	83/84	84/85	85/86	86/87	87/88
Person-Years	52	52	54	54	54	54
Operating Exp.						
- Salaries	2,100	2,146	2,592	2,592	2,592	2,592
- O&M	480	483	704	704	704	704
- Other Exp.						
Revenue	$122,800 paid in punative fines to CRF					
Subsidies						
Capital		11	150	--	4	--

Problem Identification

Private Sector:

This program was not identified as a problem by private sector contacts. The general assessment of the air safety program was positive.

Program Department:

The program contributes to the sustained, stable and long-term economic development of the aviation infrastructure. Program output includes reductions in the costs of accidents and progress has been made in this regard. The ratio of accident cost-reduction (benefit) to safety related activities (cost) has been estimated to be 20:1. The Program focus is on the small to medium air carrier, reflecting their relatively high frequency of accidents. The "A-base" review has recommended additional enforcement PYs for this program.

Intergovernmental:

The federal mandate is clear. However, the Ontario Provincial Police and the Quebec Provincial Police occasionally report violations to TC. There is close liaison and frequent exchange of safety and regulatory information with foreign government civil aviation authorities (e.g. FAA in the U.S.; CAA in the U.K.).

Observations

The program appears to be an appropriate means of contributing to aviation safety; the enforcement program is a necessary part of the air safety regulatory function. It is difficult to separate the effect on aviation safety of this program from the other TC regulatory programs.

Options

The Study Team recommends to the Task Force that the government consider the following:

1. The efficiency of the aviation safety program might be enhanced by greater involvement of the general aviation community in promoting aviation safety.

LICENSING, REGISTRATION, TRAINING & TESTING (AIR) - TC 440

Objectives

To ensure the safe and efficient movement of civil aircraft in Canadian and adjacent international airspace.

Authority

Aeronautics Act

Description

This program groups a number of activities directed at the maintenance of aviation data bases and the application of skill and safety standards. Specific initiatives are flight test standards and guides, aircraft journey logs, civil aircraft register, aircraft flight permits, aircraft registration, civil aviation personnel licensing, aviation personnel licensing guides, flight instructor courses, and flight crew and aircraft engineer licensing examinations.

Resources

($000's)	82/83	83/84	84/85	85/86	86/87	87/88
Person-Years	33	34	34	34	34	34
Operating Exp.						
- Salaries	989	1,018	1,043	1,043	1,043	1,043
- O&M	85	91	95	95	95	95
- Other Exp.						
Revenue	9	9	10	10	10	10
Subsidies	59	65	72	76	76	76
Capital	48	50	52	54	56	58

Problem Identification

Private Sector:

While the program was not identified as a problem, there were some criticisms by major commercial air carriers about the extent of inspection. These carriers have been authorized to develop and implement training programs and certification procedures. However, they are reportedly subjected to a level of inspection that does not reflect this delegated responsibility.

Program Department:

The program is viewed as a "non-discretionary regulatory function" and required by Canadian law and the ICAO Convention. There are no feasible alternate methods of ensuring that Canada meets the ICAO personnel standards. The "A-base" review may lead to organizational restructuring or resource reallocation.

Intergovernmental:

The federal mandate is clear and there are no competing or duplicative programs administered by other levels of government.

Observations

Overall, the program is an appropriate way of maintaining basic data for aircraft identification and enforcement and airworthiness purposes, and of ensuring that basic standards are met by aircraft operators. However, in the Study Team's view, it is questionable whether it is appropriate to review alternative aircraft journey logs when a standardized one is available. It is also questionable whether the subsidization of flight instructor refresher courses is of significant benefit. The Treasury Board indicates that an annual saving of $132,600 and 2.5 PY would be achieved by eliminating these activities.

There is limited cost-recovery in the program (1984-85 revenues were $10K, from licensing examinations, compared with costs of $108.1K, excluding the $182.6K cost of aircraft journey log and flight instructor courses). There is potential for full cost recovery in the program. Since the public served is clearly defined, administration of cost recovery would be straightforward.

Options

The Study Team recommends to the Task Force that the government consider the following:

1. The program modifications and increased cost-recovery represent the primary optional approaches to delivering this program.

545

CANADIAN AVIATION SAFETY BOARD - TC 600

Objective

To prevent aviation accidents through their investigation and analysis and through the identification of aviation safety deficiencies.

Authority

Canadian Aviation Safety Board Act

Description

The Canadian Aviation Safety Board (CASB) was created following recommendations made by the Dubin Commission and was proclaimed into law on May 1, 1984. Prior to that, a portion of the CASB's mandate was performed by the Aviation Safety Bureau (ASB) in TC. The bulk of the ASB's resources were transferred to the CASB to form the nucleus of the new organization. The CASB does not perform a regulatory role, but a diagnostic and advisory role.

Resources*

($000's)	82/83	83/84	84/85	85/86	86/87	87/88
Person-Years	55	58	139	198	210	210
Operating Expenses						
- Salaries	2,311	5,213	7,224	10,946	12,150	12,150
- O&M	1,075	1,320	1,820	1,485	1,677	1,677
- Other Exp.						
Revenue						
Subsidies						
Capital	--	--	900	1,190	896	584

*   Resources prior to May 1984 are those of the ASB.

Problem Identification

Private Sector:

This program was not identified as a problem. It shared the general positive assessment of the other TC safety programs. The creation of an independent agency was supported, as some identified the possibilities for conflicts of interest within the Air Administration. Most believed that the CASB should report to the Minister of Transport and not to another Minister (as recommended by Justice Dubin). The cost of carrying out the Gimli accident investigation was criticized by one Winnipeg group.

Program Department:

The CASB is viewed as providing benefits that greatly exceed its costs, although there has been a limited period during which to make observations.

Intergovernmental:

The federal mandate is clear and there are no competing or duplicative programs administered by other levels of government.

Observations

The CASB is resourced to maintain a minimum level of activity with respect to accident investigations and has a standing authority to seek additional funds to carry out investigations of major accidents. The Gimli investigation, involving no loss of life or serious injuries, has cost $2M because of the type of investigation and length of inquiry carried out by the Commissioner.

Options

The Study Team recommends to the Task Force that the government consider the following:

1. The CASB should be incorporated into a multi-modal, independent transportation safety agency.

2. The Commission of Inquiry approach to the investigation of major transport accidents should be replaced by special study team directed by the new transportation safety agency. (See overview paper on air safety.)

OVERVIEW

RAIL REGULATION

The bulk of the observations regarding rail are made in the Grain Transportation and Handling Overview. The two programs examined in this section are rail safety and railway economic analysis. The safety regulation-making function and the accident investigation function are currently being carried out by the same unit within the Canadian Transportation Commission (CTC). In the view of the Study Team, they should be separated, with accident investigation being performed by an independent agency. The question as to whether the CTC should retain responsibility for rail safety is also raised, since Transport Canada administers safety programs for the other modes. Finally, the issue of an independent multi-modal safety agency is examined and substantial evidence of support for this proposal is put forward.

The rail economic program, like many of the CTC's activities, involves a very high level of detailed bureaucratic regulation of the railway industry with unnecessarily slow, complicated and costly decision-making processes. The Study Team concludes that a comprehensive review with the objective of substantial regulatory reform is needed for this program.

RAILWAY ECONOMIC ANALYSIS AND QUALITY OF SERVICE - CTC 40

Objective

To ensure the provision of adequate railway services in Canada.

Authority

Railway Act.
National Transportation Act.
Western Grain Transportation Act.

Description

Regulation of railway service is achieved by developing and refining accounting and costing methodology, auditing the charges imposed by CN Rail and CP Rail upon VIA Rail Canada Inc., monitoring the quality of freight and passenger service and undertaking the financial and socio-economic analysis employed in the consideration of branch line abandonment and passenger train discontinuance applications.

The auditing function focuses upon the statutory requirement to ensure that the railways do not engage in predatory pricing by permitting their freight rates to fall below an established minimum compensatory level. The costing methodology is also employed in determining the existence of uneconomic services which may be required under the provisions ot the Railway Act.

The monitoring responsibility of the CTC is interpreted as requiring CTC investigations into a wide range of the day-to-day activities of the railways.

Resource

($000's)	82/83	83/84	84/85	85/86	86/87	87/88
Person-Years	78	74	74	71	71	71
Operating Exp.	3,500	3,530	3,680	3,506	3,560	3,560
- Salaries						
- O&M						
- Other Exp.						
Revenue	-	-	-	-	-	-
Subsidies	-	-	-	-	-	-
Capital	28	30	35	35	35	35

Problem Identification

Concerns were expressed by the rail industry and other respondents with respect to:

1. Unnecessary regulatory requirements placed upon the CTC such as control over the removal of station agents, station buildings and sidings.

2. Unnecessarily restrictive approaches to interswitching arrangements in terms of distance limitations which can adversely affect shippers freight costs.

3. The slow, complicated, tedious and costly decision making process of the CTC.

The CTC itself is conscious of the limitations placed upon the freedom of the railways by its regulatory activities and recognizes that such constraints can impede initiative because of the uncertainties and delays thus created.

Provincial and municipal concerns relate to the often time consuming approval processes that relate to the transfer of railway property with their attendant cost implications for urban renewal and rail line relocation programs.

Observations

1. Notwithstanding the criticism that has been levelled at the CTC, some notable progress has been achieved in recent years in the field of railway costing. The CTC has been a catalyst in a process which has placed Canada in the forefront of relatively sophisticated railway costing techniques.

2. The role of the CTC in auditing railway operating charges to VIA Rail may change significantly when the current study on VIA Rail completes its assessment.

3. The review of the Western Grain Transportation Act scheduled for 1986 and the ongoing reviews of methods of subsidy payment by Justice Emmett Hall could result in further changes in the role of the CTC.

4. The present heavy regulatory burden imposed by the CTC could be ameliorated by exempting detailed operating

matters such as agent centralization, station building removal and the abolition of sidings from CTC jurisdiction. These decisions could be more appropriately left in the hands of railway management.

Options

The Study Team recommends to the Task Force that the government consider the following:

1. There should be an in-depth review of all CTC regulatory responsibilities with a view to reducing the overall burden they represent to railways, shippers and communities.

2. The review should take into full account the team's further recommendations that:

   a) The powers of the CTC should be amended to allow it to exempt day-to-day railway management decisions such as removal of station agents, station buildings and sidings from regulation.

   b) The CTC should develop new "short form" hearing procedures that expedite decisions and reduce the delays and costs of the parties involved.

   c) Revisions should be made to the long established interswitching arrangements so that they more adequately reflect the growth and dispersion of shippers within urban areas and stimulate greater competition between the major railways.

   d) Canadian railways should be permitted to enter into negotiated contract rates with shippers on a confidential basis in order to maintain their competitive position with U.S. (deregulated) systems. In so doing they should be exempted from the provisions of Section 279 of the Railway Act.

RAILWAY SAFETY - CTC 45

Objectives

To ensure that railways are operated safely for the protection of both employees and the public, including the railway-related aspects of the transportation of dangerous goods.

Authority

National Transportation Act
Railway Act

Description

The program develops and enforces safety regulations, standards and procedures for railway operations, equipment and infrastructure. The program also administers contributions towards safety improvements at railway-highway crossings.

Resource

($000's)	82/83	83/84	84/85	85/86	86/87	87/88
Person-Years	137	151	152	154	154	154
Operating Expenses						
- Salaries	5,560	6,455	6,840	7,140	7,140	7,140
- O & M	1,150	1,350	1,400	1,400	1,400	1,400
- Other Exp.						
Revenue						
Subsidies	15,380	10,000	9,100	10,000	10,000	10,000
Capital	20	12	24	15	15	14

Problem Identification

Private Sector

The railways criticized the CTC's overly-bureaucratic inspection activities and its emphasis on the enforcement of technical standards and procedures rather than an actual railway safety performance. They indicated that it is in the railways own interest to ensure the safety of their operations, since accidents are costly. The general public is most concerned about rail safety and groups such as MTRAC in Toronto are critical of railway safety practices.

Program Agency

The CTC is very aware of the need to balance safety against economic costs. While it is most difficult to estimate the savings from accident prevention, the CTC believes the benefits of the program exceed its costs by several orders of magnitude. The CTC does not believe self-regulation by the railways to be a reliable option.

Intergovernmental

The federal mandate is clear and there are no competing or duplicative programs administered by other levels of government.

Observations

This program is difficult to assess. On the one hand, the railways claim to be over-regulated and over-inspected by CTC officials and that accident or incident investigation procedures are excessively time-consuming, legalistic, complex and costly. On the other hand, citizens groups and those concerned with safety criticize the CTC for being too easy on the railways and for making safety regulations that are not tight enough.

Options

The Study Team recommends to the Task Force that the government consider the following:

1. The accident investigation function should be divested from the safety regulation-making function and both should be moved out of the CTC.

2. The regulation-making function should be transferred to TC and the accident investigation function should be transfered to the new multi-modal transport safety agency.

554

OVERVIEW

GRAIN TRANSPORTATION AND HANDLING

Program reviews have drawn attention to the exceptionally high degree of regulation that permeates all aspects of this industry. Reference has also been made to the existence of markedly differing philosophies regarding required levels of regulation and the institutional structures related to them. These have been mirrored at the political level. This together with the inertia effect created by memories of the historical development of the industry have sometimes deflected attention away from what the Study Team considers to be the following fundamental imperatives:

- Regulation in an internationally competitive industry such as grain is justified where it assists rather than impedes the maximization of sales opportunities and producer income.

- Regulation should not inhibit innovation and entrepreneurial activity.

- Regulation should not impose a cost burden which is not commensurate with the benefits to be derived therefrom.

- Regulation should not shelter producers from an awareness of the market place or inhibit rational business decisions.

- Regulation, insofar as it is a response to a specific problem or situation at a given point in time, should be subject to periodic review and sunset provisions.

- Regulations create regulatory structures and they in turn become vested interests that can inhibit change.

- Undue secrecy, lack of accountability and arbitrary behaviour on the part of some regulators can bring the entire regulatory system into disrepute and create a perception that inefficiency and mismanagement exist.

The complexity of the regulatory structure requires evaluation on a comprehensive basis. It is doubtful that the terms of reference of the forthcoming review of the Western Grain Transportation Act will provide an opportunity

555

to address the full range of basic questions. In the Study Team's view, the following qauestions require special attention.

- Is the industry overregulated?

- Should special treatment be accorded to the transportation and handling sector by the federal government on an indefinite basis?

- Should transportation regulation be used as a vehicle for the achievement of social and other objectives?

- Should grain producers be shielded from direct subsidies?

- Are there lessons to be learned from the less regulated systems of our competitors on world grain markets?

- What would be the likely impact of unleashing innovative and entrepreneurial management upon this sector?

- What would be the consequences for Canada if more of its grain producers became increasingly market conscious like their U.S. counterparts?

- Should the institutional constraints imposed by various federal regulatory structures be subject to critical periodic review and sunset provisions?

- What constitutes the indispensable core of regulatory activity in this industry?

- How can greater accountability on the part of regulators be assured in the future?

The issues are complex and the evolution of regulation continues to be contentious and occasionally regionally divisive. Some basic elements of the regulatory framework are presented in tabular form for purposes of clarification. A direct comparison on a point-by-point basis with practice in the U.S. could prove illuminating. The major issues require dispassionate evaluation by outside experts.

A SUMMARY OF MAJOR REGULATORY ELEMENTS IN THE GRAIN TRANSPORTATION
AND HANDLING SECTOR

ACTIVITY	SECTOR	REGULATORY AGENCY	FORM OF REGULATION	IMPACT	SUGGESTED REGULATORY REFORM OBJECTIVES
1) Choice of crop variety	Production	Canadian Grains Commission, Agriculture Canada	Grading System Licensing of approved varieties	Price incentives/disincentives. Slower response to markets.	Greater responsiveness to changing market conditions
2) Application to deliver grain to primary elevator	Production	Canadian Wheat Board	Issuance of producer permit book	Variety of controls placed on right to deliver.	Loosening of control in response to enlarged system capacity.
3) Selection of primary elevator delivery point	Production	Canadian Wheat Board	Designation of delivery point (reserve power only)	Evolution of grain handling system	Lift all restrictions.
4) Producer trucking to delivery point	Production	Provincial Government	Motor vehicle licensing, fuel tax exemptions. Prescribed weight limits (seasonal) on rural roads.	License fees Reduced loads (higher unit costs)	Selective investment in rural grid road network.
5) Direct producer loading of rail cars	Production	Canadian Grains Commission Grain Transportation Authority	Approval of application on system allocation (car split)	Prolonged delay before placement Cash saving (elevation fees)	Place producers in same position as other shippers vis-à-vis railways.
6) Delivery to primary elevator	Production	Canadian Wheat Board Canadian Grains Commission	Delivery quota Grading and Weighing	Limitation of delivery opportunity Investment in on-farm storage Equality of delivery opportunity Payment of handling tariff	Phase out controls as handling industry modernizes. Periodically reassess grading system.
7) Receipt of initial payment	Production	Canadian Wheat Board	Pooled price for each type and grade	Offsets natural geographical advantages, removes incentives	Modify pooling system to provide incentives where natural advantage exist.
8) Commercial Trucking (farm to elevator)	Trucking	Provincial Governments	Licensing	Alternative to high cost (to system) branch line operation.	Encourage development of Prairie trucking industry.
9) Recording deliveries	Handling	Canadian Wheat Board	Entry in Permit Book	Control of delivery quotas	Replace with primary elevator receipt with CWB current price less handling and rail charges.
10) Grading and Weighing at Primary elevator	Handling	Canadian Grains Commission	Licensing & Inspection	Reflected in handling charges and producers initial payment Bin segregation by type, grade, protein level (higher handling charges).	Simplify grade segregation system where feasible.

557

ACTIVITY	SECTOR	REGULATORY AGENCY	FORM OF REGULATION	IMPACT	SUGGESTED REGULATORY REFORM OBJECTIVES
11) Storage at Primary elevator	Handling	Canadian Grains Commission	Tariff Setting	Charge upon Pool account (producers income)	No change.
12) Loading of rail cars at primary elevators	Handling	Canadian Wheat Board	Block Shipping System Management	Constraints on car supply. Inhibits competition between companies.	Management by railways (linked by computerized inventory monitoring system to primary elevators) in response to CWB and Grain trade requirements.
13) Operation of primary elevator	Handling	Canadian Grains Commission Labour Canada	Licensing and Inspection Canada Labour Code	Maintenance of prescribed standards, Hours of work, safety	No change.
14) Delays in loading cars at primary elevators	Handling	Canadian Transport Commission	Demurrage changes do not apply to grain cars	Encourages inefficiency	Normal demurrage charges payable by grain companies or producers (producer cars).
15) Storage in Terminals	Handling	Canadian Grains Commission	Tariff setting	Charge upon Pool account (producers income)	No change.
16) Cleaning grain at terminals	Handling	Canadian Grains Commission	Tariff setting	Charge upon Pool account (producers income)	Incentives for more cleaning at Prairie points (benefits for livestock industry)
17) Discharge of grain into vessels	Handling	Canadian Wheat Board Canadian Grain Commission (for export)	Authorization/Prohibition Inspection and grading	Terminal throughput Issuance of certificate	No change.
18) Terminal Operations	Handling	Canadian Grains Commission Labour Canada	Licensing and Inspection Canada Labour Code	Maintenance of prescribed standards, Working conditions, safety, dust extraction, etc..	No change.
19) Establishment of delivery quotas	Central Regulatory	Canadian Wheat Board	Periodic issuance of orders	Triggers producers deliveries within prescribed limits.	Phase out.
20) Control of grain deliveries to primary elevators	Central Regulatory	Canadian Wheat Board	Quotas (by quantity, type, time period).	On farm storage (transfers part of storage costs to producers). Equality of delivery opportunity.	Phase out quotas. Develop three tier system of high capacity/high throughput inland terminals, fill up and close primary elevators and emergency storage.

ACTIVITY	SECTOR	REGULATORY AGENCY	FORM OF REGULATION	IMPACT	SUGGESTED REGULATORY REFORM OBJECTIVES
21) Initial Allocation of rail cars for Board grains	Central Regulatory	Grain Transportation Authority	Weekly decision	Permits CWB to plan block shipping system	Management by railways.
22) Initial Allocation of rail cars for non Board grains	Central Regulatory	Grain Transportation Authority	Weekly decision	Permits grain companies to respond to market demand subject to primary elevator space availability.	Management by railways.
23) Secondary Allocation of rail cars for Board grains	Central Regulatory	Canadian Wheat Board	Block shipping system management	Allocates cars to grain companies within each shipping block based on modified Bracken formula	Management by railways.
24) Tertiary allocation of rail cars to delivery points	Central Regulatory	Grain Companies (as agents of Canadian Wheat Board)		Use of modified Bracken formula in the second stage of allocation creates distortions in company operations, inhibits new entry, competition and rationalization.	Decision by elevator companies. Phase out modified Bracken formula
25) Planning of train runs	Central Regulatory/ Railways	Canadian Wheat Board (in conjunction with the railways).	Block shipping system management	Car spotting at primary elevators rostering of train crews, allocation of rolling stock & locomotives	Railway Management.
26) Branch line rail service	Railways	Canadian Transport Commission Grain Transportation Authority	Branch Line Subsidy Program Performance Monitoring WGTA subsidy	Maintenance of high cost lines (cost burden on producers). Federal branch line rehabilitation program	Phase out low volume/high cost operations. Incentive rates to promote diversions to high capacity delivery points.
27) Main line rail service	Railways	Canadian Transport Commission Grain Transportation Authority	WGTA subsidy Performance monitoring	WGTA subsidy $660 million per year. Report of G.T.A. to Minister of Transport	Redirect WGTA subsidy to producers. Railways to offer variable (incentive) rates. Enlarge car spot capacity at selected points.
28) Provision of hopper cars for grain service	Central Regulatory	Canadian Wheat Board	Block shipping system	Purchase of 13,120 cars and leasing of 2,000 cars at federal expense (implied subsidy to industry)	Transfer car ownership to industry organization or G.T.A.

559

ACTIVITY	SECTOR	REGULATORY AGENCY	FORM OF REGULATION	IMPACT	SUGGESTED REGULATORY REFORM OBJECTIVES
29) Allocation of cars to terminal elevators (Vancouver/Thunder Bay)	Central Regulatory	Grain Transportation Authority	Local Coordination Officers	To improve car cycles and terminal efficiency	No change.
30) Grain shipments to U.S. markets/ports	Central Regulatory	Canadian Wheat Board	Issuance of special permits or prohibition	Inhibited due to CWB reluctance to permit use of primary elevators and ban on use of U.S. terminals.	Abolish controls in order to widen shipping options and system flexibility.
31) Setting of rail grain rates	Railway	Canadian Transport Commission	Rates set in accordance with Western Grain Transportation Act	Investment and rationalization (handling facilities) retarded. Incentive based variable rates are prohibited. Railways claim inadequate contribution to constant costs.	Permit incentive based variable rates.

560

CGC WEIGHING DIVISION — CGC 234

Objective

To provide official monitoring of scale weights at licenced terminals and transfer elevators and within the grain trade in general; to perform weighover inventory audits of grain at terminal and transfer elevators; to inspect elevator facilities and elevator scales.

Authority

Canada Grain Act

Description

The program provides the following operational services: surveillance and certification of grain weights, monitoring of railcars for leaks and seals and defective storage equipment, investigation of all grain weight discrepancies, monitoring of weighscales for accuracy and acceptance, and grain inventory audits at terminal and transfer elevators.

Resources

($000's)	82/83	83/84	84/85	85/86	86/87	87/88
Person-Years		221	218	245	245	245
Operating Expenses						
- Salaries		9,135	9,078	11,238	11,238	11,238
- O&M						
- Other Exp.						
Revenue		11,817	12,500	13,000	13,000	13,000
Subsidies						
Capital						

Problem Identification

Private Sector:

The CGC was given good marks for its regulatory role in quality certification and the high regard in which it is held internationally. This has had a positive effect on the export of Canadian grain.

<u>Program Department</u>:

The CGC's programs make a significant contribution to the marketability of Canadian grain, particularly in the important and highly competitive export market. The CGC provides a service to the industry and responds to the demands placed upon it. The fact that the industry pays fees, and in some cases actual costs for the services performed, is an incentive to efficiency as the industry appreciates that greater efficiency on the CGC's part equates to lower fees. There has been general consensus that the CGC's costs are more than offset by the benefits.

<u>Intergovernmental</u>:

The federal mandate is clear and there are no competing or duplicative programs administered by other levels of government.

Observations

The grain-weighing function of the CGC appears to be carried out with efficiency and effectiveness. The CGC has the strong support of all sectors of the grain industry.

Options

No practicable options were suggested by private sector contacts or by others with expert knowledge of the industry.

CGC GRAIN INSPECTION - CGC 235

Objective

To regulate, control and certify grain quality at licensed grain elevators.

Authority

Canada Grain Act

Description

The program provides inspection services for all domestic and export grain. It establishes quality standards and quality certification for all grains entering or leaving licenced terminals. It provides entomological and inspection services, guaranteed level of protein content for marketing, grain documentation services and management of grain inspection policies.

Resources

($000's)	82/83	83/84	84/85	85/86	86/87	87/88
Person-Years		419	417	435	435	435
Operating Expenses						
- Salaries		18,055	18,589	21,404	21,404	21,404
- O&M						
- Other Exp.						
Revenue		21,466	18,406	21,320	21,320	21,320
Subsidies						
Capital						

Problem Identification

Private Sector:

The CGC was given good marks for its regulatory role in quality certification and the high regard in which it is held internationally. This has had a positive effect on the export of Canadian grain.

The one contentious issue involves the acceptance of new varieties of wheat. The CGC has been slower to grant certification to certain high yield, new varieties of wheat than some grain

563

companies would wish. However, these critics are quick to state that there are two sides to this question and that it will take years to determine which side is right.

Program Department:

The CGC's programs make a significant contribution to the marketability of Canadian grain, particularly in the important and highly competitive export market. The CGC provides a service to the industry and responds to the demands placed upon it. The fact that the industry pays fees, and in some cases actual costs for the services performed, is an incentive to efficiency as the industry appreciates that greater efficiency on the CGC's part equates to lower fees. There has been general consensus that the CGC's costs are more than offset by the benefits.

Intergovernmental:

The federal mandate is clear and there are no competing or duplicative programs administered by other levels of government.

Observations

The grain inspection function of the CGC appears to be carried out with efficiency and effectiveness. The CGC has the strong support of all sectors of the grain industry.

Options

No practicable options were suggested by private sector contacts or by others with expert knowledge of the industry.

LICENSING, REGISTRATION AND DOCUMENTATION - CGC 901

Objective

To supervise the bonding of licensees and to ensure that licensees comply with the Act.

Authority

Canada Grain Act

Description

This program provides the following services: issues licences and monitors the performance of licensees to ensure their compliance with the provisions of the Canada Grain Act and regulations; registers and cancels negotiable elevator warehouse receipts for grain received and shipped at licensed terminal and transfer elevators; provides documentation on certified grades and weights and inward grain accounting service to the industry; and allocates railway cars to producers for self-loading.

Resources

($000's)	82/83	83/84	84/85	85/86	86/87	87/88
Person-Years		61	72	72	72	72
Operating Expenses						
- Salaries		2,331	2,380	2,571	2,571	2,571
- O&M						
- Other Exp.						
Revenue		3,431	3,214	2,953	2,953	2,953
Subsidies						
Capital						

Problem Identification

Private Sector:

The CGC was given good marks for its regulatory role in quality certification and the high regard in which it is held internationally. This has had a positive effect on the export of Canadian grain.

Program Department:

The CGC's programs make a significant contribution to the marketability of Canadian grain, particularly in the important and highly competitive export market. The CGC provides a service to the industry and responds to the demands placed upon it. The fact that the industry pays fees, and in some cases actual costs for the services performed, is an incentive to efficency as the industry appreciates that greater efficiency on the CGC's part equates to lower fees. There has been general consensus that the CGC's costs are more than offset by the benefits.

In recent years, there has been an increase in the numbers of small, independent grain dealers who require licensing. A small number of them (two or three a year) have become insolvent, thereby disrupting an otherwise stable market. Even though the producers dealing with these dealers are protected by insurance, the CGC views these developments with some concern.

Intergovernmental:

The federal mandate is clear and there are no competing or duplicative programs administered by other levels of government.

Observations

The grain inspection function of the CGC appears to be carried out with efficiency and effectiveness. The CGC has the strong support of all sectors of the grain industry. The dealer insolvency problem is one that might best be left to market forces and information programs.

Options

No practicable options were suggested by private sector contacts or by others with expert knowledge of the industry.

CANADIAN WHEAT BOARD — CWB

Objective

The purchase, receipt, storage, handling, transportation, transfer, insurance, sale, shipment or other disposal of wheat, barley and oats (and specified products) for international or domestic markets from within the designated area (Manitoba, Saskatchewan, Alberta and part of British Columbia). Collectively this range of activities is characterized by the Board as "orderly marketing".

Authority

The Canadian Wheat Board Act.
The Western Grain Transportation Act.

Description

In support of its prime responsibility for the marketing of wheat, oats and barley on an international basis, the Board administers the delivery point system which records producer grain deliveries to primary elevators. The Board fixes producer delivery quotas (on the basis of seeded acreage) within specified periods and regions. It may prohibit the delivery of any grain or quality grade and regulates the allocation of railway cars by grain shipping blocks (comprising the elevators located on local networks of rail lines which reflect the pattern of train runs). It controls the delivery of grain to terminal elevators, process elevators and lake vessels and can require all individuals and companies involved in the delivery, receipt, storage, transportation and handling of grain to report to the Board on related activities and facilities.

Normally the Board maintains monopoly powers over the export or import of wheat, oats and barley, interprovincial trade in wheat and wheat products, and the purchase of all wheat, oats and barley offered for sale to its agents, the elevator companies, at railheads in the designated territory.

The Board makes initial and final payments from pool accounts to grain producers after deducting the cost of elevator tariffs imposed by the Canadian Grains Commission and allowing for CWB overhead.

567

Resources

The absence of detailed resource data in the files of central agencies in Ottawa and the continuing refusal of the CWB to participate in the review exercise have combined to prevent the preparation of a resource profile.

Problem Identification

In the private sector there remains a clear division between those groups supportive of the "orderly marketing" concept as espoused by the Canadian Wheat Board and those with a "free market" orientation who tend to be highly critical of the Board.

Supporters argue that the Board protects producers from the threat of predatory and discriminatory behaviour by grain companies (including several multi-nationals). By virtue of its quota and pooling systems the Board provides a needed level of income guarantee to all producers regardless of geographical location. The block shipping and quota systems are seen as sustaining long established patterns of highly dispersed small capacity grain elevators (with alleged benefits to producers in terms of short truck hauls). Since most of Canada's major grain trading partners purchase through various state controlled organizations, the CWB is perceived to be best equipped to negotiate with such entitles.

Opponents of the Board argue that the Board is unnecessarily secretive and is accountable to no one. The private sector is reluctant to openly criticize the Board because of a fear of reprisals (in terms of car allocations, etc.). As a result of the regulatory burden, there is a deeply-rooted attitudinal malaise in the industry. Regulation by incentives rather than penalties is preferred. The CWB should return to its original role of a purely marketing agency now that rail capacity problems are largely solved. Excessive regulation (with respect to statutory freight rates, limitations on rail abandonment, and CWB control mechanisms) have in the past necessitated massive public investment in the grain sector that could have been avoided if normal market forces had operated. The CWB, by virtue of its dominant role, from time to time inadvertently or deliberately impedes the movement of "non-board" grains and oilseeds (marketed by the private grain trade) to the detriment of producers, the trade and the diversification of the western farm economy. The Board is regarded as being

568

inflexible in the enforcement of regulations. The CWB is preoccupied with maintaining equality of delivery opportunity for producers at the expense of system efficiency. The railways cannot assume management of the transportation system until the Board withdraws from that sector and "variable" rates are permitted on the same basis as for other traffic.

Federal agencies in Ottawa expressed concern regarding the lack of accountability of the CWB. A federal agency in western Canada considered that the modified Bracken formula (for car allocation to elevator companies) as used by the CWB, is impeding new entries to the primary elevator industry and inhibiting plant rationalization. While support for the CWB remains constant in Manitoba and Saskatchewan, the Government of Alberta has frequently questioned the role of the Board.

Observations

1. Criticism of the CWB is focused primarily on its regulatory role in transportation. There is wide support of its role in international marketing.

2. The all pervasive presence of the CWB makes grain transportation and handling one of the most highly regulated industries in Canada (see overview paper).

3. Excessive secrecy, lack of accountability and arbitrary postures are not appropriate (although commercial sensitivities in a highly competitive industry must be considered).

4. Preservation of equality of delivery opportunity inflicts heavy costs in terms of inefficient rail and elevator operations.

5. In the view of the Study Team, grain transportation policy and CWB regulation should not be used as vehicles for achieving social objectives (protection of small farms, maintenance of rural communities).

6. The development of the "non-board" grain and oilseeds sector should not be impeded by CWB actions.

Options

The Study Team recommends to the Task Force that the government consider the following:

1. It is suggested that a major review should be conducted of the Canadian Wheat Board's regulatory roles in the transportation and handling sectors. The assessment should employ the full range of criteria employed in socio-economic analysis and should draw heavily on outside expertise.

2. In order to more effectively assert its authority, the federal government should authorize the Auditor General to conduct a regular audit of the Canadian Wheat Board.

3. A guiding principle for the reduction in the regulatory burden should be the encouragement of greater entrepreneurial initiative and innovation on the part of producers, grain handlers and the transportation sector.

4. On an interim basis, steps should be taken to more effectively separate the non-boards and oilseeds transportation system from that of Board grains.

WESTERN GRAIN TRANSPORT - CTC 10

Objective

The determination of grain freight rates based on total volume of grain shipped and total rail system costs.

Authority

Western Grain Transportation Act

Description

The CTC prescribes, on an annual basis, the scale of grain freight rates applicable in accordance with the provisions of the Western Grain Transportation Act. This Act replaced the statutory "Crow" rates by a new rate-setting formula which includes federal government payments (subsidies) to the railways and progressively increasing payments within prescribed limits by grain producers to cover the new cost related freight rates.

Payments are made by the Minister of Transport to the railways on an annual basis in accordance with the recommendations of the CTC. The cost determinations made by the CTC similarly affect the contribution to total rail transportation costs made by grain producers.

The Commission also reviews the annual statement of grain related investment plans submitted by the railways and monitors the implementation of railway programs concerning grain dependent branch lines (where grain is the dominant traffic) and investment in grain related rail infrastructure such as rolling stock, track maintenance and bridge renewal etc.

The Commission is further obligated to complete a review of the volume related variable costs of grain movement on grain dependent branch lines before March 31, 1986 and every fourth year thereafter.

Resource

($000's)	82/83	83/84	84/85	85/86	86/87	87/88
Person-Years			13	15	15	15
Operating Exp.			974	1,045	1,045	1,045
- Salaries						
- O&M						
- Other Exp.						
Revenue		-	-	-	-	-
Subsidies		-	578,200	654,400	685,500	695,500
Capital		-	-	-	-	-

Problem Identification

Private sector concerns relating to this program are largely reflective of the alignment of philosophies within the grain sector. These contrasting views can be characterized as follows:

1. Groups that are supportive of the notion that grain producers should be more generally exposed to market forces where sales, bulk handling and transportation decisions are concerned tend to favour payment of subsidies to the grain producer rather than the railways.

2. Groups that support payment of subsidies directly to the railways are fearful of the impact of increased exposure to market forces on the viability of small farm operators, the survival of small prairie communities and established grain collection and marketing systems.

3. The railways view the continued payment of subsidies to them and the absence of variable freight rates as factors which deprive the grain producers of the opportunity to make rational transportation decisions based on actual costs and perpetuate the existence of a network of high cost branch lines which inflate the overall costs of the grain transportation system. These costs must be shared by all producers.

4. The alternative approach of paying grain transportation subsidies directly to the producers is seen as an administratively difficult option by those who support the present method of payment to the railways.

572

Federal agencies expressed concerns regarding the lack of incentives provided by the present subsidy arrangements and asserted that heavy financial burdens are thereby placed on producers and taxpayers in general. These result from the continued operation of high cost, low traffic density branch lines and the persistance of control mechanisms such as those operated by the Canadian Wheat Board that inhibit economies of scale in the grain handling and transportation sector.

One western provincial government tended to favour payment of subsidy to producers whereas two other western provinces are more supportive of the present program.

Observations

1. The program is one element in the overall high level of federal control of the grain handling and transportation sector, which is also addressed in profiles relating to the Canadian Wheat Board and CTC Branch Line subsidy regulation.

2. There is an urgent need to reconsider the costs and benefits of paying subsidies to producers rather than to the railways.

3. On purely economic grounds, there are prospects of significant gains to be derived from a reorientation of grain transportation subsidies from the railways to the producers.

4. The gains so derived would accrue to the majority of grain producers, the railways and the federal government (in terms of reduced subsidy payments).

5. A reorientation of subsidy policy could imply a major restructuring of the primary elevator industry at main line points in western Canada where better service at lower cost would be available.

6. Payments to producers could diminish the rationale for continuing CTC management of this program, which could be admnistered by another department such as Agriculture Canada.

7. The method of payment question is currently being addressed by the Honourable Mr. Justice Emmett Hall.

Options

The Study Team recommends to the Task Force that the government consider the following:

1. It is suggested that the subsidy be paid to producers. The 1985/86 review of the Western Grain Transportation Act should include a comprehensive review of the costs and benefits of the subsidy payment options to confirm or not the validity of this reform.

2. There should be a phased approach to the introduction of "variable" rates (which reflect the cost differentials between main and branch line operations, individual carload and multiple carload shipments and daytime versus evening and weekend loading at country points) by the railways regardless of change in the method of subsidy payment. This position should be adopted if the review confirms it.

RAILWAY BRANCH LINE SUBSIDY PROGRAM - CTC 50

Objective

To subsidize the railways for losses incurred in the continued operation of branch lines that have been judged uneconomic but necessary by the Canadian Transport Commission.

Authority

The Railway Act
National Transportation Act

Description

In order to qualify for a branch line subsidy, railways must first file for abandonment under the provisions of sections 254 and 256 of the Railway Act. This action triggers a formal hearing process during which the Canadian Transport Commission determines the validity of the operating losses claimed in accordance with the uniform classification of accounts costing methodology and considers the range of public interest factors raised by shippers and other interested parties.

If the line is found to be uneconomic, the subsequent CTC decision may permit abandonment or may require continued operation with provision of a subsidy not exceeding 80 per cent of the certified loss. No allowance is made in the determination of subsidy payments for a contribution to constant costs. Service continuance on this basis is subject to further statutory review within a period not exceeding five years.

With the exception of a very limited number of mixed train services in remote areas, this program no longer applies to passenger services. The latter are now operated by VIA Rail Canada and are subject to separate funding arrangements.

Since the advent of the Western Grain Transportation Act, which raised the level of grain rates to a compensatory level there has been a marked reduction in rail mileage subject to this program.

Resource

($000's)	82/83	83/84	84/85	85/86	86/87	87/88
Person-Years	15	15	11	11	7	7
Operating Exp.	775	305	605	605	380	380
- Salaries						
- O&M						
- Other Exp.						
Revenue		-	-	-	-	-
Subsidies	453,000	320,500	44,000	9,000	9,000	9,000
Capital	10	10				

Footnote: The decline in subsidy payments between 1983/4 and 1984/5 is attributable to the provisions of the Western Grain Transportation Act which, by means of a direct subsidy, compensated the railways for western grain traffic at a level considerably in excess of the superseded statutory "Crow" rates. The new subsidy program had the effect of reducing the number of uneconomic grain related lines in western Canada and thereby decreasing payments under the Railway Branch Line subsidy program. Branch line subsidy payments in regions other than the Prairie Provinces were not affected.

Problem Identification

Concern was expressed by the private sector in terms of:

1. The slow, complicated, tedious and costly decision-making process of the Canadian Transport Commission.

2. The major railways claimed that excessive resources must be allocated to handling the regulatory burden (of which the branch line subsidy program is a part).

3. The 1981/82 payments on branch line subsidy claims are only now being finalized, implying an unduly bureaucratic process.

4. The lack of a contribution to railway constant costs in the subsidy payments is considered by the railways to be counter productive in terms of removing any incentive for innovative marketing effort or investment on uneconomic branch lines.

5.   Subsidies are seen as impeding rationalization and
      investment in the viable components of the rail network
      where overall national economic benefits are most
      readily generated (particularly in relation to the
      grain transportation system in western Canada).

6.   Public interest advocates suggested that the regulatory
      process be made more accessible to the public with
      protection provided against intimidation by railway
      lawyers and that Commissioners sometimes took a strict
      constructionist approach in their interpretation of the
      Railway Act which tended to inflate branch line costs.

7.   There was support for the concept of giving subsidies,
      where necessary, to the shipper rather than the railway
      so that logical decisions regarding modal choice would
      be made.

8.   One federal agency expressed concern regarding the
      politicization of the western arm of the Canadian
      Transport Commission with respect to rail line
      abandonment and other issues. The CTC considers the
      program to be of declining significance.

      Provincial governments are generally supportive of the
protection offered to branch lines by this program.

Observations

1.   There is a general disatisfaction with the time
      consuming processes which trigger eligibility for
      branch line subsidies.

2.   In the Study Team's view, the political sensitivity of
      the CTC Western Division in dealing with abandonment
      cases, particularly in the Prairie Provinces, is
      impeding the modernization of the grain handling and
      transportation sector.

3.   The branch line subsidy program is diminishing in scale
      but can be expected to persist as long as other policy
      options are ignored.

Options

      The Study Team recommends to the Task Force that the
government consider the following:

577

1. Alternatives to the continuation of the present program should be pursued where feasible other than complete cancellation. Options include: the so-called "short line option" whereby selected branch lines are sold or leased to shipper groups, municipalities or entrepreneurs to ensure continued service (currently the subject of a CTC study) without subsidy, or selective subsidies to shippers rather than the railways so that modal choice is subject to market forces. Also, the "Use it or Lose it" criterion could be applied to uneconomic branch lines whereby abandonment would apply if prescribed tonnage levels were not attained.

2. The CTC should take steps to tighten and accelerate procedures in general.

OTHER REGULATORY PROGRAMS

EMERGENCY PLANNING CANADA — EPC 2

Objective

Emergency Planning Canada is responsible for coordinating the planning of the federal response to emergency, whether in peacetime or wartime, and for encouraging emergency planning in Canada.

Authority

Emergency Planning Order P.C. 1981-1305

Description

Emergency Planning Canada consists of a headquarters in Ottawa which is comprised of two groups, Planning and Operations.

The Planning Group coordinates the emergency planning activities of federal departments, agencies and crown corporations and provides training and education through formal courses at Arnprior, Ontario.

Within the Operations Group there are 11 regional directors who ensure liaison with federal agencies in their regions, and coordinate federal emergency planning with that of the provinces, and through the provinces, that of municipalities. The Operations Group has a Public Information Division and an Administration Division.

Funds are provided to the provinces for certain approved emergency planning projects, and the sponsoring of courses, conferences and research for representatives of the public and private sectors.

Emergency Planning Canada is also responsible for planning for continuity of government in time of national emergency, coordination with agencies of the United States of America and the North Atlantic Treaty Organization.

Post-disaster financial assistance to the provinces is administered on behalf of the Canadian government.

Resources

($000's)	82/83	83/84	84/85	85/86	86/87	87/88
Person-Years		79	80	83		
Operating Exp.		5,429	7,114	7,509		
- Salaries						
- O & M						
- Other Exp.						
Revenue	-	-	-	-	-	-
Subsidies		27	60	60		
Capital		252	946	232		

Problem Identification

The program is not questioned in principle as it ensures a minimal capacity to respond to emergency situations involving the safeguarding of life, food supplies, energy reserves and essential services.

Observations

As currently constituted, the program does not strictly fall into the regulatory category. Doubtless, during a major national emergency the federal government would bestow a variety of special regulatory powers upon Emergency Planning Canada. It is not possible to accurately anticipate the nature of such special powers and post facto assessment would be redundant.

Options

The Study Team recommends to the Task Force that the government consider the following:

1. Continue with present program.

2. Subject continuing program to periodic reassessment for relevance and efficiency.

BUILDING CODES (HOUSING STANDARDS) - CMHC 1

Objective

To ensure that the housing needs of Canadians are met in an orderly market and are of a technical quality to support CMHC's role as a mortgage insurer.

Authority

National Housing Act, National Housing Act Loan Regulations, Canada Mortgage and Housing Corporations Act.

Description

The primary instrument of building regulations in Canada is the National Building Code of Canada (NBCC). This is reviewed every five years and involves public consultation. Residential Standards is produced by the NBCC Secretariat for use by CMHC and others including provincial housing corporations. CMHC has a major input into its preparation. Residential Standards includes the NBCC, Builders Bulletins produced by CMHC to reflect federal policy affecting housing and introduce new technical requirements, and Building Materials Evaluation Reports that are used to qualify materials to national standards and to permit use of products that are not subject to standards.

CMHC can only apply Residential Standards to NHA programs or in support of its own mortgage insurance. CMHC conducts compliance inspections to enforce its requirements. It may withhold the benefits of subventions under NHA programs or refuse to insure. Development and maintenance of Residential Standards is centralized in Ottawa with application and compliance inspection decentralized through regional and district offices.

The legislative authority for regulations in the building field resides with the provinces. Generally, the provinces enact building codes using the NBCC as the technical model. Provincial and municipal officials enforce code requirements. They can withhold permission to build and/or impose fines for non-compliance or infractions.

The CMHC requirement of Residential Standards is usually met where local building regulations comparable to the NBCC are in force.

Resources

($000's)	82/83	83/84	84/85	85/86	86/87	87/88
Person-Years	395	515	415	372		
Operating Exp.						
– Salaries	10,733	14,378	13,688			
– O&M	3,385	4,871	4,161			
– Other Exp.						
Revenue	3,550	7,572	4,704			
Subsidies						
Capital						

NOTE: CMHC is privately audited.

The majority of the person-years shown are for the inspection function of CMHC, i.e. CMHC Technical Services. Only 24 PY's are involved in building standards activity.

Problem Identification

1. Extensive duplication and overlap with provincial and municipal jurisdictions. Even where provinces support the use of the NBCC (Ontario, B.C.) duplicate organizations exist. Municipalities often establish their own codes and inspection services. Home warranty programs exist in many provinces.

2. Standards produced under the auspices of the Standards Council of Canada are referenced in the NBCC and form the basis of much material evaluation. However, among the provinces there are different requirements in law governing the adoption of standards by reference in building regulations.

3. The role of the Federal Government in the development and application of building codes primarily supports CMHC's role as mortgage insurer and less the

requirement to meet the quality housing needs of Canadians. Justification of the mortgage insurance program is questioned.

4. Confusion over the appropriate use of building codes (especially where new materials are introduced) and the approval process at two or three levels of government lead to increased costs and undue time delays experienced by architects, developers and contractors.

5. The language of building codes is technically complex and many requirements are not understandable to smaller contractors, suppliers and building inspectors.

6. CMHC inspection has been regarded by some as both intrusive and redundant.

7. There are no standards for housing renovation and rehabilitation.

Observations

1. Studies and evaluations (CMHC, Treasury Board, Standards Council) have shown cost/benefit disadvantages to this program. CMHC has moved to eliminate redundancy of regulations and enforcement and is prepared to see greater involvement of provinces, industry and consumers.

2. Consultations with the provinces indicate that they have certain difficulties with various dimensions of federal housing regulation, including the National Building Code.

3. Recent policy changes introduced by CMHC indicate that it is no longer necessary to carry out inspections at the same level of intensity pursued during the early years of mortgage insurance.

4. CMHC is participating with the Standards Council of Canada to develop technical standards.

Options

The Study Team recommends to the Task Force that the government consider the following:

1. Privatize standards setting, testing of materials, and compliance inspection.

2.   Maintain status quo for standards setting only.
      Privatize inspection services/contract out.

3.   Provinces to establish standards and administer
      compliance.

4.   CMHC to continue its strategy of withdrawal from this
      regulatory field and its support to improve
      provincial/municipal capability and enhanced industry
      self regulation.

MORTGAGE INSURANCE - CMHC 2

Objective

Promote a sufficient flow of mortgage funds to facilitate access to homeownership and investment in rental housing in all regions of Canada.

Authority

National Housing Act (Part I), National Housing Loan Regulations, Canada Mortgage and Housing Corporation Act.

Description

CMHC as administrator of the Mortgage Insurance Fund (MIF) insures eligible mortgage loans made by private approved lenders. The risk covered is the loan in the event of the borrower's default on the mortgage. By shifting the risk of default from the lender to the MIF, mortgage insurance enhances the investment power of the mortgage instrument and thereby attracts more private funds to the mortgage market.

The need for mortgage insurance arises from both the requirement to spread the risk and financial institution legislation which prevents major lenders from making mortgages in excess of 75 per cent of the value of the property, unless the excess above 75 per cent is insured.

Insurance is made subject to approved lender status, conditions on the mortgage and that the property meets construction standards and market tests. In 1984, 42 per cent of all institutional mortgage loans were insured, of which 89 per cent were insured by CMHC. The program is intended to be self sufficient through fees and premiums. Currently, it is in a deficit position. The program is administered both centrally in Ottawa and through regional and branch offices.

The mortgage insurance market also includes private insurers and one provincial crown corporation (Alberta). The Federal Department of Insurance enforces the solvency standards for private mortgage insurers and advises on the solvency of the MIF.

Resources

($000's)	82/83	83/84	84/85	85/86	86/87	87/88
Person-Years	1,218	1,394	1,289	1,349	1,420	1,319
Operating Exp.						
- Salaries	58	66	66	72	78	74
- O & M						
- Other Exp.						
Revenue	72	83	89	119	160	1,189
Subsidies	–	498	210	108	–	–
Capital						

NOTE: CMHC is privately audited.
          Subsidies represent a deficit position for the
          Fund.

Problem Identification

1. Net contribution of public mortgage insurance is considered small today relative to its introduction in 1954 - maturity of the mortgage market, presence of private insurance, quality housing of Canadians.

2. Increased risk exposure to Government due to design features of the program, including the establishment of a reasonable premium structure, which are inadequate given current market realities.

3. Subsidizes through tax dollars lenders' risk, and hence the depositors and shareholders of financial institutions.

4. Design features of public mortgage insurance make it difficult for private insurers to compete.

5. Deficit reduction of current program.

6. Long-term role of the Federal Government in the mortgage market.

Observations

1. In the Study Team's view, the fundamental issue is whether the Federal Government should be in the mortgage insurance business and if so, to what extent.

2. Relevance of the program is questioned today despite its past success in meeting objectives.

3.   The first full evaluation is currently underway (as per
     1981 Cabinet decision) conducted by the Program
     Evaluation Division of CMHC with expected completion
     date - Autumn 1985.

4.   This program is linked with the Buidling Codes Program
     and the concern for multi-jurisdictional overlap in
     compliance inspection.

Options

     The Study Team recommends to the Task Force that the
government consider the following:

1.   Priority should be given to the internal evaluation
     currently underway.

2.   Should the government decide to exit the mortgage
     insurance business, two options are possible:

     a)   Short Term Renewable Policy offered by private
          insurers. Mortgage insurance premiums renewed
          annually or on the maturity of each term of the
          mortgage. This would allow insurers to price the
          premium for a shorter more predictable period.

     b)   Development of mortgage-backed securities to
          facilitate flows of funds into longer term
          mortgages.

3.   Should the government decide to maintain its presence
     in the market then a re-insurance scheme may be
     appropriate.

CANADA POST CORPORATION - CPC 100

Objective

    To establish and operate a postal service for the collection, transmission and delivery of messages, information, funds and goods both within Canada and between Canada and places outside Canada.

Authority

    Canada Post Corporations Act

Description

    Canada Post's aim is to provide a universally accessible postal service at a universal price. Thus, Canada Post's exclusive privilege protects the revenue and volume base required to maintain its postal service infrastructure.

    Under the Canada Post Corporations Act the corporation may make regulations:

a)   prescribing what is a letter, and what is a non-mailable matter and undeliverable mail other than undeliverable letters, and providing for the disposition of non-mailable matter, undelivered mail on which sufficient postage is not paid, including the disposition of anything found therein;

b)   classifying mailable matter, including the setting of standards for any class;

c)   prescribing the conditions under which mailable matter may be transmitted by post;

d)   prescribing rates of postage and the terms and conditions and method of payment thereof;

e)   regulating or prohibiting the installation of machines for vending postage stamps, postal remittances or other products or services of the Corporation;

f)   regulating or prohibiting the manufacture, installation
      and use of postage meters;

g)   regulating or prohibiting the making or printing of
      postage impressions;

h)   governing the preparation, design and issue of postage
      stamps.

Canada Post has an "exclusive privilege" granted by
Parliament over letter mail. A "letter" has been defined as
any message or information in any form whose weight does not
exceed 500 grams, whether or not enclosed in an envelope,
and intended for transmission to any destination, or
delivery to any addressee in Canada. There are a number of
exceptions (goods, books, magazines, newspapers, catalogues,
items addressed only to householder, boxholders, etc.)

The CPC Act stipulates that the rates of postage shall
be fair and reasonable, and provide a revenue sufficient to
defray the costs incurred by the corporation in the conduct
of its operations under the Act. The Corporation may
prescribe by regulation the rates of postage for its
products and services.

Resources

The Corporation has a responsibility to become
financially self-sufficient.

The Corporation continues to receive annual
transitional subsidies which (substantially) cover the
difference between its revenues and expenses, i.e. from
establishment of Canada Post on October 16, 1981 to March
31, 1982, the target set for government funding was $300
million. The amount actually received was $178 million. In
the first fiscal year, 1982-83, the target was $400 million
of which $262 million was required. In 1983-84, the target
was $300 million and $306 million was required.

RESOURCE PROFILE

($000's)	1982/83	1983/84	1984/85*	1985/86[2]	1986/87[2]
Revenues	2,258,400	2,400,000	2,486,000	2,714,000	2,870,000
Expenses	2,573,400	2,706,200	2,892,000	2,973,000	2,962,000
Profit (Loss)	(315,000)	300,100	396,000	(259,000)	(92,000)
DOC 2nd Class Mail Subsidy	50,000	53,200	55,600	58,900	58,900
Infrastructure Subsidy[1]	170,000	170,000	170,000	100,000	000
Government Funding Requirement	262,000	305,000	350,000	200,000	000

*   Preliminary unaudited figures.
1. Included in revenues.
2. 1985/86 Corporate Plan not yet approved; figures taken from 1984/85 Corporate Plan and are likely to change significantly.

592

Problem Identification

Many private sector responses identify CPC as a major problem in terms of most if not all evaluation criteria. The Team's impression is that this reflects frustration over CPC quality of service and business efficiency.

The definition of a letter, approved in May 1983, met some of the concerns of specific business groups, but few of consumers. The Auditor General, in his March 31, 1981 report, identified several deficiencies in the management information system of Canada Post: losses not identified in meeting government objectives; no accounting for cost centres; no information on costs of different levels of service. Small businessmen complain about discrimination in bulk rates, vis-a-vis large businesses (violators are won back through incentive rates and other marketing efforts). Canada Post itself feels that it is providing what Parliament mandated -- universally accessible service at standard letter rates -- and feels its definition of a Letter Regulation has considerable public support.

A review of the list of second class publications shows over 4,000 names, comprising, in addition to every newspaper and magazine mailed in Canada, newsletters for every conceivable type of organization (trade, community, religious, farm, consumer, research, sport, etc.). It appears that any group, however defined, appear to be able to claim second class registration to communicate to others in that group. Thus, the subsidy for such mailings is widely used.

Observations

Basically, Canada Post Corporation has become a focus for public dissatisfaction. This dissatisfaction has been fueled by the absence of service measurements and standards which have public understanding and support, and a lack of financial justification for rate increases and bulk rate discounts.

The strongest criticism of CPC comes from those who are captive customers who cannot access alternative hard copy delivery services (self-delivery, telex, couriers) such as consumers and small business. The Team has been unable to identify public frustration fully with the current regulatory framework for CPC. In our view, not even the most comprehensive form of public utility regulation (as practiced by the CRTC) can reasonably be expected to turn public attitutes around over the short term. In fact, the process used to develop the definition of a letter under the current regulatory framework was commended by many private sector groups for its openness.

Options

The Study Team recommends to the Task Force that the government consider the following:

1. Leave program as is for the time being: review regulatory process and CPC mandate at end of first five year plan; encourage CPC to diversify services and be more entrepreneurial.

2. If there is no turnaround consider:

    (a) Deregulation: remove CPC exclusive privilege over letter mail and Cabinet approval of postal rates.

    (b) Public Utility Regulation: CPC must get approval for rate increases from an independent agency (e.g. CRTC) after detailed public hearings.

    (c) Modest Regulatory Reform (light handed, market-oriented):

        (i) Require CPC to solicit competitive bids in rural and remote areas using level of service specifications; awards based on least subsidy payment required.
        (ii) Require detailed profit centre cost and revenue reporting in Annual Report.
        (iii) Order no internal cross-subsidization of services not subject to exclusive privilege.
        (iv) Eliminate requirement that couriers charge at least three times first-class rate: require them only to affix a first-class stamp to every separately addressed piece of mail.
        (v) Require consultative development of service quality measurements and standards and make rate increases dependent on them being met.

FIREARMS CONTROL - NOP

Objective

To design and implement measures to encourage the safer use of guns and to control their irresponsible use. The new gun control laws of 1978 have three major objectives:

1. To reduce the criminal use of guns.

2. To keep guns out of the hands of dangerous persons.

3. To encourage and ensure responsible gun ownership and use.

Authority

Criminal Code ss. 82-106.
Restricted Weapons and Firearms Control Regulations
Criminal Law Amendment Act, 1977

Description

1. To achieve the above objectives, initiatives introduced include: revised prohibited and restricted weapons categories; controls established to reduce availability of dangerous weapons; stiffer penalties for gun-related offenses; greater police search and seize powers; requirement of a Firearms Acquisition Certificate to obtain a firearm; inspection and licensing of firearms businesses; an appeal procedure for refused applicants.

2. On an administrative basis, the establishment of a National Firearms Advisory Council to review and recommend any necessary changes to improve the Firearms Program. Serving on the Council are the Chief Provincial Firearms Officers representing each province and territory and representatives of gun clubs, wildlife associations, and others directly affected by the gun control measures. The gun control administration consists of the following:

    a) **The Commissioner of the RCMP**
    The Commissioner is responsible for the coordination at the federal level of the Firearms Acquisition Certificate system, Business Permit System and the registration of restricted

weapons. The Commissioner is required to report annually to the Solicitor General of Canada.

b) <u>Chief Provincial Firearms Officer</u>
The Chief Provincial Firearms Officer is responsible to the Provincial Attorney-General. His function is to oversee and coordinate the Firearms Acquisition Certificate system and the administration of permits at the provincial or territorial level. The Officer also serves as a member of the National Firearms Advisory Council and coordinates provincial firearms safety education, competence training and testing programs.

c) <u>Programs Officer</u>
A Firearms Officer, usually a local police officer, issues Firearms Acquisition Certificates and Minors' Permits.

d) <u>Local Registrar of Firearms</u>
The Local Registrar of Firearms, usually a local police officer, will process applications for restricted weapons.

<u>Resources</u>

	82/83	83/84	84/85	85/86
Person-Years				
Solicitor General	-	-	4	4
RCMP	23 1/2	23 1/2	23 1/2	23 1/2
Solicitor General Operating Exp.			$180,000	$180,700
RCMP				
- Gun Control [1]	1,718,000	2,209,000	2,500,000	2,700,000
- Firearms Registration[2]	546,000	585,000	610,000	640,000

1 Payments made to provinces for administering Firearms acquisition Certificates.
2 Costs by person year allocated by RCMP for central registry of Firearm Acquisition Certificates.

* Fees charged and revenues collected by RCMP are turned over to local Registrar (in every province) who retain them as payment for issuing Firearm Acquisition Certificates.

Problem Identification

Private Sector:

1. $10 fee too low and could be increased substantially; requires legislative change because the fee now is specified in the statute.

2. Registrars of firearms have discretion to insert "reasonable conditions" to certificates and permits resulting in lack of uniformity particularly across provinces.

3. No appeal procedure available for refused applicants for restricted weapons (e.g. hand gun); though available for firearms (e.g. rifles).

Observations

1. There is a general impression that anyone with no criminal record and $10 can apply and be granted a certificate to own a gun.

2. A three-year evaluation study of gun control legislation found that the proportion of violent crimes committed with firearms declined in the post-legislation period and that when firearms were used in violent crimes there was an increasing trend for the firearms to be a hand gun. However, there is no finding as to whether firearms offenders have been granted FACs in order to determine whether firearms involved in violent crimes are generally obtained through legal means.

3. The policy group has just submitted a proposal consisting of administrative changes to the legislation to effect greater convenience for gun users and the administration. This may be perceived by the general public as looser gun control.

4. The policy administration at Solicitor General carries out studies in gun control and coordinates provincial and territorial input and develops gun control policies.

5. Policy changes and recommendations are also developed by the National Firearms Advisory Council which is well represented by interested groups.

6. There appears to be an overlap amongst the RCMP Administration, Policy Group at Solicitor General and the National Firearms Advisory Council.

7. An increase in fees could generate increased revenue. The provinces would be the beneficiaries unless a revenue sharing arrangement were instituted.

Options

The Study Team recommends to the Task Force that the government consider the following:

1. Cost-recovery: by increasing the fee, the federal contribution to the provinces could perhaps be reduced.

2. Determine the effectiveness of the program, for example, through the analysis of the proportion of firearms offenders that have been granted FACs.

CANADIAN GENERAL STANDARDS BOARD - SSC 9

Objective

To provide standards development and maintenance and, where necessary, qualification and certification listing of products and services, in support of federal government programs for procurement, health and safety, consumer protection, international trade, energy conservation and regulatory reform.

Authority

The Department of Supply and Services Act, the National Research Council Act and various orders-in-council transferring responsibilities between Ministers.

Description

The Canadian General Standards Board (CGSB) programs provide voluntary product standards development and maintenance and, where necessary, qualification and certification listing of products and services meeting the standards. CGSB programs are developed and maintained in response to the needs and initiatives of the federal government in support of government programs for procurement, health and safety, consumer protection, international trade and other programs such as energy conservation and regulatory reform. The consensus standards development work is carried out by more than 300 committees consisting of representatives from the three levels of government, industry, consumers and labour interests. The CGSB is accredited by the Standards Council of Canada as a National Standards Writing organization.

CGSB is not a regulatory body. However, consensus standards developed by CGSB are used by other government departments and bodies in their regulations. DOT uses standards for flotation devices developed by CGSB in their regulations concerning requirements for operating small boats; CCA uses CGSB standards in their regulations for garment sizes, care labelling. The majority of CGSB standards are used on a voluntary basis in lieu of mandatory regulation. CGSB programs involve the three levels of

government, industry, consumers and labour, both in the
committees for developing standards and in the Minister's
Advisory Council on CGSB. The program provides a medium of
Federal/Provincial/Municipal/industry for dialogue on issues
of standardization. The CGSB's staff is centralized in
Ottawa but its various committees are decentralized
throughout the country and involve, in addition to the three
levels of government, industry, consumer and labour,
representation from small and big business. Committee
members serve on a voluntary basis and are not paid by the
federal government for their work.

Resources

($000's)	82/83	83/84	84/85	85/86	86/87	87/88
Person-Years		43	42	42	42	42
Operating Exp.						
- Salaries		1,500	1,700	1,600*	1,600*	1,600*
- O & M		700	800	600*	600*	600*
- Other Exp.						
Revenue		2,700	2,700	2,200*	2,200*	2,200*
Subsidies						
Capital		2,200	2,500	2,200*	2,200*	2,200*

* Included in "B" Budget for Qualification and Certification
Listing Branch

Problem Identification

Private sector responses were generally positive. The
CGSB considers that the voluntary consensus standards it
establishes, and its role as certification body of last
resort within the National Standards System, facilitates
economic development by allowing easier entry into domestic
markets by new firms while avoiding excessive
standardization, or anti-competitive consequences from the
standards setting process.

Many CGSB standards have been incorporated by reference
into mandatory standards regulations of both the federal and
provincial governments. This approach allows for greater
flexibility and adaptability of regulations when compared to
writing the standard directly into the regulation.

Observations

The CGSB is a largely self-funding through user charges. It acts as a principal standards writing organization within the National Standards System (NSS). The NSS is a loose group of independent standards writing, certifying, and testing bodies in both the public and private sectors supervised by the Standards Council of Canada. These bodies generate voluntarily sought standards through consensus among the various economic interests affected by the standard, some of which are referenced in trade practices and building codes. These standards can have both product quality/performance and product safety attributes.

Generally, voluntary standards are viewed by industry and academic observers as a mechanism for facilitating trade and new entry and promoting exports. Some economists consider, in theory, that voluntary standards can act as a facilitating device for anti-competitive agreements. However, a study currently being conducted by the Bureau of Competition Policy of CCA has found few instances in the U.S., and none in Canada, where it has been established that voluntary standards have had this result. The CGSB's consensus approach (where users, government and labour, are involved with the industry in standards formulation) is designed to minimize this possibility and prevent voluntary standards from acting as a brake on technological change and product innovation.

In the Study Team's view, the reliance on volunteers to write standards also fosters good citizenship, reduces interest group demands for mandatory regulation, and minimizes the overall cost of standards development to government and the private sector. Nevertheless, the incorporation by reference in regulations of CGSB product composition or design standards which are not necessitated by health or safety considerations can create barriers to entrepreneurial product innovations.

Options

The Study Team recommends to the Task Force that the government consider the following:

1. Adopt a policy that where mandatory standards are required in federal regulations, suitable standards developed under the National Standards System should be incorporated by reference.

2. Shift the responsibility for designing product information and product quality (excluding health and safety) standards from government to National Standards System. Rely on industry self-regulation to enforce compliance.

STANDARDS COUNCIL OF CANADA - STCC

Objective

To promote standardization in the construction, manufacture, production, quality, performance and safety of buildings, structures, manufactured articles, products, and other goods.

Authority

Standards Council of Canada Act (1970).

Description

The Standards Council (SCC) acts as a national coordinating body through which accredited organizations concerned with voluntary standardization may operate and cooperate to recognize, establish and improve standards in Canada and develop a comprehensive Canadian Standards program to meet both the national and international requirements and responsibilities. The SCC is empowered, among other things, to:

1. Promote cooperation between organizations concerned with voluntary standardization and departments and agencies of government at all levels in Canada.

2. Develop criteria and procedures for the preparation of voluntary standards for testing and certification activities.

3. Accredit standards-writing, testing and certification organizations which meet criteria established by the Council.

4. Approve standards submitted by accredited organizations as National Standards of Canada;

5. Represent Canada as the Canadian member of ISO (International Organization for Standardization), IEC (International Electrotechnical Council) and similar international organizations engaged in the formation of voluntary standards.

All 10 provinces are represented on the SCC through a representative usually from a Ministry dealing with Industrial and Economic Development, Commerce, Trade or

Small Business. Head office is located in Ottawa.
International Standardization Branch is located in
Mississauga.

Resources

($000's)	82/83	83/84	84/85	85/86	86/87	87/88
Person-Years	67	71	74	82	82	82
Operating Exp.						
- Salaries						
- O & M	5,762	5,978	6,612	5,424	6,935	7,102
- Other Exp.						
Revenue						
Subsidies						
Capital						

Problem Identification

The SCC considers that it contributes to economic
development and job creation by ensuring that Canadian
business has a strong voice within international
standards-setting organizations, thereby improving the
access of Canadian goods and services to foreign markets.

No adverse comment has been received from the private
sector concerning the SCC in principle or with respect to
its operations.

Observations

The Standards Council can be viewed as an institution
created to fill two needs:

1. Coordination of Canadian voluntary standards-setting
    bodies and the process of establishing voluntary
    industry-initiated standards.

2. Representation of Canadian interests in international
forums.

Accreditation by the Standards Council is a
prerequisite to membership in the NSS. Despite the
possibility that accreditation may act as a barrier to
entry, providing accredited standards setting bodies a
measure of market power, no evidence has been received to
date to suggest that this has occurred.

No evidence has been obtained that the consensus approach to standards setting promoted by the SCC operates to favour any particular stakeholder(s) or that the approach has resulted in too much or too little standardization or excessive time taken in standards development amendments.

Because no truly regulatory powers are exercised by the Standards Council, the manner in which it seeks to meet these needs is likely to amount to a set of largely ad hoc measures aimed at selected "targets of opportunity". As a result, the Standards Council's activities are more likely to appear somewhat unfocussed or uncoordinated. Measurement of the Standards Council "output" is, therefore, very difficult. Its contribution to economic development, if any, turns on the extent to which voluntary standards of the NSS are generating net economic benefits and the benefits of Canadian representation in international standards fori.

The Team's view is that significant net economic benefits are generated by the Standards Council in its domestic activities. It has not been possible to assess whether the Standards Council generates net benefits through its international role.

Options

The Study Team recommends to the Task Force that the government consider the following:

1. Privatize the National Standards System coordination functions of the Standards Council and absorb international activities in External Affairs.

2. Have the Standards Council supervise shifting product quality (excluding health and safety) standards setting and compliance from government to the private sector.

3. Adopt a policy of employing consensus standards formulated within the National Standards System by reference in mandatory standards to the fullest possible extent.

EXPORT-IMPORT CONTROL PROGRAM - EAC 9
(Special Trade Relations Bureau)

Objective

Import controls are designed to ensure adequate supply of scarce goods, and to support action taken in support of poultry products, eggs, meat, dairy products and certain animal feeds. Controls implement intergovernmental stabilization arrangements such as the International Coffee Agreement and the Convention on the International Trade in Endangered Species. Further objectives are limitation, following inquiry by the Canadian Import Tribunal or the Textile and Clothing Board, of the importation of goods causing or threatening serious injury to domestic producers. It provides increased access to Canadian markets for textiles and clothing from less developed nations and from new exporters thus providing low cost goods to consumers.

Export controls apply to strategic goods in accordance with foreign policy objectives and security requirements. Non strategic export controls can be invoked in the event of supply problems, intergovernmental arrangements such as the Convention on Endangered Species, bilateral voluntary restraint arrangements with the U.S. and the maximization of economic advantage from raw or processed materials of Canadian origin.

Authority

Export and Import Permits Act, Agricultural Products Board Act, Canadian Dairy Commission Act, Textile and Clothing Board Act, Special Import Measures Act, Meat Import Act, etc.

Description

Import controls range from prohibition to controls, monitoring, the issuance of discretionary permits and the issuance of permits subject to the importer possessing export certificates from country of origin. The Bureau is responsible for policy development, implementation and enforcement, and consists of four divisions which address

Import Controls (Textiles and Clothing), Import Controls (Agriculture, footwear, etc..) Export Controls and Data Processing (for the issuance, control and audit of permits).

The Coordinating Committee for Multilateral Export Controls (COCOM) in Paris consists of most NATO members and Japan. It is informal mechanism for monitoring embargo lists, clearing specific sensitive export requests and coordinating enforcement. An export control list and an area control list specify the embargoes which are enforced by the Bureau.

Overall enforcement is shared by External Affairs, Customs and Excise, the RCMP and The Attorney General.

Resources

($000's)	82/83	83/84	84/85	85/86	86/87	87/88
Person-Years			72	74	89*	90
Operating Exp.			5,325			
- Salaries			2,625	2,700	3,100	3,150
- O & M			2,600	2,650	2,200	1,900
- Other Exp.			100	100	100	100
Revenue			1,000	1,100	1,210	1,350
Subsidies			-			
Capital			-	1,340	300	-

* Assumes assumption by STRB of computerized permit issuance service previously contracted out.

Problem Identification

Importers tend to regard the Bureau as a component of an obstructive bureaucracy whereas exporters were generally supportive, though noting occasional problems due to insufficient advance notice regarding permit issuance. Exporters also suggested some doubts concerning the attitudes displayed by the Bureau in relation to certain strategic exports, the defence orientation of COCOM members and the impediments that are placed in the way of trade with Taiwan and Israel. Retailers echoed the concern of importer groups and asserted that the present system of bilateral import controls is not keeping up with the dynamic shifts of manufacturing from one developing nation to another. Protection was suggested on the basis of commodity, quantity and source.

Concerns expressed by federal departments focused on a wide range of questions relating to the effectiveness of specific import controls, the fairness and responsiveness of the import quota allocation system, the relationship of import controls to supply management programs and the impact on consumer prices. Questions were also raised regarding the effectiveness of export controls and the somewhat vague relationship to the pursuit of foreign policy objectives.

No major provincial concerns are on record although specific restraint actions have triggered adverse responses.

Observations

1. Export controls are generally based on logical and readily intelligible criteria although delays are sometimes attributable to the multi lateral approval (COCOM) process.

2. Notwithstanding the avowed aims of the import control program to foster job creation and protect domestic industry, it nevertheless contains potentially irreconcilable elements. Protective measures for the benefit of specific sectors can have a deleterious impact on Canada's overall position in world markets in terms of retaliatory measures that reduce export and job creation opportunities.

3. The complexity and changing pattern of import controls tends to confuse importers, creates uncertainty and results in occasional inconsistency in trade policy.

4. There is a need to ascertain the degree to which the import and export programs are achieving their objectives.

5. The export-import control program is to be considered in the forthcoming green paper on trade.

Options

The Study Team recommends to the Task Force that the government consider the following:

1. Initiate a comprehensive review of import-export controls that takes full account of the broader

interests of Canada's international trade and
manufacturing sector adjustments, and is based on a
sound economic basis and the interests of consumers.

2.   The objectives of the review should be to simplify
procedures, increase the transparency of regulations,
and to eliminate inconsistencies between programs
culminating in a gradual phase out of import protection
measures where feasible.

BACKGROUND

EXPORT-IMPORT CONTROL PROGRAM

In the Study Team's view, the proposed review of import-export controls should focus on the following issues:

- Are the principles of fairness, equitability and market responsiveness fully adhered to in the allocation of import quotas?

- Do the special privileges (economic rents) gained by long established importers from the retention of import quotas deter the entry of new participants in the import trade and otherwise create rigidities in business?

- How effective are the range of voluntary restraint measures in safeguarding the interests of Canadian manufacturers?

- How flexible are existing import restraint programs in responding to rapid shifts in manufacturing activity to nations that have not hitherto been subject to restraints?

- Is the practice of issuing supplementary import permits by the Special Trade Relations Bureau for specified agricultural products incompatible with or supportive of domestic supply management programs?

- Are consumer interests adequately protected by import controls on selected meat, poultry, footwear and clothing imports?

- Have import controls proven to be effective vehicles in achieving the restructuring of the footwear, clothing and textile industries?

- How can the uncertainties, attributable to import controls, that are inherent in retail sector buying strategies be minimized?

- Are the penalties for contravention of import controls adequate as deterrents?

- Does the relationship between the Import-Export Act and the attainment of foreign policy objectives require further clarification?

- Should the objectives of export controls be subject to periodic review?

- How much export trade to restricted nations such as Taiwan and Israel is moving through U.S. ports with U.S. documentation?

- How protectionist is Canada in its trade policies as compared to other western nations?

- What has been the overall impact of import restraint policies in terms of domestic market stability, loss of export opportunities and retaliatory measures by trading partners?

There are certain inherent contradictions in programs that impede the free flow of commerce. Thus, while import controls may confer tangible benefits on the manufacturing sector in terms of sustaining production and employment, consumers may be subject to higher retail prices with subsequent impact on other sectors. Export controls, on the other hand may restrict sales opportunities for Canadian manufacturers and thereby reduce employment opportunities, while at the same time responding to broader national security or bilateral concerns. The attainment of an optimal balance between these various objectives is a moving target, subject to the government's current policy priorities. The current structure of control is not in tune with the Team's assigned priorities. For this reason, a comprehensive review of export-import control policy has been suggested.

CANADIAN IMPORT TRIBUNAL - CIT 1

Objective

To protect Canadian producers from injury resulting from an influx of dumped or subsidized imported goods.

Authority

Anti Dumping Act and subsequent amendments
Special Import Measures Act

Description

The Tribunal undertakes investigations, acts as a court of record and conducts formal hearings and inquiries to determine the existence of material or serious injury to Canadian industry due to the importation of goods.

The Tribunal consists of five members and a secretary appointed by the Governor-in-Council and a support staff. It holds hearings, undertakes statistical and financial analyses, conducts in-house research, maintains liaison with Canadian manufacturers, importers, associations and government officials and inspects production facilities.

Where the Tribunal establishes that injury has occurred anti-dumping duties are levied by Revenue Canada which represent the difference between export price and normal value in the country of export.

An in-house monitoring and review process relating to prior findings determines the degree to which changes in production and marketing conditions have occurred that might justify adjustments, extensions or rescindment of findings.

The Tribunal and its enabling legislation are designed to conform to the criteria and procedures set forth in the GATT Anti-dumping Code.

Resources

($000's)	82/83	83/84	84/85	85/86	86/87	87/88
Person-Years	31	31	31	41	40	40
Operating Expenses	1,410	1,416	1,624	2,464	2,381	2,381
Revenue						
Subsidies						
Capital						

Problem Identification

Apart from one horizontal organization that views the Tribunal as an unacceptable constraint on trade, there is acceptance of the need for the protection offered by the Tribunal within the private sector, although certain reservations were expressed:

1. The preservation of the confidentiality of information presented to the Board remains at the discretion of the Board.

2. Board objectivity is best served by in-house research and information gathering rather than reliance on inputs from government departments.

3. Perspectives are mixed on the relevancy of a merger with the Textile and Clothing Board. Protectionist arguments favour the retention of a separate Textile and Clothing Board.

4. Common concern that commissioners may identify with the interest of parties. A fixed term, rotating board with industry reprsentatives was seen as an alternative.

5. A strengthened and more independent body in line with U.S. practice was favoured as a means of increasing the credibility of the board.

From the perspective of the public sector some concerns were expressed regarding the period of 120 days that generally elapses from initiation of appeal to decision. While there is no overlap or duplication of a jurisdictional nature, the involvement of public utility commissions, provincial Crown corporations or provincial government departments in Tribunal hearings always carries with it the risk of strained federal-provincial relations.

Observations

1. There would appear to be a justification for maintaining an equivalent injury appeal process to that which exists in the United States.

2. As an investigative and adjudicative body, the regulatory process within the Tribunal is considered to be minimal.

3. There has been continuing consideration of a merger between the Canadian Import Tribunal and the Textile and Clothing Board. The activities of the two bodies are to a great extent similar although the former takes cases on referral from the Minister whereas the latter is more discretionary and determines quotas.

4. Industry representation on the Tribunal may be feasible but care would be necessary with respect to conflicts of interest in the hearing of specific cases.

Options

The Study Team recommends to the Task Force that the goverment consider the following:

1. Remove ongoing uncertainty by merging the Textile and Clothing Board with the Canadian Import Tribunal.

2. Streamline Board procedures and reduce delays by imposing a 20 day time limit on Revenue Canada for completion of the first two steps in the review process and a sixty day limit on the Tribunal for the subsequent rendering of its decision.

3. Review ways of strengthening the independence of the Tribunal to conform more closely with its U.S. counterpart.

4. Examine further the case for a fixed term rotating tribunal with industry representation.

TEXTILE AND CLOTHING BOARD - TCE

Objective

To provide advice to the Minister of Regional
Industrial Expansion which forms the basis of decisions by
the government to restrict imports of textiles and clothing
as permitted under the GATT and the Multi-Fibre Arrangement
and in support of the National Textile Policy.

Authority

Textile and Clothing Board Act

Description

The mandate of the Board is to determine in response to
requests from the industry, whether specific imports are
causing or are threatening to cause serious injury to
production and employment in Canada. In making this
assessment, the Board is also required to establish that
manufacturers are taking steps to enhance their competitive
ability.

Recommendations of the Board are generally passed by
the Minister to Cabinet Committee and the ensuing decisions
trigger the negotiation or imposition of special measures of
protection to limit imports by the Special Trade Relations
Bureau of the Department of External Affairs.

The Board initiates special investigations and studies
and maintains an ongoing review of protective measures that
are in place.

Informal and non-adversarial hearings are conducted at
centres of the clothing and textile industry and
manufacturers, importers, retailers and trade unions
participate in the inquiry process.

While the Board is essentially an advisory body it is
nonetheless a first stage in a regulatory process.

Resources

($000's)	82/83	83/84	84/85	85/86	86/87	87/88
Person-Years			17	17	17	
Operating Exp.			1,11	1,200	1,305	
- Salaries						
- O & M						
- Other Exp.						
Revenue			-	-	-	
Subsidies			-	-	-	
Capital			-	-	-	

Problem Identification

Manufacturers generally support the import quota system and regard the Board as an efficient and respected organization. They perceive the Board as a knowledgeable and impartial body which maintains a close working relationship with the industry.

Importers took a negative view of the Board in terms of its justification and activities.

Retailers suggested that the Board has not adequately fulfilled its mandate. Its posture was seen as essentially reactive. All special measures of protection should be subject to sunset provisions. They claimed that the Board has not adequately monitored restructuring in the industry and should have acted as a catalyst for change by focusing attention on new symbiotic relationships between manufacturers and retailers. They perceive the textile and clothing industry in terms of three components – competitive, non-competitive and a marginal sector which could benefit from short term protection. Retailers view Board reports as defensive in tone, supportive of continued protection and primarily of academic interest.

The Board asserted that it has maintained a high degree of independence, impartiality and credibility and has been instrumental in assisting the restructuring of the industry and the preservation of employment.

The Special Trade Relations Bureau in the Department of External Affairs expressed concerns relating to the performance of the Board in discharging its mandate of ensuring the restructuring of the industry. It considered that the Board could be vulnerable to "capture" by the industry it serves. Questions were raised as to whether the self-initiating powers of the Board should be retained or whether action should be taken only on the basis of ministerial referrals. This could justify a merger with the Canadian Import Tribunal, which under the provisions of the Special Import Measures Act, is permitted to determine "threat of injury" and to monitor the situation. It suggested that the dubious reasoning employed in certain publicly released Board reports could impede international trade negotiations.

Provincial governments are generally supportive of the Board in terms of the protection it creates. However, differing approaches by provinces to minimum wage levels are contributing to industry restructuring. This is particularly evident in the shift of some components of the garment industry from Quebec to New Brunswick.

Observations

1. The program is one element in overall federal control of import trade and should be considered in conjunction with the Canadian Import Tribunal, the Special Trade Relations Bureau and the Tariff Board. The continuance of the Board is inextricably linked with protectionist trade policies.

2. There is little evidence that the rate of restructuring of the clothing and textile industries in Canada has outstripped that of other nations lacking equivalent specific protection mechanisms.

3. Perpetuation of special treatment for one manufacturing sector may be retarding rather than encouraging the restructuring of the industry.

4. Merger with the Canadian Import Tribunal, while having little impact on resource allocation could enable the government to provide closer guidance for investigation of complaints.

Options

The Study Team recommends to the Task Force that the government consider the following:

1. The Board should be merged with the Canadian Import Tribunal.

2. Future government policy should provide clear
    guidelines for the CIT and the Department of Regional
    Industrial Expansion regarding the restructuring of the
    industry.

3. Insofar as government policy is concerned, protection
    should be extended on a short-term basis only.
    Continuing protection should not be provided for
    non-competitive manufacturing operations.

TARIFF BOARD - TRFB 101

ider all appeals registered with the Board from
by the Revenue Canada, Customs and Excise and
e upon all those that are not withdrawn.   To
quiries into tariffs and trade matters as
the Minister of Finance.

oard Act (1931)
Act
ax Act
mport Measures Act
ministration Act

e as a court of appeal, panels of three
Board hold public hearings at various
ada and declare on appeals from rulings of
da, Customs and Excise with respect to the
stoms duties, excise taxes and other charges
sales taxes.   The Board may also adjudicate
n petroleum and petroleum products or on
f any oils under the Petroleum
.

of the Tariff Board are final and
conclu   subject only to appeal to the Federal
Court   d the Supreme Court of Canada.
Declarat   e Board affect liability for duty, tax and
other c   thereby have economic impact.   The rules
of the B   nformal in order to ensure ease of access
by appel

The B   es inquiries, upon request of the Minister
of Finance   instruction by the Governor in Council may
inquire into   atter or thing relating to the trade and
commerce of Ca   a.

A recent survey (1985) conducted by the Chairman indicated a high level of support for the fairness and equity of the Board's decisions.

Resources

($000's)	82/83	83/84	84/85	85/86	86/87	87/88
Person-Years		38	40	40		
Operating Exp.		2,095	2,336	2,685		
- Salaries						
- O & M						
- Other Exp.						
Revenue	-	-	-	-	-	-
Subsidies	-	-	-	-	-	-
Capital		16	13	13		

Problem Identification

The Board is perceived by the private sector as exercising a very significant regulatory role in view of its role as adviser to the Department of Finance, Tariff Division in addition to its prime responsibilities.

The program is not questioned in principle although the private sector has expressed the following general concerns:

1. Timing of the appeal process leads to regulatory lag.

2. Occasional lack of regional focus with respect to hearings.

3. Question as to whether the Board will hear appeals on services as trade in this sector increases.

4. The Board may eventually become too powerful and be less sensitive to the interests of the organizations or constituents they were appointed to serve.

5. Anticipate value of industry appointments to the Board on a fixed term and rotation basis.

6. One private sector organization expressed a preference for the research and information gathering activities of the Board to be conducted in-house rather than placing reliance on other government departments which may provide biased perspectives.

The program department noted that any attempt to reduce the regulatory lag ought to be undertaken within the Revenue Canada where the three-step initiation of the appeal might be reduced. It considers the program to be free of major problems. Recent discussions have focussed on combining the responsibilities of three tribunals involved in investigative and adjudicative activity - the Tariff Board, the Canadian Import Tribunal and the Textile and Clothing Board. However, the cost savings appear to be minimal.

Observations

1. It is likely that the Board may be subject to some changes during the next decade as the harmonized system of customs nomenclature is implemented and as the international trade in services grows in significance.

2. Few problems exist and no high profile issues are expected in the near term.

Options

The Study Team recommends to the Task Force that the government consider the following:

1. Maintain the role of a regulatory organization.

2. Review the costs and benefits of combining the Tariff Board with either the Canadian Import Tribunal or the Textile and Clothing Board or both of these organizations.

3. Review Revenue Canada procedures with a view to reducing delays in the overall appeal process.

OFFICE OF REGULATORY REFORM - TB 6

Objective

To improve public administration through reform to the regulatory process and to reduce the regulatory burden on the Canadian economy by improving the efficiency and effectiveness of government regulation. The Canadian government's regulatory reform program is aimed at improving equity, economy, efficiency and growth, as well as private sector/government relations.

Authority

Prerogative

Description

The Office of Regulatory Reform was established as a Task Force in October 1979 and in 1980 the President of the Treasury Board was assigned responsibility for coordinating the federal government's regulatory reform activities. The functions of the Office are to advance and coordinate action on regulatory reform in conjunction with central agencies, regulating departments, and regulatory agencies; to provide policy advice on regulatory matters to the President of the Treasury Board and to regulatory departments and agencies; and to provide analysis of proposals for deregulation and reform to the regulatory process. The program was scheduled for review at the end of 1985/86.

Resources

($000's)	82/83	83/84	84/85	85/86	86/87	87/88
Person-Years	5	7	10	10		
Operating Expenses						
- Salaries	189	277	408	520		
- O&M	155	210	187	157		
- Other Expenses						
Revenue						
Subsidies						
Capital						

Problem Identification

The majority of private sector respondents did not comment on the Office of Regulatory Reform on the program questionnaires. Two respondents, however, indicated a major problem existed with the adequacy and relevance of the program.

The office is responsible for managing the Regulatory Agendas Program which has received strong private sector and departmental support.

There are no provincial concerns with the program as such. In fact, one of the major reasons for the office's establishment was the need for a central office to maintain liaison with provincial and territorial offices of regulatory reform and to promote coordinated reform across the country.

Observations

As an instrument of regulatory reform policy, the role and utility of the Office of Regulatory Reform depends entirely on the nature of the government's policy and work plan in this area. For several years there has been neither central policy nor consistent program direction and ORR's contribution has been correspondingly limited. In the continuing absence of a reform policy requiring central coordination, officials in ORR would recommend termination of the program.

The government's future institutional requirements for regulatory reform and management will no doubt flow from the policy it identifies as a result of the work of the Ministerial Task Force.

To the degree a coordinating function is required in any new regulatory policy, the present diversity of somewhat overlapping and uncoordinated activities (e.g. the SEIA function of the Decriminalization Project in Justice, etc.) should be harmonized, if not integrated.

Options

The Study Team recommends to the Task Force that the government consider the following:

1.   Terminate the program.

2. Continue the existing Office as a source of advice and expertise on innovative regulatory and systems change, and as a source of operational support to the Minister responsible for regulatory reform.

3. Reconfirm the Office, or create a new one with authority to coordinate a clearly defined and comprehensive regulatory strategy.

4. Integrate ORR's current role and activity into another existing unit in Treasury Board or elsewhere in government.

NOTE: Anti-Conflict of Interest Section
            Since the Regulatory Programs Review Team is composed of several members of ORR, private sector members of the team were asked to provide their own views concerning the future of ORR on the supplementary page in this section.

Private Sector Comments

On programs in which public servant members of the Regulatory Programs Review Team might be perceived to have a conflict of interest, the practice in the Team was to invite comments only from the private sector members.

The following are their comments on the Office of Regulatory Reform and the Technical Advisory Group.

"The six private sector members of the Regulatory Program Review Team, representing consumer, labor, small and large business interests, comment as follows:-

Office of Regulatory Reform

- Terminate ORR as is. Although the ORR has performed superbly in coordination and support of the Task Force on Regulatory Program Review, it has not achieved most of its objectives approved by Cabinet in November 1980, nor has there been sufficient political support to be able to achieve these objectives.

- Create and establish a new department of Regulatory Affairs with:

  - a clear federal regulatory affairs policy statement

  - a reporting relationship through a Minister of Regulatory Affairs to the Office of the Deputy Prime Minister

  - the Minister of Regulatory Affairs should not also be the President of the Treasury Board

  - a review of all federal regulatory programs every five years, with ten major programs being selected by Ministers annually

- a clear mandate to integrate these programs listed below to a consistent set of objectives:

> Technical Advisory Group (SEIA)
> Evaluation of Regulatory Programs (OCG)
> Privy Council Office (Justice)
> Administrative Law Reform
> Federal Offences Decriminalization and Compliance Enhancement Program

- to report activities/results annually to Parliament

Technical Advisory Group (SEIA's)

- Seriously consider having SEIA's done by the private sector, based on competitive bids, with evaluation of bids based on technical competence, as well as least cost.

- Broaden coverage, from present narrow focus on health and safety, and based on voluntary requests from departments."

TECHNICAL ADVISORY GROUP – TB 901

Objective

To promote thorough and systematic analysis of the socio-economic impact of new health, safety and fairness (HSF) regulations; to ensure uniformity in the methodologies and assumptions used in such analyses; and provide an opportunity for increased public participation in the regulatory process.

Authority

Financial Administration Act, TB Minute Number 766982 (establishment of policy, 1978), TB Minute Number 782699 (current authority, policy revised 1982).

Description

The socio-economic impact analysis (SEIA) policy was implemented by the federal government in August, 1978, in response to growing concerns about the inflationary impact and efficiency effects of government regulations. It requires departments and agencies to consult with affected parties when considering new HSF regulations, and to perform and make publicly available an analysis of the expected impact of major HSF regulations (as well as feasible alternatives to them) before they become law.

In terms of systematic coverage and uniformity, all proposed regulations are subjected to a screening exercise to determine their costs and eligibility for analysis. Generally, any regulations where the direct and indirect social costs of implementing the proposal will exceed $10 million, and other variations of this base amount are subject to a SEIA. The policy directs the participating departments and agencies to submit documentation on this exercise to the PCO section of Justice when regulations are sent for legal examination. These forms are then forwarded to TAG.

The Technical Advisory Group on impact assessment (TAG), within the Treasury Board Secretariat plays an active assistance and advisory role to departments and agencies in promoting the adoption of consistent and acceptable techniques for SEIA. The policy currently applies to the following departments and agencies: Agriculture; Consumer and Corporate Affairs; Energy, Mines and Resources; Environment; Fisheries and Oceans; Health and Welfare; Indian Affairs and Northern Development; Labour; Transport; AECB; CTC; CMHC and the NEB.

Resources

($000's)	82/83	83/84	84/85	85/86	86/87	87/88
Person-Years	4	4	4	4	4	4
Operating Expenses						
- Salaries	185	195	195	195	195	195
- O&M*						
- Other Expenses						
Revenue		N/A				
Subsidies		N/A				
Capital		N/A				

*   TAG is not a separate reporting unit, so the O&M figures are unavailable, however, O&M budget is negligible.

Problem Identification

The majority of private sector respondents did not rate TAG on the program questionnaire. Comments from the private sector on the methodological quality of the eight analyses produced to date has been mixed, though generally critical. A number of the parties affected by these regulations have called for third-party review or even preparation of the SEIAs.

Federal departments and agencies have found the SEIA requirement a useful, beneficial, and cost-effective contribution to regulation-making. Several departments indicated the policy ensures that proponents of regulatory action have considered the social and economic impacts of the proposed action. The majority, however, indicated their work on SEIAs had not caused them to change the details of proposed regulations. Fifty percent of departments and agencies believed SEIAs should be extended to all federal regulations with the potential for significant impact on the private sector.

Observations

1. As the instrument of the SEIA policy, the future of the TAG program would be judged in relation to any changes in the policy itself.

2. Since the beginning of the policy in August, 1978, eight SEIAs have been completed.

3. In order to effect change in the regulatory process, especially from the point of view of considering alternatives to regulations, impact analysis must come before the fact, and not after the fact, when the interested parties have expended considerable time and effort and commitment in preparing the drafted regulations.

4. Relative to the large number of HSF regulations generated, it appears the criteria for inclusion in the SEIA policy are too limiting, in that only eight SEIAs have been completed in seven years.

5. There is no verification or post audit function to determine whether the participating departments and agencies are correct in the information contained in the screening documents establishing whether or not a SEIA is needed for a particular regulation - this leaves lots of room to departments to ignore the inconveniences of the policy.

Options

The Study Team recommends to the Task Force that the government consider the following:

Re SEIA

1. Maintain the policy's current threshold of $10 million, but extend it to cover all regulatory initiatives, including, for example, economic rate setting, immigration, cultural regulation and conditions of entry into markets.

2. Departments and agencies should be required to substantiate information contained in screening documents and a minister responsible for regulatory affairs should have authority, where reasonable doubt exists, to require a SEIA.

<u>Re TAG</u>

1.   The Group's role should be maintained but integrated in a single bureau responsible for regulatory affairs.

> Technical Advisory Group (SEIA)
> Evaluation of Regulatory Programs (OCG)
> Privy Council Office (Justice)
> Administrative Law Reform
> Federal Offences Decriminalization and Compliance Enhancement Program

- to report activities/results annually to Parliament

<u>Technical Advisory Group (SEIA's)</u>

- Seriously consider having SEIA's done by the private sector, based on competitive bids, with evaluation of bids based on technical competence, as well as least cost.

- Broaden coverage, from present narrow focus on health and safety, and based on voluntary requests from departments."

REVIEW OF THE FEDERAL REGULATORY SYSTEM

Introduction

The Terms of Reference for the Study Team on regulatory programs stipulated that the team examine the federal regulatory system and, in its report to the Ministerial Task Force, provide observations and advice concerning the efficiency, appropriateness and adequacy of:

(a) the system as a whole, with special emphasis on regulatory prior assessment, approval and review procedures;

(b) private sector co-ordination and consultation practices;

(c) interdepartmental and intergovernmental coordination and consultation procedures;

(d) enforcement and compliance under existing regulations and consistency of administration.

The Study Team was not asked to address issues concerning the relationship between government and federal regulatory agencies (except to identify problem areas) since these questions are to be the subject of a separate study.

On the whole, the Study Team found significant weaknesses with regard to each of the four aspects of the system which it was asked to study.

A Snapshot of the Federal Regulatory System – More than Meets the Eye

The federal regulatory system involves considerably more than just the processes used to develop and approve "regulations". The system includes all government activities relating to (1) the development and approval, (2) implementation, (3) adjudication, and (4) evaluation of federal regulatory intervention.

As was explained elsewhere in this report, regulation in the generic sense, is defined as the imposition of rules backed by the threat of government sanctions, with the intention of modifying or controlling private behavior.

These rules can be established in statutes, subordinate legislation ("regulations"), administrative procedures, orders, directives, guidelines, manuals and implicitly, in administrative and quasi-judicial decisions. All of these involve different aspects of the federal regulatory system.

The content, interpretation, and implementation of these rules is determined by regulatory policies which are developed and approved by a variety of actors in the regulatory system including officials, the police, independent agencies, ministers, and Cabinet all of whom have distinct roles in the federal regulatory system.

Regulatory requirements, like other types of law, establish rights and duties for individuals. The processes of adjudication respecting those rights and duties, carried out by independent tribunals (including regulatory agencies) and by the courts, are equally part of the regulatory system.

Finally, the mechanisms for evaluating our existing stock of regulation -- for determining whether it is still needed and if it should be changed -- form or should form part of the system.

The previous chapter of this report dealt with certain areas of federal regulatory activity that have been identified by the study team as being "problem programs". In some cases, the problems identified relate not to the substance of the regulatory activity (i.e. the content of the rules), but to the process through which the rules are developed and applied by federal regulators. To that degree, there is an important link between the programs and the overall system. However, it is clear that many process difficulties in existing regulatory programs could have been avoided if there had been a solid foundation, that is, a better regulatory policy development system in place.

A Summary of Major Problems

The regulatory process problems addressed in this section are generic and pervasive. Most are not new. They were recognized years ago and have been the subject of recommendations by bodies such as the Economic Council of Canada, the Standing Joint Committee on Regulations and Other Statutory Instruments, the Special House of Commons Committee on Regulatory Reform, the Law Reform Commission of Canada, the Federal Statutes Compliance Project, the Privy

Council Office Task Force on Regulatory Agencies Reform, the Department of Justice Administrative Law Reform Project, and the Office of Regulatory Reform.

Having reviewed the range of studies and expert opinions as well as the response to its system questionnaires, the Study Team concludes that, over the years, some improvements have been made to federal regulatory process. However, overall little has been attempted and even less accomplished. The "system" is neither efficient nor adequate.

The major problems can be stated quite plainly:

(1)   There really is not a federal regulatory "system" per se. Scanning across the government, what the Study Team discovered was a largely unstructured, uncontrolled, highly variable, and thoroughly confusing mixture of legal requirements, policy guidelines, and ad hoc administrative practices.

(2)   The government currently has no effective mechanism to plan or control, on an overall basis, federal regulatory intervention in the private sector.

(3)   There is a multiplicity of arrangements for developing, approving, and implementing regulation. The combination of inconsistent policies and procedures from department to department and agency to agency seriously detract from the efficiency effectiveness, and fairness of federal regulation. This works to the disadvantage of the government as a whole by antagonizing the private sector and undercutting the legitimacy of regulation as an instrument for achieving the government's social and economic objectives.

(4)   The Socio-Economic Impact Assessment (SEIA) process is inadequate, poorly supported and appears to be largely ignored.

(5)   One of the parts of the system that is structured - the examination process under the Statutory Instruments Act - has been the cause of serious bottlenecks and delays in the regulatory system as a result of inadequate or inappropriate resources and overwhelmed management.

(6)   The government does not have an effective
        mechanism for systematically evaluating existing
        regulatory programs and for deciding whether to
        continue, abolish, or modify them. The large
        number of "problem programs" identified by the
        Study Team in Section B shows the inadequacy of
        existing arrangements.

(7)   Existing activities within the government aimed at
        improving aspects of the federal regulatory system
        are fragmented, inadequately coordinated and, to
        some extent, duplicative.

(8)   None of this should be surprising, because there
        has never been a government policy setting out its
        principles on regulatory intervention.

Because of the scope of regulatory activities and their
importance, problems in the regulatory processes should be
cause for concern.

Describing the Federal Regulatory System

(a)   ### The Key Players

        Other than private individuals, unions or
        companies, the key government players in the
        regulatory system are Parliament, the Cabinet, the
        Prime Minister, Ministers, the departments, the
        independent regulatory agencies, the courts, the
        central agencies and the police. Individually, or
        collectively, they develop, review, and approve
        regulatory policy and requirements, implement
        regulatory programs, adjudicate under the
        provisions of the rules, and assess performance of
        the regulatory programs.

        The departments, or the officials in them, carry
        out a variety of functions in the regulatory
        system, such as formulating regulatory policy,
        developing and analyzing regulatory proposals,
        consulting, preparing draft legislation, servicing
        the government's legislative activities in
        Parliament, informing and educating the private
        sector about regulatory requirements, inspecting,
        investigating, laying charges for violations,
        making orders and other rules, and adjudicating.

Most federal regulatory programs are housed in departments, and departmental officials have more contact with the private sector than all the other players in the system combined.

The central agencies (the Privy Council Office, the Department of Justice, Treasury Board Secretariat, and the Office of the Comptroller General) play a very important role in the regulatory system. They have control over, or participate in, several of the processes within the system. The Privy Council Office provides secretariat services and policy advice to the Cabinet committees that review and approve regulatory policy and legislation. It also services the Prime Minister, who has important powers and responsibilities within the system. So too does the President of the Privy Council who chairs the Special Committee of Council. The Clerk of the Privy Council, in conjunction with the Deputy Minister of Justice, has a statutory responsibility to advise in respect of subordinate legislation (see below).

The Department of Justice has a statutory responsibility to advise on the legality of all government activity. It participates in regulatory policy development, drafts statutes, advises on interpretation of regulatory requirements in legislation, develops and advises on regulatory procedures, advises on enforcement, and undertakes prosecutions and other forms of litigation. The Deputy Minister of Justice has a statutory responsibility to advise on the legality and propriety of subordinate legislation, a function that is carried out on his behalf by the Department's Privy Council Office Section. The Department's Federal Statutes Compliance Project is responsible for implementing the government's policy on limiting and reducing the use of criminal sanction and processes in all federal (regulatory) legislation. This Project is developing a range of proposals on decriminalization and compliance system reform for consideration by Ministers. The Department's Administrative Law Reform Project is engaged in studies on statutory instruments law and practice,

Crown law, administrative procedure and administrative appeals mechanisms, with the objective of developing reform proposals for consideration by Ministers.

The Treasury Board Secretariat services the Treasury Board committee of Cabinet which has statutory authority over the approval of any (regulatory) proposals that involve increases in the resources of the government. It also reviews and briefs the President of the Treasury Board on submissions directed to the "policy Committees" of Cabinet (including those dealing with regulatory matters). The Technical Advisory Group within the Secretariat is responsible for administering the government's SEIA policy, which requires that department proposing "major" health, safety, or fairness regulations conduct a socio-economic impact analysis and prepublish the draft regulations. The Office of Regulatory Reform is responsible for advising the minister responsible for coordinating regulatory reform, contributing to reform initiatives and administering the government's Regulatory Agenda system, under which 15 departments and agencies publish semi-annual Agendas providing information to the private sector on possible regulatory intervention. The Office of the Comptroller General reviews and briefs the President of the Treasury Board on submissions directed to the "policy committees" of Cabinet. It is also responsible for administering the government's Program Evaluation policy which requires that Deputy Heads in specified departments and agencies, establish and implement arrangements for periodic evaluation of their programs (including regulatory programs).

The Independent Regulatory Agencies are much more than just specialized courts. Depending on the agency, they adjudicate, develop, announce and implement regulatory policy; advise the government on regulatory matters; develop, draft, consult on and approve subordinate legislation; inform, educate, investigate, inspect and enforce regulatory requirements; set prices, control entry to and exit from regulated markets, and control the quantity and quality of regulated goods and services.

Ministers have control over the regulatory policy
and legislative proposals that emanate from their
departments. In some areas, and subject to
limitations specified by statute, Ministers may
have the authority to issue binding policy
directives to independent regulatory agencies or
to veto their decisions. In some cases, they have
legal authority to approve subordinate
legislation. Some regulatory statutes require the
consent of the responsible Minister before
enforcement proceedings can be commenced.
Ministers also have a variety of adjudicative
functions under federal regulatory legislation.

The Cabinet reviews and approves major regulatory
policy, and the content of government bills to be
put before Parliament. In some areas, and subject
to limitations specified by statute, Cabinet may
have the authority to issue binding policy
directives to independent regulatory agencies.
Most subordinate legislation requires Governor in
Council approval, a function that is usually
performed by the Special Committee of Council.
Some decisions of the independent regulatory
agencies can be appealed to Cabinet or reviewed by
it on its own volition.

The Prime Minister has significant responsibilities in the regulatory system and as great
influence as he chooses to exercise over the
substance of federal regulation. The Prime
Minister controls the "machinery of government",
which involves the allocation of ministerial
responsibilities and anything else that could
affect the relationships among Ministers. He
controls all appointments of senior officials in
the government (including those who will be
responsible for regulatory areas). He controls
all appointments to positions on the independent
federal regulatory agencies. He appoints the
Chief Justice of the Supreme Court of Canada. In
large measure, he determines who will be making
the decisions on regulation within the federal
jurisdiction.

The Police investigate some violations of
regulatory legislation and carry out enforcement
activities.

The Courts adjudicate. They rule on violations of regulatory legislation, on the rights of individuals under regulatory arrangements and, within the limited grounds of judicial review, on the proceedings and decisions of the independent regulatory agencies.

Parliament's role is to hold the government accountable for its (regulatory) actions. It approves regulatory legislation, delegates through statute the authority to make subordinate legislation, reviews and approves the spending estimates of (regulatory) departments and agencies, and sometimes holds inquiries into matters of regulatory policy. The Standing Joint Committee on Regulations and Other Statutory Instruments reviews regulations and reports to Parliament on their legality and propriety.

(b)   The Key Activities in the Federal Regulatory System

There is no standard, or generally accepted, breakdown of the federal regulatory system. In fact, there really isn't a system at all. At best, there is a variety of systems -- and that is a charitable interpretation of the current situation. So, for the purposes of this report, the Study Team has divided the various regulatory processes into the four major dimensions of activity:

(1)   The first area captures development of and decision-making on new regulation. In reality, there are at least two distinct activities here. One handles development and approval of major regulatory policies and regulatory statutes. This stream feeds into the so-called "policy committees" of the Cabinet and, in many cases, into Parliament itself. The other involves development and decision-making on subordinate legislation. Subordinate legislation is not passed by Parliament but is made by other authorities such as independent regulatory agencies, individual ministers, or Cabinet. Technically speaking, "regulations" are a particular type of subordinate legislation.

(2)   The second category of activity involves the implementation of regulatory programs. This area focuses on the wide range of activities carried out by departments, agencies, and other authorities to administer regulatory programs. These activities are concerned mainly with securing compliance with the rules and dealing with non-compliance.

(3)   The third category of activity focuses on the adjudication function. This task is performed by the courts, by government officials, Ministers, Cabinet, and by the regulatory agencies which combine it with policy development, program implementation, and legislative functions.

(4)   The fourth set of activities involves the evaluation of existing regulatory programs and requirements. Evaluation, in one form or another, and for a variety or purposes, is carried out through a number of mechanisms.

These dimensions are described in detail in the attachment to this chapter.

Problem Identification

It will be clear from the description of the Federal Regulatory System that it is misleading to think in terms of one single coherent system. Indeed, the layers and threads of the system make it very difficult to discuss either the system or its problems in general terms. While exceptions to many of the problems identified may be found, the context of the Team's study was the system taken as a whole and generalizations or "common denominators" are necessary to reflect the general flavour of the concerns expressed about the system.

The problems described below were identified by three means:

(1)   questionnaires and contacts with the private sector;

(2)   questionnaires and contacts with departments and agencies; and

(3)   reference to problems identified by and, in many
       cases, the subject of recommendations from groups
       such as the Economic Council, the Special House of
       Commons Committee on Regulatory Reform, the Law
       Reform Commission of Canada, the Standing Joint
       Committee on Regulations and other Statutory
       Instruments, the Office of Regulatory Reform, the
       Privy Council Office Task Force on Crown Agencies,
       the Federal Statutes Compliance Project, and the
       Department of Justice Administrative Law Reform
       Project.

1.   <u>Lack of system.</u>

        The federal regulatory system is not a system but
appears to the observer, inside or outside the government,
as a bewildering array of legal requirements, procedures and
administrative practices varying from one department or
agency to the next. In the Team's view, the parts do not
add up to what should be a clearly delineated,
comprehensible regulatory system which citizens can
understand and accept as reasonable and fair.

        On the contrary, the impenetrability of the federal
regulatory process hinders the government's ability to
assess its performance and ensure that objectives are being
achieved efficiently and effectively.

        Indeed, the Study Team noted throughout government a
generally poor understanding of the regulatory process as a
whole, and of its performance. This is, in part, due to the
noticeable lack of articulated policies governing many parts
of the federal regulatory process. For instance, no
guidelines exist for the structure and powers of new
regulatory agencies created by legislation.

        The lack of a coherent system makes it difficult for
the government to exert overall direction and control over
federal regulatory intervention and easier for poor
regulatory management to escape unnoticed. Under these
conditions, accountability for the efficiency of regulatory
activities becomes merely theoretical.

        There are consequences within the private sector as
well. The unnecessary complexity of federal regulatory
process gives rise to the view that this important area of
government activity is so technical and complex that it
requires expertise to understand it or participate in it.
(This is especially unacceptable in the case of the small

business operator, the union local and the private citizen.)
Naturally, this sense of intimidation compounds and
entrenches the original problem and the resulting lack of
scrutiny, input, and involvement undermines public
accountability. It encourages regulators to deal largely
with specialists in the regulated sector and hence it
consistently favours organizations which can afford to
invest in and pay for specialized regulatory expertise.

Ultimately the lack of a simple, understandable and
easily accessible regulatory system shelters regulatory
activity from public and parliamentary scrutiny -- to the
long-term disadvantage of good government.

2.   A Lack of Regulatory Policy

In contrast to other means of government action, such
as taxation and expenditure, an overall regulatory policy
setting out principles for using regulation as an instrument
of public policy has never been articulated.

To the extent that elements of such a policy exist,
there is no effective mechanism in place to ensure that a
regulatory policy is implemented and adhered to and,
specifically, to advise Ministers concerning specific
regulatory initiatives and ongoing regulatory activities
that appear to diverge from the policy.

3.   Lack of Regulatory Planning Mechanism

There is currently no mechanism for an overall planning
of federal regulatory intervention. Nor is there a
systematic means to set priorities among different federal
regulatory initiatives to insure that drafting, legal,
analytical, Cabinet, Parliamentary and other scarce
resources are all used in proportion to the importance of a
specific regulatory initiative.

4.   Inadequate Arrangements for Giving Early Notice

There is no overall policy concerning the timing,
content and response procedure for giving citizens advance
notice of regulatory initiatives. The existing arrangements
for giving advance notice of regulatory initiatives are
largely ad hoc, inconsistent, and in the eyes of many in the
private sector, often inadequate.

The Regulatory Agendas which were experimented with as a means of _early_ notice, do not cover all regulatory departments and agencies, the quality of information in the Agendas is not adequately policed and the Agendas are not published in the most cost-effective fashion. On the other hand, the Agendas constitute the sole reform in recent years oriented to making the "system" more accessible by the public. It is strongly supported by the private sector and by a majority of participating departments and agencies. But many called for improvements.

5.   Inadequate Arrangements for Prepublishing Draft Regulations

Very few federal statutes contain provisions legally requiring prepublication of draft regulations and there is only limited voluntary prepublication of draft regulations. No overall policy exists in this area.

6.   Inadequate Arrangements for Private Sector Consultation

There is no systematic or generally understood policy ensuring adequate consultation with the private sector on proposed regulatory intervention. While the Team's contacts generally perceived the government as being receptive to input from the private sector, federal consultation on proposed regulatory intervention was seen as uneven and inconsistent. Thus, some departments and agencies get good marks from the private sector for their consultation efforts but there remains a substantial level of dissatisfaction with both the degree and effectiveness of existing consultative arrangements and many charge that "even where there is consultation there is no listening" or "consultations take place only after the department has made up its mind".

7.   Lack of Sensitivity to Small Business

There is a general sense in the small business sector that there is inadequate sensitivity to the special circumstances and interests of small business. Federal departments and agencies do not assess, as a matter of course whether their regulatory proposals are likely to have an adverse differential impact on small business. Decisions are being made on new regulations without analysis of the potential for adverse differential impact on small business.

There is no consistent effort to adjust or "tier" regulatory requirements to take account of the ability of small business to comply with rules or to supply required information and there is little formal provision for flexibility in applying regulations to small business.

8. Imbalance of Interests in the Regulatory Process

There is no encouragement of procedures and approaches by regulators designed to ensure that all interests have a reasonable opportunity for participation and involvement in the regulatory process.

Private citizens are at a disadvantage compared with businesses, unions and other entities which have sufficient resources and tax write-offs for expenses incurred in connection with participation in the regulatory process. The result is that regulators (including both departments and independent agencies) may make decisions on new regulation without necessarily having a full appreciation of the expertise or perspective of interested individuals or small interest groups.

9. Compliance and Enforcement

Too much federal regulatory legislation relies on the use of criminal sanctions to achieve compliance. Too much legislation is subject to "unwritten rules" of enforcement with the result that the private sector does not know how regulators will respond when problems occur. This type of uncertainty undercuts regulatory activities. There is considerable evidence that carefully defined compliance strategies oriented to the special circumstances of each relevant piece of legislation would greatly enhance the fairness, efficiency and effectiveness of the regulatory program.

The strategies should include measures to facilitate, encourage and monitor compliance, as well as deal with non-compliance. Among the elements that seem most needed in a fair and cost-effective regulatory program are: a clear policy purpose in the legislation; ways to involve regulatees closely in the design of the rules and policies that may affect them; an explicit information and education program on the content of rules and ways of complying; a wide variety of modern compliance enhancement techniques for use by regulatees; and monitoring techniques that rely as fully as possible on the procedures and participation of regulated companies and individuals.

10. Statutory Instruments

The definition of "regulation" and "statutory instrument" in the Statutory Instruments Act have been found to be confusing, and the way in which they are implemented, especially through enabling clauses in statutes, is not based on any articulated policy. This creates the risk that some statutory instruments may escape the legal review, registration, publication, and parliamentary scrutiny provisions of the Act.

Insufficient steps have been taken by the government to identify and make accessible to Parliament (i.e. the Standing Joint Committee on Regulations and Other Statutory Instruments) the statutory instruments that it is required by law to scrutinize.

Some administrative guidelines, manuals, and other internal procedural instruments amount to regulation because of the way they are applied but are not subject to legal scrutiny, ministerial approval, or parliamentary review. "Administrative" regulation of this sort is questionable in principle but remarkably prevalent.

The existing requirements covering the content and distribution of Explanatory Notes accompanying regulations are inadequate with respect to reasons for and effect of proposed new regulatory requirements.

11. Legal Review - a major system bottleneck

The government's existing arrangements and procedures for legal review of draft regulations pursuant to the Statutory Instruments Act are inefficient, unnecessarily time-consuming and fraught with delays running into years. Although the Department of Justice Privy Council Office Section (PCOJ) was intended to carry out a proof-reading and legal vetting function, it redrafts about 80 per cent of all instruments channeled through it. On average, a regulatory manager cannot be assured that a regulation will receive PCOJ clearance in less than nine months.

The PCOJ has operated, at least until recently, with too little staff, inadequate accommodation and services, overwhelmed management, no priority system and no formal groundrules. It is a major problem area in the regulatory system and the subject of considerable concern among regulating departments. However, as such, it has been under intensive senior management scrutiny and important reforms are currently being implemented.

644

12. Internal Decision Making

There is no standard approach or recognized policy regarding the information Ministers require before approving proposed regulatory initiatives. Indeed, most regulations have traditionally been approved with minimal ministerial participation. Notwithstanding a policy calling for major new regulatory initiatives to be reviewed by the relevant Cabinet policy committee, this rarely occurs.

Even if the policy were honoured, existing requirements governing the form and content of Cabinet submissions (including the new Executive Summaries) do not encourage analysis of regulatory impacts or alternatives or require that the necessary relevant information be presented in a way that makes it easier for Ministers and their advisors to find it and judge its adequacy.

Federal departments and agencies are not systematically required to consider alternatives to regulation when dealing with a problem, nor are they challenged to select the least intrusive or least costly regulatory approach when developing and proposing regulatory proposals.

There has been a tradition of approving all proposed new regulations put before the Special Committee of Council without requiring any indication of the need for or the potential impact of the new requirements. The Committee has had no independent source of analysis and advice so that it can make informed judgments on proposed regulations.

13. The SEIA Policy and Program

The existing Socio-Economic Impact Assessment (SEIA) policy does not apply to proposals for regulatory statutes, is too limited in its coverage of regulations, and requires more detailed analysis than could be reasonably justified for most regulations. The Study Team questions whether the policy is being adhered to when only 8 SEIAs have been completed since the policy was implemented in August, 1978. This important regulatory technique should be reinvigorated and given teeth or scrapped. If maintained, there should be provision for contracting out elements of the work and for ensuring other types of private sector input.

14. Mechanism for Review of Existing Regulation

There is no mechanism other than internal program review (which itself has been inadequate in the regulatory area) for systematically evaluating existing regulatory programs and for deciding whether to continue, abolish, or modify them. In the Study Team's view, an outside challenge function applied periodically to regulatory programs is highly practical and desirable.

15. Overlapping of Regulatory Reform Activity

Existing activities within the government aimed at improving aspects of the federal regulatory system tend to be fragmented, inadequately coordinated and, to some extent, duplicative.

16. Lack of Accountability for Regulatory Activities (Administrative or Political)

The impenetrability of the regulatory system and lack of policy guidance on specific regulatory procedures ensure that there cannot be effective bureaucratic or political accountability for individual regulatory activities.

Current arrangements for performance review of officials, particularly senior officials, are not sufficiently sensitive to the effective management of regulation.

Parliament, and its committees, are not effective in exercising oversight and ensuring public accountability for the regulatory activities of the federal government.

The Standing Joint Committee on Regulations and Other Statutory Instruments has made progress but has not yet succeeded in forging as constructive a role as it would appear vis-a-vis the regulatory system.

Options for Improvement

To respond to the problems identified above, the Study Team identified suggestions and options for change in the federal regulatory system, falling within three broad categories:

      (A)   Overall System Improvements

      (B)   Responses to Private Sector Concerns

                (C)   Improvements to Internal Regulatory
                       Management.

        In many cases the possible changes are not mutually
exclusive -- a combination of them would be possible.

        The Study Team, therefore, recommends to the Task Force
that the government consider the following measures:

(A)   Overall System Improvements

       Multiplicity/Inconsistency of Regulatory Processes

       1   Achieve maximum consistency by standardizing
               rule-making and other procedures for all
               departments and agencies through generalized
               statutory requirements, such as a Regulatory
               Procedures Act.

       2   Improve consistency by setting minimum procedural
               requirements for all departments and agencies
               through legislation, while allowing flexibility
               for maintenance of those existing arrangements
               that are working well and for the adoption of new,
               innovative practices and procedures.

       Lack of a Regulatory Policy

       1   Develop, announce, and implement an overall
               federal regulatory policy focusing solely on
               government responsibilities, setting out
               principles for when and how regulation could be
               used.

       2   Develop, announce, and implement an overall
               federal regulatory policy covering the roles and
               responsibilities of both the government and the
               private sector.

Develop Mechanisms for Overall Planning of Federal
Regulatory Intervention

1   Require all departments and agencies to include
       specified information on their proposed regulatory
       activities for the upcoming year in their Multi-year
       Operational Plans (MYOPs), such proposals to be
       specifically considered and approved in principle by
       Cabinet. The purpose of Cabinet review should be to
       ensure consistency of proposed activities with the

relevant policy requirements of the government,
particularly the overall Regulatory Policy, if one
exists.

2   Require all departments and agencies to prepare and
        submit to Cabinet for review and approval in principle,
        separate annual Regulatory Plans providing specified
        information on their proposed regulatory activities for
        the upcoming year. As with the Option 1 directly
        above, the review should focus on the consistency of
        the proposals with relevant government policies,
        particularly the overall regulatory policy, if it
        exists.

3   Publish or make available to the public on request,
        the annual Regulatory Plans submitted by departments,
        or the relevant excerpts from the MYOPs, depending on
        whether option 1 or 2 is selected.

4   Establish a federal "Regulatory Budget" system under
        which Cabinet would set limits on the overall economic
        costs to be imposed through federal regulatory
        intervention, and would allocate "shares" of that total
        cost to the various departments and agencies. In
        connection with Options 1 or 2, require
        departments/agencies to estimate the potential cost of
        their proposed initiatives and to demonstrate that they
        will not result in the department/agency exceeding its
        Regulatory Budget.

5   Institute procedures so that the Special Committee of
        Council can establish overall government priorities for
        the preparation, vetting, consideration, and approval
        of subordinate legislation (regulations), through a
        planning process specific to subordinate legislation,
        on the basis of information disclosed by
        department/agencies in their annual Regulatory Plans
        (Options 1 or 2), or on an ad hoc basis when requested
        by those responsible for advising on the legislation.

Improve Capacity for Oversight of Regulatory Activities to Ensure Consistency with Government Policy

1   Distinguish two oversight streams: legal vs.
        economic. Co-ordinate, but do not integrate, existing
        legal function (PCOJ) with economic, which would be
        carried out by a Bureau of Regulatory Management and
        Economic Analysis.

2.   Integrate the two oversight functions, so that they are
      performed by a single unit, a Bureau of Regulatory
      Affairs.

Institutional Location for Regulatory Oversight Functions

1   Establish Bureau of Regulatory Management and Economic
      Analysis (single focus) or Bureau of Regulatory Affairs
      (dual focus) in Treasury Board Secretariat -- because
      of "regulatory management" aspects.

2   Establish either bureau in Department of Justice --
      because of legal dimension of regulation.

3   Establish either Bureau in Privy Council Office --
      because of statutory responsibilities of Clerk of Privy
      Council under Statutory Instruments Act, machinery of
      government aspects of regulatory oversight, and
      linkages with existing PCO secretariat functions to
      Cabinet policy committees and Special Committee of
      Council.

4   Establish either Bureau as a distinct unit, reporting
      directly to the President of the Privy Council, Deputy
      Prime Minister, or other Minister with
      specially-designated responsibility for regulatory
      affairs.

Improving and Enhancing the Consistency of Early Notice

1   Establish an overall policy on early notice _allowing_
      flexibility, but setting as a minimum requirement that
      all federal department and agencies give the private
      sector early notice of all possible regulatory
      initiatives through publication of Regulatory Agendas,
      with freedom to supplement the Agendas through other
      notice mechanisms.

2   Stipulate that no initiatives should come into effect
      sooner than 60 days after giving early notice, subject
      to exemptions for emergencies, the principle of budget
      secrecy, dislocation of markets, impairment of
      federal-provincial-territorial relations, impairment of
      international relations, impairment of national
      security, breach of Cabinet confidentiality, or in
      other specific instances approved by the designated
      minister(s).

3   Encourage the development and use of alternative
     supplementary early notice techniques; establish a
     clearing-house function to ensure dissemination of
     information on alternative techniques within the
     government.

4   Establish an overall policy on early notice <u>with
     emphasis on maximum consistency</u>, requiring the use of
     stipulated uniform early notice mechanisms including
     the requirement for publication of Regulatory Agendas
     by all departments and agencies (subject to the same
     exemptions as in Option 1).

5   Create a new, less costly section (Part IV) of the
     Canada Gazette for publication, on a cost-recovery
     basis, of Regulatory Agendas, other forms of notice,
     draft regulations and other materials.

Improving Prepublication of Draft Regulations

1   Establish an overall policy requiring prepublication of
     all draft regulations (including amendments to existing
     regulations) in the Canada Gazette subject to specified
     exemptions (e.g. dislocation of markets, housekeeping
     matters, emergencies, regs exempt from publication
     requirements in Statutory Instruments Act, regs that
     make no material change in existing requirements).
     Allow exemptions in other specific instances approved
     by designated minister(s). Implement policy through
     Cabinet (administrative) directive, not through
     legislative requirements.

2   Establish overall policy on prepublication as in Option
     1 but implement through legislative requirements in
     federal statutes. All new statutes to include a
     standard-form prepublication requirement as a matter of
     course unless Cabinet specifically directs otherwise
     when approving legislative proposals prior to drafting.

3   In addition to injecting legal prepublication
     requirements in new statutes, review all existing
     statutes and inject standard-form prepublication
     requirements either on a piece-meal amendment basis,
     through an omnibus amendment bill.

4   Create a new, loss costly section (Part IV) of the
     Canada Gazette for publication, on a cost-recovery
     basis, of Regulatory Agendas, other forms of notice,
     draft regulations, and other materials. (See identical
     option under "Early Notice", above.)

5   Revise the existing government policy on the content of
     the Explanatory Notes which are published together with
     draft and final regulations, extending the information
     that must be disclosed to include matters such as the
     underlying specific policy objectives, the reasons for
     the regulation, the content of the regulation, changes
     from existing requirements, processes for and timing of
     consultation, approval and coming into force,
     identification of contact person(s), results of
     previous consultations, summary of any impact analysis,
     consistency with overall Regulatory Policy, if one
     exists.

Improving the Quality and Consistency of Private Sector Consultation

1   Establish an overall policy on promoting private sector
     participation in the regulatory process, requiring
     consultation on policy, objectives, rules, methods and
     approaches to program delivery and compliance, setting
     out fundamental principles for the consultative
     process, but allowing flexibility in the specific
     consultation arrangements used by various
     departments/agencies.

2   Encourage the development and use of innovative
     consultation arrangements; establish a clearing-house
     function to ensure dissemination of information on
     alternative arrangements within the government.

3   Establish an overall policy on private sector
     consultation with emphasis on maximum consistency,
     requiring the use of stipulated uniform consultation
     arrangements.

Improving Sensitivity to Differential Impact on Business

1   Establish an overall policy on equitable regulatory
     treatment of small business.

2   Implement the overall policy, in part, through a
     Cabinet (administrative) Directive requiring that all
     proposals for new regulatory legislation (statutes and
     regulations) or for changes in regulatory program
     administration/enforcement take account of the
     potential impact on small enterprises, and ensure that
     small units are not burdened disproportionately by the
     imposition of uniform regulatory requirements,
     including paperwork requirements regardless of size

(e.g. through "tiering" of regulatory requirements). This requirement for small business impact analysis could form part of a more general requirement for a Regulatory Impact Analysis of all regulatory proposals.

3   Implement the overall policy, in part, through enactment of statutory requirements (i.e. the equivalent of the U.S. Regulatory Flexibility Act) stipulating that proposed regulations which are likely to have a significant economic impact on a substantial number of small entities be prepublished together with a preliminary assessment of their potential impact and that the final regulations be published with a final assessment.

4   Implement the overall policy, in part, by reviewing all existing federal legislation (statutes and regulations), and developing tiering amendments where appropriate to bring the legislation into conformity with the policy. Implement the changes either through piece-meal amendments or through an omnibus amendment bill.

5   Implement the overall policy, in part, by adding a "Small Business Impact" heading to standard form for entries in the Regulatory Agendas and requiring departments/agencies to briefly indicate the potential impact of each proposed regulatory initiative on small business.

Ensuring a Balance of Interests in the Regulatory Process

1   Establish an overall policy on government assistance to interests that are inherently at a disadvantage in the regulatory process.

2   Implement the policy, in part, by encouraging the development and use of innovative procedures and arrangements by departments/agencies to facilitate the participation of such interests in regulatory processes; establish a clearing-house function to ensure dissemination of information on alternative arrangements within the government.

3   Implement the policy, in part, by immediately increasing federal support for funding Public Interest Group intervenors in proceedings before federal independent regulatory agencies.

4   Affirm need for increased support for public interest
        group intervenors, but defer decisions on increased
        funding for two years, or until fiscal situation of the
        government has improved.

Improving Arrangements Aimed at Achieving Compliance with Regulatory Requirements

1   Either as a supplement to an overall government
        Regulatory Policy (with no duplication of principles),
        or on its own (with some duplication), develop,
        announce, and implement an overall government policy
        on Compliance which would, among other things, reaffirm
        the government's policy on limiting the use of criminal
        sanctions and processes in federal legislation.

2   Continue the work now being carried out by the
        Department of Justice Federal Statutes Compliance
        Project which will, in its proposed Phase II, involve
        the review of all existing federal legislation and
        compliance systems (including all regulatory programs)
        to identify areas where compliance arrangements can be
        improved and to develop and implement needed changes.
        The project also contemplates a review of all new
        legislative proposals to ensure consistency with good
        compliance practices.

Improving and Expediting the Drafting and Legal Review of Statutory Instruments

1   Continue the current internal efforts by the Department
        of Justice to improve and expedite drafting and legal
        review of statutory instruments.

2   Limit the PCOJ function to examination of statutory
        instrument -- eliminate its de facto drafting
        activities.

3   Fully or partially decentralize the legal review and
        advice function required under the Statutory
        Instruments Act to Departmental Legal Services Units,
        maintaining a slimmed-down central unit in the
        Legislation Branch of the Department of Justice or in a
        Bureau of Regulatory Affairs, primarily as a source of
        expert advice and assistance to the DLSUs.

4   Increase the resources for PCOJ.

Helping Ministers Make More Informed Decisions on Regulation

1   Maintain the status quo (maintaining SEIA requirement as is for the "major" health, safety, or fairness regulations).

2   Establish an overall policy specifying the types of information to be provided to Ministers when they are asked to approve regulatory initiatives (e.g. evidence of a problem, justification for government intervention, identification of alternative ways for the government to handle the problem (non-regulatory alternatives), justification for the recommended course of action, assessment of the costs and benefits, information on consultation).

3   To implement the policy, require that specified regulatory impact analysis information accompany all regulatory proposals that require ministerial approval (including regulatory policies, statutes, and subordinate legislation). A flexible approach would be taken under which the level of detail required would be in direct relation to the potential significance of the proposal. The information could be conveyed in the form of a separate standard-form Regulatory Impact Analysis Statement (RIAS) or through inclusion in existing briefing materials such as Memoranda to Cabinet, Executive Summaries, and Submissions to Council. Revisions to the format and content requirements of these documents would likely be necessary to ensure that the information would be easily accessible and clearly conveyed.

4   Extend the SEIA analytical requirements to regulations in all areas, either maintaining the cost thresholds at current levels ($10 M per year in current year dollars) or reducing them so that more regulations will be subject to the analytical requirements.

5   Combine the overall RIA requirement (Option 3) with an extended SEIA requirement (Option 4), so that the more detailed SEIA analysis would generate the required RIA information for very significant regulatory proposals in all decision-making streams.

Strengthen Ministerial Decision Making and Control over Subordinate Legislation

1 Special Committee of Council to continue decision-making, as opposed to former practices of rubber-stamping proposals for new regulations.

2 More strictly interpret and enforce existing government policy which requires that Cabinet policy committees review and approve any proposals for subordinate legislation that have significant policy implications. Ensure that Cabinet policy committees review significant regulations that are subject to approval by individual Ministers or other authorities.

3 Establish a committee of Parliamentary Secretaries to vet all proposals for subordinate legislation prior to their consideration by the Special Committee of Council. (Note: This arrangement has been used by the Province of Ontario for several years.)

4 Provide Staff support to the Special Committee through an integrated Bureau of Regulatory Affairs, so that ministers will have access to an independent source of legal and economic analysis and advice.

Improve Arrangements for Review/Clean-up of Existing Regulation

1 Establish an overall policy on the use of sunset or mandatory review clauses in federal regulatory legislation.

2 Implement the policy, in part, by stipulating that all new regulatory statutes include a sunset or mandatory review clause as a matter of course unless Cabinet specifically directs otherwise when approving legislative proposals prior to drafting.

3 In addition to injecting sunset clauses in new regulatory statutes, review all existing statutes and regulations and inject sunset or mandatory review clauses either on a piece-meal amendment basis as the legislation comes up for revision, through an omnibus ubmission to Governor in Council (for regulations subject to Governor in Council approval).

4   Establish a distinct policy on the evaluation of
     regulatory programs (separate from the general Program
     Evaluation Policy) stipulating that regulatory programs
     are to be reviewed every five years according to a
     timetable and with reference to criteria established
     externally (i.e. by Cabinet or by the central agency
     responsible for the system), authorizing a proactive
     quality-control challenge function for the responsible
     central agency, and requiring that evaluation reports
     be submitted by the responsible central agency to
     Cabinet for Ministerial review and direction.

5   Periodically conduct in-depth major policy reviews
     of target regulatory programs identified by ministers,
     through the use of joint public-private sector Study
     Teams.

To Ensure Co-ordination of Efforts for Regulatory System Reform

1   Integrate all system reform activities into one
     operation under the authority of a designated
     Minister (e.g. ORR, OCG Regulatory Program
     Evalution, TAG, PCOJ, JUS Admin. Law Reform
     Project, JUS Federal Statutes Compliance
     Project, Special Committee of Council briefing
     function).

2   Retain separate operations, subject to overall
     co-ordination based on a Cabinet approved Regulatory
     Program.

3   A hybrid of Options 1 and 2: integrate key functions
     in one unit, retain others as separate operations
     subject to co-ordination under a Cabinet approved
     Regulatory Program.

Improve Accountability for Regulatory Activities

1   Ensure that more instruments having regulatory
     effect are available for review by the Standing Joint
     Committee on Regulations and Other Statutory
     Instruments by amending the definition of "regulation"
     and "statutory instrument" in the Statutory
     Instruments Act.

2   Ensure that more instruments having regulatory effect
     are available for review by the Standing Joint
     Committee by establishing policy guidelines for the

drafting of new enabling clauses, instituting administrative arrangements for identifying and making available statutory instruments to the Committee, and by taking steps to ensure that manuals, directives, guidelines, etc. with regulatory effect are made available to the Committee for scrutiny.

3   Include regulatory management/compliance performance in the annual assessments of Deputy Ministers.

4   Ensure that the Treasury Board policy governing the Access to Information Register requires clear disclosure of the existence of manuals, directives, and statutory instruments.

5   Propose to Parliament that the mandate of the Standing Joint Committee be expanded to include the right to review the subject matter of enabling clauses in all bills placed before Parliament. Amend the Statutory Instruments Act to enshrine the criteria used by the Standing Joint Committee in legislation.

A Somewhat Detailed Description of

The Federal Regulatory System

The federal regulatory system can be broken down (some would say it is <u>always</u> broken down) into four layers:

(1)   development and approval processes

(2)   implementation processes

(3)   the adjudication processes

(4)   the evaluation processes

1.   <u>Development and Approval of New Regulations</u>

The federal regulatory system is difficult to grasp. This is because, except for the legal approval process corresponding to the requirements of the Statutory Instruments Act, there is no single, recognized (let along understood) system. However, there are procedures which operate at different levels on an ad hoc or traditional basis which taken together pass as the "system".

This attempts to describe how the system, such as it is, goes about developing and approving new regulatory initiatives.

To facilitate understanding, three approval or process streams corresponding to a hierarchy of regulation types are identified:

(a)   regulatory statutes

(b)   subordinate legislation

(c)   administrative rules, guidelines and procedures.

(a)   <u>Regulatory Statute and Policy Stream</u>

All new regulatory initiatives originate in more or less the same way. Somebody either in the private sector, or in one level of government identifies a problem and concludes that the way to solve it is for the federal or another government to make or change a rule. This function is carried out predominantly by departmental or agency officials.

At some point, hopefully early in the game, somebody in the government decides to inform the private sector about what's going on. There are several different techniques used among federal departments and agencies to give advance notice of regulatory initiatives. However, the only standardized arrangement for advance notice is the Regulatory Agendas program. Under a two-year experimental program, 15 departments and agencies published semi-annual agendas disclosing basic information on possible regulatory actions.

Arrangements for consultation with the private sector on proposals in the regulatory statutes/policy stream are highly variable. In some cases, private sector consultation is completely ad hoc; in others long-standing formal structures are used. In still others, no consultation takes place at all. Sometimes the opportunity for consultation is left open to all affected interests; sometimes it is limited to a few key interests that would be most directly affected or that could significantly influence the chances for success of failure of a government initiative.

The approach to consultation can vary considerably, as well. At one extreme, it may amount to "negotiation" or true joint development of regulatory requirements. At the other, it takes the form of simple notice or"information sessions" in which communication is largely one-way - from the government to the private sector. In response to the Regulatory Study Team's questionnaires and contacts, a common theme was the way in which "there is consultation" but nobody listens."

Interdepartmental and intergovernmental consultation like private sector consultation, takes a variety of forms. Most of it is carried out through informal, ad hoc bilateral contacts. The lack of consultation contributes to regulatory overlap and inconsistencies which are detrimental to the economy as a whole.

The policy development and analysis function is especially important for this stream of activity since each individual initiative is likely to have the potential for very significant social and/or economic impact on the private sector. The methods and content of this function vary across the government. In fact, they vary within departments and agencies depending on the regulatory area or specific matter involved.

Sometimes the government will release a draft of a proposed policy or statute for public comment or distribute it to a few key interests for reaction. This approach is not generally adopted, however, because of the principle of parliamentary privilege which restricts the distribution of a draft bill unless it has been tabled (not necessarily for First Reading) in Parliament.

Once a proposal has "gelled" sufficiently, it is documented in a submission to Cabinet and presented by the responsible Minister. The form and content of Memoranda to Cabinet and the Executive Summaries that accompany them are subject to standardized requirements. The main reference document for Ministers, the Executive Summaries, are supposed to contain, among other things, information on the objectives of the proposal, the issues, the background, recommended action, departmental positions, and possible adverse consequences.

Cabinet submissions must be filed with the Privy Council Office 96 hours before they are to be considered by the relevant policy committee. During the intervening period they are duplicated and distributed to other Ministers, to departments, and to central agencies. Briefings on the submissions are routinely prepared for Ministers by officials in the PCO, the Treasury Board Secretariat, and the Office of the Comptroller General. The perspectives of these briefings varies depending on the agency involved; none have an orientation focused on regulatory impact.

If Cabinet approves a major regulatory policy proposal, it is usually left to the responsible Minster to implement the decision and announce the new policy. If a statutory change is involved, the responsible department must convey drafting instructions to the Legislation Section of the Department of Justice which prepared the draft bill. The bill must then be submitted to the Legislation and House Planning Committee of Cabinet for review and final approval before tabling in Parliament. After Parliamentary consideration and approval, the bill is given Royal Assent.

It may come into force upon Royal Assent or upon a date that is set by Proclamation. It is not uncommon for legislation or parts of legislation to be passed by Parliament and left unproclaimed indefinitely pending the coming to pass of circumstance for which it was legislated. (e.g. Part III of the National Transportation Act). A variant on this occurs where "umbrella" legislation is passed and proclaimed but requires subordinate legislation (i.e. regulations) to have any effect and these are not passed for the time being (e.g. the Interest Act).

(b) Subordinate Legislation Stream

While all paths in the regulatory statutes and policy stream lead to the Cabinet, the paths in the subordinate legislation (regulations) stream feed through a variety of decision points. Depending on the statute under whose authority they are to be made, regulations may be made by the Governor in Council (Cabinet), a Minister, an independent regulatory agency, or an official. The early decision-making stage is usually the same in all cases, however. Somebody, in most cases a minister or an official, but often someone from the private sector, identifies a problem and concludes that the way to solve it is for the government to make or change a rule.

There are many techniques and instruments used by federal departments and agencies to give advance notice of new regulations. In general, because changes in subordinate legislation are more common than changes in statutes, the notice arrangements are somewhat more routine and better established. The Regulatory Agendas cover all regulatory initiatives, including those that will be implemented through subordinate legislation. The Agendas constitute the only system providing the potential for comprehensive, standardized, early notice of new or amended regulations.

As with the regulatory statutes and policy stream, a myriad of arrangements exists for consultation with the private sector on new regulations. The approach to consultation, the timing, the coverage, all vary depending on the department or agency and the matter involved. Consultation is required as a matter of policy in one area, however. Under the government SEIA (Socio-Economic Impact Analysis) policy (see below), departments and agencies proposing new regulations in the health, safety, or fairness area must consult with directly affected parties at the problem definition stage (i.e. on realizing that government intervention may be required). The 13 departments and agencies subject to the SEIA policy are required to maintain a public list of affected parties who will be notified with respect to regulatory initiatives in the health, safety and fairness area.

The policy development and analysis functions for subordinate legislation are highly variable. But unlike the statutes and policy stream, there are requirements for impact analysis of some regulations. Under the government SEIA policy, departments and agencies proposing "major" regulations in the health, safety, or fairness area must carry out a cost-benefit or cost-effectiveness analysis of the proposals, publish a summary of the study in the Canada Gazette together with the draft regulations, and make the full study available to the private sector. All this must occur no later than 60 days before the regulations are to come into effect.

As noted above, the principle of parliamentary privilege imposes limitations on the prerelease of draft bills. Although this is not a concern with subordinate legislation, there are no general requirements for prepublication of draft regulations. Prepublication, however, does occur in some circumstances. The SEIA policy require prepublication of "major" health, safety, or fairness regulations. Moreover, prepublication has been voluntarily adopted as standard practice in some federal regulatory operations, and is a legal requirement in 24 federal statutes.

Every government bill that is to be put before Parliament must be drafted by lawyers in the Legislation Section of the Department of Justice. Regulations, on the other hand, are drafted in departments. However, government procedures require that all draft regulations be submitted to the Privy Council Office Section of the Department of Justice (PCOJ) which examines the draft to ensure that:

 (a) it is authorized by the statute pursuant to which it is enacted;

(b) it does not constitute an unusual or unexpected
     use of authority pursuant to which it is made;

(c) it does not trespass unduly on existing rights and
     freedoms and is not, in any case, inconsistent
     with the purposes and provisions of the Canadian
     Bill of Rights; and

(d) the form and craftsmanship of the proposed
     regulation are in accordance with established
     standards.

At this point the paths that regulations can take begin
to diverge. Regulations that are to be approved by an
independent regulatory agency or by a Minister return from
PCOJ to the originating institution where the decision-
making procedures are handled internally. Most regulations,
however, require approval by the Governor in Council.

These regulations must be presented to the Special
Committee of Council with a formal recommendation signed by
the sponsoring Minister.

The recommendation must cite the precise legal
authority for the regulation being proposed and must also
indicate, in cases where the enabling Act requires it, that
any "conditions precedent" to the making of regulations have
been met.

The Minister's recommendation together with the draft
Order in Council stamped by PCOJ and an explanatory
memorandum including relevant background material are then
sent to the Assistant Clerk of the Privy Council to be put
before the Special Committee of Council.

The sponsoring department or agency must also send a
covering "Letter of Transmittal" to the Assistant Clerk
stating any special instructions concerning publication or
timing of submission of the proposed regulation to the
Governor in Council. This letter must indicate whether the
proposed regulation has any financial implications for the
government.

Once the Assistant Clerk of the Privy Council has
received the appropriate documentation he will have the
recommendation and draft Order placed before the Special
Committee of Council, one of the ten committees in the
current Cabinet, for approval.

The Special Committee is composed of ten ministers with a quorum of four. This committee generally meets once a week (or as required) to consider submissions for Orders in Council -- the formal instrument by which regulations and other statutory instruments are made. Until recently, the Special Committee has routinely approved, without scrutiny or questioning, most substantive submissions for Orders in Council dealing with new or amended regulations.

Regulations approved by the Special Committee are then presented to the Governor General for signature. After that, they are returned to the PCO and the sponsoring department or agency.

At this point in the process, the approved regulations will normally be registered by the Assistant Clerk of the Privy Council (Orders in Council) pursuant to Section 6 of the Statutory Instruments Act. A regulation does not normally come into legal force until the day on which it is registered. After registration, the new regulations are published in Part II of the Canada Gazette.

In the final stage of this process, the regulations are reviewed by Parliament. Pursuant to Section 26 of the Statutory Instruments Act, regulations and other statutory instruments, except those lawfully kept secret, stand permanently referred to the Standing Joint Committee on Regulations and Other Statutory Instruments. This Committee examines the regulations using its own criteria but including the identical criteria used by the PCOJ Section. Although the Committee has no power to approve, disallow, or vary any regulation, it exerts influence through this continuous contacts with responsible departments and agencies, and through its periodic reports to the House and Senate.

(c) The Third Main Stream - Administrative rules, guidelines, procedures

Not all new regulation takes the form of major policies, statutes, or regulations. Sometimes rules that can be made under the authority of a statute, do not fall within the definition of "regulation" in the Statutory Instrument Act. A good example of this is the power given to the Fishery Officers under the Fisheries Act to vary catch limitations that are established in regulations. Because of the way that enabling power is set out in the statute, the variances do not qualify as "regulations" under the Statutory Instruments Act and are not, therefore covered

by the requirements for legal vetting by the PCOJ ,
publication in the Canada Gazette, or registration.
Nonetheless, they have regulatory effect.

Similarly, a department or agency will often
establish internal procedures or guidelines, either formally
or not, that have equivalent and often powerful effect on
regulators. Obviously, how a department or an enforcement
agency interprets the letter or spirit of a law or
regulation can make all the difference.

Documents relating to the interpretation, application
or other aspect of regulatory implementation are not made
public. Usually ministers and sometimes even deputy
ministers are unaware of them.

2.   Implementation

After a regulatory policy has been developed and
approved in one form or another, it is put in place as a
regulatory program or simply as yet another regulation.

Implementation of regulatory programs involves
everything that is done by the government to ensure
compliance with regulatory requirements. A lot more than
just enforcement of the law is involved. In fact,
investigations and prosecutions, which have in the past been
seen as the primary functions of regulatory authorities,
play a relatively minor part in the real world of
regulation. Providing information on regulatory
requirements through educational programs and materials as
well as through inspection activities is a far more
significant and effective method of obtaining compliance.
Gathering information on compliance with those requirements,
through self-reporting, third-party monitoring, and on-site
inspections is another significant function.

3.   Adjudication

Adjudication functions are performed by the courts,
the independent regulatory tribunals, agencies, Ministers,
the Cabinet, and by officials. The types of decisions
involved include:

-       determining whether persons have contravened
        regulatory requirements, imposing sanctions,
        ordering remedial action;

-   determining whether persons have qualified for
    exclusions or other benefits under regulatory
    legislation.

-   controlling entry into an exit from regulated
    markets by granting, reviewing, and revoking
    licences, and by attaching conditions to them;

-   controlling the prices of regulated goods and
    services, by approving rates of return, approving
    specific prices, setting production quotas, etc.

-   controlling the quantity and quality of regulated
    goods and services;

-   controlling other characteristics of regulated
    goods and services.

4.   Evaluation of Existing Regulations

Evaluation of existing regulatory activities is
possible through a variety of mechanisms. The Cabinet or a
Minister may direct that a legislative or policy review be
carried out. Most departments and agencies conduct ad hoc
review of their regulatory activities. But these tend to be
concerned with efficiency or effectiveness as opposed to
the need for the activity in the first place. Internal
audits can focus on specific regulatory programs. The
Program Evaluation System, administered by the Office of the
Comptroller General, is supposed to ensure periodic and
systematic evaluation of all programs over a
three-to-five-year cycle. The Auditor General may review
the regulatory programs of a department or agency. However,
notwithstanding the available mechanisms for evaluation, the
reality is that they have rarely been used for substantive
regulatory review in recent years.

RECORD OF CONSULTATION

FEDERAL/PROVINCIAL/TERRITORIAL CONSULTATIONS

The Regulatory Programs Team's mandate was extended to permit time for comprehensive consultations with provincial and territorial representatives. The purpose of the consultations was to ensure that the provinces and territories had a full opportunity to contribute to the Study Team's work.

The Chairman of the Ministerial Task Force wrote to provincial and territorial heads of government in June proposing meetings with representatives of the Study Team. All responded positively albeit, in some cases, rather warily. Subsequently, meetings were held in every provincial and territorial capital between July 25 and September 19.

With the exceptions of Quebec and, to a certain extent, Manitoba, the provinces and territories responded openly and positively to the opportunity to discuss federal regulatory programs and reform initiatives. Notwithstanding the good atmosphere of the meetings, nearly all provincial and territorial representatives reiterated certain common themes almost in identical terms:

a) they have certain concerns about the Ministerial Task Force;

b) the meeting with the Study Team should be seen as "technical" discussions among officials", not formal intergovernmental consultations;

c) there should be formal political level consultations on any regulatory reforms that might negatively impact on them;

d) it would be unacceptable if the federal government "dumped" its regulatory activities on them without compensation.

Once the cautionary formalities were over, every meeting involved worthwhile discussion and new insight into the web of regulatory linkages in Canada.

II. Shared Provincial and Territorial Views

There were several common threads among the areas of
provincial/territorial concern. Environment, fisheries and
transportation were the most persistent and repeated
problems and evoked the strongest expressions of concern.
Financial institutions and food regulation came next,
followed by substantial commentary on regulatory agencies.

While provincial and territorial concerns were similar
in substance, there was a quite distinct approach to the
consultations on the part of the territorial governments.
The territories view regulatory reform as central to their
devolution objectives vis-à-vis the federal government.
Consequently, they addressed their concerns at a high level
of political and constitutional generality and called for
changes which in fact go beyond the strict domaine of
regulatory reform.

The one-day round-table format of the meetings served
to provide an excellent overview of issues, but several of
the provinces indicated that the Team's consultation
meetings should be seen as only the first step of a
continuing dialogue on regulatory issues - several suggested
a schedule of further meetings at each of which two or three
key issues could be discussed at length.

Most of the provincial contact points are officials in
central agencies. Many commented that the meetings with the
Study Team demonstrated a need for occasional "central
agency" meetings to take a panoramic view of regulatory
issues that otherwise are hidden to view (often for years)
in the myriad of consultative mechanisms between line
departments.

III. Conclusions

The Study Team draws the following major conclusions
from its review of federal/provincial regulatory relations.
(Its views vis-à-vis the territories can be found under
relevant programs such as those of the Department of Indian
Affairs and Northern Development).

1. Day-to-day administrative relationships among
    federal and provincial regulators are generally
    very good - and much better than they were a few
    years ago.

2. Several provinces are more advanced than the
    federal government in improving their regulatory
    systems, but only Ontario seemed to have a more
    highly developed sophistication with regard to the
    theory and principles of regulatory reform and
    economic deregulation.

3. All provinces are keenly interested in regulatory
    administration and are eager to see resumed
    federal leadership in a field they believe was
    largely abandoned by Ottawa a few years ago. The
    majority of provinces called for the
    reinvigoration of the Federal/Provincial/
    Territorial Committee on Government Regulations
    which was active from 1978-82 as a result of
    agreements by First Ministers in the late 70s.
    (It has only met once since 1982 - in March of
    this year when it met to be briefed on the work of
    the Regulatory Programs Study Team.)

4. With regard to regulatory programs, there is
    significant overlap and duplication between both
    levels of government, notably in areas of shared,
    delegated or concurrent jurisdiction.

5. The Study Team remains convinced that the number
    one regulatory issue in the country is the
    cumulative burden of regulation both on
    individuals and on the economy stemming from the
    multiple layers of regulatory authority. Thus,
    even more important than overlap/duplication, is
    the question of whether or not an individual or
    group is subjected to too much different
    regulation. The Team considers Canadians vastly
    over-regulated for their own good as supposedly
    free citizens and for the good of the country's
    economy. How to cope with this layering of
    federal/provincial/territorial/municipal
    regulation - how to shrink it - should be the
    primary objectives of future federal/provincial
    regulatory cooperation.

IV. Options

The following options are suggested by the Study Team to the Ministerial Task Force for consideration by the government, with a view to initiating improvements in the country's overall regulatory system and activities:

1.   Consider pursuing a federal/ provincial strategy of national regulatory reform directed to shrinking the overall regulatory burden on Canadians.

2.   Consider assigning authority for the development and implementation of the strategy to the Minister responsible for regulatory affairs.

3.   Federal-provincial initiatives should be included among the distinct elements of a federal regulatory improvement strategy. The initiatives could be of two sorts:

     (i) initiatives to resolve overlap/duplication problems;

     (ii) initiatives of a "horizontal" nature - that is, problems in major economic sectors which are regulated at two or more levels of government and by multiple regulatory programs.

4.   As initial targets in the strategy outlined above, the Study Team suggests:

     (i) a federal-provincial joint study involving officials and possibly private sector representatives (not restricted to environmental specialists) to address solutions to problems of overlap and duplication in the area of environment regulation;

     (ii) a federal-provincial joint study involving burden in the tourism industry, with a view to identifying an intergovernmental action plan to rationalize and shrink that burden;

(iii) a federal-provincial joint study on the regulatory burden in the building industry, with a view to identifying an intergovernmental plan to rationalize and shrink that burden.

5. The Study Team suggests that consideration be given, as part of a larger federal regulatory improvement strategy, to the inclusion of a regulatory cooperation item on the agenda of a federal/ provincial meeting of First Ministers.

6. It is suggested that the Ministerial Task Force conveys the specific views of provincial and territorial officials to individual Ministers with relevant policy and program responsibilities.

FEDERAL/PROVINCIAL/TERRITORIAL CONSULTATIONS

FREDERICTON, NEW BRUNSWICK

Mr. Basil D. Stapleton
Director
Law Reform Division
Office of the Attorney General

HALIFAX, NOVA SCOTIA

Ms. Ann Janega
Coordinator of Regulations
Executive Council Office
Policy Board

ST. JOHN'S, NEWFOUNDLAND

Mr. Douglas M. Brown
Director
Resource Programs
Intergovernmental Affairs Secretariat
Executive Council

CHARLOTTETOWN, PRINCE EDWARD ISLAND

Mr. Doug Boylan
Clerk of Executive Council

WHITEHORSE, YUKON

Mr. William Oppen
Senior Projects Officer
Department of Intergovernmental Relations

VICTORIA, BRITISH COLUMBIA

Mr. Stuart Goodings
Assistant Deputy Minister
Ministry of Consumer and Corporate Affairs

EDMONTON, ALBERTA

    Mr. William Samis
    Coordinator
    Regulatory Reform Project

QUEBEC, QUEBEC

    M. Marc Morin
    Directeur
    Affaires Economiques et Financieres
    Secretariat aux affaires intergouvernementales
        canadiennes

SASKATOON, SASKATCHEWAN

    Mr. Graham F. Parsons
    Secretary
    Economic Policy
    Saskatchewan Executive Council

WINNIPEG, MANITOBA

    Mrs. Barbara Carroll
    Federal Provincial Relations
    Department of Finance

YELLOWKNIFE, NORTHWEST TERRITORIES

    Mr. Stien K. Lal, Q.C.
    Deputy Minister
    Justice and Public Services

TORONTO, ONTARIO

    Mr. Kent McLure
    Legal Director
    Public Trustee's Office

PRIVATE SECTOR CONTACTS

Air Canada
Air Transport Association of Canada
Alberta Chamber of Resources
Alliance of Canada Travel Association
American Motors of Canada
Apparel Manufacturing Council
Arctic Petroleum Operators Association
Association of Canadian Distillers
Association of Canada Film & TV Producers
Bell Canada
Bradley Air Services
Brewers Association of Canada
B.C. Council of Fishermen
B.C. Federation of Labour
B.C. Mining Association
B.C. Telephone Company
B.C./Yukon Chamber of Mines
Business Council on National Issues
Cadbury Shweppes & Powell
Canada Grains Council
Canada Safety Council
Canadian Air Line Pilots Association
Canadian Air Traffic Association
Canadian Air Traffic Controllers
Canadian Arctic Resources
Canadian Association of Broadcasters
Canadian Association of Custom Brokers
Canadian Association of Immigration Lawyers
Canadian Association of Management Consultants
Canadian Association of Manufacturers of Medical Devices
Canadian Bankers Association
Canadian Bar Association
Canadian Cable Television Association
Canadian Canadian Chemical Producers Association
Canadian Chicken Marketing Agency
Canadian Civil Liberties Association
Canadian Conference of Teamsters
Canadian Council of Social Development
Canadian Drug Manufacturers Association
Canadian Exporters Association
Canadian Federation of Agriculture
Canadian Federation of Independent Business
Canadian Federation of Independent Grocers
Canadian Federation of Labour
Canadian Food Brokers Association

Canadian Food Processors Association
Canadian Grains Commission
Canadian Growth Assistance
Canadian General Electric
Canadian Health & Life Insurance Association
Canadian Home Builders Association
Canadian Importers Association
Canadian Industrial Transportation League
Canadian Institute of Chartered Accountants
C.I.L.
Canadian Labour Congress
Canadian Labour Relations Board
Canadian Life & Health Insurance Association
Canadian Manufacturers Association
Canadian Marine Transportation Centre
Canadian Merchant Service Guild
Canadian Mining Association
Canadian Motor Bus Association
Canadian Motor Vehicle Manufacturers' Association
Canadian National Transport Ltd.
CN Rail
CNCP Telecom
Canadian Organization for Peoples Entitlement
Canadian Organization for Small Business
CP Air
Canadian Petroleum Association
Canadian Pulp and Paper Association
Canadian Real Estate Agents Association
Canadian Railway Labour Association
Canadian Standards Association
Canadian Tanners Association
Canadian Trucking Association
Canadian Trust Companies Association
Canadian Wildlife Federation
Canadian Holdings
Cargill Canada Ltd.
Carleton University
Jacques Cartier & Champlain
CDIC Task Force
Chamber of Commerce
Chrysler Canada
Clothing & Textile Workers Union
Coalition of Provincial Organizations of the Handicapped
Colgate - Palmolive Canada
Cominco
Communication Workers of Canada
Conseil du Patronat
Construction Trade Union

Consul General of Canada
Consumers Association of Canada
Continental Grain Co.
Cooperative Union of Canada
Corporate Growth Assistance Ltd.
Dairy Farmers of Canada
Dalhousie University
Dangerous Goods Transportation Association
Dene Haltion
Dome Petroleum
Dominion Marine Association
Domtar Inc.
Economic Council of Canada
Electric Workers Union
Engineering Institute of Canada
Environmental Law Centre (Alberta)
Esso Resources
Federation of Associations on the Canadian Environment
Federation of the Blind of Quebec
Fisheries Council of Canada
Friends of the Earth
Further Processing Association of Canada
General Motors of Canada
Grain Transportation Authority
Granger Ron
Green & Apiegel (Barristers)
Grocery Products Mfg.
Groupe Provincial & l'Ind. du Medicament
Groupement d'Entreprises Quebecoises
Gulf Canada
IBM Canada
Independent Petroleum Association of Canada
Institute for Research on Public Policy
Jackman Barbara
Klondike Placer Miners Association
MacMillan Bloedel
McCarthy and McCarthy
Manitoba Farm & Business Association
Manitoba Pool Elevators
Mining Association of Canada
Montreal Association for the Blind
Motor Vehicle Management Association
S.A. Murray & Co.
National Anti-Poverty Organization
National Association of Canadians of Origins in India
National Congress of Italian Canadians
National Dairy Council
Newfoundland Fish & Food Allied Workers

Noranda Inc.
Norman Wells Pipeline
Northern Sales Ltd.
Northwest Air
Northwestel Inc.
N.W.T. Association of Municipalities
N.W.T. Chamber of Commerce
N.W.T. Chamber of Mines
N.W.T. Construction Association
N.W.T. Territorial Government
Nova Alberta Corporation
Ontario Council of Agencies Serving Immigrants
Ontario Fruit & Vegetables Growers Association
N.W. Paterson & Sons
Packaging Association of Canada
Pan Arctic Oils
Parrish & Hermbecker Ltd.
Petro Canada
Petroleum Association for Conservation of the Environment
Pharmaceutical Manufacturers Association
Pioneer Grain Co.
Polar Gas
Proprietary Association of Canada
Public Interest Advocacy Centre
P.S.A.C. (Agriculture Union)
Quebecair
Quebec Federation of Labour
Regina University
Retail Council of Canada
Roads and Transportation Association of Canada
Rogers Cable
Royal Lepage Real Estate
Safeway Stores
Saskatchewan Wheat Pool
Special Trade Relations Bureau
Steel Workers Union
Stelco
Telecom Canada
Textile & Clothing Board
Textile & Clothing Workers Union
Transport 2,000
Tourism Industry Association of Canada
United Grain Growers
United Fish and Allied Workers Union
University of B.C.
Washington State Government
Western Food Processors Association
Weir Foulds

Winnipeg Commodity Exchange
Yukon Chamber of Commerce
Yukon Chamber of Mines
Yukon Livestock Agriculture Association
Yukon Territorial Water Board

APPENDIX A

CATEGORIZATION OF PROBLEM PROGRAMS

PROGRAM	YUKON	B.C. F.	ALTA	SASK	MAN.	QUE.	N.B. P.	N.S.	NFLD	PEI.	NWT.	ONT.
CDC 200												
CDIC 901			J	D J								
CGC 234												
CGC 235								Po				
CGC 901			E					E				
CHRC 1				D J					J			
CLKB 1												
CMHC 1				E				Po				
CMHC 2				Po R								D J R
CPC 100				E	E							
CRTC 901								Po	R			
CRTC 902				D		InPo	D J	J	J Po			
CTC 2					E							
CTC 10												
CTC 12				E				E				
CTC 20								In				
CTC 30										OpPo		
CTC 40				R	E							Po
CTC 45				E								
CTC 50				E								
CWB 1			E	E	Po			E				
DI 1				D			D					
DOC 100					J Po		D Op	J	OpPo			
DOC 901									Po			

KEY: D – Duplication/Overlap   E – Economic   I – Inconsistency   O – Others   R – Revision
In– Information/Input   Op– Operational   Po– Policy (Consultation)   J – Jurisdictional

CATEGORIZATION OF PROBLEM PROGRAMS

PROGRAM	YUKON	B.C.	ALTA	SASK	MAN.	QUE.	N.B.	N.S.	NFLD	PEI.	NWT.	ONT.
EAC 1												
EAC 9				Op								
EC 18		D J		Op								
EC 903		D J			D J	DEJ		Po				
EC 23		D J										
FC 25	J		D Op	D			D J		D		D E	O
EC 97		D J	D R					Po	I			
EC 98			J					Po				
EC 901			J Po	E				J				
EIC 901			Po					Po				
EIC 902			Po									
EMR 2			D J				R	E		E J	D Op	
EMR 12			J		Po							
EMR 30			D J I									
EMR 114				J								
EPC 2		D J	Op	Op					Po			
F&O 1		D J										
F&O 7		D J	J PoR				I	R				J Op
F&O 8		D J	J PoR				J	E	D			J Op
F&O 902	J			D J			D Po					J Op
FC 2			J	J								
FC 901				E R								
HWC 17												
HWC 18							D J					

KEY: D – Duplication/Overlap   E – Economic   I – Inconsistency   O – Others   R – Revision
     In– Information/Input   Op– Operational   Po– Policy (Consultation)   J – Jurisdictional

680

CATEGORIZATION OF PROBLEM PROGRAMS

PROGRAM	YUKON	B.C.	ALTA	SASK	MAN.	QUE.	N.B.	N.S.	NFLD	PEI.	NWT.	ONT.
HWC 22							E					
HWC 100				I			J					
HWC 101				E								
HWC 102												
INAC 58	I										D J	
INAC 79	J OpR										E J Po	
INAC 201	Po											
INAC 201.1	J EPo											
INAC 201.2												
INAC 201.3	E Op										J	
INAC 201.4	Op											
INAC 226												
JUST 18												
JUST 901												
JUST 902												
LC 4											J	
LC 6				J					D J		J O	J
LC 20											J	
LRC 1												
NCPC 1											J	
NEB 100		J	D Op	E J	Po		E J		E		D E	
NFPMC 1				Op			Po					J
NFPMC 2				Op								

KEY: D - Duplication/Overlap   I - Inconsistency   O - Others   R - Revision
     In- Information/Input   J - Jurisdictional

     E - Economic   Po- Policy (Consultation)
     Op- Operational

681

CATEGORIZATION OF PROBLEM PROGRAMS

PROGRAM	YUKON	B.C.	ALTA	SASK	MAN.	QUE.	N.B.	N.S.	NFLD	PEI.	NWT.	ONT.
NPAC 1												
PCO 100									Op			
RCCE 2												
RCCE 3								Po				
RCCE 4												
RCCE 14			I	In				Op				
RCCE 29				E In				Po	R			
RCCE 34												
RCMP 4												Po Op
SS 1												
SSC 9												
STCC 11												
TB 6												
TB 901												
TC 4												
TC 27												
TC 47												
TC 57				J								
TC 61												
TC 67												
TC 93			D InJ	D	E J	D				D Op	J	R
TC 275												

KEY: D – Duplication/Overlap   E – Economic   I – Inconsistency   O – Others   R – Revision
In– Information/Input   Op– Operational   Po– Policy (Consultation)   J – Jurisdictional

682

CATEGORIZATION OF PROBLEM PROGRAMS

PROGRAM	YUKON	B.C.	ALTA	SASK	MAN.	QUE.	N.B.	N.S.	NFLD	PEI.	NWT.	ONT.
TC 310												
TC 315												
TC 320			Op									
TC 325							Op					
TC 330			D J	J								
TC 405												
TC 420												
TC 425												
TC 430												
TC 435												
TC 440												
TC 500												
TC 600												
TC 610							E					
TC 999							E					
DRIE 902												
TRFB 101												

KEY: D - Duplication/Overlap E - Economic I - Inconsistency O - Others R - Revision
In- Information/Input Op- Operational Po- Policy (Consultation) J - Jurisdictional

683

CATEGORIZATION OF PROBLEM PROGRAMS

PROGRAM	YUKON	B.C.	ALTA	SASK	MAN.	QUE.	N.B.	N.S.	NFLD	PEI.	NWT.	ONT.
AFCB 1				DJ			DI	J	J			
AGC 18				E	J							
AGC 211												J
AGC 213			D	Op E	J							Po
AGC 214				E								
AGC 215				D Op			D	E				
AGC 902				E								
AGC 223-6				E								D
CIT 1				E								
CCA 2				D Op			Op	Po				
CCA 4				J				Po				
CCA 5												
CCA 9			R									
CCA 10			R	Op								
CCA 12					Po							
CCA 13				R			Op					
CCA 14				R								
CCA 31												
CCA 32				E								
CCA 100				E								
CCA 101								R				
CCA 102												
CCA 103												
CCA 901												

KEY: D - Duplication/Overlap   E - Economic   I - Inconsistency   O - Others   R - Revision
    In- Information/Input   Op- Operational   Po- Policy (Consultation)   J - Jurisdictional